One Man's Blues

One Man's Blues
The Life and Music of Mose Allison

patti jones

Quartet Books

First published in 1995 by Quartet Books Limited
A member of the Namara Group
27 Goodge Street, London W1P 2LD

Copyright © Patti Jones 1995

Song copyrights appear on p. 321

A catalogue record for this book is available from the British Library

ISBN 0 7043 7086 7

Typeset by Contour Tyesetters, Southall, Middx
Printed and bound by WBC Bookbinders, Bridgend, Mid Glamorgan

All rights reserved. No part of this book may be reproduced in any form or by any means without the prior written permission of the publisher.

In memory of my brother Richard P. Jones (1947–1963),
to Pete Townshend and their generation

ACKNOWLEDGEMENTS

Special thanks to the Allison family, immediate and extended, with much gratitiude to Amy, Alissa, Janine, Maxine and especially to John for his research and assistance and to Audre for her continued inspiration, support and encouragement.

To everyone who took the time to contribute to this project, Mose's friends acquaintances, and colleagues, recording artists and their cooperative staffs, journalists and writers. Many thanks to Ralph Hughes and Nicola Joss.

To my former music students in Kansas City and New Orleans, Mose listeners, all.

To the pedigogues – Dr. Raymond Stahura at Ripon College, Ripon, Wisconsin, Dr. Eph Ehly at the Conservatory, University of Missouri, Kansas City and the late Dr. Jack Stephenson.

To the faculty and administrative staff of Suffolk University Law School, Boston who indulged reserach on this book during my study of American jurisprudence and especially to Sally Gaglini, Esq.

To Frank John Hadley, Charlie Backfish, James Austin, Bill Anthony, Jon Pareles, Bill Levenson and Bas Hartong at Polygram Records, John Snyder, David Shanen, Harry Weinger, Fred Goodman, Adam Block, Chris Parker, my man Pat McGrath at Looney Tunes, Boston and cool cat Fred Cohen at Jazz Center Records, N.Y., Jonathan Love at ASCAP, Ray Whitehead in the U.K., Ron Free, Ben Sidran, Wayne Naus and John Voight at The Berklee School of Music, Bill Ferris at The Center of Southern Culture at the University of Mississippi, Millard at The Boston Public Library, The Ulrichs Mika El Baz, Nancy Meyer and Scott Cameron, Mike Kappas, Chris Blackwell, Ken Goes, David Beiber, Denis Richardson, Margaret Breitenstein and Jeffrey Hirsch, to the many devoted fans I met at Mose's shows.

To Stephen J. Garvin, where ever you are, for the teen–age introduction to Mose's music.

To John, Bob and Mary Jane Liepold.

To Dingles, Buster, Bill, Ruth, Zachary and Alex Jones.

To my girls Julia and Veronica.

To my hero Jeremy Beale at Quartet.

To Mose for the years of puttin' up with me.

To the Great Almighty and His Son for every blessing and lesson.

CONTENTS

1	TIPPO, THE FIRST CROSSROAD	1
2	UP FROM THE SWAMP	20
3	DIDACTICS, BARTÓK AND CURLY'S	35
4	HALCYON DAYS	51
5	BACK COUNTRY SUITE	68
6	LOCAL COLOR	83
7	A PRESTIGIOUS COMMITMENT	96
8	DETRIBALIZATION AND TRANSFIGURATION	114
9	THE WORD FROM MOSE	132
10	WHEN YOU MEET YOUR DESTINY FACE TO FACE	161
11	HELLO THERE, UNIVERSE	179
12	STILL NO TOP FORTY RECORD	202
13	ALMOST SUCCESSFUL	218
14	TOWARDS A PIANO STYLE	235
15	MOSE ALLISON: A SOURCE	260
	APPENDIX: ARTISTS ON ALLISON	268
	Bonnie Raitt	
	Bruce Lundvall	
	Robert Palmer	
	Jack Bruce	
	Pete Brown	
	Black Francis	
	Zoot Money	
	John Hammond	
	Brian Auger	
	Jorma Kaukonen	
	Georgie Fame	
	Al Kooper	
	Susannah McCorkle	
	Ray Davies	
	John Mayall	
	Pete Townshend	
	REFERENCES	312
	LEAD SHEETS	317
	DISCOGRAPHY	321
	INDEX	346

1

TIPPO, THE FIRST CROSSROAD

"I am often questioned, especially in Europe, about my childhood in racially segregated Mississippi. It usually comes down to 'How did a white guy like yourself get involved with black music there?' These days, when we've all been made aware of racial crimes and tensions worldwide, I hate to make generalizations about any racial group because I believe that 'individuals differ as much within races as they do between races.' Ironically, I first heard that in a psychology class at the University of Mississippi in 1947 and I think it is definitive. However, the answer to the question is: 'I followed my ears.'"

Mose Allison

"If You Live"

Ah well, if you live your time will come
I say, if you live your time will come
So child don't mess with that cotton sack
It's gonna scratch your knees and bend your back
And if you live your time will come

Ah well, if you live your day will come
I say, if you live your day will come
So child don't play with those pots and pans
They're gonna soon enough ruin your pretty hands
And if you live your time will come

Ah well, if you live a day will come

I say, if you live a day will come
When the sun will shine and the crops will grow
And you'll think that you're a not gonna worry no mo'
But if you live your time will come
Your time will come

> Mose Allison

Highway 49, the Mississippi state highway connecting Greenwood to Clarksdale, ambles north through the sultry swamps, weeping vines and vast farm flatlands of the Delta. In their heyday, the rich fields bordering Highway 49 yielded a cotton crop that fetched a dollar a pound at market. From World War I until the Great Depression, the period marking the zenith of the region's economic prosperity, the abundant cotton harvests were as valuable to the Delta as gold was to California or oil to Texas. But it was primarily the white landowner who profited during the Delta cotton boom. Although freed from slavery for over fifty years, African-Americans remained subjugated in a white-dominated economic and social structure. Like their enslaved ancestors, black sharecroppers and field laborers could only dream of owning the fields where they continued to toil for a white landlord.

Born of the anguish experienced by slaves in the Delta cotton fields, but also articulating a spirit of eternal hope, the music from this north-west corner of Mississippi was the country blues. The agrarian hamlets and towns that spawned the music and its creators sprawl around Highway 49 like the Great River's tributaries. From Clarksdale came Son House, Willie Brown and John Lee Hooker; from Glendora came Sonny Boy Williamson; Big Bill Broonzy from Scott; and from further south in Rolling Fork came McKinley Morganfield, who named himself "Muddy Waters" after the river itself. These artists were among the black blues prophets who established a musical tradition destined to transcend both racial and national boundaries. For Mose Allison, a native Delta son and a white man, the social and economic circumstances, artistic traditions and folklore of this bucolic province would provide the chief artistic inspiration for his unique musical identity.

Mose John Allison, Jr. could have appropriately personalized his popular cover of bluesman Willie Dixon's "Seventh Son" by renaming it "Eleventh Son," for he was born during the eleventh hour of the eleventh day of the eleventh month of 1927, in Tippo, a small farming community located ten miles east of Highway 49 in Tallahatchie County, Mississippi. The county was immortalized by country singer Bobby Gentry in her 1967 crossover hit "Ode to Billy Joe." Gentry's ballad depicted the public indifference towards teenage tragedy when the fictitious Billy Joe MacAllister jumped off the Tallahatchie Bridge, a few miles from Allison's hometown. The county was also site of a real-life tragedy, the lynching of Emmett Till, a young African-American from Chicago. During a visit to relatives in the Delta in the summer of 1955, the fourteen-year-old Till allegedly whistled at a white woman and paid for it with his life. When his body surfaced in the Tallahatchie River, his murder ignited the fire of the civil-rights movement in the South. Today, Till's story still stirs up strong emotions in and around Tallahatchie County.

Mose Allison was born in his grandfather's wood-frame farmhouse which still stands on what is technically an island three miles from the village of Tippo. Completely surrounded by Tippo Creek and accessible only by dirt road and a rickety wooden plank bridge, the farmhouse on "the Island," as residents call it, was built in 1914 by John Robert "Papa" Allison, Mose's paternal grandfather, and the family patriarch. He was a pioneer and farmer whose family came from South Carolina. He married three times, his first two wives apparently succumbing to malaria, then a common disease due to the massive populations of mosquitoes in the South. In fact, Mose himself had several bouts of the disease during his childhood and it also claimed the lives of both his paternal and maternal grandmothers.

Before malaria struck, John Robert's first wife, Minnie Holland, bore one son named Lacey. Allison then married Texana Paul. Their only child, Mose John Allison, was the celebrated musician's father. Finally, Papa Allison married his third wife and third cousin, Ollie Cox, whom the family fondly called "Mom Ollie." Each of the four girls she had with John Robert was given a boy's name: Frances, Farris, Sammie, and Johnnie.

John Robert was considered a visionary by Delta standards. He owned the first automobile and radio in Tippo, furnished his homestead with the modern convenience of an "in-house" bathroom instead of the typical outhouse and built innovative recreational facilities on his property, a tennis court and a swimming pool with a sand bottom. In addition to a fine house, Allison's 1,500-acre spread boasted a goldfish pond, numerous horses and a buggy, several mules, a blacksmith shop, a sorghum mill and a cotton gin in Tippo.

A prominent and respected member of the community, John Robert was known locally as "Captain John." He supervised the county highways for twenty years, laying the first gravel roads in the region. Allison kin remember him for his artistic talent and, more significantly, for his humanity and compassion. His exemplary service to the community set the standard for the rest of his family. On weekends, Papa Allison's home was a gathering place for family and friends, black and white, his front porch resonating with laughter, dancing and the music of the day.

Mose Allison's mother, née Maxine Collins, was born in Booneville, Mississippi, in 1905. Located in the north-eastern corner of the state, Booneville sits in the region known to native Mississippians as the "hill country."

Maxine attended college at the Mississippi State University for Women in Columbus, graduating in 1924, and settling in Tippo sometime in 1925 to teach high school History. A colorful and ebullient personage who in later years gained celebrity for her "about town" column in the Charleston, Mississippi newspaper called "Miz Mose's Musings," when she splashed on to the Tippo scene in the mid-1920s the entire hamlet sat up and took notice. She quickly assumed her place in the community by marrying the town's most eligible bachelor, Mose John Allison. They were a couple of complementary characters. The flamboyant and fashionable flapper and ukulele player Maxine formed a perfect alliance with the dapper, reserved Mose Allison, Sr., son of a respected Delta landowner. The Tippo townsfolk affectionately embraced the out-of-towner, even dubbing Maxine "the little Colonel," a nickname reflecting her "take charge" personality.

"Miz Mose" still embodies the brand of Southern fire celebrated by Mississippi novelist Eudora Welty. Now in her eighties, a diminutive, ivory-skinned, white-haired lady with the sparkling blue eyes her son Mose inherited, Maxine is independent and spunky, a commanding presence in the Delta. She has travelled the globe, her journeys proudly marked by pins on a world map hanging on the wall of her rambling Tippo home, but she can entertain for hours by spinning tales about the towns in the Delta, the county events, the colorful inhabitants and, in particular, Southern-style food: greens, cornbread stuffing, chicken and apple pie.

Much of Maxine's wry wit and independent spirit prevail in her son. Mose himself freely credits the Collins side of his family for his sense of humor, particularly his maternal grandfather and his Aunt Maurine, Maxine's sister, whose irreverent attitude and ironic nature made early, lasting impressions. He recalls:

> Cliff Collins, my maternal grandpa, was sort of a comedian. He drank, and his euphemism for getting drunk was "Pa's got a bear." He once had a snapshot made standing by a stuffed bear and sent it to friends. Also, my Aunt Maurine was a deadpan type who always said the outrageous thing that everyone else was thinking and was able to get away with it.

Mose John Allison, Jr., Maxine's first child, was born a year after she was married. She took a short leave from teaching high school but, committed to her work, decided to return almost immediately. Thus, for the first two years of his life, Mose Jr. lived with his grandparents, Papa Allison and step-grandmother, Mom Ollie, and he spent most of his time with them until he was five, developing a close bond with them both, but especially with Mom. Frances Butts, Mom Ollie's eldest daughter, remembers:

> Mose was the little boy Mother always wanted. My mother had four girls, so when he came along he was heaven-sent. It was wonderful that he lived on the island for five years while Mother taught school. Mose had a great imagination. He grew up all alone because we lived in an isolated area, and he had an imaginary playmate. Whenever he played, he called his little playmate by name and Mother had to set a place for him at the table at lunchtime. As a child he was always very intelligent and even a little eccentric. When he was five, I left the Island to go to school and eventually married. I always remember little Mose crying and crying when I left, saying he was going to "shot" my husband for taking me away.

Two years after Mose's birth, Maxine lost her job when the local high school moved to the county seat, Charleston, a few miles north east of Tippo. At that point, Maxine did not actually need to work, but economic circumstances swiftly changed.

The onslaught of the Depression wreaked havoc on the Delta economy and the Allisons, major landowners in Tippo, were not spared. When they nearly lost the family farm, Maxine had to resume teaching at a local grade school. Mose, Sr. doubled his farming duties with tending to his primary responsibilities, running a general store and service station in Tippo. The younger Mose remembers that his "parents had to work hard to keep things together to get out of the hole. That was the way it was until the Second World War, when the cotton farmer regained prosperity."

Mose John Allison, Sr. strikingly resembled his mother, Texana Paul Staton, John Robert's second wife. According to Maxine, Ruth Staton, Texana Paul's daughter from a previous marriage, coined the name "Mose" for her baby half-brother. The six-year-old Ruth evidently mistook the name "Mose" for her preference, the more common biblical name, "Moses." Appreciating the novelty, the Allisons decided to retain the name.

Mose Sr.'s personality traits are distinctly reflected in his eldest son and namesake. The elder Allison was a soft-spoken, pensive and sensitive man highly regarded in the county. The same Southern grace and charm, laced with offbeat humor, characterize the younger Mose. The elder Mose also handed down a great passion and prowess for music to his son, particularly for the piano.

Mose John Allison, Sr. was an accomplished self-taught stride pianist who learned the ragtime style from watching and imitating piano rolls on player pianos. Primarily a "parlor pianist," he played semi-professionally around the county, entertaining audiences with his renditions of "The Twelfth Street Rag" and "Sweet Sue." Maxine describes him as "kind of quiet but a charmer. Everywhere he went, he'd sit down at the piano. Someone would hum a tune and Mose, Sr. could play it right off. Then, he had an unexpected stroke when he was fifty-six. He was partially paralyzed on one side and had to stop playing." The rollicking Sundays at Papa Allison's farmhouse on the Island often featured Big Mose at the piano. His step-sister Frances Butts, remembers:

> There was a Negro chauffeur named Percy Walker who used to drive for Theo Thornton down the road. He was a one-man band. On Sundays, he would come over to the house on the Island and play his instruments. Big Mose would play the piano. We'd throw down some sawdust and everyone would dance to the boogie-woogie. Sometimes they would play some blues songs that were considered to be quite raw and Mother wouldn't allow those songs on Sundays.

Mose Allison, Sr.'s reputation in the community paralleled that of his father, John Robert. A deeply religious and compassionate man, Mose Sr. was a landowner and leading merchant in the hamlet who used his status to break from racist Southern traditions and treated sharecroppers with dignity and fairness. Whenever possible, Allison promoted ownership of the land by blacks, frequently financing the ventures with his own funds or paying for their college tuition. To show their appreciation for Allison, when he died in February, 1973, the citizens of Tippo erected and dedicated a monument to him. The monument contains the original plantation bell from his father's farm, rung to summon workers into and out of the fields. It stands adjacent to the Methodist church in Tippo where Mose Allison, Sr. was a lifelong member of the congregation. His father's funeral forced the otherwise punctilious and dependable Mose Allison, who by the early seventies was mostly playing six nights a week and touring much of the year, to cancel a club engagement, an occurrence occasioned only twice in the forty years Allison has performed on the road. A major blizzard caused the other cancellation.

Mose was two years old in 1929 when his family permanently moved from the comfort of his grandfather's house on the Island. A weathered wood-frame, the Allisons' first house was situated on the banks of Tippo Creek, down a dirt road about a mile from the village. Mose's earliest memories of their place on Tippo Creek were of waiting excitedly for a Model T Ford to meander down the dirt road to deliver the funny papers and an incident where his father was shot, but not seriously wounded, during an attempt to settle an argument between two neighbors.

A year later, the family moved from their place on the Creek to the village of Tippo proper, where Mose spent the remainder of his youth. In 1947 while Mose was in the Army, the Allisons moved from his boyhood home to the oldest residence in Tippo, a 100-year-old Southern ranch-style house where Maxine had always wanted to live and where she still resides. Mose remembers his childhood home:

> My years from ages three to seventeen were spent in Tippo proper and we moved into a slightly ramshackle, weather-beaten house with gaps under the doors, one fireplace, and no electricity. Oil lamps, an outhouse, and toting water from the well were all a part of it. I was about twelve when the TVA [Tennessee Valley Authority] and electricity came to the area. I remember the first night they got electricity in

Tippo and turned on the lights in the two general stores and service station. It was a spectacular sight!

Technological advancements provided Tippo farmers with an increased capability to gin cotton. By the 1940s, a cooperatively-owned electric cotton gin replaced the original diesel-engine gin owned and operated by the Allison Brothers where Mose Jr. had worked as a teenager. Originally owned by his grandfather, it was located approximately a quarter of a mile south of town. The "new" electric gin still hums at harvest time and occupies a convenient central location in the tiny Tippo crossroads. Maxine Allison recalls:

> Our general store was where the Tippo Pub is now, but it burned. We had a service station right across the street from where the welding shop is. Right across from my yard is another big general store we owned. We only ran one store at a time and the service station. The station is where everybody met, the social gathering place of the town. Negroes were allowed in both places. Mose Sr. furnished Negroes with their crops, he lent them money through the store for the crops and charged a percentage of interest for them.

When Mose was five years old, he began his formal studies on the piano. His teacher, "Miss Jimmy" Oliver, was a local piano teacher to whom Maxine sent her three children, for what she describes as "a little music." Young Mose had an immediate affinity for the instrument but shunned the discipline of practicing for Miss Jimmy's lessons. He was happiest and most comfortable plunking out tunes by ear, showing a remarkable facility for this skill at an early age. However, Mose did honor Maxine's only request for her pianist son. Before terminating his formal piano lessons at age eleven or twelve, he learned to play "The Rosary" for his mother. Although he learned that particular piece from sheet music, Allison never became truly adept at reading the four-part musical scores familiar to most pianists. He comments that his illiteracy in musical notation sometimes "cut him from certain markets once out on the road." Nevertheless, he more than compensated for the deficiency later, mastering big-band charts and lead sheets, the printed language of jazz rhythm sections. Mose has clear memories of his first steps in music:

> Miss Jimmie was a good teacher but the piano lessons for me were sort of a chore. My folks used to have to bribe me to take them. I used what my piano teacher called the "hunt and peck system" so she doesn't take much credit for teaching me. When I was in grade school, I started to pick out my own things myself. That's when I began to get interested in playing. Once I discovered I could pick out things by ear, it became an outlet for me. I liked to pick out the boogie-woogie tunes, anything bluesy or bouncy, tunes I heard around there in the 1930s. As a consequence, I didn't learn how to read very well. It's fair to say that I'm primarily self-taught.
>
> Considering the extreme poverty and provincialism in the area, I was relatively privileged. I never suffered any actual material deprivation and in some ways it was an idyllic childhood. But I was a fairly solitary kid. I spent a lot of days in the house, and the piano, an old upright, was there. My dad enjoyed playing but he was caught in the economic circumstances which prevented him from playing music full time. He didn't encourage me to play that much, but he never discouraged me either. He just let me go my own way.

Mose Allison's memories of a hermit-like childhood existence are disputed by some family accounts, but they might possibly be attributed in part to the considerable difference in age between him and his two siblings. Six years older than his sister Joy, twelve years older than brother Tony, he could hardly have been considered a suitable childhood playmate for either of them. However, Allison cannot be described as anti-social or introverted, and his childhood sounds relatively happy. Although somewhat reserved in temperament, Mose has always made friends easily, and his mother maintains that in his youth he was no different. Like every other Southern boy growing up in the 1930s and 1940s, he partook of the local Delta camaraderie and his pastimes included swimming in the local creeks, going to parties, playing sports, living the lifestyle of a "middle-class white boy" in Mississippi. Always in step to his own drummer, though, the young Mose chose football and tennis as his favorite activities instead of the more traditional Southern passion of duck hunting. Maxine remembers: "Mose, Jr. was quite popular and had friends all over the county. Why, he even wrote a song for a girlfriend once!" His active social life as a teenager notwithstanding, Mose explains that he did not shirk his work duties around his family's farm:

> My dad wanted me to learn the value of the dollar as it related to the various forms of manual labor around there, so I was introduced first to yard work, then to the fields; stuff like plowing with a mule (I'm probably one of the few remaining blues singers with *that* experience), picking, chopping, and hauling cotton and hay, a lot of which took place in temperatures approaching 100 degrees. Later, I graduated to the cotton gin and the general store, but I had already decided by then that I didn't want to make a career of any of that.

Allison wrote his first song when he was in grade school, around the age of thirteen or fourteen. A song already featuring the sardonic lyrics that would become his trademark, it is a parody on radio commercials, alluding to one of the era's most popular soap ads. It castigated the frequent commercial interruptions of radio programs and qualifies best for what he terms his "slapstick" song category. He called it "The Fourteen-day Palmolive Plan." Allison describes the piece as "a Louis Jordan-type of tune that I used to play at parties, that sort of thing. It was my hit and it was popular all over Tallahatchie County."

"The Fourteen-day Palmolive Plan"

I woke up this morning feeling low
Thought I'd turn on my radio
I tell you, man, it grieves me so
When they tell how Lifebuoy stops B.O.

His mother recalls her reaction on first hearing the song:

One night Mose, Jr. was in there and was composing one about ads – a commercial about the fourteen-day Palmolive Plan. That was the first one he ever composed. It was the cleverest thing. He was singing and I walked in and said, "Mose, Jr. who did that?" And he said, "I made it up." And I said, "Isn't that clever?" It was the first time I realized how good he was.

From the outset, Allison's parents never discouraged young Mose in his love for music and, unlike some of his peers, he was never coerced into carrying on the family business. Instead, his musical talents flourished under the guidance and support of key family members. His father, a versatile and gifted pianist, provided a strong musical role model but also maintained the necessary distance to allow Mose to find his own voice and shape his own ideas. Maxine encouraged her son's musical and emotional development, counseling him through his adolescent bouts of low self-esteem and depression. Mom Ollie, his step-grandmother, was also a powerful force in his life at this time. Mose describes her as "a sweet person, an angel in the background who would never say anything bad about me, no matter what I did. She was the person I could always rely on, the most unselfish person I ever knew."

Allison's first musical influences sprang from the styles indigenous to his Mississippi environs: the boogie-woogie and the blues. These styles were successful musical exports from the South, created and popularized by African-Americans, their sonorities figuring prominently in the rural outreaches of the Delta, where the black population significantly outnumbered whites. The jukebox in his father's service station was Allison's most fertile source for this influential music. It was stacked with recordings known collectively as "race records," a generic term that record retailers in the 1930s used to identify and classify music by artists of color, released on independent record labels. The boogie-woogie strains of Albert Ammons, Pete Johnson and Meade "Lux" Lewis, and the shuffle rhythms of Louis Jordan often blared out from the filling-station jukebox and Mose soon discovered that Earl "Fatha" Hines and Count Basie, both giants of swing, also dabbled in boogie-woogie, a style particularly favoured by both Mose and the entire country in the late 1930s.

The bouncy boogie riffs immediately captured Allison's musical fancy. Internalizing the melodic, rhythmic and harmonic patterns, he sat at the piano for hours woodshedding the notes of the boogie-woogie masters by ear. His early successes at this practice signaled an uncanny ability to learn music through osmosis, a talent later to serve him in discerning and replicating the harmonies and complex left-hand patterns of the twentieth-century piano sonatas composed by Charles Ives and Paul Hindemith.

A jukebox in a cafe hangout in Charleston, where he attended high school, became another one of his hot spots for music. Maxine Allison recalls:

When Mose was in high school, they had a sandwich shop over in Charleston that had a nickelodeon. Mose had lunch money for school and he'd put half of it in the jukebox. That's when the boogie-woogie first came in. First thing I knew Mose, Jr. was in there playing the boogie-woogie on the piano. I said, "Where did you pick that up?" And he'd say, "On the jukebox at Tracy's Kitchen."

The country blues had a more pronounced and dramatic impact on Allison. Its plaintiveness, sincerity, joy, and simplicity sprang naturally from the culture surrounding him. It permeated the working fields, radios, porches, junctions and backyards of the Delta, reflecting the mood and pace of life in the South. As Mose himself points out, "The blues was in the air. A few people around the area had guitars and there was always a lot of singing. Someone sitting on a porch would be whistling the blues. There was also an occasional itinerant blues singer."

But Allison was not only breathing the homespun blues from Tallahatchie County; his father's filling-station jukebox was also spinning race-records "hits" by blues artists Memphis Slim, Tampa Red, Big Maceo, Memphis Minnie, Big Bill Broonzy, Louis Jordan and His Timpany Five and Roosevelt Sykes.

Mose Allison thus had the opportunity to establish his musical persona from a unique vantage point while growing up in Tippo. It was Allison's sense of pathos, coupled with his musical acuity, that precipitated the adoption of the blues as *the* crucial ingredient of his style. A sensitive and perceptive young listener drawn to the language of his African-American neighbours, although conscious that the segregated society around him treated blacks differently than whites, Allison never allowed the deplorable racial attitudes in the South to impede his curiosity about and enthusiasm for the music indigenous to his home.

Indeed, unusually for both the era and the region, the Allison family appeared to pay less attention to racial differences than did most Southerners. They espoused a relatively liberal attitude of social tolerance and acceptance of the region's music which fostered their son's exploration of a genre largely eschewed by the white population. In granting their teenager this freedom, his family allowed a critical musical osmosis to take its natural course. Mose recalls:

> My folks never gave me any racist propaganda line and when I started listening to and playing music that was usually associated with blacks, no one ever expressed any reservations to me. When you're a kid and have never been out of your environment, you don't make objective analyses of the situation. To a child, it seemed that the blacks were having more fun. It was later, after getting out of Mississippi and coming back, that I began to see things more clearly. Then I admired the blacks for being able to survive and maintain some dignity while being denied basic

rights, subjugated economically and in many instances brutalized. Add this to the fact that most of my musical heroes were black and you will understand why, like all good white jazzmen, I couldn't wait to get to a place where I could play with black musicians legally.

In this way the prescient Mose Allison became privy to the cultural language of his neighbors, expressed through black music. Allison identified with the blues, with its fundamental truths, its texts rich in aphorisms and allegory, finding the rhythmic inflections of its musical phrasing reflected in his own everyday speech. At an early age, he also discovered that the simple musical structure and tonality of the blues allowed him quick access to the style as a player. If he could play it on the piano, he could write his own blues tunes.

Throughout Allison's subsequent career, the blues form remained the foundation, an integral element in his unique style. In personalizing the blues, Allison frequently employed the form to produce ironic, pithy apologues. Within the simple three-chord blues structure, he was able to insert singular improvisatory sections derived from a plethora of sophisticated and disparate influences. Mose himself comments:

At the time, I was conscious of the blues thing. Where I grew up the regional music, phrasing and idiom were all-pervasive. When I was a boy, the ratio of blacks to whites was about eight to one. Black culture was all around and whites talked the same way. Most people think of the South as the white people on one side of town and the black people on the other, but that's not the case in rural areas where everybody worked on the same job and went to the same stores and all that, so I don't see how you could grow up unaware of it. Since then, nobody's known just what to call what I do. I mean, I never copied a particular style, even though I used the blues as a starting point.

With no other public schools in close proximity, beginning in the sixth grade, Mose attended public school in Charleston,

Mississippi and remained there for his entire grade-school education. The trip to Charleston, fifteen miles north-east of Tippo, was not a simple one, Mose having to take the one bus that departed early every morning and returned late every afternoon. The long trips paid off, however, and by junior high school he was a thriving musician gaining recognition among both his teachers and peers. Mose's earliest performing experience took place in the school in Charleston. He recalls:

> By the time I was in grade school, I was listening to a lot of music and writing little songs. It had become something that I liked to do and something I had a knack for. The teachers knew I had an ability to play, a good ear and all that, but the consensus at that time was that I wouldn't apply myself well enough to amount to anything. My first public performance was a talent contest at Charleston High School when I was in the seventh grade. I played a Fats Waller tune called "Hold Tight." There's a line in it, "Foodarakasaki want some seafood, Mama." I always remember that. I was about fourteen and came in second. The guy who won played the "Washington and Lee Swing" on the fiddle. It would be interesting to see that on videotape sometime! I can imagine what all the teachers thought of me. It was a small town and a small school. I was considered talented but nothing spectacular. At that time, I was actually doing better as an artist. I had won a drawing contest and even though I drew a lot, it got to the point where it just didn't interest me as much as playing. I often wondered if I could have gone off in that direction.

Mose also picked up the trumpet at this time and joined the school's marching band. Some Mose Allison fans may be unfamiliar with his trumpet playing, but it was first cameoed in a lyrical solo on Richard M. Jones's blues "Trouble in Mind," recorded on his second album, *Local Color*, for Prestige Records. His original tune "Stroll," from his third Prestige release, *Young Man Mose*, also features a trumpet solo, but one more indicative of his personal style on the instrument.

Music, especially playing the trumpet, became Mose's first priority in high school, although football also played a major role in his life at this time: "I guess I wasn't big enough to be a star football player, and I did pretty well as a musician. I didn't get a good foundation as a trumpet player, though. I learned how to play from the band director, Mr. Yerbie, a saxophone player, who 'taught' me how to play by giving me some elementary instructions."

Soon thereafter, the young Allison got his first taste of gigging in a nightclub. On a few weekends during high school, the aspiring trumpeter played dates at a honky-tonk called The Rising Sun on the outskirts of nearby Greenwood. The job was a short-lived rustic adventure, but afforded Allison a valuable preliminary glance at a musician's life in a setting that was to become the mainstay of his performing career. Mose recalls: "The Rising Sun was filled with local color. They served bootlegged whiskey, had illegal gambling, and dancing to a live band. I was impressed with the scene because the other members of the band were mostly college boys and I was just a high schooler."

Allison's newfound trumpet playing won out over the piano during his teenage years. His chief influence on trumpet at the time was Buck Clayton, whose performances with Count Basie he found fascinating and inspiring. Mose's affection for the instrument lingered far from both the band room and the din of the honky-tonk, the sounds of his sultry trumpet refrains reverberating in the steamy, calm Delta summer evenings. Frances Butts recalls:

> Mose used to practice his trumpet out in the yard during the summertime just when everybody else was about going to bed in that sleepy little village. My mother used to love to hear him play "Tenderly," one of her favorites. He often played that song sitting out in the moonlight on the Island.

Allison also began to show signs of a talent for arranging at this time, showcasing his ability in a Dixieland group he formed in high school called the Feet Warmers. In this band, he was the only player who could improvise, and so he used to write out solos for the other instruments. He still maintained an interest in the piano, though, and once he met Bill Woods, a student at the University of Mississippi, he improved as an arranger. Woods showed him a few things about the piano, for example, breaking away from the walking bass with the left hand.[1] A saxophonist and arranger for the Mississippians, the university's premier dance band, Bill Woods led the group while Mose was a student at "Ole Miss." He was also responsible for introducing Mose to the music of Nat Cole and the Nat Cole Trio, one of Allison's major influences.

Mose Allison attributes his first exposure to the jazz idiom to his first cousin Elizabeth Staton, daughter of his Aunt Ruth. A jazz aficionado, Elizabeth's influence on Mose's musical education and listening habits played a pivotal role in his development. Being a few years older than Mose, she had sophisticated musical taste, gravitating towards swing music. Her record collection included the latest hits of Duke Ellington, Count Basie, Fats Waller, Earl Hines and Louis Armstrong, and she often played them for her precocious and impressionable cousin.

As with the blues, jazz had a marked and lasting effect on Allison's musical sensibilities. He discovered tonal variety, rhythmic independence and a fundamental exuberance in the style, characteristics which became the hallmarks of his own approach to music. Fusing jazz with his solid blues base, the mature Allison fleshed out, refined and embellished his style, eventually arriving at an original and personal synthesis which combined the sophistication of jazz with the simplicity of the blues. He comments:

> Up until recently, all the great jazz players have played the blues. Louis Armstrong played and sang the blues all the time. So when the country blues players were discovered later, people started to discriminate between that type of blues and the kind of blues jazz players played. You don't hear too much classic blues playing today when you hear jazz but all the great jazz players did it.[2]

The musical traditions of Mississippi, its indigenous

pervasive country blues, the boogie riffs from its jukeboxes, the rhythm and meter of its dialect, and the introduction to jazz imparted by his cousin Elizabeth left indelible stylistic imprints on the young Mose Allison. The sights, sounds, and smells of Mississippi fashioned his impressions of life. As a songwriter, Mose Allison looked first to his familiar surroundings, to the folklore, characters, life and aphorisms of rural Mississippi. Through his music, he was thus able to introduce Southern culture in the United States to a curious, young, and growing international audience. Mose comments:

> Playing and singing is what I always want to do. I was always a piano player. I always felt that what I've been doing for the last forty years is what I was doing in the sixth grade. In Phoenix years ago, I ran into a person who I went to high school with. She reinforced my ideas on this. She said, "You know, you're doing the same thing you were doing in grade school." Of course, I *have* stretched it out a bit since then.

Allison, the quintessential droll soothsayer, looks back at the Mississippi roots which played such a vital role in defining both his personal and musical identity:

> The older I get, the more I think about my childhood. In a way, I think that I probably learned everything that motivates me now before I left Tippo, Mississippi. I can pick out attitudes that I have now and trace them back to my childhood. I think there's a continuity there and you might have it all before you even get started. It just takes a while to unravel because you're showing it to yourself. I think that it probably takes a while to show it to yourself.

2

UP FROM THE SWAMP

"I left Ole Miss as a naïve provincial and when I returned, I was a fledgling hipster. When I went back to Ole Miss after the Army, I had become a bebop fanatic; bebop was my crusade. Dizzy Gillespie was my hero and I wrote arrangements for the dance band which were not particularly well received by the student body. This was my period for the 'pathetic exaggerations of youth.' I followed Dizzy's big band all over the south east. I heard them in Jackson, Mississippi; Jackson, Tennessee; and even at the Grand Ole Opry in Nashville. That was one of the most exciting bands ever. I would go up to Memphis on weekends and try to sit in at the black clubs when possible. There were some good musicians there at the time, both black and white."

Mose Allison

"Swingin' Machine"

Are you tired, are you uninspired?
If you're bored, you just can't afford
To miss out on the scene
When I turn on my little swingin' machine

I worked years through sweat and tears
I made tests tryin' to find the best
You know just what I mean
When I turn on my little swingin' machine

Sometimes it gets a little hard to start
Sometimes I think it's going to come apart
But when it's workin' just like a charm
Keeps me from going back to the farm

So, look neat, don't you drag your feet
Just turn loose, have a drink of juice
You'll know just what I mean
When I turn on my little swingin' machine

When my machine ain't runnin' right
I walk the floor, can't sleep at night
But when it really starts to percolate
I feel like I'm the master of my fate

Take a tip, don't be over hip
Just reach out, see what it's all about
You know it's much more felt than seen
I'm talkin' about my little swingin' machine

I'm talkin' about my little swingin' machine

Mose Allison

Soon after his high-school graduation, Mose Allison, like his father before him, decided to attend college at "Ole Miss," the University of Mississippi, Oxford, majoring in chemical engineering. Choosing the major was largely a whim, but Allison hoped it would be a practical career choice because he had read that chemical engineers were in great demand. The real motivation, however, was satisfying his *wanderlust*, which also turned out to be a factor in his ultimate career choice: professional musician. Allison thought that as a chemical engineer, he might be able to travel frequently to places around the world. The travelling mystique of a chemical engineering major soon dissipated, however, when he found himself subjected to six-hour science labs and could only look forward to four years of an equally lackluster curriculum.

    Mose broke the tedium of his freshman summer schedule

by taking up with another Southern social tradition when he joined Kappa Alpha, a fraternity on campus at Ole Miss. Still an avid football fan, he joined the house primarily because one of its members was a star on the Ole Miss football team, but Allison's affiliation with the fraternity proved short-lived. When he returned to Oxford after his eighteen-month stint in the Army, the worldly, recalcitrant musician had turned decidedly against the herd mentality as he knew it and was now clearly out of step with the hardline Southern "brotherhood."

Conversely, Allison's association with the University of Mississippi dance band, the Mississippians, survived his Army enlistment. Mose mostly played trumpet in the brass section during his freshman year, when pianist Dick Calloway led the band. Buck Clayton remained his favorite on trumpet, although Louis Armstrong's playing had also made a strong, lasting impression. Big-band swing music was in vogue at the time and musicians such as Count Basie and Lester Young were the most important influences on many young players at Ole Miss. However, Mose remembers that most college bands in the South actually played in the white swing-band style, fashioned in the vein of the Tommy Dorsey and Les Brown bands.

The Ole Miss dance band was no exception to this rule. The group played mostly parties and dances, and from his freshman year until he left Ole Miss in January, 1950, Mose Allison was always one of its prominent members. In this forum, Mose Allison, the soloist, stepped into a more public spotlight, often performing as the band's featured singer/pianist during short interludes between dance sets. Typically, he played one or two standard numbers, styling his performances after his great musical inspiration, singer/pianist Nat Cole. Allison later also adopted Cole's relaxed approach to phrasing in interpreting the blues. Although it remained latent in his repertoire at Ole Miss, Allison had not forgotten nor abandoned the blues genre. The modern style of jazz had only temporarily superseded his interest in the Mississippi roots music during this critical stage of his music education.

Another crucial period in Allison's musical maturation was

right around the corner. In an ironic twist of fate, the United States Army bolstered the further development of Allison's musical persona in two ways. First, it reneged on the conditions of Allison's enlistment. Second, instead of shipping him out overseas as planned, the Army stationed him in Colorado Springs, where he took the initiative to secure a position for himself as trumpeter in the 179th Army Ground Forces band. The eighteen-month tour of duty had a profound impact on the boy from Mississippi, expediting his metamorphosis from country bumpkin to "fledgling hipster" in both music and attitude.

Allison joined the Army on February 4, 1946, as a private. World War II had been over for six months, but the draft, for most eligible young men, remained viable and inevitable. Instead of waiting for the Army to draw his number, with only two full semesters of college completed, Allison volunteered for military service. He explains:

> I joined the Army for eighteen months because the officials told me that if I volunteered with my two buddies, we could stay together. One of my buddies, named Dudley Fedric, was from Tippo. He was my high-school pal and we went to Ole Miss together. The other guy was Benjamin Harrison, who in later years in Oklahoma called me up and identified himself as General Harrison. He stayed in. The ironic thing is that I was the one that got split from those two guys. Those two stayed together and went to North Carolina to the Quarter Master Corps and I went to Fort McClellan in Alabama, to the Infantry. I found out later that Fort McClellan was where Lester Young took his basic training. Most people who have done basic training know that Fort McClellan was one of the worst places in the world to do it. In fact, I had another bout with malaria when I was there, but the medics I went to said that nobody got malaria anymore, so they gave me something to soak my feet in! I had to wait until I got home on leave to go to my doctor and get cured of the malaria I had.
>
> After basic training, I went on a troop train from Memphis to Seattle and that was a hell of a trip. It was after

the war, so the soldiers had lost a lot of their charm. They had us on old discarded cars, filthy and such, and it must have taken about a week to get there. We'd go a few miles and stop somewhere. When I did get to Seattle, the idea was that I was supposed to be shipped overseas to the Orient, probably to Japan or Korea. While I was in Seattle, Congress changed the law about sending troops overseas who had limited training, ten weeks or whatever it was. So after getting the shots to go, and getting out there, I couldn't be sent overseas because I didn't have enough basic training. Then, they sent me back to Colorado Springs and as soon as I got there, I got into the band. It was the 179th Army Ground Forces band.

During his stint in the Army, the nineteen-year-old Allison played both trumpet and piano. In addition to his trumpet duties in the Army band, which required him to play formal and official ceremonies, he also played piano in small combos, groups with horns and a rhythm section, that provided music at officer and NCO clubs and dances. Mose preferred and was more proficient at playing piano in combinations, especially when he could feature center stage as the singer/pianist for an occasional number as he had done at Ole Miss:

> I was still playing both trumpet and piano in the Army. But, there were some good trumpet players in the band who made me realize that I wasn't as prepared on trumpet as I might have been. It was because I never had the consistency on the instrument. Sometimes I could play it, other times I had problems. So, I was really the piano player.

This exposure to a diversity of musicians, their advanced level of musicianship and life experiences, changed Allison. Disconnected from the protected enclave of his provincial Southern college campus, playing music full-time in the company of urbane, professional players had a galvanic effect on the young Mississippian. A new "hip" culture enveloped and influenced him, and he quickly fashioned his attitudes, lifestyle, fads, fashions, language and interests after the aesthetic of the professional musician. He recalls:

> There were several good musicians in the Army band but the phenomenon, the first jazz virtuoso that I was ever around, was Tommy Turk, the trombonist from Pittsburgh. He was the first serious hipster that I had met and I was very conscious of being the yokel. I played trumpet in the band, but piano in the small dance groups, and we stayed busy playing officer and NCO clubs, my first experience performing with musicians of that caliber. Just being around players like that gave me some enthusiasm. Playing in the Army band was a new experience. It resulted in my becoming an outsider at Ole Miss and my eventually going out on the road.

Mose also remembers playing at one memorable ceremony while he was stationed in Colorado Springs. The occasion was the dedication of the first ski lift at the world-class ski resort at Aspen, Colorado, and he became the first musician to play the blues on the lift:

> The 179th Army band was attached to the 10th Mountain Division. The commander of Camp Carson decided that the band should take ski training, so we travelled up to Cooper Hill, Colorado in trucks and we lived in tents for about six weeks and took ski training. We walked around in the snow up there, mostly going uphill. One of the things we did while we were up there was take a truck over to Aspen; the band was hauled up on the ski lift and we played for the opening ceremonies of the ski lift. At that time there was nothing in Aspen but an old run-down hotel, a bunch of weatherbeaten houses and a run-down bar. We played marches at the top of the ski lift for the opening dedication ceremony of the new ski lift. Coming down on the ski lift, the tuba player Bob Ploetz, was in front of me on the chair lift and he played a blues line. I played some blues with him. So, one of my undeniable accomplishments was that I was the first person to ever play the blues on the Aspen ski lift.

By the time Allison completed his military service in the Army, the trumpeter had achieved the three-stripe rank of T4 or Technician 4th class, and received an honorable discharge in August, 1947. He immediately re-enrolled at the University of Mississippi, Oxford for its fall term, this time as an economics major. Bill Woods was still with the Ole Miss band, leading the group when Mose returned. Although Woods's wife, Sarah Chatham, was the band's official singer, Mose was frequently showcased in his former role as singer/pianist. He continued to play dances with the Ole Miss band and a few off-campus jobs during the holidays, but Mose admits he returned to Ole Miss transformed:

> I don't think I was very rebellious about home until I left and came back to Mississippi. When I first went to Ole Miss, I was just your average Ole Miss freshman, but when I went into the Army and came back, by that time, I had become interested in bebop and seen the world a little. It was the whole idea of being a musician and cool and different from other people there. Stuff you'd read about musicians and the romance of a musician's life was part of it. I think everybody that's interested in something that doesn't exist where they live goes through that. My folks began wondering after I came back what was happening to the boy. I was twenty when I came back to Ole Miss. I had the long hair, slicked back with the DA, was trying to talk hip talk and spent most of the money I saved in the Army at the Beale Street tailors in Memphis on zoot suits. I was a bit of an embarrassment at that point. I've seen two or three generations of that now, so I believe that it's just a part of the sequence of things. Every generation picks something that it likes and it's usually something that older people are going to hate. It's just a normal procedure that goes on and I guess it always will.

After Allison returned to Ole Miss, he took regular weekend trips to nearby Memphis, fuelling his newfound hipster image. In 1947 and 1948, he spent most of his spare time there, going to clubs to listen to and meet musicians, encountering the phenomenal talents of a teenage prodigy, pianist Phineas Newborn, and a white alto player, Don Brooks, in the city. On one of these excursions to Memphis, Mose met Shenny Walker, the bass player for bluesman B.B. King. Walker provided an important entré into the black music world, sneaking Mose into the black clubs on the "chitlin circuit" and passing the white Allison off as his "cousin" when necessary. He also held sessions at his Memphis home and invited Allison to sit in. But for a white boy from Mississippi already interested in the blues, a monumental "whites only" musical event sent him reeling back to his musical roots. Allison remembers:

> On one of my trips to Memphis in 1948, I heard the first Sonny Boy Williamson at the Beale Street Auditorium, an afternoon performance for whites, a "Sepia Review", as it was called then. I went primarily for the high-note trumpet players and the dancing girls. Toward the end of the program, this guy comes out on stage in an old suit with a harmonica. I don't even think he was billed. He did ten minutes alone and it was one of those moments. The emotional force and rhythmic purity that he was able to generate were in complete contrast to the rest of the proceedings. It turned out to be the original Sonny Boy Williamson, who was killed soon afterwards. He reopened my eyes to the blues.

In fact, the original Sonny Boy Williamson, John Lee Williamson, was murdered by muggers in Chicago after performing at the Plantation Club on June 1, 1948 and Allison had witnessed one of his final performances. Mose also recalls that he was similarly impressed by the second Sonny Boy Williamson, Rice Miller, when he heard him play a few years later at a club on the south side of Chicago.

In 1947, also in Memphis, Mose had also heard the strains of what he believes was the first "rock and roll." A group called Tuff Green and His Rocketeers was in the vanguard of the style, but has since gone unrecognized in popular-music history. Whether he was hearing music defined as rock and roll or rhythm and blues, during his jaunts to Memphis, Allison was certainly attuned to the first stirrings of a revolution in popular music:

> Tuff Green and His Rocketeers played "a tastier version" of what became rock and roll later. Their big number was "We're Gonna Rock This House Tonight" and at the Mitchell Hotel, I heard a black singer do a slow-drag version of "Rock Around the Clock." I also started listening to B.B. King at the Mitchell Hotel on Beale Street in 1947. Turns out B.B. actually made his first recording with Tuff Green and His Rocketeers, on Memphis's Bullet label.

With college credits behind him and substantial experience on the bandstand, Allison was poised to play professionally during summers off from school. In the summer of 1948, he drove to Illinois, first to Chicago, then from town to town, going to clubs and sessions, meeting and sitting in with musicians there.

> I drove up to Chicago with my friend John Earle McDade, a trombonist with the Ole Miss dance band who was from Winona, Mississippi. He got a day job and ended up staying there. But the sequence of finding a cheap place to stay (YMCA), then checking out where the music was, trying to find out where you might be able to sit in and meet local players, was typical. I met some guys that were there with Lionel Hampton's band and one of them, a horn player named Lester Bass, taught me the quintessential bebop tune of the day, "Half Nelson," written by Tadd Dameron. When I got to New York City eight years later, it turned out to be one of of the "must-know" items at all of the sessions.

All told, Mose spent about six weeks in Illinois, eventually landing a two-week job in a Rock Island nightclub playing piano in a "jobbing band" directed by Tony Papa, a bandleader from Chicago.

The following summer, 1949, Allison was hired full-time to play piano and trumpet in a band at Rockaway Beach, a summer resort at Lake Taneycomo in the Ozark Mountains of south-western Missouri, near Branson, a short distance from the Arkansas border. Don Gilbert, a guitarist from Arkansas, led the band and organized the job. Mose remembers he was hired because Gilbert was assembling the band with players mostly from Mississippi. That summer he also met and performed with a reliable bass player named Taylor LaFargue and a trombonist/drummer named Dale Hampton, both from DeWitt, Arkansas, the two future members of his first professional trio.

At Rockaway Beach, Missouri, Mose also met Audre Schwartz, a lovely, dark-haired girl from St. Louis who was vacationing at the resort with her girlfriends. Two and half years later, they were married. Audre recalls:

> I was seventeen, had just finished my freshman year at the University of Missouri and was on vacation with my sister and five friends. After the first night I saw Mose, I wrote in my diary, "The band has a cute singer. He sang "Fools Rush In" just like Billy Eckstine." I never dreamed I'd meet him, but the next afternoon one of my outgoing friends came running down to the beach and said, "Come on up to the pavilion. The band is there and we're talking to them." I didn't talk to Mose, but later that afternoon he came driving up to our cabin and asked if I'd go out with him that night. Though I was apprehensive about going out with "a musician," Mose proved to be truly a Southern gentleman. Instead of the usual college boy bragging about sporting accomplishments and fraternity events, Mose looked up at the clouds and described what he imagined he saw. That night I wrote in my diary, "I feel like I've just met myself."

Returning to Ole Miss in the fall of 1949 for what would be his last semester, Allison assumed leadership of the Ole Miss dance band, writing band arrangements and rehearsing the group. That semester the economics major also enrolled in a course called "Cotton Economics." The substance of this course brought Mose new insight into the financial structure of Southern commerce, changing his thinking forever.

A percipient witness to the plight of sharecroppers, black and white, Allison was already familiar with the human condition of the African-American in the Mississippi; his black neighbors, for the most part, led impoverished, physically demanding lives. A step above slavery, they farmed in torrid temperatures, working in intolerable conditions amid mosquitoes, mules, and horseflies. In "Cotton Economics," Mose learned for the first time the full extent of the economic deprivation his neighbors in the Delta actually experienced. The course taught him that for every dollar spent on cotton products in the marketplace, the men and women actually toiling in the Delta cotton fields received only two cents of the profit. On the same dollar, white brokers and related business administrators made twenty cents. Enlightenment to the stark reality of Mississippi economics only exacerbated Allison's mounting anxiety about his native surroundings.

By 1950, the rebel among "Rebels" had clearly fallen out of the pack at Ole Miss. Disenchanted and restless, floating now without academic direction, Allison decided to hit the road, to try his hand at playing music professionally. In the first January of the new decade Mose and his trombonist/ad hoc drummer college roommate Dale Hampton connected with their Rockaway Beach cohort bassist Taylor LaFargue to propose a venture out of Mississippi in search of a music scene. Following rumors that beboppers and jazz clubs were thriving in Houston, the three packed up and headed south west. They drove only as far as Lake Charles, Louisiana, however, before stopping at a local roadhouse to eat. They ended up as the establishment's regular band, playing six nights a week for six weeks. It was Allison's first six-nighter, his first road tour with his first trio; the beginning of his peripatetic career as a professional musician. Taylor LaFargue recalls:

> Mose had a band at Ole Miss and Dale Hampton went up there to play in the trombone section after the summer of

1949. I had dropped out of college. Then, Dale and Mose left Ole Miss during the second semester and the three of us were supposed to go to Houston because Chubby Jackson, a bass player with Woody Herman, was supposed to have a big band. We were going down there to be around that band because it was supposed to be so great. In January, 1950, I picked them up in my car. We were on Highway 90 going across southern Louisiana when we stopped in Lake Charles at a place called Sammy's Restaurant and Bar to get a cup of coffee and some refreshments. We stayed there for six weeks because we got a job right then and there with the trio, starting that night. We went down to the local music store and picked up a snare drum, cymbals, a stand and some brushes and Dale was playing drums. We had a group that somewhat resembled a little King Cole Trio. We played swing music and also ballads, all the great standards like "Body and Soul," "I Can't Get Started," and "Stardust." Mose hadn't really started composing.

Allison named the group the Nat Garner Trio after his two musical heroes, singer/pianist Nat Cole and pianist Erroll Garner. The trio performed songs in the styles of both players, leavening their act with Louis Jordan numbers and whatever pop tunes they needed to "keep the dancers happy." When the six weeks in Lake Charles ended, the threesome drove west to Lafayette, Louisiana, landing a three-week job at Carlo Listi's Bar and Mardi Gras Lounge. The Nat Garner Trio broke up after the Lafayette job, but Allison continued alone, finding work as a pianist with a group playing a club in Panama City, Florida. Shortly thereafter, LaFargue rejoined Allison at the Panama City job, bringing with him drummer Bill Patey and a pianist from Little Rock, Walter Norris. Allison remembers:

After the Nat Garner Trio jobs played out I got a gig with a band called Four Satans and an Angel. We were playing in Florida for a few weeks but a squabble came up between two of the Satans in regard to the Angel and the band disbanded. Then, I called up a few of my buddies and we took over the job. I doubled on trumpet and piano and Walter Norris, who is now a well-known, distinguished pianist, doubled piano and saxophone.

Taylor LaFargue takes up the story: "We only got fired from one job in our lives and that was in Panama City. It was because the young lady doing the tap dancing couldn't dance and she blamed the band. She was attractive enough and she convinced the bar/nightclub's proprietor to fire us." After this débâcle, Allison joined a Southern territory band led by the well-known Burt Massengale, a group whose members, interestingly, came mostly from Pittsburgh. Mose remained with the Massengale troop for much of the remainder of 1950, starting out playing trumpet and later moving to piano; he remembers the experience with mixed emotions:

> A lot of good young players worked with Burt Massengale over the years. He would let them play a little but the jobs were mostly in conservative clubs with dancing and floor shows. I had trouble with the floor shows because I couldn't sightread well enough. This sort of thing came up several times during this period, cutting me out of some jobs and getting me into some unpleasant scenes with some of the "stars."

While Mose was playing for Massengale, Bill Bennett, an alto sax and clarinet player, converted an old house into a nightclub on the outskirts of Jackson, Mississippi. For a decade, Bennett owned and operated several clubs in the state. The clubs were always local hot spots, acting as jazz havens and attracting some of the South's best musicians. Allison and his various trios worked Bennett's clubs extensively from 1950 until he relocated permanently to New York City in 1956.

Mose was working Bennett's club in Jackson on New Year's Eve 1950 when he invited Audre to come down from St. Louis to meet his family. The holidays over, on the way to the airport for Audre's return trip, they decided instead to make a detour to the Justice of the Peace in Hernando, Mississippi on January 2, 1951. She recalls:

> Two and a half years after I met Mose in Rockaway Beach, after a romance almost entirely by mail, we married. I had actually seen him only a total of twenty days in short spurts, including that first week at Lake Taneycomo. Mose invited me to meet his parents in Mississippi two years later and as he was driving me to the airport for my return to St. Louis, he asked me to marry him instead. On that trip from Tippo to Memphis, we discussed any obstacles we might have to overcome, decided we could do it, that he'd apply to LSU, I'd get a job and we'd move immediately to Baton Rouge in time for the spring semester.

Following a trip to St. Louis to visit Audre's family, Mose did indeed apply to Louisiana State University, located in the state capital of Louisiana, Baton Rouge. For some time he had been considering returning to college to finish his bachelor's degree and, now married, the time seemed right to complete his education. The Allisons moved immediately to Baton Rouge, and Mose entered the spring semester, 1951 at LSU as an English major.

For Mose Allison, one advantage to attending school at LSU was the access it provided to the Baton Rouge music community. Because Louisiana was not a "dry" state like Mississippi, where state law prohibited liquor to be served in clubs, Mose knew that Baton Rouge could boast a hopping club scene. He was also aware that several good jazz players lived in and around the town and that the jazz hub of the South, New Orleans, was right on his doorstep, a few miles to the south east.

Taking up residency in the local clubs would provide him with ample opportunities to develop his style and work out with a few exceptional local players later to become world-famous. Just as important, Allison's seminal years at LSU would enable him to look inward. Mose Allison could now immerse himself in the subjects he truly enjoyed: literature, creative writing and philosophy. His intellectual development would expand his artistic horizons and help to ground his work in a solid ideology, thus laying the foundations for his lengthy career in the music industry.

3

DIDACTICS, BARTÓK AND CURLY'S

"I tried to use this music [blues] as a way of expressing myself. I had aesthetics in college and before I began performing full-time, I already had an idea of how I wanted to approach my music. I picked up ideas from a philosophy of art course, such as the difference between the artist and entertainer and the difference between the betrayal of emotion and the expression of emotion. These influenced me."

Mose Allison

"Foolkiller"

I was walkin' down a back street just the other night
I got a funny feeling that things weren't right
I heard some heavy footsteps right behind
And I know it wasn't just my mind

The foolkiller's comin'
Gettin' closer every day
The foolkiller's comin'
I got to try to make my getaway

I been livin' in this concrete ant hill	*Alternative version*
Scrapin' and a scrapping for that dollar bill	Eight million
Eight million people livin' on the brink	people livin' on
Got no time to stop and think	the make
	Waitin' for that
	one big break

The foolkiller's comin'
I do believe it's true
Ah well, the foolkiller's comin'
I think he's got his eye on me and you

If you've never been a fool then you don't have to worry
If you know you have better get in a hurry
Just to be on the safe side
Get yourself a place to hide

Because the foolkiller's comin'
Gettin' closer every day
The foolkiller's comin'
I got to try to make my getaway

Mose Allison

"Art is the removal of surpluses," wrote Walter Pater, nineteenth-century English aesthetician, Oxford scholar, and author of *Marius the Epicurean*, the celebrated reflection on late-Victorian society. Allison studied Pater's writings among those of other essayists in a course on aesthetics at Louisiana State University, Baton Rouge, taught by a favorite philosophy professor, Dr. Carmichael. Finishing his bachelor's degree in English, Mose's contemporaneous academic expeditions into subjects like metaphysics and aesthetics illuminated his studies in literature, criticism and creative writing. Allison, a voracious reader and a great admirer of literature from around the world, was now afforded the luxury of most college students: studying the topics that interested him. Moreover, with respect to his music, his academic pursuits helped create his personal style and later buttressed his ideological approach to it. Although the young Allison had established himself, at least in his own mind, as a musical renegade at Ole Miss, a mature and intellectually assertive Allison surfaced at LSU. A pliant student, he thoughtfully synthesized information and experience, eventually molding the artist the public would come to know and appreciate. During his Baton Rouge years, Allison independently explored various styles of music, defined and developed his own musical ideas and fashioned an artistic rationale with which to defend them.

For instance, Pater's eloquent dictum "Art is the removal of surpluses" translated more simply to "I do the most with the least" for the musician from Mississippi. At the time, "art," as applied to Mose Allison, remained an amorphous term, since he was engaged in multiple creative endeavors, writing short stories, performing music and composing. Although deeply committed to and serious about his music, Allison leaned, in both his studies at LSU and his interests at that time, more towards writing prose. His personal definition of art, therefore, required elasticity and breadth. Consequently, Pater's definition of art served Allison well, presenting him with an artistic modus operandi.

Allison's true bible on aesthetics, however, became R.G. Collingwood's *Principles of Art*, a treatise written in 1938. He was introduced to the book and studied it extensively in the aesthetics course at LSU. From the outset, Allison derived the substance of his artistic ideology from Collingwood's definition of "art proper": "Artistic activity is the experience of expressing one's emotions, and that which expresses them is the total imaginative activity called indifferently language or art. This is art proper."[1]

To fully grasp the meaning of Mose's statement that he based his approach to his music on "being aware of the differences between the artist and the entertainer, and the betrayal versus the expression of emotion," it is necessary to refer to Collingwood's academic, somewhat abstruse theories on art, since these were the cornerstone for Allison's thinking in establishing an "artistic conscience." Collingwood asserts: "When an emotion is aroused for its own sake as an enjoyable experience, the craft of arousing it is *amusement*; where for the sake of its practical value, *magic*."[2] Here, Collingwood asserts that neither "amusement" nor "magic" holds any true artistic value because each exists simply to entertain an audience, "while magic is utilitarian, amusement is hedonistic."[3] Conversely, Collingwood maintains that a work of "art proper" can stand on its own merit because by itself, the work represents the expression of true emotion.

What is important to consider here is that, according to many music scholars and critics, Collingwood's definition of "art proper" might not apply to the popular-music genre at all, and therefore not to Mose Allison, a musician whose blues-based jazz is considered a style of American popular music. Throughout its evolution, popular music, "music of the people," has in the main not been recognized as possessing true artistic merit, artistic legitimacy, by the "serious," classical-music community. It could be argued that popular music is largely a by-product of an era's "popular culture," invented to amuse and entertain the masses rather than express the human condition, communicate experience through art. Allison, however, enthusiastically embraced Collingwood's notion of "art proper," treating the expression of emotion as paramount, rather than seeking merely to entertain his audiences.

When Allison explains that he learned the difference between the "betrayal of emotion and the expression of emotion," he refers again to Collingwood's principles as applied to his music. Collingwood suggests that if an artist is committed to producing true art, no preconception of his audience's emotional reaction to it should exist in the artist's mind.[4] Rather, through the artist's chosen medium, whether paint or clay, dance, drama, or music, if the artist's own emotions are explored before the audience, and the audience is, therefore, allowed to discover itself similarly and simultaneously through the artist's work, that process creates true art. In a radio conversation with Ben Sidran, Mose summed these ideas up thus:

> I'm trying to do the best that I can with what I've got and I'm trying to make it mean something without being pompous about it. I like to think that if you analyze my songs, you'll get something out of it other than the surface swing. A lot of people approach me and tell me they got something out of it. People tell me there's a therapeutic quality to the songs and that they've helped them get through bad times. That's what they've done for me.

> I'm playing for my audience by playing for me. I'm not that much different from them. If the song means something to me, the fact that I'm pretty much like everybody else will make it appeal to other people.

The philosophy of art Allison gleaned from his education and experiences at LSU was to sustain him through his career. In the world of commercial music, Allison's artistic ideology would be repeatedly tested by powerful, influential forces. But Allison always stuck to his principles, resisting pressures from the record hucksters and corporate demands to mass-produce and eschewing the gimmickry of record-production techniques and fads. Inevitably, his uncompromising attitude would militate against commercial success, but Allison was mentally and emotionally prepared for the path he chose. Unlike many artists, who set themselves artistic limits only once their career is on the upswing, Mose Allison was fully committed to his chosen artistic path while still an idealistic college student and struggling musician in Louisiana.

Interestingly, Mose enrolled in only one formal music class at Louisiana State University, a mandatory course in the curriculum called "Music Appreciation." He was required to listen to several classical compositions in the course, mostly symphonies, which he found somewhat mundane. Months earlier, however, he had first heard the music of Béla Bartók, a composer celebrated for weaving the folk song of his native Hungary into large-scale orchestral compositions and solo instrumental pieces. Mose remembers going to the Music Department at LSU one day specifically to listen to Bartók's piano suite, "Hungarian Sketches." The piece gave him the idea for his own "Back Country Suite." Listening to how Bartók had personalized the form, he realized that using the suite could also enable him to compose a program using the stylistic elements of his own musical traditions, jazz and blues. Experimenting with this musical concept, Mose composed, bit by bit, the music which would become his "Cotton Country Suite."

Meanwhile, Allison was still playing professionally in clubs. A thriving live music scene existed in Baton Rouge in the early 1950s, and the town's nightclubs welcomed the newcomer pianist. Allison kindled relationships with several good musicians at this time, playing frequently with trumpeter Lee Fortier, who led a local band; a talented trombonist, Carl Fontana; and his friend Bill Patey, who played drums. Another local bandleader was Buddy Boudreaux, and he often hired Mose on piano and trumpet for six-nighters at a Baton Rouge club called the Golden Slipper. The Boudreaux group also included Fortier, Fontana, and Patey. Allison also recalls another club: "There was a black club across the river, the Blue Moon, I think, where I used to go and sit in with Joe Houston's band. He had a trumpet player named Walter Miller who was fantastic. I think he later played with Ray Charles."

One musician whom Mose respected and admired was another native Mississippian, tenor saxophonist Brew Moore. Mose and Taylor LaFargue, who had also relocated to Baton Rouge to find work as a professional musician, frequently travelled to New Orleans to listen to Moore, who was working strip joints in the Big Easy. Eventually, Mose ended up on the bandstand with him. He recalls:

> Brew Moore was from Indianola, Mississippi. He was a few years older than me and one of my early heroes. When I met him he had already made the New York scene, recorded with other Lestorians like Al [Cohn] and Zoot [Sims] and also with Machito. He was a very colorful, artistic guy who eked out a living on the fringes of the jazz world and died under-appreciated. He had inherited a little money, gone to Europe and was killed in an accident.
>
> I played with Brew across the river from Baton Rouge, in West Baton Rouge. They had gambling over there, so there were clubs. I got a job one time and I asked Brew to join me. He was living then in New Orleans. He always played well no matter who he played with and I heard him play well with some awful bands.

Although Mose was playing with musicians of the caliber of Brew Moore in Baton Rouge, he was nonetheless receptive to playing music in any available venue:

> Sometime during this period, I also worked odd jobs with whomever I could work with. I remember working a Cajun wedding one time and some jobs with an alto player named Bill Yiengst. He was an older guy who had a "jobbing" band that played weddings, dance halls, etc. I played this one job with him one time that was way out in the swamps of Louisiana in somebody's front room. They'd taken the furniture out. We were playing just standard tunes, anything people could dance to, "Stardust," "Rosetta" and "Honeysuckle Rose."

During the summer of 1951, Allison ventured to New York City for the first time, both to explore the possibilities of transferring to New York University to finish college and also to investigate the city's economic and artistic climate as far as jazz was concerned. When he first arrived in the city, he stayed with his cousin Marianna Staton, his Aunt Ruth's daughter. Ruth had moved from Mississippi to New York after her husband died in a cotton-gin accident. Her daughter, Marianna, had also lost her husband and lived alone in a pleasant apartment on Park Avenue and 96th Street. She thus had room to spare for her visiting cousin who stayed with her for a month, before moving into an apartment vacated by a friend, pianist Cookie Norwood. Audre then moved up from Louisiana to join him in Norwood's apartment and the couple spent the rest of the summer there.

Mose's impressions of New York University were not entirely favorable. The Southerner was somewhat overwhelmed by the NYU campus, located as it was in Greenwich Village amidst cement, noise, traffic and calamity. It was a completely foreign atmosphere to him, especially compared with the peaceful campuses of Ole Miss and LSU, with their green trees, rolling hills, and stately buildings. He knew that finishing his degree at NYU might hold academic advantages, but he also understood that relocating to New York City would require major life adjustments to enable him to cope with the pace of life and the city surroundings generally. With only a few credits left to finishing his bachelor's at LSU, he decided that moving to New York would not be worth the effort this readjustment would entail.

Also, a cooled climate for jazz in New York City in 1951 confirmed the wisdom of Allison's decision to head back to Louisiana. Mose scanned the Manhattan scene for jazz musicians, eager to determine whether any remnants of the prosperous club culture of the late 1940s still existed. He discovered that many of New York's established venues were alive and well, but a combination of the summer months and a decline in the general demand for the music had definitely lulled the action. Since the scene had dried up and he saw "many jazz stars out on the corner trying to borrow five dollars," he resolved to return to the South, finish school, perhaps embark on a writing career or get another degree and teach English. Meanwhile, although Baton Rouge was certainly not the jazz hub New York was, he knew he could always get some kind of work playing music there.

Returning to Baton Rouge, Allison was confronted with another ironic twist of fate when Bill Harvey, B.B. King's first musical director and tenor saxophonist, called him. Mose had befriended both Harvey and Shenny Walker, King's bass player, in Memphis clubs during the late 1940s while a student at Ole Miss. Harvey had heard Allison sing the blues, and was telephoning Mose in Baton Rouge to ask if he would be interested in recording a couple of tunes at a Memphis studio which had expressed interest in recording a white blues singer.

An interesting parallel arises here with another white singer interested in black music, then a teenager, who was rumored to have been making the rounds at the same Memphis clubs Allison frequented in the late 1940s, particularly the B.B. King shows. His name was Elvis Presley; he also hailed from Mississippi, and he made his first recordings at Memphis Recording Service, a studio owned by former D.J. Sam Phillips. Phillips had also recorded bluesmen B.B. King, Howlin' Wolf, and Bobby "Blue" Bland at his facility on 706 Union Street, establishing his label Sun Records shortly after Bill Harvey called Mose Allison. Sun Records, of course, was the record label that launched Elvis Presley in 1954. The rest is history.

At Harvey's request, Mose composed two "Charles Brown"-style numbers for the Memphis sessions. For reasons unknown to Allison, the sessions never materialized and the deal never proceeded. Presumably, Harvey was contacting Mose as a potential recording artist for Sun Records and Allison believes that the studio probably "got someone else," to wit, another white blues singer, who may very well have been Elvis Presley:

> I just happen to have been one of the people that came out of the New Orleans, African-American style which was developed mostly by Southerners and Midwesterners who were active in the 1920s, '30s, and '40s. It started with Louis Armstrong, then went to swing with Count Basie and Lester Young, then to bebop with Charlie Parker and Dizzy Gillespie.
>
> There were also the country-blues people like Muddy Waters, Lightnin' Hopkins, and John Lee Hooker. This whole thing is the bedrock, the foundation for all the music that is happening now, and I just happened to be one of those people who learned it from the ground up in the Mississippi Delta. I was doing it before it was big business. After one of my first records, John S. Wilson of the *New York Times* wrote a review that said I did the country blues so authentically, the phrasing was so authentic, that I could turn the raw country blues into a commercial item. I laugh every time I think about that, because not only was it turned into a commercial item, it became a billion-dollar business. It turned out that I wasn't the one who turned it into a commodity, although I was one of the people who was doing it first.

Allison finally graduated with a bachelor's degree in English from Louisiana State University in the spring of 1952, forgoing the formal graduation ceremony to play a night at his familiar stomping ground, Bill Bennett's honky-tonk on the outskirts of Jackson, Mississippi. A few great artists passed through Jackson that spring, namely B.B. King and Percy Mayfield, who played only in all-black clubs. Mose remembers that his friend Bill Harvey was able to get him into B.B. King's show, but having no connection into the black club where Mayfield was playing, he had to listen to his show from the street.

Shortly after the Bennett club gig, Allison embarked on what would become another four years of "on the job training" taking him throughout the Southern United States again. During these four years on the road, Allison interrupted his constant touring only during lulls in club business or when he and Audre were in need of a respite, returning to Tippo for a month or two's recuperation.

Allison's "on the road" period in the early 1950s provided him with valuable experience, enabling him to cope more easily with his eventual arrival on the New York scene in the later part of the decade. Together with Taylor LaFargue, a constantly shifting group of drummers and the occasional horn player, he led a rather bohemian lifestyle, travelling in search of local lounges and saloons back and forth from Florida to Texas. Audre accompanied her husband on the road, locating furnished apartments and day work for herself in each town, sometimes doing odd jobs, while the band settled in to perform nightly. Without the trio, Mose made it as far west as Denver, Colorado in 1953 and 1954, where he played piano in various clubs with drummer Shelly Rym, guitarists Bob Grey and Joel Cowan, and sometimes trumpet with the celebrated pianist Cedar Walton. Always drawn to the music of mambo bands, Allison also performed with a few Latino bands while in Denver. It was also in Denver, in 1954, that his first child, his daughter Alissa, was born, an event that precipitated his move to New York, with the hope of breaking in to the jazz world proper. Audre recalls:

> I think Mose thought that once we had a baby we had to start thinking about how we were going to get to New York for him to determine if he could play for a living. The idea was that you had to go to New York to find out if you could make it in music. He just always acted very respon-

sibly and now that we had Alissa it was time to find out, so we began to save money in anticipation of going there.

At this juncture, the trio was still frequently playing the Southern territory. Mose and the ever-present Taylor LaFargue alternated the group name Nat Garner Trio with the new sobriquet, the Johnny Garner Trio. LaFargue had remained Mose's constant travelling companion and musical comrade, the two sharing a common enthusiasm for and relaxed approach to playing swing and blues. Mose remembers:

Taylor LaFargue was very significant in my early years. He was a good basic four-four-type bass player and was always ready to go find a gig. He was also a Count Basie fanatic and it was through him that I heard a lot of those Basie with Lester records. We sort of had a good relationship. When I played with him down South for those years, the drummers and horn players always fluctuated; we had trouble getting reliable drummers when we started out. One drummer we worked with was Sparky Falkenhagen. I think we played music based on what ultimately became known as rhythm and blues, I suppose, but with elements of jazz like Nat King Cole and Erroll Garner. But definitely dancable.

Taylor LaFargue also has fond memories of this time:

We were on a kick one time about Erroll Garner and Mose could play a lot like him, usually good standard swing tunes. The style was strictly swing-era then. It wasn't very progressive jazz and didn't go off the deep end. Of course, the blues was one of our biggest deals. We had "group vocals" and learned Spanish songs. When we played in this Spanish bar, especially down in Texas, we sang in Spanish, we learned the songs. The music was great down there, like Tito Puente, because we loved that kind of music too. We also really tried to sing like the Nat Cole Trio. We did group vocals like "Call the Po-lice," one called "I Got Fish for Supper," and "Route 66." Of course, Mose was the feature focus because, like Nat Cole's group, when you hit the bridge, Mose got a solo.

On occasion, Mose was successful in persuading a club owner to add another salary and versatile Ralph Hughes, a trumpeter and drummer, joined the duo on the road. Originally from Ruleville, Mississippi, Hughes met Mose through his uncle, a trombonist Mose met after he returned to Ole Miss from the Army. Ralph became a close friend of the Allisons', moving to New York City a year after they had moved to Queens, and eventually marrying Mose's cousin, Susan Staton, another of Ruth's daughters and Marianna's sister. Hughes played his first job on trumpet with Allison in 1950 at Bill Bennett's in Jackson and continued working with him intermittently until 1956. He too has fond memories of this time:

> The audience especially liked Mose's singing. Occasionally, Mose would play a song he'd written, but they weren't featured or anything; he wasn't pushing them. We were pretty much just hanging out and we had a pretty loyal following at these clubs. The audience would keep coming back night after night. Because Mose took jobs that didn't pay as much, we didn't have to be too commercial and take a lot of guff. We didn't make a lot of money but we had a lot of fun hanging out together. Mose always had a good sense of humor; I guess you could call it droll.

Allison's itinerary was hectic during these four years on the road. He and his band toured extensively in Texas, where jobs appeared to be plentiful. Before Ralph Hughes joined the group, Allison, LaFargue and drummer Sparky Falkenhagen played a short trio job in Dallas, Texas in a lounge and bar by the side of the Adolphos Hotel, where Audre got a job as secretary to the sales and catering manager. The next stop was Pete Baggett's 49 Club in Waco, where the trio played frequently at different times, generally weekends and once during the Christmas holidays. Hughes joined the group in Waco and a drummer from New Orleans, Paul Logos, replaced Falkenhagen. The quartet then continued on to Curly's in Longview, Texas. At that point, the drummer left the band and its remaining members expanded their repertoire to include rumbas and cha-chas, performing in a Latin club in Houston with Ralph Hughes now playing drums. In fact, Allison's affinity for Latino music, elements of which are traceable in his own style, particularly in the rhythmic sensibility of his originals, made him feel right at home in certain parts of Texas:

> When I was out on the road in Texas once, the band was out of work but I got a job for a couple of nights with a mambo combo way over the Mexican part of San Antonio. I was the only gringo around and the dances were just fantastic.

Ralph Hughes has clear memories of this period of touring:

> The places I played in Texas were Waco, Houston, and Savannah. Mose also played Texarkana but I wasn't with him. I remember Curly's in Longview, Texas. There was a waitress at Curly's named Maudie Dempsey who used to say, "Honey, I don't worry about a thing 'cause I know nothin's gonna be alright." That was always Maudie's story. I don't know it for sure but I think Mose may have gotten that line from her.

After Houston, LaFargue tired of the road, and returned promptly to DeWitt, but before long, Mose was reconnecting with him and offering new employment, this time with a quartet. The re-formed group featured Harry Johnson on drums and a tenor saxophonist from Mississippi named Toby Tehnet and they played a month at Bill West's nightclub in Odessa, Texas. Then, after two weeks in Austin, the quartet disbanded again. Allison and LaFargue headed back north east to Jackson, Mississippi to play Bill Bennett's club, adding Don Brooks on alto sax. Their latest Jackson stint completed, tenor sax player Bunky Lane from Meridian, Mississippi joined the group and they played a quartet job in Natchez. Mose, Audre and Taylor then drove south to Miami to investigate opportunities to play there. Miami was completely devoid of a jazz-club scene, however, and after a month of sunshine, their restlessness brought them back to their staple gig at Bill Bennett's in Jackson.

Allison's four years of playing on the road in the South were replete with colorful characters and spiced by a few dangerous adventures. Although gunfights, not getting paid or both are considerable drawbacks in a touring musician's life, the illegal gambling and alcohol-induced brawls also staved off the tedium of the road. These hazards did not seem to affect Mose, and his marriage to Audre also provided a stabilizing factor:

> About 1954, I was playing in a place one night in Mississippi where one guy got shot. Some of those places I used to play in were really tough. I never got involved. I just kept playing. In this place where the guy got shot, he was shot by a gambler. They had illegal gambling there. It was during the Christmas holidays and when the pistol went off you could hear it all over the club. This gambler had the presence of mind to come running out screaming, "Somebody threw a firecracker in here." It was Christmas and everybody thought it was a logical explanation. Turns out it was some football player who lost some money at the gambling table and was giving them a hard time, so they shot him in the leg.

Ralph Hughes, like Mose, is philosophical about the hazards of the road life:

> We were playing at a place called the Pine Hill Club managed by Bill Bennett and they had a gambling thing going on. One morning, Bennett came over to the motel, woke us up and said, "Well, what do you think is the worst thing that could happen?" We said: "Alexander (who was the guy responsible for the money at the time) skipped out with the money." And Bill said, "No, somebody shot him dead in a card game last night." That was the end of that job.

The romance of their lifestyle on the road was further enhanced when the group adopted aliases, a measure they were forced to undertake in at least one Florida locale. Hughes recalls:

We used aliases at the time because we were underground. We were sort of avoiding getting hassled by the union, so each of us took on an alias. As the Johnny Garner Trio, "Jug" LaFargue's alias was "Sam Taylor;" I was "Danny Williams" and Mose was the leader, "Johnny Garner." Everybody knew who we really were but wouldn't admit it.

Taylor LaFargue particularly remembers an Orlando gig:

Ralph and I had been playing in Puerto Rico with a guy named Gene Corber. He had a little band and also booked a job at an NCO club at Fayetteville, North Carolina. I got Mose to play piano with Gene and Ralph since I'd played with them before. This same band went to Orlando to play a little club that R.J. Reynolds, the tobacco magnate, was trying to get off the ground. Reynolds had a club with a trotting track. Rick Caseres, who was a full back with the Chicago Bears at that time, and JoJo DiAgostino, whose father had an Italian restaurant there, opened up this club. It was sort of run-down but they spruced it up. We went down there to play a weekend with Gene Corber. They ended up hiring Mose, myself and Ralph Hughes to play drums.

Audre Allison also has vivid memories of that gig:

I worked as a waitress and saved about $800 from tips (that I put under the bed!) for our trip to New York. The R.J. Reynolds place was incredible. It was like a hotel upstairs, with giant rooms where Reynolds' guests stayed. We were the only ones there and had the upstairs to ourselves. The lobby had a carved piano and there were two beautiful staircases leading upstairs. The nightclub was run by two famous football players who were the drawing cards, attracting every young woman in the Winterpark area. Alissa was two years old, and when I worked at night, I would leave my job and run upstairs to check on her.

Orlando would be the end of the line for the "Johnny Garner Trio" as well as for Allison's extended jobs in the Southern states. In the four years he had also passed through and played in Georgia, South Carolina and Alabama. When he later returned to his native South as a well-known jazz artist, Mose would have established a distinct personal style for himself, a melange of downhome and uptown. Dave Brubeck's face on the cover of *Time* magazine in 1954 heralded the renaissance in jazz, generating a renewed interest in the music. Mose realized it would soon be time to turn north east again to Manhattan, the jazz metropolis, to try his hand at carving out a niche in his new "city home":

> When the jazz boom started there was a lot of national publicity about it and people who were struggling before were finally making a living playing jazz. I decided I wanted to go where the action was just to see what I could do. When I worked the small towns in the South, I learned that unless you have a lot of publicity, you can only go so far. Going to New York was an attempt to put myself in a better position for surviving. I got tired of working cocktail lounges and saloons down South and I needed a change.

Taylor LaFargue recalls that, despite their life on the road, he and Mose appeared relatively respectable:

> I know wildness is associated with jazz musicians but we weren't wild. I, personally, never was interested in raising hell, so to speak. We were, for those days, weird enough. We wore mustaches, goatees and zoot suits and tried to look like the guys we admired. This was an eye-catcher to the populace in itself. I guess they thought we were pretty far out according to their standards. But we did wear suits, white shirts, and neckties. Even though we had long hair, it was always groomed. We had a nice group—eating a lot of meals together, conversing a lot, and just hanging out.

4

HALCYON DAYS

"When I first came to New York, some people thought I was saleable as a 'colorful rustic.' I didn't cooperate in that role. I had a person approach me when my first record came out, someone in the promotional field, and the implication was, if you want to go on and stress this thing about being from Mississippi and being a colorful rustic, we can do something with that. But, if you want to play like everyone else, develop yourself, we can't do anything with that. I have no complaints. I feel really fortunate that I've been able to do what I wanted to do. A friend of mine once said that white Southerners, except for writers, are only acceptable by the national media as either buffoons or psychopaths."

Mose Allison

"City Home"

I'm thinkin' 'bout a place
I'm waitin' for the day
When I will make my getaway
'Cause as any fool can see,
There's nothin' here for me but
"Hurry up, boy, bring that water,
Don't do things you shouldn't oughta"

But, when I go away and find my easy street
I'll have a smile for all I meet
And they will welcome me I know

Everywhere I go,
I'll see the town in all its glitter
How can anyone be bitter
And there's a chance that I may
Find my big romance
When I get to my City Home

Mose Allison

"If You're Goin' to the City"

If you're goin' to the city
You better have some cash
If you're goin' to the city
You better have some cash
Because the people in the city
Don't mess around with trash

When you get up to the city
You better lock your door
When you get up to the city
You better lock your door
You know they'll take what you got, boy
Then they'll ask for more

When you get up to the city
You got to learn to shout
When you get up to the city
You got to learn to shout
'Cause if you don't stand up and holler
You gonna get left out

If you stay up in the city
There's just two things I hope
I said, if you stay up in the city,
There's just two things I hope
That you don't take money from a woman
And you don't start messin' 'round with dope

Mose Allison

The zeitgeist of the New York jazz scene in the late 1950s seeped into clubs like Birdland, Cafe Bohemia and the Village Vanguard, via jam sessions held in lofts and basements around the city. These sessions sustained many musicians in their off hours from clubs, and served as social centers and outlets for music where stars convened and mingled with unknowns and wannabes. For some struggling musicians, the "big time" proved elusive; others survived the endurance test in the city, their talent connecting with established jazz figures willing and able to provide aspiring players with exposure before an appreciative audience and with the opportunity to make a few dollars by indulging their passion, playing music.

One session spot which had a notable impact on the New York jazz scene was held in a loft downtown at 335 East 34th Street. Clyde Cox, a trombonist from Mississippi, founded and organized the sessions in his loft apartment, beginning in 1956. They continued into the early 1960s, when the building was demolished, surviving the departure both of their chief organizer, Cox, and of the host of musicians who roomed there. Since 1953, Clyde Cox had found steady employment as a trombonist in various touring bands based out of New York. When he discovered that his fellow Southerner and Ole Miss alumnus, Mose Allison, had relocated to the city, he immediately contacted him and invited him to join the recently-convened sessions.

Cox had first encountered Mose Allison in 1948 while he was at high school attending a band festival at the University of Mississippi, Oxford. Mose was playing trumpet in the Mississippians, reputed to be one of the best college dance bands in the South, and Cox recalled Mose's boogie-woogie piano feature as a showstopper. Yet when Cox matriculated at Ole Miss the following year, he had no personal contact with Mose on campus. He remembers that he often watched Mose conduct dance-band rehearsals and was aware that Mose was their arranger as well as a band member. The wayward Allison left Ole Miss shortly thereafter, touring on the road in the South, but frequently passed through Oxford to visit and sit in on sessions. Cox remembers him as the college idol because Mose was actually a "professional musician" out playing while everyone else was "just diddling with it."

Clyde Cox soon followed in Allison's footsteps as a career musician, playing in road bands and rooming with bass player Paul Worthington, also an acquaintance of Mose Allison. It was Worthington who leased the 34th Street apartment, sharing it with Cox, and when the bassist ran into Mose in New York, he mentioned the Mississippi connection and the sessions that Cox was organizing. Cox recalls:

> Paul Worthington had a place on 34th Street and I had a law suit pending at the insistence of Mario Bauzá. I was in a trombone section in 1954, I think with Machito's band, a jazz mambo band. They had to release the trombone section and Mario said the only way we could get severance pay was to sue him and he'd sue whomever it was running the job. I was on the road and had forgotten all about it. Then, when I came back to New York in 1956, I had a check for $150 waiting for me. I went down, bought a piano, put it in the loft on 34th Street and just started calling people and planning sessions. We started to session there about every night of the week and Mose was a steady. He either played trumpet or piano and would play there well into the sixties when he wasn't working.

In addition to the 34th Street sessions, Allison also remembers frequenting a basement session in Greenwich Village that Sonny Simpson put together. When he first arrived in New York City, Mose also visited the Musicians' Union each Wednesday afternoon, joining the many unemployed jazz musicians who gathered there to pick up weekend work:

> I don't remember my first job in New York but I remember hanging out at the union where everybody else hung out. The work was usually awful and didn't pay anything, but there was always something to keep you going. A few of those were some of the worst jobs I ever played in my life. I never got into the "jobbing bands" that played weddings

and such, but I was on the fringes of that at first. I would end up playing lounges on Friday or Saturday night, sometimes six hours for fifteen dollars.

Allison's break in playing clubs, however, came not from contacts he made at sessions or at the Musicians' Union but from having accompanied singer Marilyn Moore on piano in Galveston, Texas during his touring days in the South. Moore's husband was tenor saxophonist Al Cohn and when Allison arrived in New York City in the fall of 1956, Cohn asked him and Audre to their home for dinner in Flushing, Queens. Already a popular name in the jazz community, Cohn had garnered steady work in several well-known clubs in the city. He asked Allison to join his quartet on piano, offering him occasional work. Mose remembers:

The first job I ever worked with Al was a club in Queens. I hadn't been in town too long and I played with Al a couple of days. I think I worked my first six-nighter with him. At that time, when you first got to New York, you weren't supposed to work a steady job because of union regulations. You were supposed to be in New York six months before you could work a steady job. You had to go down to the union and apply for a transfer, and it took six months before you could work regularly. You could only work weekends and one-nighters until your transfer went through. So, I worked a lot of odd jobs; some of it was hardship, playing long hours for short money in terrible situations. Little by little, I began getting better work. Al Cohn was the first guy who started giving me work. He also gave me my first record date. It was in 1956 shortly after I moved to New York with Al, trombonist Bobby Brookmeyer, Teddy Kotick on bass and Nick Stabulas was the drummer.

Not long after meeting Al Cohn, Mose was introduced to tenor saxophonist Zoot Sims at the loft on 34th Street. In the early 1950s, Zoot Sims formed an on-stage partnership with fellow tenor player Al Cohn, the two having met playing in

Woody Herman's band. Mose had always been impressed by the duo's records, which he had heard when touring the South. By the time he finally met the two tenor saxophonists in 1956, they were established, well-known international players, both individually and as a duo. Over the years, the two tenors fronted various jazz ensembles and Allison became one of their regular pianists.

Mose had been without steady employment for several months, but once he connected with Zoot Sims and Al Cohn, he worked consistently as their sideman. His days of hanging around the union on Wednesday afternoons were over; from this time on, he would always have steady work as a musician. Mose continued as a regular Sims–Cohn sideman both for their live performances and record dates, until 1960, even after he had recorded with his own trio and was gaining widespread recognition in his own right.

Allison's work with Al and Zoot was significant because he gained valuable on-stage experience backing expert players, and was thus able to demonstrate to a wide audience his adroitness at "comping," the technique of accenting chords behind the solo instrumentalist. His relaxed approach to rhythm and phrasing, derived largely from Southern influences, and his affinity with the Lestorian tradition soon made him a much-valued commodity in certain jazz circles.

One extended performance that Allison remembers with the Cohn–Sims duo took place at the Half Note Cafe on Spring Street, the site of their live recording *A Night at the Half Note*, which also featured bassist Nabil "Knobby" Totah, Paul Motian on drums and alto saxophonist/clarinetist Phil Woods. At the Half Note, the sextet played what would now be considered a grueling night's work, a six-set performance between 9 p.m. and 3 a.m., for ten weeks each year. He also played piano for more collaborative efforts by the duo, 1957's *Al and Zoot*; *Either Way*, recorded in 1959; and *You 'N Me*, recorded in 1960. He is also heard on one of Cohn's solo records, *Al Cohn Quintet featuring Bobby Brookmeyer* recorded in 1956.

In addition to the Cohn–Sims jobs, Allison's debut years in New York City found him playing as a sideman for other name jazz artists. Juggling his schedule with Cohn and

Sims, he also became a regular sideman on piano for tenor saxophonist Stan Getz. The flamboyant tenor player was an international jazz superstar when Allison began his association with him in the late 1950s. The Woody Herman band had given Getz his break, his extraordinary sax solo on the recording "Early Autumn" launching a stellar career that spanned several decades. Getz was constantly touring both in the U.S. and abroad, and Mose Allison accompanied him on many of his U.S. apppearances in 1957 and 1958, especially on the east coast, in Manhattan, Philadelphia and Long Island, New York, also siding on Getz's 1957 recording entitled "The Soft Swing.".

In addition to his work with Stan Getz, Mose also played piano for baritone saxophonist Gerry Mulligan, traveling with him to Baker's Lounge in Detroit and locally, to another well-known jazz venue, the Cork and Bib in Westbury, New York, where he had previously played with tenor saxophonist Freddie Greenwell. Allison also played one weekend with the legendary trumpeter Chet Baker, returning to the Red Hill Inn in New Jersey where he had previously sided for Stan Getz. Between Al Cohn, Zoot Sims, Stan Getz, Gerry Mulligan and Chet Baker, Allison was now professionally associated with a number of the most celebrated jazz figures of the day, musicians around whom the movement in modern jazz rallied. At the same time, though, Allison was developing his own original musical ideas, preparing himself for his entrée into the music world as a solo artist:

> I was working with Al, Zoot and Stan at the same time. In fact, I remember specifically working at Birdland one matinee with Al and Zoot and the same night with Stan in Newark New Jersey. Birdland was the jazz corner of the world. It was *the* place and had an aura about it. It was considered the peak, the mountain top. I never really felt part of it, though. I thought I was there temporarily, sort of passing through. I never thought about making it or about being one of the princes of Birdland. For somebody who was new in town, especially someone from the South, Birdland was sort of an imposing place, a little intimidating.

Later, I did work there with my trio on the same bill with John Coltrane.

When Allison first arrived in New York City, he had not yet settled on his solo course, so accompanying famous jazz artists satisfied him momentarily. Eager to work and grateful for the opportunity to play, he was especially thrilled at finding himself on stage playing with musicians he admired. Further, the role of sideman did not stifle his artistry. Every night of "on-the-job learning" in New York bolstered his confidence as a musician. He had come a long way from Bill Bennett's in Jackson, Mississippi. Thrust into the limelight before swelling crowds in major metropolitan centers, Mose's eyes were opened to a phenomenon new to him: audiences actually *listened* rather than simply dancing to the music being played:

Playing with those people was gratifying and it was a learning experience for me in every way. There were no drawbacks to it at all. I was able to express myself as well as I wanted to when I was playing piano with well-known musicians. It was great fun and I remember when I first began to see how many fans some of these guys had. I think I was on the road with Getz and the adulation being showered on him was completely overwhelming to me, because down South where I had been playing, the musicians had about the same status as a bus boy. What was really an eye opener to me was realizing that once a musician had a lot of fans, all he had to do was get to the job and play.

Allison's humility about his work and his easygoing demeanor notwithstanding, factions in the New York jazz community immediately attempted to disparage and devalue his work by categorizing him and his style. As with every performance art, many different approaches to jazz existed at that time and Allison, along with his contemporaries, whether amenable or not, became victims of labeling, musical dissection and contrived classification. Mose Allison, an eclectic musician, was not keen on being lumped into a particular camp, especially after he had established his own direction and identity, and he became even more hostile to the descriptive tag "colorful rustic," with which certain people in the New York music community attempted to label him, stereotyping him because of his Southern agrarian background:

> There had been run-ins with people at jam sessions in New York when I first got there. But most musicians are megalomaniacs anyhow. There are clannish instincts about it, there were always cliques and I'm sure there still are. Since everyone is striving to make it, that's the way it is. It was no different when I got to New York. The classic example of this is the two forms of playing that were prevalent at the time when I first came to New York. Some admired Lester Young, others Charlie Parker. These were two completely different approaches to rhythm. Lester Young's style was more of a Southern, laid-back, relaxed, pastoral type of playing. Charlie Parker was more intense, frenetic and torrential.

Initially, the 34th Street loft had a Southern air, serving as it did as the New York oasis for uprooted white Southerners. Mose Allison was a familiar figure at the loft during his off hours, and soon became a dominant musical force there on both piano and trumpet. Also, Clyde Cox quickly gained two roommates from the South: Taylor LaFargue and Ralph Hughes, who had also moved north to Manhattan to try their hands at playing professionally. Ronnie Free, an experienced drummer from South Carolina, also made frequent appearances there. Eventually, however, a growing number of players from around the country attended the jams at the loft and although this tended to dilute the homogeneity of the Southern group, its hospitality and geniality lingered. The loft thus quickly earned a reputation around the city as a music haven, noted for its relaxed ambiance and comfort, both of which facilitated the artistic happenings occurring there.

The location at 335 East 34th Street was not typical of most lofts. Sandwiched between two woodworking shops on the middle floor of a three-story building, the physical accommodations on 34th Street were smallish, resembling more an apartment than the cavernous shape of a traditional Manhattan loft. Like the conventional floor plan of a loft, though, the space on 34th Street was one large room which its occupants had separated in two by means of bamboo drapes. Clyde Cox remembers that someone had hung a dartboard in the back half of the apartment, which also helped to emphasize the division of the space.

Aside from the woodworking shops, there were no other residents in the building. However, the location was surrounded by street traffic and other buildings, both potential impediments to conducting noisy all-night jam sessions. To soundproof the area, Ralph Hughes, an expert carpenter, led a small group in constructing sound drops. After 9.30 p.m., the attending musicians would hang the drops outside the buildings, lifting them only in the short respites punctuating the playing.

As word of the loft spread and its residents became acquainted with more musicians, the sessions became increasingly crowded. Admittance was by invitation only, and players alternated throughout the night, coming and going, guests bringing with them other musicians. Up to twenty players might pass through in a single evening, with one musician playing sometimes for two hours at a stretch and another player waiting in the wings to replace him.[1] One regular visitor to the loft was the celebrated pianist/vocalist Dave Frishberg from St. Paul, Minnesota, who often brought musician friends with him. Frishberg was familiar with Allison's trumpet playing from the loft jam sessions and he also knew Mose played piano for Cohn and Sims. But when Ronnie Free played him Allison's newly-released *Back Country Suite*, Frishberg was more than impressed:

I loved the singer and I asked who it was. When Ronnie told me it was Mose singing, I thought, "What else does this guy do?" I learned then that Mose was also a composer and lyricist and, most important to me, a unique stylist. I've always been partial to musicians who put their own personal stamp on the music, and Mose's music was, and continues to be, his very own—impossible to imitate convincingly.

I thought of the regulars at Clyde's as the Southern contingent. I remember they liked to talk seriously about literature and were fans of William Faulkner. When I first began writing songs in the early sixties, I ran into Mose one night in the Village, and I invited him up to my apartment to hear some of my tunes. He didn't have much to say about the songs but he did suggest that I learn to sing more in tune, and that's a suggestion I took seriously, even though I still wouldn't represent myself as a standard for good intonation. But I still haven't read any Faulkner.

The steady stream of musicians patronizing the loft on 34th Street included many New York jazz players whose careers were on the rise. Allison frequently attended the jam sessions with bassist Buddy Jones and Seattle tenor saxophonist Freddie Greenwell. Those present at the loft recall that Greenwell sessioned there more often than any other tenor player, even living there intermittently. Mose also met well-known pianist George Wallington at the sessions, and connected with two drummers who eventually became sidemen: Frank Isola, the drummer on his first record; and Ronnie Free, who played several record dates and toured with him in the 1960s. Among other regular participants at the loft were pianist Don Friedman and popular bass player Henry Grimes. In addition, trumpeter/pianist Jerry Lloyd (Jerome Hurwitz), a sideman for Charlie Parker, and tenor player Don Janes from Sedalia, Missouri often dropped by.

Among the more celebrated musicians who played the sessions regularly on 34th Street were Mose's employers Al Cohn and Zoot Sims. Sims usually arrived at the loft with pianist Johnny Williams, and occasionally he brought Stan Getz with him. Al Haig, the singular and influential pianist, would often attend these sessions and renowned tenor saxophonist Sonny Rollins, often with bassist Henry Grimes, was also a frequent participant. Even the legendary pianist Bud Powell passed through the 34th Street loft before he moved to Paris in 1959. Powell had already been plagued by a series of mental breakdowns by then and Clyde Cox remembers that in the two or three visits Powell made to the loft, he never played but simply sat and stared around him.

The drug trouble plaguing Powell and many of his contemporaries was conspicuously absent from the 34th Street loft. From the inception of the sessions, the musicians collectively declared that using hard drugs would be taboo and the participants had to commit themselves to being drug-free. Although marijuana smoking was not unusual, hard-drug incidents were thus exceptionally rare. In one incident, however, Clyde Cox discovered a hidden set of heroin "works" hanging out of one of the windows. By cutting them loose and letting them drop to the street, he sent a clear message to their owner that drug activity was not welcome at the loft.

Freedom from drugs was one factor that allowed the music to prosper and friendships to flourish at the loft. Freedom from ego battles, serious musical competition and petty infighting also engendered a supportive and spirited environment which advanced the cause of playing and creating music. In all accounts of the 34th Street sessions, participants recall the cameraderie and serious approach towards making music there.

Pianist and composer Dave Frishberg was so enamoured of the place that he described the idyllic era of the converging of music and people as "the halcyon days of the loft." Clyde Cox recalls:

> The loft was not a competitive place at all. We had what I guess you could call a "cutting session" one time but it was wonderfully friendly. Dizzy Utley came in one time when Zoot was there and they played literally for seven hours. It was a memorable night, a head-to-head, and they played until five in the morning. There may have been two horns going at it like this but in terms of the fierce and blistering

tempos, strange keys and meters of the classic cutting session, none of that ever went on. The whole idea of the loft was not to exclude. The exclusion was done on the basis of who was invited in the first place. It was pretty much word-of-mouth, but there was no wholesale inviting people because there was not enough room.

In 1957, Mose was working clubs with Stan Getz when Taylor LaFargue finished up a tour with Buddy Morrow's band in New York City. LaFargue and Allison had parted company earlier in 1956 after touring the Southern states, and while Allison journeyed north to work in New York, LaFargue withdrew to Arkansas. LaFargue's initial communications with Allison indicated that Mose was disgruntled with the New York jazz scene, was struggling to find work, and intimated that he was interested in re-forming their Southern state touring band.

By the time LaFargue arrived in New York, however, Mose's situation had improved. Allison was enjoying his career as a sideman with various name players, working steadily and was able to introduce LaFargue to Stan Getz at one of the sessions at 34th Street. Mose was about to embark on a multiple-city tour with Getz, and he knew that Getz needed a bass player. After Mose introduced the two, Getz hired LaFargue for the tour, taking the quartet to Rochester, New York, Detroit, Chicago, Providence, Norfolk, Va. and Philadelphia.

The Allison-LaFargue rhythm section also backed Getz for several performances in the Manhattan area, some lasting a week at a time. LaFargue then became a regular sideman when Allison formed the Mose Allison Trio in 1957, and was invited to play on Mose's first record date for Prestige Records that March. Altogether, though, Taylor LaFargue found it difficult finding steady work as a jazz bassist in New York. A few months after recording Mose's album, he grew disenchanted, realizing that he was sitting around discussing music at Junior's or Charlie's Bar more than he was actually standing up playing bass. He was studying voice regularly with Margaret Haymes, mother of the popular singer Dick

Haymes, but realistically eventually realized he felt he could no longer depend on a career in music. With his father's death, LaFargue inherited his family's rice farm in DeWitt, Arkansas, and moved back there, closing a chapter in his life as a musician and winding up his ten-year professional association with Mose Allison.

Fortunately, after his arrival in New York City, Allison had worked consistently at building up a strong network of eminent jazz players. He had never abandoned his plans to lead his own trio, continued to compose and kept up with his singing. When the time was right, he was determined to gather the right players together and work autonomously, as he had in the South. His New York network provided him with numerous outstanding players, among them bass player Addison Farmer, twin brother of the well-known trumpeter Art, and the gifted drummer Paul Motian, whom Mose met on Cohn-Sims and Getz dates.

Motian was the drummer on Allison's first New York trio gig at the Cafe Bohemia in 1958, a nightly job that lasted two weeks. Allison notes that Horace Silver and Herbie Mann were also on the bill and that on his first night out as the Mose Allison Trio, he was "virtually ignored." Paul Motian, however, became a favorite accompanist for Allison during his early career. Because the drummer was a highly sought-after player, Mose often had to fill the spot with other drummers, but as the first sideman to play Allison's original material in public, Paul Motian quickly formed both a professional and amicable relationship with Mose Allison which subsequently weathered both their hectic international careers. Motian played on several of Mose's Atlantic record dates and for over forty years has enjoyed accompanying him when schedules allow. At their first meeting, Motian was acquainted only with Mose's sideman work for the celebrity saxophonists Cohn and Sims, but he was immediately intrigued by Allison's original material and his singing of the blues.

Mose Allison's vision and determination to carry out plans for his solo project, the Mose Allison Trio, did not end with the Cafe Bohemia job, and New York audiences seemed receptive enough to his brand of artistry. Allison's appearances on the local bandstand with recognized jazz artists had already made him a familiar New York figure. Moreover, his personal musical style, a hybrid of jazz and blues, was original, not to say unique, even to the sophisticated ears of New York jazz listeners. The country-blues song form Allison introduced to the New York music scene had had little previous exposure in the North. Considered "exotic," even "primitive," this musical legacy of his Mississippi upbringing was immediately welcomed as a refreshing, "authentic" novelty by jaded New York jazzers. Mose comments:

> While I was in college, I studied aesthetics, and I had decided that the blues was an art form. I was trying to incorporate my experiences with the form of music of my childhood into jazz elements. This was in the fifties and I wasn't the only one doing it: Horace Silver, Hampton Hawes and Wynton Kelly were into that same process to varying degrees at the same time. I've always said that you have to get a style and transcend that style. That's what I've been doing ever since I got to New York. I got my style together, basing it on the African-American blues, and now I'm trying to maintain the essential ingredients of that style but still with enough embellishments to keep it fresh and not fall into any petrified, standardized type of thing. That's what I do every time I play.

Clyde Cox adds:

> The only original tune I can remember Mose playing in the loft was from his first record. It was called "Spring Song." This was the sort of deliberate, artful, downhome stuff, shouts and such, that I would call "popularized primitivism." The first person I heard doing it and talking about it was Mose Allison. Ray Charles was also starting to become big and Mose mentioned him, so I promptly went out and bought those records. I think Mose was into this way before anyone else because I remember, in 1949, I heard Mose playing "Move" and he had his own treatment

of it that was very much his own style. He sure wasn't playing like Miles. He was playing like Mose.

It was imperative to achieve success with the Mose Allison Trio, because as the father to a growing family, Mose required economic stability. For over two years, the Allisons' first apartment in Manhattan, located on the upper west side at West 106th Street and Columbus Avenue, had served as a warm hearth for the couple, their young daughter, Alissa, and friends. During that time, Mose was an active participant in his family's life, spending playful afternoons with his daughter after picking her up from the Hansel and Gretel nursery school at noon while Audre worked at a Manhattan advertising agency. Central Park was a convenient playground for Mose and Alissa, but after the birth of their second daughter, Amy, in 1958, the family decided to relocate to an apartment in the more residential area of Jackson Heights in Queens, a short distance from Manhattan, a home which offered more room and a backyard. In 1959, the twins John and Janine were born, completing the Allison brood. By 1963, the Allisons had moved even farther out to Long Island to the home in Smithtown, New York where Mose and Audre still reside, close to the high school where Audre has taught English and creative writing for several years.

The Allisons had adapted well to their new urban lifestyle, adjusting to the stability of remaining in one place for an extended period of time, and quickly becoming New Yorkers. Socially, Mose easily integrated into the circle of personalities in the New York jazz world, swiftly developing a core of supportive musician friends. Professionally, at thirty years old, he had also succeeded in carving out a musical niche in New York, both as a highly regarded sideman on piano and trumpet and as leader of his own trio. His collaborations with a diverse group of players had brought the standard of his musicianship to a high level, and his new urban setting gave a new edge to the art he had based so solidly on his appreciation of Southern culture.

In leaving the familiar South, Mose Allison had confronted the ultimate challenge. For most, moving to the urban jungle,

New York City, to try and "make it" playing music, was at best a speculative proposition. But both he and Audre had often agreed that he would forever regret never having made the attempt had he stayed in the South. Through luck and perseverance and courtesy of his unique musical gift, his efforts were beginning to bear fruit, and after only a few short years on the New York circuit, Mose Allison was well on his way towards making an indelible mark in jazz. Clyde Cox remembers the Mose of this period with affection and respect:

> Mose was always—I don't want to use the word gentleman because it sounds out of context if you say a jazz player was a gentleman. What I mean is that I cannot remember a single unpleasant incident ever involving Mose, and there were people who were unpleasant sometimes in terms of conduct. Mose has a wonderful sense of humor, and that was part of the loft. In describing the ambiance, "fellowship" doesn't do it, "a bunch of cats" doesn't do it either. It wasn't a bunch of damn fools sitting around trying to be hip. There were people who were serious about it, who loved to play music, and Mose seemed to be committed and more serious than any of us about what he was doing. There was never any ego nonsense. He'd sit down and play with anyone.

5

BACK COUNTRY SUITE

"Sometimes I like the angrier songs like 'Foolkiller' but I think that I have no real favorites apart from *Back Country Suite*, which was the first thing I heard so I'll always have a special feeling about that. I don't think I actually have a favorite song. It might be a strange thing to say but when I listen to Mose, I can put anything on. It's like I'm receiving the whole man, the whole atmosphere. I suppose what I'm trying to say is that if we thought about him in Eastern terms, if he were Indian, for example, he would be considered saintly in that respect. I get some kind of meditative message from all of it, therefore, I don't want to get too attached to the superficialities in the music. I don't want to get too involved in it. And that's why his voice is so important. I do love the words, I do like the songs, I do like the self-effacement, I do like the humor, I do like the brevity and the cascading modern piano style that he's using these days. He gets better and better as a musician, more lyrical, more fluid, more bright and dangerous. But this is the evolution of the body and mind in his case.

"The reason I'm so happy he sings is because I think the voice, to use the eternal cliché, is the window to the soul. I think that he seems to have a very good soul and the goodness that is there comes across in it."

Pete Townshend

"Young Man Blues"

Well, a young man
Ain't nothin' in this world these days

I said a young man
Ain't nothin' in this world these days

In the old days
When a young man was a strong man
All the people stand back when a young man walk by
But nowadays
The ol' man got all the money

And a young man
Ain't nothin' in this world these days

Mose Allison

The material for Mose Allison's *Back Country Suite* filtered through his mind for nearly ten years but was largely complete when he arrived in New York in 1956. Alluding to its inspiration and Southern agrarian theme, Allison originally titled the piece "Cotton Country Suite," a name that his record company, Prestige Records, later changed, presumably to proffer greater market appeal. Allison's introduction to the Prestige label is attributable to the late pianist George Wallington, who recommended him to Prestige president Bob Weinstock. Allison had met Wallington at a session at Clyde Cox's loft on East 34th Street, and discovering they were neighbors in New York City's upper west side, became acquainted with him, providing arrangements for one of Wallington's record dates.

One evening, Wallington threw a party in his Manhattan apartment, inviting his guests to participate in a jam session. Allison joined in on the piano, performing various sketches from his *Back Country Suite*. Wallington had previously heard Allison's original work, but the material Mose played that evening particularly impressed him. Personally acquainted with Bob Weinstock at Prestige Records, a growing New York independent label that was gaining momentum in successfully recording jazz artists, Wallington offered to contact the record company president on Allison's behalf. Having failed in his own attempts at obtaining a record date for his material, Mose was keen to have his colleague provide his introduction to Prestige Records.

After Mose made a rough tape of his *Cotton Country Suite* in the loft on 34th Street, Wallington brought him to meet Bob Weinstock. With the three present in his New York office, the Prestige president listened to Allison's tape and immediately offered the pianist/vocalist a recording contract with his label. Allison agreed to a two-year, six-record deal with Prestige, receiving $250 for the first two records and $350 for the remaining four. In retrospect, the money for Allison's work was a pittance, but as a career move, Weinstock's company turned out to be a good first investment for Mose: not only would Allison be on a roster that included jazz artists such as John Coltrane, Miles Davis, Charles Mingus, and Thelonious Monk, but as a young independent label, Weinstock's company was small and interested enough to pay attention and actively participate in his music and career.

On March 7, 1957 in Hackensack, New Jersey, Rudy Van Gelden, a celebrated recording engineer, recorded Allison's first solo album, *Back Country Suite*, for Prestige Records. Appearing as the Mose Allison Trio, his long-time Southern colleague Taylor LaFargue accompanied him on bass and Frank Isola, a musician he had met during sessions at the 34th Street loft, performed on drums. Allison was less than pleased with the result:

> My remembrance of the whole thing is that the tape I made in the loft on the old piano was ten times better than the record I was able to make. The studio cramp and the whole unfamiliarity of recording and being put off by the process of stopping and starting bothered me. Recording is a completely different world. I still feel like that. It was a painful and completely different experience than just playing.

Taylor LaFargue agrees:

> I guess I was nervous for that record. When we did it, it was a hurried deal. We did it in one afternoon in New Jersey at a

recording studio. The owner of Prestige Records was there and I think everyone was a little nervous. Even though the critics like it, in retrospect, I wasn't very comfortable with my performance because I felt like the whole process was hurried and nerve-racking.

The harsh self-criticism of its performers notwithstanding, *Back Country Suite* was an instant hit with critics, especially with the venerable and influential jazz magazine *Downbeat*. The five-star review written by *Downbeat*'s music critic Dom Cerulli and those of other music journalists substantially boosted Allison's first effort. Mose acknowledges the important role the press played in his early success:

I remember the first review of *Back County Suite*. I was completely astounded because it got a real rave review in *Downbeat* and all over, which really launched me. It helped other people show interest in my work.

Allison's ideas for *Back County Suite* had germinated while he was a student at Louisiana State University studying English and philosophy and listening to a diversity of musical styles, including classical music. He was aware that many composers had used folk motifs in their orchestral works and that the technique had become a trend prevalent in American twentieth-century classical composition. He had also learned that, decades earlier, the composers in the American neoclassical movement, led by Igor Stravinsky and Aaron Copland, had used the baroque form of the dance suite for composing ballets.[1] Further, he was greatly inspired by the music of Duke Ellington, who often approached jazz composition from a perspective generally adopted by classical composers. Ellington's suite *Black, Brown and Beige*, a programmatic piece for jazz orchestra, made a particularly deep impression on Mose.

Interestingly, in composing *Back County Suite*, Allison turned directly to Béla Bartók who is known for his skill in utilizing his country's folk music to provide color and substance for his orchestral compositions. Allison became something of a

Bartók devotee, listening to many of the Hungarian's compositions, and being particularly impressed by his Second Piano Concerto and Concerto for Orchestra.[2] It was, however, a piece from Bartók's piano repertoire, the Hungarian Sketches, a suite of folk impressions for solo piano, that Allison used as the paradigm for *Back Country Suite*:

> I first heard Bartók's Hungarian Sketches when I was at LSU. I thought, here is a guy who's taken folk themes and songs and put them together to create a piece which reflects the whole society. I thought I could probably do the same thing with the society I came from, so I decided to set down my impressions in music.

The album *Back Country Suite* broke new stylistic ground, marking out Mose Allison as a singular, refreshing voice in American music. Following Bartók's lead, Allison composed his own set of Southern sketches for solo piano, using the suite as his framework. While the classical composers, including Bartók, used the traditional instrumental form, one comprised of several movements based musically on the rhythms, tempos and motifs of classic dances, Allison composed his suite using both instrumental and vocal movements reflecting musical elements characteristic of American popular music, jazz and blues. Allison's musical program for the suite was thematically based on Southern culture, presenting a musical montage of impressions depicting Southern scenes. *Back Country Suite* utilized indigenous American musical styles and through its program, Allison was able, convincingly and naturally, to synthesize the Delta folk music, the blues, with the sophistication and rhythmic vitality of modern jazz.

Back Country Suite features ten musical vignettes of varying tempos, nine short piano pieces written for the standard jazz trio/rhythm section, piano, bass and drums, and one vocal placed midway through to break up the density of the instrumentals. Ten tone poems comprise the suite and each receives a short, colorful title, descriptive of some aspect of life in the South. In *Back Country Suite*, Mose Allison introduces his audience to his unique stylistic traits, compositional techniques and musical subjects as well as foreshadowing elements that feature strongly in his mature style.

For instance, one theme that pervades Allison's work is ambivalence. In his first major opus, the composer immediately invokes antithetical musical ideas, countering the tonal simplicity of the blues and the consonance of his jazz melodies with dissonant voicing in his harmonic writing. The discordant minor second placed in the inner voices of the chord and his repeated use of the tritone, cornerstones of Allison's later harmonic writing style, also recur throughout *Back Country Suite*.

Another paradox springs from Allison's adoption of the blues as a song form, a controversial decision for a white musician in an era predating both the civil rights movement and the subsequent wide-based acceptance of the country blues. Allison's espousal of the blues may have also appeared anomalous because he was earning impressive credentials in New York City as an accomplished pianist in the modern jazz idiom, a more sophisticated musical style harmonically, melodically and rhythmically. Although a white jazz pianist playing blues may have appeared controversial, Allison had, in fact, arrived at the decision to incorporate the blues into his music years earlier, while studying aesthetics and formulating his pragmatic definition of art:

> In college I became more conscious of what I was doing. I had played the blues first because they were cute and naughty, and then I saw the possibilities of universal types of songs. I began to see that form of music as a form of literature that had been pretty much neglected.[3]
>
> The blues hadn't really caught on when I first got to New York. No one had really heard of Muddy Waters and Lightnin' Hopkins. It was a little later that it all started happening. In fact, later I played one job where I was on the bill with Muddy Waters. It was an all-white audience in Hartford, Connecticut. Muddy Waters got up and before he played he said, "I'm glad to be here, even though I did have to come to you through the Rolling Stones." So, the

English thing is what really triggered the blues. Of course, it was beginning to happen in the late 1950s and early '60s. Ray Charles was around and was starting to get real big.

The scope and range of the piano pieces on Allison's 1957 debut recording provide evidence that Mose Allison was initially considered first and foremost a pianist whose singing was something of an afterthought. He had successfully established himself as a sideman for saxophonists Al Cohn, Zoot Sims and Stan Getz, but his piano playing on their recordings was often subdued, restricted to "comping" in straightahead jazz accompaniments, laying down a solid Lestorian swing to showcase the talents of saxophone soloists. In his solo venture, Allison was finally able to carve out his own personal musical identity, to stretch out on the piano with original ideas.

Back Country Suite was swiftly hailed as an innovative addition to the jazz repertoire. Each musical sketch is characterized by elements of both the jazz and blues genres, although one style often predominates in a specific segment. For example, Allison's ballads in the suite are composed primarily in the jazz vein, featuring more complex melodies and harmonies, but a pronounced compositional technique appearing in many of the tone poems is the fragmented phrasing that Allison derived from the blues. In these pieces, Allison employs an antiphonal style, a "call-and-response" phrasing that harkens back to the field-holler origins of the country blues, and imbues the pieces with a strong blues feeling. The tonality of many of the pieces also hovers around the blues scale. However, Allison garnishes these blues-based pieces with his personal musical twist, performing them in a jazz swing style, jazz tempos and phrasing governing the basic groove of the piece. At one point, Mose even considered taking the *Back Country Suite* into a "third stream" direction through the addition of orchestration. In an interview with *Downbeat* in May, 1958, Allison commented, "I've thought about doing it [*Back Country Suite*] wih a larger group. The way I hear it is with different instrumentation for different sketches. I hear 'New Ground' as a string quartet. There are some places in the suite I felt a need for tambourines... even a gong."[4]

A closer look at each piece emphasizes the suite's subtle and imaginative interweaving of blues and jazz ideas.

"New Ground," the opening piece, is an "eight-to-the-bar" swing number written in the twelve-bar-blues format. Its call-and-response phrasing serves as an introduction, then bass, drums and piano exchange melodic and rhythmic ideas. "Train," a slower New Orleans shuffle also constructed on the call-and-response motif, is based on the blues. The first melodic idea evokes the "train" metaphor using major seconds, then the second melody develops the motif on the blues scale. "Warm Night" is reminiscent of a typical jazz standard, with traditional chord changes. The seminal "Blues," Allison's first recorded vocal, is compelling and colorful, his singing adding variety to the instrumental scheme. "Saturday" swings in the tradition of Lester Young, slipping in and out of an E flat minor blues. The ubiquitous minor second and tritone melodies alternate with a single-note blues riff. Flowing in a melodic line of sixteenth-note runs, "Scamper" is a virtuoso piece, primarily jazz-based, executed in bop style with a time out for trading fours with the drums. "January," a wistful ballad, tempers jazz and blues motifs, its melody and harmony mostly jazz-oriented, while the improvisation section hovers in a heavy blues scale on the tonic chord. "Promised Land," based on a variation of the twelve-bar harmonic blues form, swings in a medium tempo and is infused with boogie-woogie piano licks. "Spring Song," a slow ballad, is a delicate melody with standard jazz chord changes. "Highway 49," the final tone poem depicting the "real-life road to Tippo, Mississippi," is the funkiest of the set. A twelve-bar blues, its backbeat captures the dancing spirit of downhome, combining a hoedown, squaredance motif with boogie-woogie and rhythm and blues. The coda closing the suite flourishes the quintessential Allison trademark, the minor second voiced inside each of the outer voices in the chord on the way out of the tune.

Mose Allison's vocal on "Blues" made a powerful social statement and a historic musical impression. Mose recalls that he wrote the song in 1955 before he left Mississippi, its genesis in a phrase he once heard someone say.[5] In the song, Allison's expressive, allegorical text, performed in a free-form chanting blues style, wraps symbolism and irony around its central theme of impotence. His lyrics dramatize an ironic reversal of roles in the social hierarchy; the old man's wealth gains him the social power, prestige and community respect normally reserved to the virile young man who, in Allison's song, "ain't nothin' in this world these days." "Blues" finds its young narrator displaced, hopelessly alineated from society, mourning his lost status and mired in the futility of a meaningless existence.

Twelve years later, Allison's song took on fresh meaning when it was adopted by the rock music of the next generation. The Who embraced the truth in Allison's text, and the gripping angst of their strident, thrashing rendition of "Blues" (retitled "Young Man Blues") made musical history on their album *Live at Leeds*. The UK rock group's version focused on the musical and poetic anger and violence in the song; Pete Townshend's distinctive guitar, a rabid extemporizing on Allison's simple blues motif, Keith Moon's turbulent drumming and the continual pulsating undercurrent of bassist John Entwistle laying down a solid rock foundation for lead singer Roger Daltrey's impassioned interpretation of Allison's lyrics.

Far from the battle cry of the Who's angry young man, Allison's straightforward, laid-back delivery of "Blues" on *Back Country Suite* is a poignant lament, sung in a straight, vibrato-less tone, impeccably in tune. Allison's youthful baritone understates the vocal line, approaching each phrase with a pure, boyish rounded tone, naturally high, with a resonating, nasal quality. His use of a relaxed rubato evokes a plaintive and delicate simplicity, and creates a mood that perfectly expresses the ironic subtlety of the text.

The compositional technique in "Blues" also underscores the meaning of the text. Breaking from the twelve-bar format, Allison writes artfully, using irregular call-and-response phrasing and sustained notes in the melody to carry and highlight the song's drama. True to the spirit of call-and-response, he sings the phrases unaccompanied, freeing himself from a regular meter. As is traditional in the blues form, the phrases follow an AABA pattern, the melody repeated with each A phrase: "Well, a young man ain't nothin' in this world these days," while the B phrases develop the song's text. Allison cautiously varies his use of the piano, filling the spaces in the text with an alternation of an animated repeating blues riff in regular meter of four with drum brushes and bass accompanying, and a simpler, single unaccompanied melodic line. Each vocal phrase ends on a somber note, the final cadence resonating with a sustained dramatic octave doubling in the bass.

Like a poet reading his verses, Allison punctuates certain words in the text, using his voice creatively to amplify the song's poetic elements. In a manner reminiscent of the field holler, Allison's voice falls off the pitch on the word "man" at the end of the short phrase, the answer continuing the length of the melodic line. The lyric then sends his voice deep into its bass register, Mose nearly speaking the pivotal word "money" to focus attention on the thematic crux of the song. This free and imaginative interpretation of the blues song form establishes Allison's unique style for the first time on record. It is a style that he was fully to develop over the course of his career, and one which was destined to influence a host of admirers, from Michael Franks and Ben Sidran to jazz/cabaret singer Susannah McCorkle and British R&B singer/keyboardist Georgie Fame.

The most noticeable technique in "Blues," and one for which Allison has received both acclaim and disdain, is his use of "sforzando" in his phrasing. Sforzando is the conventional musical term describing the accenting and abrupt retreat from the pitch, creating a mini-explosion or emphasis on a note. The articulation of a phrase using repeated sforzando accents creates a speaking style or conversational inflection in the phrase. In addition to this sforzando phrasing, in certain instances Allison might also employ a spoken manner termed in popular, jazz and musical theater as the "throwaway line," where the phrase is sung under the breath, intoned or "thrown away" from the sung to the speaking voice.[6]

By contrast, the "bel canto," or "beautiful song" style requires the singer to connect pitches, perfecting the beauty of the vocal line in creating legato or smooth flowing phrases.[7] Many popular vocalists use the bel canto style to sing ballads, where phrasing the melody beautifully simultaneously demonstrates the beauty of the voice. Allison's earliest vocal influences by and large qualified as bel canto singers.

Many reviewers, critics and listeners allude to the laid-back, laconic style of American singer/songwriter/pianist and showman of the 1930s and 1940s, Hoagy Carmichael, when describing Mose Allison's style. Mose, however, was chiefly influenced by the singing of Nat Cole, his vocal model since high school, and by Percy Mayfield, an underrated rhythm and blues singer from Louisiana. Carmichael and Allison are similar musical stylists in that they write, sing, accompany themselves on piano and present their songs with a relaxed demeanor. Carmichael, however, wrote popular songs with mass appeal whereas Allison has always fostered an intimacy with smallish, cult-like audiences through employing an esoteric, highly individual musical style. Allison himself has never attributed his style to Carmichael, consistently naming his vocal heroes as Nat Cole and Percy Mayfield. He finds both Cole's and Mayfield's approaches honest and uncontrived, their styles chiefly concerned with shaping the vocal line with unpretentious, relaxed and natural phrasing. In addition to Nat Cole and Percy Mayfield, Mose was also inspired by Texas bluesmen Charles Brown, T-Bone Walker and by Tennessee's Willie Mabon. These singers were also popular with club and cabaret audiences and influenced Mose's delivery of standards from the blues and pop repertoire while he was touring with combos down South in the late 1940s and early 1950s. Yet, as soon as Mose began seriously to compose his own music and formulate his own philosophies, he realized the critical need to transcend this hero worship and develop a personal singing style.

Although faithful to the Cole and Mayfield styles as a point of departure, Allison eventually added to their relaxed phrasing, rounded tones, clear diction, and perfect intonation, his own idiosyncrasies. A young lyrical baritone with forward placement of tone and a full, colorful timbre in the bass register, he slowly explored the possibilities of his range and tone color as well as developing an approach to phrasing based in the natural dialectic inflections of his Southern accent. Allison soon discovered that his natural approach to singing also incorporated elements of his instrumental playing. Mixed with his attempts at creating a smooth, legato line were the percussive instincts of a lifelong trumpet player and pianist. These conflicting influences shaped his singing style, and naturally, he often found himself thinking like a horn player, adding melodic embellishments and executing phrases like the instrumentalist he was.

Once Mose freed himself of the influence of his stylistic predecessors and focused on his own natural inclinations, his conversational style of singing appeared to evolve on its own. Allison concedes that the only drawback to his "speaking" style of singing, developed over several decades, is having consciously to control the weight of the accents, avoiding his innate inclination to "punch" pitches:

> I was really surprised the first time I heard my voice on tape. It sure didn't sound like Nat Cole; my voice was deeper. Part of it was just my physical equipment, where my voice comes from. Part of it was my accent. The thing about that whole type of music, blues and all, really amounts to a difference in the way you move, I think. That's the key to it, just a subtle thing having to do with the way you move.[8]

The other vocal featured on *Back Country Suite* is Mercy Dee Walton's straight twelve-bar blues, "One Room Country Shack." A big hit in Texas that Mose believes he may have heard on the jukebox in Tippo, it premiers his personalized approach to the traditional country blues. His stylized, relaxed vocals and the delayed, Southern approach to phrasing, are also influenced by Nat Cole. Allison comments:

I always accompanied myself and my first model for that was Nat Cole. When I was in high school, I used to sing things in the style of Nat Cole and the trio he had at the time. He was the model, I guess, for all vocalists who accompanied themselves.

Some of the accompanying took in the Southern approach to phrasing. When I was hanging out with black musicians in the late forties in Memphis and going to black clubs, that's when I became really conscious of the difference in phrasing, and the laid back, delayed phrasing, the split-second delay in the phrasing.

You can trace that back to Louis Armstrong. The Southern style was to overemphasize the phrasing. It was already present in the classic players like Louis Armstrong. The kind of music they played was even more laid-back.

Mose Allison's singing and piano style, first heard on "Blues" and "One Room Country Shack," impressed an influential figure in England, founder of that country's blues revival movement, John Mayall:

Mose is only a couple of years older than I am, so about the same time I was listening to blues on record over in England, he was listening to blues back in Mississippi. I think we shared the same influences. When I first heard his album *Back Country Suite* it was quite a novelty because I heard it on the "Voice of America," which was broadcast on the shortwave we got in England. When he sang "One Room Country Shack" and "Blues" from *Back Country Suite*, those were the things that started me finding out more about him and following the subsequent albums that came out.

Scotsman Jack Bruce, former bass player with the psychedelic "supergroup" Cream and a talented songwriter whose powerful voice raised rock and roll singing to a new standard, was similarly impressed with Allison's vocal delivery:

The straightness of Mose Allison's style was important, the actual vocal sound, the lack of vibrato. The sound was very pure and very much a thing of the time. Like Ornette Coleman's plastic sax, there was this wide-open voice with no vibrato which didn't relate. It was kind of opposite to what was happening vocally at that time since certain singers then were a lot more florid. Mose's sound has a purity, and a dusty, desert feeling that I later found out was more of a Texan type of sound. At the time, where it came from didn't count.

Also on *Back Country Suite*, Mose's Lestorian, swinging, up-tempo rendition of the rhythm and blues tune made famous by New Orleans singer Fats Domino in 1956, "Blueberry Hill," and an original, elegiac ballad Allison titled "In Salah" after reading a Paul Bowles novel, are worth hearing.

Both in its own right and as a precedent for Allison's subsequent work, *Back Country Suite* is a true American original, balancing a variety of musical forces to produce its portrait of the culture of the Southern United States. Further, *Back Country Suite* has probably had the greatest impact of all the recordings Mose Allison has released to date. In the United States, radio disc jockeys immediately hailed the work as a classic and, unbeknownst to Allison, it soon attracted an audience from coast to coast.

By the early 1960s, the record had made it to a European audience; it was widely played in the United Kingdom and in continental Europe via American Armed Forces Radio. This European airplay and the resultant record sales helped to build a sizeable and diverse international audience for Allison, particularly in the young British population, whose fledgling pop musicians were demonstrating a keen interest in American music, largely in the country blues. As the young Britishers prepared to launch a musical invasion that would forever change the course of popular music, a few considered Mose's album to be their primer. One such musical revolutionary from England touched by Mose Allison's debut recording was the Who's guitarist, singer and songwriter Pete Townshend:

I first heard Mose Allison through records, specifically on *Back Country Suite*, which was released through Esquire in the U.K. I discovered it at the same time I discovered a lot of blues music. I had a friend called Tom Wright who was the son of a U.S. Air Force man based in the U.K. I was in art school in 1961 and the only blues music I'd heard up to that point was Leadbelly and Big Bill Broonzy and the country blues artists. I lumped those in with a lot of other American political folk like Pete Seeger and Woody Guthrie, who to me sort of added up to roughly the same thing. I think of all the music I heard, of all the records in that collection by Tom Wright, there was one record that struck me as being the kind of music that I would have aspired to, that was rich, that was the blues, but was also intellectually challenging and that was *Back Country Suite*. I still think that is a masterpiece.

Mose Allison himself acknowledges the importance of his first recording:

The *Back Country Suite* is sort of my primer, my foundation. Everything I do now pretty much has a precedent in the *Back Country Suite*. I don't concentrate on the local-color aspect now because that era is gone and I'm not into nostalgia or revivalism as regards that. I'm trying to keep playing and developing my style, letting it go wherever it will and keeping it as interesting to me as possible.[9]

6

LOCAL COLOR

"'Parchman Farm' was on an album called *Local Color* during the period when I was trying to evoke the sound and flavor of the South, the Southern style and the Southern pace. Tippo, Mississippi, where I grew up, wasn't very far from Parchman Farm, the state penitentiary, and so I sort of had a morbid fascination with the place. Every once in a while, there would be a sheriff's posse coming through with bloodhounds and the whole thing. I remember after I got to New York, a local blues aficionado played me Bukka White's version of 'Parchman Farm' and it was similar but different, too. The content and verses were different but there was a slight similarity in the overall tone to my version. I was sort of amazed by that. It's possible I might have heard it as a child on the jukeboxes because the jukeboxes in that area had about 70 percent country blues. I'll never really know."

Mose Allison

"Parchman Farm"

Well, I'm sittin' over here on Parchman Farm
Well, I'm sittin' over here on Parchman Farm
I'm sittin' over here on Parchman Farm
And I ain't never done no man no harm

Well, I'm puttin' that cotton in a-leven-foot sack
Well, I'm puttin' that cotton in a-leven-foot sack
I'm puttin' that cotton in a-leven-foot sack
With a twelve-gauge shotgun at my back

I'm sittin' over here on number nine
I'm sittin' over here on number nine
I'm sittin' over here on number nine
And all I did was drink my wine

Well, I'm gonna be here for the rest of my life
I'm gonna be on this farm for my natural life
Well, I'm gonna be here for the rest of my life
And all I did was shoot my wife

I'm sittin' over here on Parchman Farm

Mose Allison

Local Color, Mose Allison's second album on Prestige Records, was recorded on November 7, 1957 only eight months after his debut recording *Back Country Suite*. Like its predecessor, it had a rural Southern theme, and similar musical effects and motifs also bring the earlier recording to mind. The later album's ten cuts capture the musical spirit and pastoral ambiance of *Back Country Suite*, particularly in five of the six original compositions found on side A.

In *Local Color* Allison rendered a memorable solo trumpet performance on the blues tune "Trouble in Mind" and, more significantly, gave listeners their first taste of his unique interpretation of the standard twelve-bar blues on "Parchman Farm." True to its title, the local-color theme prevails in songs with titles evocative of the rural South: "Carnival," "Crepuscular Air," "Mojo Woman," and "Town," but, unlike the musical montage presented in *Back Country Suite*, the later recording is distinguished by the absence of a formal unifying programmatic scheme. Rather, Allison approaches each song separately as a Southern scene, conveyed by his unique approach to both jazz and blues.

Mose wrote all but one of his original cuts for *Local Color* in the mid-1950s, prior to his arrival on the New York City jazz scene in 1957. Jazz critic Ira Gitler's program notes for the record point out Mose's Southern musical influences; for instance, Allison was especially attuned to musically communicating "local color" when composing "Carnival," a march-like motif drawing on its composer's exposure to the marching bands which performed on the midway of small Southern town carnivals.[1] And in "Town," Allison strives musically to portray the festive holiday atmosphere created when country folk, otherwise isolated, gather in their one central location.[2]

It was, however, the allegorical "Parchman Farm," also recorded on the A side of *Local Color*, that catapulted Mose Allison to celebrity, both in the United States and abroad. "Parchman" soon became the vocal chestnut of the Mose Allison repertoire and his most requested title. Though it never charted as a mainstream pop song, once progressive disc jockeys got hold of "Parchman Farm" they promoted it generously, giving it significant air play from coast to coast, helping to expand the fledgling musician's audience. "Parchman Farm" is, today, still Mose Allison's most celebrated song, recorded by other artists more frequently than any other of his compositions.

"Parchman Farm" has many of Allison's trademark musical devices in the piano accompaniment. The tune, in a straight-ahead blues, follows the standard twelve-bar progression, but is personalized through a piano style marked with dissonance and chromaticism. Allison accompanies the vocal line with his signature chord voicings, the dissonant minor seconds sandwiched between the outer voices. The progressive sequence of chromatic key lifts on each verse, which results in the song opening in the key of E flat and closing the last verse in F sharp, is novel for a blues tune and serves to keep the listener in "harmonic suspense."

The piece also exemplifies Allison's affinity for allegorical literary texts. Set in the Mississippi State Penitentiary, Parchman Farm, a real working prison farm located approximately twenty miles from Tippo, the song, delivered in Allison's stoic, almost conversational baritone, is a deeply ironic account of its subject's imprisonment and the reasons behind it. Mose dramatizes the last verse of the tune by abruptly changing the tempo, eventually taking the listener off guard with the song's punch line, "Well, I'm gonna be here for the rest of my life. And all I did was shoot my wife."

The irony in the lyric, a recurring literary device in Mose Allison's writing, backfired badly on Mose in the 1970s, the apogee of the women's movement. At this time, the text was unfortunately misinterpreted as being misogynistic, as even sanctioning male domestic violence. This misunderstanding rather bemused Allison, betraying as it does a lack of understanding of irony, but he nevertheless no longer performs the song:

> Actually, "Parchman Farm" is allegorical to start with. It means something to me other than just what it means on the surface. To me, "Parchman Farm" represents whatever you have to do. So, we're all faced with one "Parchman Farm" or another. And, the thing about "all I did was shoot my wife": in order to complete the ironical twist to that song, I had to have something very serious happen in the end. Instead of advocating shooting your wife, it's meant to mean that it's something bad to do. On the other hand, in real life, people *do* shoot their wives and wives *do* shoot their husbands, so it's not that far out. Some people do have trouble with that line, though.[3]

It was not just feminists who missed the song's irony; one venerable member of the blues community was also intrigued by Allison's biting lyric. Mose remembers the late Muddy Waters's first reaction to the song: "I played on a deal with Muddy Waters several times. The first time I met him was at this joint on the South Side of Chicago, down around 64th Street. He didn't have a band then and was working with the house rhythm section. He had heard 'Parchman' and the first thing he wanted to know was if I really shot my wife. He also thought I was black."

Allison cannot pin down the actual origin of the song, although his mother Maxine is quick to argue that the story is a Tippo legend, directly traceable to the saga of Puddin Taylor, a real-life African-American sharecropper who worked for the Allisons while Mose was growing up. Mose, on the other hand, insists that the main character of his "Parchman Farm" had nothing whatever to do with Puddin Taylor. Maxine remembers:

> Puddin was the most respected Negro locally. He was dependable and the hardest worker in the area and everyone knew him. Puddin had a young, sassy wife and one night after he came home from work, she chased him around the house with a big butcher knife. Puddin took out his shotgun and shot her dead. He was sent to Parchman Farm, but the county got together a petition asking for his release from the governor of Mississippi because he was a valuable worker and respected around here. The governor agreed to release him and he's been here working in Tippo ever since.

Allison himself thought highly enough of "Parchman Farm" to update its lyrics and rhythmic feel, compose a new accompaniment and develop an improvisatory section in its sequel, "New Parchman," which appeared on his 1964 Atlantic release, *The Word from Mose*. The new song's lyrics are variations on the first version's theme:

> Well, I'm sittin' over here on Parchman Farm
> Well, I'm sittin' over here on Parchman Farm
> Well, I'm sittin' over here on Parchman Farm
> And the place is loaded with rustic charm
>
> I went downtown tried to do what's right
> I went downtown tried to do what's right
> I went downtown tried to do what's right
> Don't let nobody tell you them dogs won't bite
>
> Well, I'm up every mornin' at the break of day
> Well, I'm up every mornin' at the break of day
> I'm up every mornin' at the break of day
> And all I did was try to have my say

> Well, it won't be long, boys, I'm gonna leave this place
> I said it won't be long, boys, I'm gonna leave this place
> Well, it won't be long, gonna leave this place
> I'm goin' somewhere to join the human race
>
> Well, I'm sittin' over here on Parchman Farm

Despite being seen as a vengeful ballad of male domination, "Parchman Farm" is still a standard in the blues repertoire, performed alongside tunes written by such blues giants as Willie Dixon, Muddy Waters, and Robert Johnson. Various versions of the apparently timeless song continue to be released, indicating that the impact of the song has not waned. Among the recording artists who have released their own versions of "Parchman Farm" are John Mayall and the Bluesbreakers, and keyboard players Georgie Fame and Brian Auger. In the United States, pop singer Johnny Rivers, bluesman John Hammond and the Jefferson Airplane blues spin-off, Hot Tuna, have all recorded versions of Allison's song.

The Britishers were the first to cover "Parchman Farm." In the 1960s, the UK's passion for American culture, especially for blues and jazz, left the scene wide open for musical novelty and Mose Allison had already created somewhat of a stir there. The release of his *Back Country Suite*, and of his follow-up recording, *Local Color*, both distributed in the U.K. by Esquire, established Allison as a refreshing and unique American voice. Having authentically captured in music a setting considered exotic to Europeans, Allison's work caught on quickly in London's trend-setting music community. British critic Oliver Howes wrote in a 1959 *Jazz Journal*:

> I began by speaking of a remarkable young man. Why remarkable? Well, consider. On the strength of two records, *Back Country Suite* and *Local Color*, issued here by Esquire, Mose Allison now possesses a reputation that amounts almost to legend. *Back Country Suite* received the sort of critical acclaim normally reserved for such records

as *Louis Armstrong plays W.C. Handy* or *The Atomic Mr. Basie*—masterworks from established stars. Yet Mose Allison was no established star; Britain did not even know he existed. Most remarkable of all, however, is that today, a full year after the release of his first record, we know little more about Mose Allison than we know about some of the legendary giants of New Orleans.[4]

The British jazz community was not the only place where the impact of Allison's music was felt. His approach also attracted the attention of London's less erudite but richly diverse pop-music scene. Allison's influence there was widespread, a phenomenon transcending the boundaries of the esoteric factions who divided themselves into camps labelled "rhythm and blues," "blues purists" or "rock and roll." Allison's "Parchman Farm" elevated him to cult status in the U.K., and among his admirers was a select group of musicians who approached their work seriously and eventually rose to international superstardom in the rock and roll world, helping to shape the popular music of the future.

Rhythm and blues singer/keyboard player Georgie Fame's version of "Parchman Farm" was the first to appear on record. Although erroneously listed as "Parchment Farm" on the 1964 EMI album *Georgie Fame and the Blue Flames: Rhythm and Blues at "The Flamingo"*, Fame's cover is performed in a British emulation of Allison's style, vocally and instrumentally, and is strongly suggestive of the esteem in which Fame held his American mentor at the time the recording was made. Georgie Fame was instrumental in spreading the word about Allison, extending the Mississippian's music out of a strict jazz context and into the popular mainstream in Britain. Fame, a highly respected musician in the U.K., was leader of the resident band at London's renowned venue, the Flamingo Club, during the 1960s. The Flamingo featured various rhythm and blues bands, catering to a somewhat diverse clientele, but on weekends its audience was comprised primarily of African-American military men stationed in England. Fame later enjoyed commercial success in the U.S.

with several pop hits including "Yeah, Yeah" and "The Ballad of Bonnie and Clyde."

Keyboard player Brian Auger also frequently played the Flamingo Club in the 1960s. Auger pioneered the jazz/rock/fusion movement, leading the 1960s bands Steampacket, whose members included Long John Baldry and Rod Stewart, and the Trinity, comprised of bassist Rick Brown and drummer Mickey Waller and featuring singer Julie Driscoll. Auger recalls:

> A lot of U.S. Army personnel, G.I.s and American Air Force people, would come into the club on weekends when I was playing at the Flamingo in London. There was much more of a black mix to the R&B music, so more black G.I.s would come there instead of going to the Marquee, which was more of a rock club. Because we were playing in this steamy environment and we had the chance to play for these American G.I.s, the music seemed very real to us. The audience would respond with "yeah" and we knew that this was it, this was get-down time. They knew what you meant and we knew what they meant. Mose's lyrics had that Southern flavor that was lifted straight from that place in Mississippi. The pictures of sitting over at Parchman Farm with eleven-foot cotton sacks and twelve-gauge shotguns being sung by a guy with a foggy Southern voice was like: "Wow, we were really there." It was also incredibly ugly, and a white guy singing about Southern justice from the American underclass was something we related to. As working-class English, the underclass, we understood everything he was talking about.
>
> Mose describes it so well that I could almost feel the humidity through that rolling swamp beat. And the song really does cover boundaries from a sociological perspective.

The most famous version of "Parchman Farm" was recorded by the versatile British musician John Mayall on *John Mayall and the Bluesbreakers Featuring Eric Clapton* in 1966 for Decca Records. A guitarist, keyboardist, singer and harmonica player, Mayall organized and fronted a number of blues bands, and it was under his tutelage that musicians such as Eric Clapton and Jack Bruce, future members of the rock supergroup Cream, as well as Fleetwood Mac bassist John McVie, learned the blues. Mayall incorporated two blues standards into the Bluesbreakers' playlist, deriving them directly from Allison's repertoire: "Parchman Farm" and Willie Dixon's "I Love the Life I Live," a version released by Allison on the Columbia label. Produced by Mike Vernon, the Mayall/Bluesbreaker version of "Parchman Farm" featured the bandleader on solo vocals and harmonica; his harp filled in the two-bar spaces between phrases with repeated riffs and he linked the verses with an extended harmonica solo. He is accompanied by bassist John McVie and drummer Peter Ward; Clapton is missing on this track. Mayall comments:

> I've always enjoyed Mose Allison's piano playing. At the time I discovered him, he was one of the few jazz pianists who was calling heavily on his blues background, which is not what the typical jazz players before him had. That really set him apart in my book. Then, he came out with "Parchman Farm." When I later put my band together, it was one of the tunes I used as a starting point for the harmonica instrumental—which is what it was from that time on. Over the years, the treatment of the song has changed and it is now completely different; I've always felt that the song lends itself very well to both the harmonica and the keyboard. "Parchman" is the only song of Mose's that I've recorded, but I also became familiar with another song I've played, "I Love the Life I Live," from Mose.

"Parchman Farm" also reverberated in the soul of another popular-music hero, the eminent rock composer, guitarist and occasional singer and keyboard player of the British group the Who, Pete Townshend. A devotee of Mose Allison, Townshend cites Allison's early piano style, notably the harmonic voicings used in "Parchman Farm," as one of his early influences and as a continued inspiration for his approach to his own keyboard style:

Musically, the Mose Allison influences really only come up when I sit and play the keyboard. On guitar it doesn't happen . . . it's when I fool around with the blues, trying to be as unconscious as possible. It's sort of like white gospel. All the Mose type patterns arise when I sit and play the piano for fun, which is what I normally spend about an hour a day doing. It's not a Ray Charles, it's not a Jimmy Smith, it's Mose's style that I like. And I like it because it will lead into European influences as well, which are obviously just as deep.

American musicians, many of whom were in the vanguard of the blues-rock movement in the U.S., also tuned into "Parchman Farm." Keyboardist Al Kooper, a longtime jazz aficionado, founder of the Blues Project and the jazz-rock band Blood, Sweat and Tears, traces his roots to the blues. He remembers hearing disc jockey Symphony Sid play "Parchman Farm" when he was a teenager in 1958, and to his ears it was a thought-provoking piece of music. He later claimed that he discovered the blues through Mose Allison, since Mose's covers of blues tunes led him to investigate the work of other blues artists. Kooper's own version of "Parchman Farm," which he insists was recorded as a joke, also ended up in Britain as his first solo venture:

> Mose led me to the people I needed to be led to. He covered Willie Dixon and Muddy Waters songs like "Seventh Son" and "Rollin' Stone." Then, strangely enough, in 1960 I was fooling around in the studio and cut a version of "Parchman Farm" just for kicks. Unbeknownst to me, my publisher sold it in Europe and it came out in England on Mercury. I had this record out that I didn't even know about, of this song that I hope none of us ever hears; very embarrassing. It was my first single under my own name.

Another of Kooper's American contemporaries, blues-rock singer Peter Wolf, former lead singer with the Boston-based J. Geils Band, also acknowledged an early acquaintance with Allison's album, *Local Color*, a recording that college kids in his

Bronx neighborhood turned him onto and one that inspired his early love for the blues. Jefferson Airplane/Hot Tuna guitarist Jorma Kaukonen and bluesman John Hammond were similarly influenced by Mose Allison. Kaukonen's brand of the electric blues helped to shape the rock of his group Jefferson Airplane, while bluesman John Hammond, Kaukonen's friend since their undergraduate days at Antioch College in Ohio, has remained a blues purist for decades. Hammond continues his performances in the country-blues tradition as a one-man blues show, singing, playing harmonica and accompanying himself on the acoustic guitar. Kaukonen and Hammond recall a momentous hearing of "Parchman Farm" when they were in college, and both went on to cover the tune, Kaukonen's band, Electric Hot Tuna, performing a version released by Epic Records in 1990.

Blues harmonica player and vocalist, Charlie Musselwhite, from Kosciusko, Mississippi, well known for his musical affiliation with young white Chicago blues players, Mike Bloomfield and Barry Goldberg, the blues rock group, the Nighthawks and for his own international career as a solo artist, recalls how "Parchman Farm" entered the blues vocabulary in Chicago when he was playing there in the 1960s:

> I'd heard about Mose Allison when I was living in Memphis growing up. A friend of mine there had a garage full of 45 records and I had collected some of Mose's records from him. "Parchman Farm" was a hit as far as I was concerned. I remember hearing it on the radio and thinking Mose was black. With a name like that and a voice that sounded black, I didn't realize he was white until I saw an album cover and thought it was interesting that he also played trumpet. Everybody does "Parchman Farm." When I was up in Chicago with all of those rock and roll people like Barry Goldberg, they all knew it and played it. The song was widely known and I couldn't name anyone who doesn't know it. But I don't think anyone does it the way Mose does it. It's a real appealing song; the story and the rhymes make it catch and you can really remember the lyrics.

American pop singer Johnny Rivers also recorded a live version of "Parchman Farm" in 1964 on his album *Live at the Whiskey A Go Go* on the Imperial label. A native of Louisiana, Rivers's distinctive style, blending rhythm and blues and country, lent a swinging, twangy pop groove to "Parchman Farm" and his version met with considerable success in the pop mainstream. Another tune that Rivers reportedly culled from the Allison repertoire and popularized on Top 40 charts was Willie Dixon's "Seventh Son."

An odder cover of "Parchman Farm" was recorded by the noisy heavy-metal 1960s band, the Boston-cum-San Francisco trio Blue Cheer. Most famous for their cover of "Summertime Blues," Blue Cheer's defiantly strident version—perhaps a satire or an attempt to replicate the rock and roll angst found in the music of the Who and Jimi Hendrix—is difficult to take seriously. A study in electronic reverb and feedback reminiscent of Iron Butterfly's rambling epic "In-a-Gadda-Da-Vida," Blue Cheer's "Parchman" features a free-style instrumental mid-section complete with a sputtering psychedelic guitar solo. For color, the lead singer also changes a few of the lyrics, adds expletives and a spoken comment about shooting his wife, "She wasn't no good." The vocalist then recapitulates the first verse on the way out of the tune and in what appears to be a feeble tribute to Allison's modulating musical setting of "Parchman Farm," lifts the key a half step higher. In a bizarre musical ending, the song closes abruptly with the final chord taken yet another half step higher.

Although "Parchman Farm" became the standout track on Mose Allison's second Prestige album, *Local Color* also includes two other noteworthy songs. One is Percy Mayfield's whimsical and wry love song, "Lost Mind," which has lasted through Allison's multi-decade career and remains a staple of his current repertoire. On his *Local Color* version, Mose's smooth, laid-back delivery is steeped in Nat Cole's balladeer influence. At some points, Mose's phrasing even evokes the work of jazz songstress Billie Holiday. Mose's most recent version of Mayfield's "Lost Mind" is sung more aggressively, in his speech-like phrasing style, emphasizing the twists in the lyric, and performed at a faster, swinging tempo.

Allison's memorable muted trumpet solo on Richard M. Jones's "Trouble in Mind" also demonstrates his excellent sense of phrasing; indeed, Mose's recorded work on trumpet was often critically acclaimed for its sensitivity. Thirty years later, when he had long put the trumpet aside, he resurrected the witty lyrics to "Trouble in Mind," recording a new vocal version of the song on his 1987 Grammy-nominated Blue Note record *Ever Since the World Ended*. Since recording the 1987 version, he has adopted the song as a standard part of his live repertoire.

Mose Allison's *Local Color* reinforced, both in the U.S.A. and abroad, his significance as a solo artist with a singular style. While musical and cultural fashions shifted around him, Allison's evolutionary trek took him further and further from his Tippo, Mississippi roots, but some tinge of "local color" has always remained in his work:

> Actually, the only thing I have to say about "Parchman Farm" is that I haven't done it in about 20 years. That's one song that I don't do anymore, but it probably got more exposure than anything else I did in those years, and maybe even in my whole career, who knows? It's hard to figure what catches people's fancy. I've pondered just why people would like that better than anything else I ever did, but it seems like that song just got around more and it caught more people's ears than I would guess, anything else; except "Your Mind's on Vacation," which has maybe now surpassed it. I still get requests for "Parchman Farm" but I don't do it.

7

A PRESTIGIOUS COMMITMENT

"Bebop got a little too brittle and frenetic for me; that's an urban thing. I was brought up in the rural South and one of my main heroes was Lester Young. I've been trying for years to capture on the piano the delicacy and accuracy of Lester Young's playing on the saxophone. That's evidenced in my early Prestige recordings very clearly if you know where to look. I'm trying to phrase like Lester Young phrased. Of course, that's hard to do on piano. I gave that up after a while, but I went through a phase of that. I came more out of the swing thing, the delicacy of the time. The problem I have nowadays with rhythm sections is they might overplay, to my way of thinking. There are so many young players who can play so much, they're into execution, so it's hard to find a player considerate of the swing, the phrasing and delicacy. These are the things I came up with and that I'm still trying to preserve. Everybody has to balance out their influences and come up with something valid. That's what we're all involved in."[1]

Mose Allison

"I Don't Worry 'bout a Thing"

If this life is drivin' you to drink
You're sittin' around wonderin' just what to think
Well, I got some consolation
I'll give it to you if I might

You know, I don't worry about a thing
'Cause I know nothin's going to be alright

This world is one big trouble spot
'Cause some have plenty and some have not
You know I used to be trouble
But I finally saw the light
Now, I don't worry about a thing
Now, I know nothin's going to be alright

Don't waste your time trying to be a go-getter
Things will get worse before they get better
Alternative version
                Don't waste your time trying to be a big winner
                If you get too fat somebody else gets thinner
You know, there's always somebody
Playin' with dynamite
Now, I don't worry 'bout a thing
'Cause I know nothin's goin' to be alright

Mose Allison

Mose Allison's first two releases on Prestige Records, *Back Country Suite* and *Local Color*, were original works that established him as a Southern impressionist adept at capturing, on a musical canvas, his native culture. While valuing him as a highly individual musical stylist, Prestige Records saw another dimension in Mose Allison. A versatile musician with extensive experience in jazz combos performing as a sideman for well-known jazz artists, Allison had consistently demonstrated great skill in playing blues and jazz standards. Keen to capitalize on his talents in this area, Prestige Records therefore directed the young musician to take time out from recording his original material in order to emphasize a more mainstream appeal as a vocalist/pianist mining the jazz and blues standard repertoire.

Young Man Mose, Mose Allison's third album for Prestige Records, recorded on January 1, 1958, embodied this artistic shift from unique stylist to more conventional jazz performer, featuring only a single original piece, a trumpet solo entitled "Stroll." In both his early work and throughout the course of his career, Allison has frequently drawn on the jazz, blues and sometimes country standards repertoire for material. In culling his selections from these diverse sources, his main criteria in choosing songs require that the tunes not be over-familiar and that they possess some unique musical or lyrical element appealing to him. Featuring Nick Stabulas, a veteran of Allison's second Prestige recording on drums, and bassist Addison Farmer, the ten-track *Young Man Mose* demonstrates Allison's artistry in simultaneously presenting distinctive twists to an eclectic song selection, and seemingly conjuring up new musical ideas within conventional jazz and blues boundaries.

Allison's singing on two of the three vocals on *Young Man Mose*, Duke Ellington's "Don't Get Around Much Anymore," and Ray Noble's "I Hadn't Anyone Till You," is strongly reminiscent of Allison's jazz ballad style, when he fronted nightclub dates during the early 1950s. Here, probably because the musical and lyrical content of these ballads demands a more traditional approach, Allison all but abandons his signature speech-like vocal style. Instead, he sings in the laid-back, legato phrasing of his vocal heroes, accompanying himself on piano in the delayed phrasing style of Nat Cole. The exception is Mose's rendition of Ray Charles's slow blues "Baby, Let Me Hold Your Hand," where his singing is demonstrably freer, more expressive.

The renditions of his six piano selections on *Young Man Mose* indicate that at the January 1958 date, the style of his solo piano playing was still heavily based on the swing tradition of Lester Young. His versions of Gershwin's "How Long Has This Been Going On," standards "Bye Bye Blues," "My Kind of Love" and a bouncy version of the popular song "Sleepy Time Gal" are particularly noteworthy.

"Stroll," on the other hand, is a telling muted trumpet solo in the bebop vein inspired by a favourite player at that time, bop trumpeter Clifford Brown. Allison's performance here demonstrates great technical ability, but it was, unfortunately, his final recorded appearance on trumpet:

I started out being influenced by Louis Armstrong and

Buck Clayton. After them, I heard Dizzy and Miles and got more into the bebop thing, more on trumpet than on piano. Of course, Clifford Brown and Fats Navarro are still two of my favorites. Their influence is more apparent in a lot of the young trumpet players.

I played trumpet a little in the early days, but mostly just sitting in. I don't think I ever played a professional job on trumpet in New York, or very few even before I moved there, because the piano player is the first guy hired and the trumpet player is maybe the fifth or sixth guy hired. I could work as a piano player, but not that much on the trumpet. I wasn't really an expert on the trumpet anyhow so I couldn't play a lot of the jobs that trumpet players have to play if they want to survive. You have to be able to read well unless you're a phenomenon and can have your own band right away. I also had a better background for the piano. I was always a piano player.

I didn't have time to keep up with the trumpet. It was sort of a hobby that I could do now and then. The trumpet is a demanding instrument and you really have to keep it up if you want to be able to play anything. After I started to work full-time in the sixties, I sort of lost interest. Also my original trumpet that I came to New York with got stolen on a job in Philadelphia. I bought another cornet but I never really liked it much.

While *Young Man Mose* was Allison's only recording coming close to an undertaking consisting entirely of cover versions, his fourth album on Prestige Records, *Ramblin' with Mose*, which included only one vocal, qualified as his nearest endeavor to an album comprising only instrumentals. Recorded on April 18, 1958, three months after *Young Man Mose*, Allison's piano and voice are again accompanied by bassist Addison Farmer, but he adds a new number to the rhythm section, the capable drummer Ronnie Free, a South Carolinian whom Mose had befriended during sessions at the 34th Street loft.

The five original compositions on *Ramblin'* do not provide evidence of an evolution in either Allison's writing style or his piano playing. He has, however, returned to his Southern musical roots, continuing to compose tone poems depicting Southern bucolic tableaux. Two pieces in the repertoire stand out, "The Minstrels," a technically challenging melody played in bebop style, and "Ramble," whose square dance theme is composed within a variation on straight blues form and includes his signature dissonances in the harmonic voicings of chords. The medium-paced blues-infused "Saritha," however, is the most notable of Allison's compositions on this date and probably also a favorite of its composer, since it can still be heard in his current repertoire as one of the piano pieces that open his live sets.

Ironically, Allison's cover tunes on *Ramblin'* are more stylistically personalized on piano than those from his previous recording. For instance, he lends harmonic color to chord voicings on the bridge and enigmatically suspends the final chord of the song without resolution to "You Belong to Me." His Latin twist to "Ole Devil Moon" is replete with the rumba beat, doubled octaves and parallel thirds which characterized the style Mose played in Texas years earlier. This Latin style remains an influence and often provides a primary approach to many of his own songs. Allison's laid-back vocal from the *Ramblin'* date, a cover of Joe Liggins's ballad, "I Got a Right to Cry," is reminiscent, in sonority, tempo, and phrasing, of the cover "I Hadn't Anyone Till You" from his previous recording.

In his interpretations of non-original piano pieces, Allison always respects the musical integrity of the song while attaining a simple, relaxed approach, but a recurring characteristic that enlivens his interpretations is his use of melodic ornaments in his single-note melody lines. These are particularly effective on "Stranger in Paradise" and "You Belong to Me." For many listeners, these florid embellishments are surprising in view of the more assertive and dramatic nature of his mature piano playing style, but for the most part Allison's recorded performances on both *Young Man Mose* and *Ramblin'* are replete with the directness and musical honesty which characterized his playing on his first two recordings. Although not one of his strongest works, Allison's own musical voice does, nevertheless, surface on *Ramblin' with Mose*.

Joe Goldberg's liner notes from 1958's *Ramblin' with Mose* paint up the difficulty involved in categorizing and marketing Allison's music:

> ... Mose [is] very difficult to categorize and from time to time [this] causes him a good deal of trouble. For instance, one recording executive thought hard about the best way to "exploit" Mose, and take advantage of his unusual talents. The result of this soul-searching was the gift to Mose of a portfolio of Gene Autry songs. They have not been recorded. But some of the frustrations have been even greater than being turned into a repository for old sheet music. Mose, by his own assessment, is not "in" enough for the hard-core jazz rooms, and not bland enough for the supper clubs. So it is sometimes difficult for him to find a place to work.[2]

Goldberg also recounts a story of one of Allison's live performances, which appears to have been conceived by one club manager/"art activist" either as a multi-media experimental event or a market gimmick, or both:

> Earlier I referred to Allison's compositions as pencil sketches, and there was one occasion when that came very close to being true. Max Gordon, impresario of New York's Village Vanguard, is always looking for unusual entertainment and at one time was indulging himself regularly in that practice every Sunday afternoon. One such Sunday, Mose shared the Vanguard bandstand with a painter. Mose would give the title and general idea of one of his pieces to the painter, and as he played, the painter, on the spot, worked out a visual complement to the music. The incident provides a good way of thinking about Mose's music.[3]

A younger and obviously more open-minded Allison it must have been who participated in this type of event; the mature artist would no doubt refuse to countenance the distilling of his music into the visual-arts medium.

Creek Bank, Mose's fifth recording in the Prestige series, recorded on August 15, 1958, demonstrates a more aggressive approach to both his piano playing and his songwriting. The "local color" theme permeates this recording, both musically and lyrically, with seven of the ten tracks containing pastoral references. Allison claims one vocal and four piano pieces as original compositions. Addison Farmer on bass and drummer Ronnie Free, his accompanists on *Ramblin' with Mose*, line up again as sidemen on this date, which comprises two vocals and eight instrumentals. *Creek Bank* is Allison's personal favorite of the six he made for Prestige, because he remembers he "had a rhythm section that played more with me than any other before we recorded."

Allison's cover version of Willie Dixon's "Seventh Son" on *Creek Bank* drew attention not only to Allison, who made it a staple of his own repertoire, but also championed its legendary composer, a prolific and gifted songwriter whom Mose has always credited in live performance.[4] The work of the late Dixon, a bassist and celebrated blues bard now considered an American "roots artist," influenced generations of musicians, crossing into the rock mainstream. "I'm Your Hootchie Coochie Man," "I Just Want to Make Love to You," "Spoonful" and "Little Red Rooster," to list only a few, are among the many contributions Willie Dixon made to the American popular-music repertoire. Dixon and Allison were friends for decades, playing on the same bill on a few occasions in New York, with Allison occasionally joining Willie's group "The Willie Dixon Dream Band," a group Dixon, despite his ill health, convened in the late 1980s. Dixon admired Mose both as a singer and a man:

> "The Seventh Son" is making a statement about the facts of life and Mose makes a beautiful statement about the facts of life when he sings those songs. He knows how to emphasize them proper and get people to understanding them and makes the people love them. That's another thing about the blues, you see, when you get the people to love it, it will go over big. People don't know that all the roots of American music is the blues. There's no doubt about the fact that the blues is an art form. It was a form that was

created in Africa generations ago and became the root of all American music. Practically anybody who sang or played music in America is playing or singing part of the blues anyway because the blues is the roots of all American music.

I love the way Mose do my songs. Actually, he made a hit out of a couple of songs of mine and I feel like those, in fact, are two of the biggest songs I ever had. When they were hits way back, it didn't help me then but it do now. He's a beautiful guy and I like the way he make his statements, especially when he's doing his musical arrangements. He knows how to emphasize what he's trying to do and he does a darn good job of it.

Mose first heard "Seventh Son" in blues/R&B singer Willie Mabon's version and decided to cover the tune. This was a fortuitous decision, and it was Allison's version that spawned the numerous subsequent covers by other artists. Like two of Allison's originals, "Parchman Farm" and "Your Mind Is on Vacation," despite being composed by Dixon, "Seventh Son" became synonymous with Mose Allison. Mose's Prestige rendering of "Seventh Son" also marks his return to the country blues, his distinctive interpretation of the tune yet another example of his expressive "speaking" style of vocal phrasing. Mose comments:

When I first started recording and I hadn't written many songs, I was looking mainly at the country blues section to try to get some material. And, I ran across that down South in one of those blues record stores. I thought that "Seventh Son" was a great song of that type—the "I'm Superman" type of thing. I mean, that's what everybody would like to feel, anyhow. And most people have felt that at one time or another in their life, I think. Felt that they were really the seventh son. So, right away I knew I wanted to do it. When I first started doing it, it probably got me through some of the early years. It was one of the tunes that everybody wanted to hear.[5]

Musically, too, "Seventh Son" is intriguing. Set in a Latin groove that Allison initially dubbed "rumboogie" (the downhome version of the rumba), Mose's piano playing, whether accompanying or improvising, has undergone a rather dramatic technical and artistic evolution. Dissonance and chromaticism, two stylistic elements that have consistently characterized Allison's playing, are boldly emphasized in "Seventh Son." Additionally, richer harmonic texture and a rhythmic independence combine to change his approach to phrasing. The denser, richer chord sonorities, evolved from the former right-hand single-note lines, appear first in an improvised introductory passage. These chords carry a blues melody where a blues tremolo, a device Allison often uses in improvisation, evokes a "blues harmonica" effect.

Allison's piano solo is also vastly different from his previous blues solos. Here, heavy-handed chords on displaced accents dominate, chopping the phrases into an asymmetrical or irregular pattern, a style prefiguring Mose's future piano improvisations. His solo melodies remain centered on the blues scale tonality, but because of the changes in rhythm and harmony, they do not qualify as blues clichés. In this early version of "Seventh Son," Allison the pianist stands at the threshold of a significant period of musical growth. The new, exploratory musical additions contrast with his earlier, simpler piano style and indicate that he has begun to listen to the works of twentieth-century composers for piano such as the American Charles Ives, the German Paul Hindemith, and the Russian Alexander Scriabin. From this point forward, Allison's improvisations employ the dense harmonic textures and melodic and rhythmic patterns these composers used in their pieces for the piano. The blues song form, with its simplicity and directness, provided the perfect vehicle for implementing these new musical ideas, and because Allison used Dixon's song throughout the years to explore, develop and hone his improvisational style on the piano, he believes "Seventh Son" has undergone the most profound musical change of any one song in his repertoire.

"If You Live," Allison's F minor blues, rounds off the vocals on *Creek Bank*. The song's lyrics follow the straight AABA song form, its theme the hardship of the laboring Southern field worker. The piano accompaniment follows the standard blues format in part, but Allison varies things harmonically by adding an interesting touch to the B section of the lyric. Here, he provides a smooth musical contrast, substituting the V chord with a four-chord sequence that hovers in the key of E flat, the dominant of the relative major key. The descending repeating blues riff in the right hand throughout the A section of the text lands an exotic melodic motif to his plaintive vocal delivery, executed as usual, in speech-like phrasing. The signature minor seconds (A and A flat) fill in the tonic chord where it appears.

The piano material on *Creek Bank* presents the mélange of jazz and blues typical of Mose Allison, the styles obliquely intertwined in specific instances, the difference between them more pronounced in others. His playing is steeped in the sophistication of a modern-jazz stylist in Charlie Parker's "Yardbird Suite," Vernon Duke's "Cabin in the Sky" and Ellington's "Prelude to a Kiss" but his bluesy interpretations of jazz tunes persist. Apart from his original, blues-infused "Mule," Jack Lawrence's "If I Didn't Care" is typical of Allison's developing piano style, chords dominating the melodic line, replacing the single-note melodies in the right hand. Other originals on *Creek Bank*, "Moon and Cypress," the boppish "Dinner on the Ground" and the title track "Creek Bank," offer the same jazz/blues blend with familiar local-color overtones. The record's liner note succinctly sums up the use of the blues in Allison's work on *Creek Bank* as well as his general approach to playing:

> The feeling is for the blues, but not "The Blues" which begs to be defined technically in terms of chord progressions and scales with flatted thirds and sevenths. What characterizes his playing, no matter how advanced it gets harmonically, is the blues sound made up (in Mose's picturesque language) of "curved notes, bent notes and smashed notes." That's the sound he perceives in the country-bluesers with whom he still identifies. Mose believes every type of music is modal and thinks of his music as being in the blues mode.[6]

The "blues mode" to which Mose alludes is the country blues scale consisting of tonic, flat third, fourth, flatted fifth, and flat seventh, intervals whose dissonances can combine, and in Allison's case, deliberately merge, into what he describes in visceral terms as "smashed," "bent" and "curved" notes. Allison's basic concept of the blues tonality governs his piano style throughout its evolution, even though his mature piano improvisations feature musical complexity and intricacy that extend the acknowledged boundaries of rhythm, meter and harmony. Also, later, he adopts a "jazz-blues" tonality where intervals of the second, natural third, and sixth are added to his musical vocabulary and characterize his piano accompanying and improvisations.

Autumn Song, Mose Allison's sixth and final album in his Prestige series, contains some of the artist's strongest work on record since his 1957 debut album *Back Country Suite*. Mose's music on this last recording puts into effect his aesthetic adage: "You have to get a style and then transcend it." The pieces still revel in blues-based tonality, but both his original compositions and piano solos undeniably reflect Allison's new musical influences and artistic development.

Inspirations from the 1950s generation of piano stylists pervade Allison's work in the *Autumn Song* sessions. Ideas derived from the keyboard approaches of Thelonious Monk, Al Haig, John Lewis and Lennie Tristano reverberate through Allison's evolving style as he explores uncharted musical territories. Here, Mose's primitive, simple diatonic right-hand lines are replaced with intriguing modal melodies, repetitive melodic figures, and sprightlier rhythms. Rhythmically, Allison's playing also signals his departure from the staid swing tradition in favor of a looser version of the genre combined with the then fashionable bebop style. During this period, traces of the influence of legendary bebop pianist Bud Powell are easily discerned in Allison's playing. Powell's pianistic genius loomed large to Mose and his contemporaries in the younger generation of players during the late 1950s, and Mose recalls that this emulation of Bud Powell's style was not conscious or intentional but merely inevitable.

For Mose Allison, however, the proclivity to follow in Bud

Powell's musical footsteps was short-lived, reaching its pinnacle in Allison's work on *Autumn Song*, and after the experience, Mose's artistry emerges mature and unscathed as far as the integrity of his own personal style is concerned. The album features compelling vocals, dynamic piano playing and intriguing compositions. Although he had delivered his final Prestige record, Mose Allison had established himself as an important artist.

A more aggressive performance by his now stock rhythm section, drummer Ronnie Free and bassist Addison Farmer, accompanies the pianist in the diverse ten-track set of *Autumn Song*, comprised of four original compositions for piano trio, three vocals covering blues and jazz tunes, and four jazz standards. Allison performs commendably on his piano covers of Dizzy Gillespie's bop standard "Groovin' High" and of the jazz pieces "Strange" and "It's Crazy." Allison excels, though, in performing his own compositions, particularly "Promenade," the title track "Autumn Song" and "Devil in the Cane Field."

The medium walking blues-based "Promenade" features a descending melodic line based on the blues scale. Like "Saritha," his piano composition from the *Creek Bank* record, "Promenade" remains in Mose's current repertoire as an instrumental set opener. The lush piano tone poem, "Autumn Song," however, is unlike any piece Allison had previously composed. It features a dense, rich, harmonic texture, a new technique that foreshadows the chord voicings he was to use to accompany himself in future vocals, "Let It Come Down," "How Much Truth," and "Hello There, Universe."

The lush-sounding harmonies in these pieces are mostly attributable to Allison's use of the interval of the perfect fourth in his compositions, primarily in chord voicings and melodies. Mose's propensity to compose using the exotic-sounding interval was probably influenced by his affinity for both ethnic folk music and the works by modern composers for the piano. Allison has always expressed a particular interest in the folk music of China, which often uses a succession of descending fourths.[7] Additionally, the piano literature of Paul Hindemith and Alexander Scriabin, two composers whose writing made strong and lasting musical impressions on Allison, is immersed in "quartal harmony," a harmonic system based on the fourth.[8] Influences from folk music and twentieth-century harmonies are also apparent in "Autumn Song," which Mose writes using a descending melody in fourths and quartal harmonies in chords, evoking an impressionistic soundscape.

Another original work, "Devil in the Cane Field," strongly suggests the influence of the two preeminent contemporary jazz pianists, Bud Powell and Thelonious Monk. Mose plays the tune's melody of sixteenth-note runs in a boppish style reminiscent of Powell, signaling his break with the euphonious single-note melodies in the right hand and demonstrating his burgeoning piano technique. Executed in a rumba tempo, repeated melodic figures, modal melodies and harmonic dissonance also dominate the tune, all conjuring up the playing of Thelonious Monk. Allison is quite happy to acknowledge Monk's influence:

> I always loved Thelonious Monk's playing. I first heard him on recording in 1947. I liked him immediately because I've always liked people who have a definite personality in their playing. I always liked Erroll Garner for the same reason. You can always tell it's Thelonious Monk when you hear him; the same goes for Erroll Garner and Nat Cole. Those were my three big heroes throughout the years. Along with John Lewis and Count Basie, they were stylists that depended more on touch, phrasings and rhythm. My mainstays were Monk, Garner, John Lewis, Al Haig and a lot of players from that era. The others were the virtuosi like Art Tatum and Bud Powell. Lennie Tristano would fall between the two, I guess. I always liked him and consider him an influence. On the style thing, my outlook is that nobody has everything. If you go in one direction, there are a lot of things that you might overlook. It matters to know what you're after and balance it.[9]

Allison's vocals also take center stage on *Autumn Song*. His memorable cover of Sonny Boy Williamson's "Eyesight to the

Blind" exemplifies his hybrid stylistic approach, intertwining jazz elements with a straight twelve-bar country-blues tune. Allison's unique rendition of this simple blues is also laced with bebop. Within a solid uptempo swing, Mose's piano solo, spun from eighth-note phrases, and marked vaguely by melodic clichés, focuses the tonality not on a strict country-blues scale but on jazz sonorities as well, adding the sixth as one tonal center. Allison's smooth, cool vocal, featuring his speech-like singing style, adds another jazz twist.

Mose's rendering of Sonny Boy Williamson's blues reverberated in the blues and rock community in London, and inspired rock musician Pete Townshend, for one, who covered the tune several years later on his 1986 live solo album *Pete Townshend's Deep End Live!* Townshend remembers: "It was Mose's version that I first heard and I actually didn't hear Sonny Boy's version until about 1987, although we worked with Sonny Boy a lot when he was living in England."

Robert Jr. Lockwood's blues, "That's All Right," has also survived for over forty years in Allison's vocal repertoire, in a relatively conventional interpretation. In a version inspired by blues singer Jimmie Rogers, Mose takes the piece downtempo in what he calls a "medium-walking-tempo blues" and approaches his singing with more conservative legato phrasing. Today, Allison performs his cover of "That's All Right" at a faster tempo and marks the vocal phrasing with heavier accents.

Mose also still performs Duke Ellington's "Do Nothing Till You Hear From Me," covered first on *Autumn Song*. This early version is distinguished from his previous Ellington remakes in that instead of caressing Ellington's melodies like a crooner, he personalizes the music as a vocal and piano stylist, hammering the vocal line with accents and smearing the piano accompaniment with colorful, rich chord voicings. In his current version, these stylistic traits are even more exaggerated. On the final phrase, he stretches to the outer reaches of his falsetto voice, putting a fermata on the word "you," singing it in falsetto a minor sixth above the written note. In his most recent live renditions of the song, when he is particularly good voice, the jocose Mose follows the falsetto on "you" with a coda of yodeling. The surprise Marx Brothers-style ending, sung above the sustained final chord, guarantees a laugh from an unsuspecting audience, embossing the song with Mose Allison's personal insignia, his droll sense of humor and penchant for irony. Arguably, the playful phrase also flows well musically, his preceding use of his falsetto voice on "you" making the yodel a logical musical ending to the song.

While today Mose appears to have ample time to invent wry new twists to the serious songs of Duke Ellington, for example, such departures might have been seen as indulgent in his two compressed Prestige years. Considering the pressures of Allison's Prestige contract, which required him to produce large amounts of recorded music in a short period, the artist doubtless had little time to exercise his imagination beyond writing and preparing for the next session. Mose Allison contracted with Prestige Records for six records over two years, or one roughly every four months. Moreover, although Allison did not protest the deal, which would have been deemed a typical independent-label agreement for that era, by today's music-industry standards, the same arrangement would, most likely, be held to be unreasonable. Prestige offered Mose Allison little money, $250 per record, with no escalation based on the financial success of his product. This was arguably an exploitative arrangement, even one that smacked of unfair dealing. Also, with respect to the development of Allison's recording career, the Prestige arrangement was not altogether favorable to the artist. From the artist's perspective, flooding the market with an overabundance of material, especially if musically inconsistent, could only be damaging to the consumer's perceptions of the artist's work. More significantly, the notion of a new, developing recording artist being legally obligated to deplete his or her catalog quickly, producing music in assembly-line fashion, is a shortsighted practice militating against long-term success. Unless the artist is naturally prolific, mass production often results in a burn-out that destroys the creative process, taking the artist's career with it.

At the time Mose signed with Prestige, however, his

arrangement was by no means unique to him. In the United States, the music business was in an embryonic state and, unfortunately, rife with somewhat Machiavellian procedures. It was not uncommon to witness record companies and music publishers promising fame and fortune in return for legal indentured servitude, where artists were sucked dry of their work for very little money, their record companies absconding with complete rights to their songs, and getting away with it. Given the average artist's naïveté, his or her lack of bargaining power at the table, and with lawyers rarely involved, musicians were easy prey and typically signed abusive but legally binding deals. By the time American jurisprudence caught up with these egregious industry practices, and acceptable standards and laws to protect the interests of both sides evolved, it was often too late. In the meantime, prevailing practices in the music industry during the 1950s often violated many musicians' rights. Mose Allison was no exception.

Allison's multi-record arrangement with Prestige clearly took a toll on his work. From a purely artistic perspective, Allison's recording career on Prestige was inconsistent, sometimes brilliant, occasionally mediocre. His first two records, his debut *Back Country Suite* and its sequel *Local Color*, earned outstanding reviews because the music for these recordings had been developing for years, the original pieces having been composed long before Mose associated himself with a label. However, shortly after the two recordings received this critical acclaim, Prestige understandably required him to produce a third record. With much of his reservoir of original material exhausted in six months on two record dates, and given roughly four months to replenish the supply, it is no great surprise that Allison's middle records for Prestige lack flamboyance and distinction. It appears that Prestige, under the guise of reintroducing Allison as a jazz-standard pianist/balladeer for his third album, *Young Man Mose*, compensated the artist by allowing him a respite from composing. Paradoxically, although his third effort is musically more conservative and quite mundane compared with his first two, it bore the title *Young Man Mose*, a title evoking the romance, mystique and local downhome color of "Young Man Blues." *Ramblin' With Mose*, his fourth release recorded only three months after his third album, is another mediocre work. In the final analysis, *Ramblin'* may not have proved detrimental to Allison's career in the strictest sense, but the lackluster nature of the album proves that he had little time to listen to his muse.

A short four-month hiatus between *Ramblin'* and *Creek Bank* proved beneficial and productive for the fledgling recording artist, who had been developing musical ideas throughout the prior recording dates. *Creek Bank* yielded some outstanding blues vocals, a version of Willie Dixon's "Seventh Son" and his own "If You Live." The record exuded Mose's renewed confidence in his musical roots and was well received by both his audience and the critics. His piano piece, "Saritha," from *Creek Bank* remains one of his personal favorites among his piano instrumentals, and is a piece that Al Cohn and Zoot Sims, his two venerated jazz colleagues, covered during his sideman days with them.

By far the strongest of the later Prestige works is Allison's last album for the label, *Autumn Song*; the six-month interval between records clearly paid off here. *Autumn Song* demonstrates Mose's musical progress, solidifying his unique style, which by now had evolved beyond simpler swing-style playing. Allison was listening astutely to new music, decoding both twentieth-century classical piano pieces and idiosyncratic modern-jazz piano styles, assimilating certain of these characteristics into his own piano playing. The longer break between recordings resulted in thoughtfully composed songs and new experiments in Mose's piano style.

What finally emerges from Mose Allison's six Prestige records is a romantic Southern musical persona performing in a style amalgamating the country blues and jazz. Allison's singular vocal style, with its cool, laid-back phrasing, captivated his audience. As a pianist, Mose Allison had commenced his recording career playing in the conventional lucid, Lestorian swing style, but his final Prestige record foreshadows the unorthodox bebop and classically-inspired piano stylist.

To be sure, Prestige Records, and the company's subsequent owner, San Francisco based Fantasy Records, have taken the opportunity to exploit and recycle Allison's catalog of sixty-five master recordings, releasing reissue after reissue since Allison's term on the label ran out in 1959. The maudlin, unoriginal album titles such as *Ol' Devil Mose* (no doubt derived from his cover of "Ol' Devil Moon") and *Mose Allison Plays for Lovers*, emotional hooks that are not reflective of the album's contents, appear to be directed at the "dinner music" market, and demonstrate a profound misunderstanding not only of Mose Allison's work but of his audience as well. Record-company kitsch, notwithstanding, each Prestige reissue sparks off a resurgence in interest in Mose Allison's music, and presents a new generation of listeners with the opportunity to hear a style that even in its infancy continues to inspire, instruct and entertain, exactly as Mose intended.

8

DETRIBALIZATION AND TRANSFIGURATION

"When I first came on the scene in New York, a lot of people saw me as a commercial product, a potential commercial product. They saw me around and talked to me and saw that I wasn't going to be too cooperative. They said, 'You might blow it, you know, you could blow it, you might not get another chance, you better sign this now.' I never looked at it the way they did. All I ever wanted to do was play. They were thinking they could get as much as possible out of me commercially and make me a lot of money, enough to do anything I wanted. The implication is that you're not doing what you want to do ... they could keep you from doing what you want to. 'You can stay a victim,' is what one guy said. I'm considered a victim because I'm still playing small clubs for a living. If I wasn't a victim and went along with the right people, I might play bigger places, playing six weeks a year and loafing the rest of the year. The music was always first with me. I always admired the people who were good musicians. I was always more concerned with staying busy and earning the respect of my peers than making a lot of money or whatever. I'm looking from a standpoint of what I'm getting out of it because it's what I want to do with my life. I'm actually quite fortunate in that I have been able to make a good living doing what I want to do."

Mose Allison

"Ask Me Nice"

I just got here day 'fore yesterday
It won't be long and I'll be on my way
For these few days that I'll be 'round
Please don't try to bring me down

I made my entrance on the Greyhound bus
I don't intend to cause a fuss
If you like my style, that's fine with me
And if you don't just let me be

I don't claim to be so great
I'm no pacesetter, no potentate
I got some kids, I got a wife
I'm just tryin to swing my way through life

So don't try to make me what I'm not
I'll just get by with what I've got
Live, let live that's my advice
If you got questions
Ask me nice

I'm not the first, I'm not the most
Of this town, I am not the toast
I'm gettin' older every day
I'm just tryin' to swing a little in my way

So don't try to make me what I'm not
I'll just get by with what I've got
Live, let live that's my advice
If you got questions
Ask me nice

Mose Allison

By the late 1950s, Mose Allison's career had taken off to the extent that he was able to tour the United States, and later Europe, leading the Mose Allison Trio, on the strength of his own recordings. Throughout the next two or three years, however, at least until he was firmly ensconced at Atlantic Records, Mose also continued to play as piano sideman for the Cohn-Sims team and for Stan Getz as well. With a wife and four children to support, these sideman jobs were more income-related than true creative outlets. Allison had clearly established himself as a solo jazz personality and although he would have preferred shows as an independent headliner, developing a solid fan base on the road would take time. Nevertheless, Allison began touring the country alone, sometimes on short road trips with a rhythm section accompanying, at other times hiring regional sidemen recommended by word of mouth, which continues to be his regular practice.

Handing the evening's bass player the black book of his charts, Allison trusts the sideman will have sufficient musical acumen to sightread his music, or at least have studied his records well enough to keep up. Although granted no time to rehearse his repertoire, in the early days his sidemen did have the opportunity to play for several nights of club engagements, for two or three sets each night, which gave them ample time to learn Allison's songs and adapt to his style of live performing. Mose Allison has always had an eccentric on-stage personality, a reserved and reticent demeanor which results in his addressing the audience directly only to introduce sidemen or credit composers. Although relaxed, Allison approaches his live performances with a serious professionalism more akin to that of a concert pianist, always commencing his set with a piano instrumental or two to warm up to allow the music to set the mood.

In his first road trips with the Mose Allison Trio, Mose remembers that audiences sometimes expected him to be black. With only radio airplay and no likeness of the Caucasian Allison on his first Prestige records, audiences were easily confused by the timbre of the Mississippi baritone singing the blues.

> That was when a lot of people assumed I was black if they heard me on records. When I first started out, I once got a

call from *Jet* magazine and the writer wanted to know if I was the first black graduate of LSU.

People would come up to me in clubs and tell me they thought I was black. I had several responses I would use, depending on the situation. My favorite was, "I thought I was black, too."

I remember my first trip to California in 1960. I played in L.A. My first job had posters of me up and they had drawings of me as an Afro-American. The job was at a high school in a predominantly ethnic neighborhood in L.A. and I definitely felt a draft there. I wish I had saved that poster because they were hand-drawn. The promoters had taken a picture off an album cover that was sort of indiscriminate and you couldn't really tell what my racial qualities were, so they made my hair a little curlier.

I wasn't aware that singing the "so-called" black blues would offend anybody or that anybody would take exception to it until I came to New York. I first became aware of racial antagonisms entering into music when I was thirty years old. It was the first time that it was brought home to me that some people didn't like the fact that I was singing the blues. There was one review of my first record that read, "the white Mississippian who's unabashed to sing the blues." And I thought, why should I be "abashed" to sing the blues? That made me aware that some people took exception to what I was doing.

Being a white man singing the blues was a bit of an anomaly, but Allison was not alone. Barbara Dane, a blond Caucasian woman from Detroit, was a relatively well-known blues singer in the 1950s and 1960s. She performed regularly with African-American blues artists such as Mama Yancey and sidemen such as Willie Dixon and Memphis Slim, even in the face of racial controversy.[1] In other jazz circles, the baritone saxophonist/composer/arranger best known at that time for his "Birth of Cool" work, Gerry Mulligan, also proved that music could transcend racial barriers, frequently joining with jazz virtuosi such as Art Farmer, Miles Davis and

Thelonious Monk. Mose Allison himself has thought a good deal about the racial question:

> I must have heard "We thought you were black" a thousand times. It's usually meant as a compliment and I accept it as such. However, if you start analyzing some of the implications, it becomes sticky: a) you're so good at playing black music that we thought you were black; b) you sound like a black man (no one ever says which one) but you're white so you must be some sort of freak or fraud. Then there's the occasional smartass who says, "I knew that you were white all along," meaning I was trying to fool them but they were too smart for it. Of course I know all of this is completely negligible and has nothing to do with the essential thing, which is whether or not what I do has merit. Part of the challenge of performing is in trying to convince *yourself* that what *you* are doing is worthwhile.

When Allison's six-record deal with the independent Prestige terminated in 1959, authorities at Columbia Records obviously considered Mose Allison a hot enough commodity to offer a recording contract to him immediately. Since the 1930s, Columbia Records had established itself as a label dedicated to the blues and jazz genres, prospering under the tutelage of CBS producer John Hammond. Hammond championed the careers of many noteworthy American artists, bringing swing master Benny Goodman and blues songstress Bessie Smith, among many others, to the label. By the time Mose Allison began his business association with Columbia, the label had more recently excelled in developing a strong roster of modern-jazz artists such as Miles Davis, Thelonious Monk and Dave Brubeck. Columbia opted for signing big-name artists with commercial, mainstream viability, and no doubt the label was contemplating market success for Allison, untried as he was in the majors, but already proving himself a successful independent-label recording artist. Allison's proven track record on Prestige indicated that he was poised to produce the goods for Columbia; already an acclaimed international artist, his devout following, novel style, and potential for crossover into the pop mainstream made him a good investment. Allison was also personally and professionally ready for the change. With a major corporate label backing his work, the promotion and distribution of his recordings would now enable his music to reach a wider audience and, he hoped, place his career in a highly visible fast track. Unfortunately, however, the relationship was not as successful as both parties had wished. Allison's stint on Columbia lasted for two years, from 1959 to 1961, and was curtailed when the artist himself eventually requested his release.

Mose Allison recorded three full-length albums under his contract with Columbia Records. On Prestige, Mose's recordings had been primarily self-produced, with occasional input from Bob Weinstock. The big-league record labels operated differently, and in Allison's case, Columbia directed the venerable producer/arranger Teo Macero to step in to supervise the recording sessions. Although their artistic relationship yielded commendable work, it somehow lacked the impact and mystique of Allison's ground-breaking first recordings on Prestige.

Columbia Records released all of the master recordings delivered for Mose's first two albums, *The Transfiguration of Hiram Brown* and *I Love the Life I Live*. His third album, an after-the-fact cut-and-paste project, merged six new tracks with selected cuts from his previous two Columbia releases. Once Allison left Columbia and the young independent Atlantic Records had launched his successful debut for them, *I Don't Worry 'Bout a Thing* in 1962, Columbia culled material from Allison's three albums as *Takes to the Hills*. Ironically, the title track was one of the songs that Columbia had decided not to release while Mose was on the label. In 1966, with Mose having a string of records on Atlantic behind him and also attracting wider name recognition, Epic Records, a division of Columbia, reissued *Takes to the Hills*, calling it *Mose Allison Sings and Plays V-8 Ford Blues*, as part of the label's "Jazz Series." Mose also appeared as a Manhattan Jazz All-star on a Columbia Records compilation tributing the Frank Loesser musical "Guys and Dolls" while he was signed to the label. Mose comments:

I don't even remember how I got to Columbia from Prestige. I must have run into this guy Nat Shapiro, I think that was his name. He must have told me to come up and talk to him when he found out I was looking for a new record company. So, I went up to talk to him and we just signed a new contract right there. But my A&R man there was Teo Macero, who has also worked with other jazz people.

Columbia Records had high hopes for Mose Allison's first outing on the label, *The Transfiguration of Hiram Brown*, which appeared to be a more sophisticated remake of his solo debut on Prestige, *Back Country Suite*. The album was recorded on December 21 and 23, 1959 and January 11, 1960, the title piece embodying side A, while a selection of covers, including two vocal tracks, comprises the flip side. "The Transfiguration of Hiram Brown," composed as an extended work of multiple movements, seven piano pieces and one vocal, revives the suite form that Allison successfully employed in *Back Country Suite*. Here, however, Allison departs from the individual-program musical sketches of his first suite, writing in a through-composed three-tiered scheme of theme-development-recapitulation, the music reflecting the passage of time and events.

One of his most brilliant achievements, yet critically ignored, Allison's opus flies in the face of the era's musical conventions and orthodoxy. It delves deep into Allison's arsenal of musical influences and references, borrowing considerably from his growing classical-music catalog and reflecting the exponential pace of his development in his compositional and improvisational skills. Allison's piano improvisations on *Hiram Brown* feature recurring dissonances, chromaticism, and an increased use of the left hand. The revered bassist sideman Addison Farmer, veteran of five Prestige albums, and a new drummer, Jerry Segal, accompany Mose on this first Columbia recording.

Hiram Brown's program resounds with autobiographical overtones marking Allison's own impressions of his transition from "country bumpkin" to "city sophisticate." Allison chronicles the "detribalization" process of the protagonist, a provincial named Hiram Brown, in a suite musically depicting the three phases in the protagonist's life cycle. The listener is introduced to Hiram Brown entrapped in his pastoral surroundings, fantasizing about escaping for a more interesting life in the city. After "Cutting Out" from the country backwater, Brown is overwhelmed by the chaos and cruelty of the big city. Disenchanted and disenfranchised, the protagonist then embarks on an introspective period, searching for his lost youth. Deciding that this exercise is futile, Brown subsequently realizes that his identity crisis has been a positive experience, resulting in the dénouement, his "transfiguration," or psychological/emotional adjustment to his new city life.

"Barefoot-Dirt Road," a blues-infused jazz piece based on a squaredance rhythmic theme, begins the suite. The opening chords feature a homophonic planing of harmonies, with the minor second retained in the inner voices, a melancholic melody in a descending fourth echoing Allison's affinity for the folk motif. The folk theme is carried forward in a squaredance rhythm, and is expanded and developed extensively in the improvisation section, which also features trade-offs with the bass.

"City Home," the only vocal in the suite, performed at a painfully slow tempo on this recording, remains a mainstay of Allison's repertoire. The lyrics are self-contained in twelve bars, yet meander in a musical freestyle of two-bar phrases with a repeated melodic phrase. An unusual harmonic direction emerges from the melodic pattern of the song, a blues. In it, Allison creates unorthodox chromatic chord progressions, key modulations and transitory harmonic passages, firmly stamping his individual style on the simple melody.

As the song modulates from its original key of E flat to the harmonically distant key of D, Allison makes the change in a three-chord passage, slipping from the V (B flat) to the unconventional tritone (E minor) before landing on the modulating chord, A minor 7, the V7 chord in the new key of D. This strange passing tonality essentially occurs in the third phrase on the pivotal word "getaway," sung on G flat where a tritone movement in the bass from B flat to E minor serves as the modulating passage out of E flat and into D. After a brief excursion in the new key, the melody modulates back to the home tonic, E flat. Mose acknowledges the unusual nature of the song:

> I never ran across another tune with exactly that same chord change. Where it goes from E flat into D and the way the melody gets there by hanging on to the word "getaway" is unusual. In other words, the combination of the melody and the way the melody is tied in with the harmonic transition taking place from E flat to D is unusual. I've played and seen a lot of songs but have never run across that particular change in another song. It could be I've never seen it before. If it's not original, it's at least unusual.

The innovative harmonies and intriguing melodic meandering of "City Home" notwithstanding, "Cuttin' Out," the next piece, is an uptempo swing variation on the blues, and marks a refreshing return to a diatonic melody and conventional chord changes.

"Gotham Day" revels in harmonic and melodic dissonance, musically capturing the ominous mood of urban confusion. Here, the compositional and piano style prefigure Allison's mature technique more closely than any other piece he had recorded until then. The ascending modal melody of "Gotham Day" suggests a whole-tone scale but is composed around the blues scale, emphasizing the augmented fourth and minor seventh. A driving ostinato bassline of descending tritones contrasts contrapuntally with the tritone ascent in the piano. Allison's offsetting melodic snags of chromatic motifs in the upper register, crashing lower-octave bass notes voiced simultaneously with dense dissonantly voiced chords on the treble register, and oblique motion in both hands, suggest that his astute listening has taken him well beyond Thelonious Monk and Al Haig to the classical world of Ives and Scriabin.

"Gotham Night" develops a descending chromatic homophonic melody reminiscent of a minor-key version of the American popular tune "Ain't She Sweet." The identical thematic material in "River" and "Echo" musically portray the protagonist's introspection. "River," a rhapsodic piece, is a short, flowing, languid melody which begins with the motif set homophonically before branching into a single-note melodic line. "Echo," a blues/jazz fantasia for piano, repeats the motif of "River," elongating it with sequential descending fourths and extending the piece with a blues-infused improvisation section. The dénouement, "Finale," is a short recapitulation of the theme to "Barefoot-Dirt Road," implying a dual thematic interpretation: that Hiram Brown either succumbed to the city strain and retreated back to his pastoral roots, or that he successfully reconciled the differences within himself.

Ben Sidran, the producer, jazz artist, radio and television host, cites "The Transfiguration of Hiram Brown" as a predominant musical influence on him while he was growing up in Wisconsin:

> I first heard the recording, "The Transfiguration of Hiram Brown" when I was in high school. I loved the song "City Home." I was sitting in a small town in Wisconsin and it really spoke to me about what I was considering doing. Mose's piano playing in particular was important because at that time I was listening to Horace Silver, but I was also listening to Bud Powell. I hadn't discovered Sonny Clark yet and was sort of listening to Mose as an offshoot with the tributary sort of like Monk. And, of course, I had followed Mose's early records in the late 1950s.

Sidran, who was to produce Mose Allison's later recordings on the EMI jazz affiliate Blue Note Records, discussed the issue of "detribalization," *Hiram Brown*'s central theme, with Mose on his talk show for National Public Radio. Mose commented:

> The detribalism theme is one that I experienced coming

from Mississippi to New York. I think you just keep getting more transfigured, if you're lucky. You keep going through all sorts of phases. That was meant to give an impression of, as I say, the detribalization process which is taking place all over the world. All kinds of people are going through it. They're going from agrarian societies into urban societies. That's one of the major themes of this century, I guess. I just feel like I had been through that and that's what it was all about. There's no end to it. I mean, you don't get from one thing to another and just stop. After you get into the urban thing, there are all sorts of ways you can go from there. I think everything is headed at some sort of synthesis. You take the best aspects, try to find the best aspects of all the different modes of living, and try to put together a new way to live that will allow us to survive.

Side B of the Columbia release presents some strong Allison performances of cover material, two outstanding vocals, both executed in his unique speaking style. Where these record dates do not find Allison in the best of voice, today the technical wizardry of vocal harmonizers would probably mask the imperfections. The best of Teo Macero's takes included apparent problems with vocal intonation and an open mike on a groaning pianist during his solos. Nevertheless, the two vocals from *Hiram Brown*'s B side, J. Williams's classic gritty blues "Baby Please Don't Go" and the jazz standard "'Deed I do," are sincere and earthy. Indeed, the recorded vocal imperfections imbue each with a striking humility, authentic character and intimacy, as if Mose were playing the songs in his living room.

Allison's rendition of "Baby Please Don't Go" also marks his formal adoption of his "rumboogie" groove, which he later renamed his "Afro-Cuban groove." Debuted in his first version of "Seventh Son," on *Creek Bank*, Allison calls this eight-to-the-bar rhythmic approach the "downhome rumba" since it crosses the timing of a Latin rumba with the boogie-woogie.

The piano pieces, Johnny Mercer/Hoagy Carmichael's "How Little We Know," Bob Merrill's "Make Yourself

Comfortable" and a stylized version of Cole Porter's "Love for Sale," fill out Mose's first recording for Columbia.

Bruce Lundvall, president of the jazz label Blue Note and a former executive for Columbia Records, remembers his first professional connection with Mose Allison in 1960 through his former employer:

> I first listened to Mose when he was playing piano for people like Stan Getz and Zoot Sims back in the fifties. Then, I fell in love with the earlier records where he sang. The first time I was somewhat involved with Mose was the first day I started work at Columbia Records in 1960. I had never met him at that point but what happened was that I was a trainee at CBS and they sent me up to Bridgeport, Ct. where the pressing plant was. The record they were pressing the very first day of my career in the record business was Mose Allison's "Baby Please Don't Go," which was released as a single. I was one of two trainees and we were both madly in love with the record and Mose's music.

The strength of the material notwithstanding, and despite the superlative performance of the cover tunes and Allison's burgeoning and dynamic compositional style, *The Transfiguration of Hiram Brown* did not perform well in the marketplace. Mose explains:

> The record company got behind the first album, *Hiram Brown*, but it didn't sell anything. After recently hearing some of that record again, I still think it's one of my better ones. My only problem with it is that I can't believe how slow I play "City Home." I play it in a completely different tempo now. I think that's one of the things I did wrong on a lot of my records. I exaggerated tempos and played some things too slow to be effective. Nobody knew how to play those tempos slow and I probably didn't either. That's why they didn't come off. But, I suppose that was one stage I had to go through.

Mose Allison's solo piano style had taken on a new,

engaging dimension, evolving from a strict adherence to the swing tradition to a more intricate, impressionistic, personalized style, but he nonetheless remained a favorite sideman of jazz colleagues Zoot Sims and Al Cohn. His accompanying their popular recording of *You 'N Me* for Mercury Records in June, 1960 followed the release of Mose's modern and urbane serio-fantasy. Ironically, Allison restrained his newfound piano style on this record, instead reverting to a conservative, muted approach in his playing in Zoot and Al's rhythm section. His only salient departure is his stretching out in the harmonic voicings to a tune he had already adapted to his own piano voice, "Love for Sale." Maintaining strict swing timing, Allison's solos on the date's rather out-of-tune piano are consistently lucid, rhythmically buoyant and completely in character with the genre his contemporaries were seeking to preserve. Mose also turned in commendable performances as a sideman for the Sims-Cohn *Either Way*, recorded in February, 1961.

With the Zoot-Al session behind him, Allison was set to begin work on his second Columbia recording, *I Love the Life I Live*. This next effort, named after a Willie Dixon standard, was recorded during June, July and September, 1960. A host of various rhythm sections share the bill on Allison's second Columbia venture, drummer Jerry Segal and bassist Addison Farmer playing in "You Turned the Tables on Me," "Mad with You," "Fool's Paradise," "Path" and "Night Ride"; drummer Paul Motian and bassist Henry Grimes accompanying on "Hittin' on One," "I Love the Life I Live," "News," and "You're a Sweetheart." Bassist Bill Crow and drummer Gus Johnson play on the cuts "I Ain't Got Nobody," "Isobel" and "Can't We Be Friends."

Allison's vocals, remakes of blues and jazz tunes, are paramount on this album, the five classics highlighting his strength at adapting a familiar repertoire to his own personal style. Willie Dixon's "I Love the Life," Johnny Fuller's "Fool's Paradise," Lightnin' Hopkins's "Mad with You," "Adamson/McHugh's pop song "You're a Sweetheart," and Graham/Williams's "I Ain't Got Nobody" are memorably presented in

Allison's inimitable speaking style of phrasing. His tone, however, appears more nasal in these renditions, suggesting that he may have been singing with a cold on these dates. Unfortunately, the date is also poorly mixed, with drums overwhelming piano, bass and vocals and frequently disrupting the album's musical flow.

"Fool's Paradise," one of Allison's best tunes both in live performance and on record in later years, is taken at a lethargic slow drag, the sluggishness of the tempo exacerbated by the obtrusive echoing beat points of drum brushes. Dixon's keen and pithy wordplay blues, "I Love the Life I Live," suffers from a similar slower-than-normal tempo, but both Allison's piano comping and his singing style make the tune distinctive. The two jazz covers swing capably; "You're a Sweetheart" and "I Ain't Got Nobody" contain more of Allison's personal vocal coloring, the voice trailing in fall-off lines, and the text almost spoken in some phrases. The strongest vocal performance here, though, is the infectious blues, Lightnin' Hopkins' "Mad with You," a song Allison has resurrected in later years. The "rumboogie groove" set down by the trio, Allison's dissonant harmonic voicings in his bluesy piano playing and his speech-like singing combine in a performance reminiscent of "Baby, Please Don't Go," his funky blues classic from the *Hiram Brown* suite.

The late bluesman Willie Dixon comments on Allison's interpretation of his song, "I Love the Life I Live," employing his own brand of logical reasoning, and sharing his philosophy about the blues:

> Anybody can sing the blues. It all depends on what they're singing about. The blues itself is a statement and when people make a statement in their music, especially about the facts of life, it's the blues. In the various songs that Mose sings, he's definitely making a statement about the facts of life, especially in "I Live the Life I Love and I Love the Life I Live." He's just telling the world how he feels about the facts of life. That song is a statement about the facts of life and that's what he's doing when he sings it.

The original piano pieces from *I Love the Life I Live*, "News," "Night Ride," "Path" and "Hittin' on One," take fewer risks pianistically than did Allison's work on *Hiram Brown*. Rather, these songs harken back to Allison's more conservative approach to jazz/blues-based composing, featuring tuneful melodic motifs that develop into lucid but conventional improvisational melodies. His covers "Isobel," "Can't We Be Friends" and "You Turned the Tables on Me" are well executed but equally uneventful.

When Mose Allison's second venture for Columbia did not fare any better than *The Transfiguration of Hiram Brown* had done, the record company was prompted to motivate Allison to reroute his thinking towards a more commercial, mainstream endeavor. Although the executives at the label were not blatant in their requests to him to change his direction in repertoire selection, the record company's subtle pressure to produce a selling record slowly mounted on the artist. But Allison stood steadfast regarding his aesthetic principles:

> On Columbia, I had freedom at first, but when the first records for them didn't sell anything, they started suggesting that I do this and that. So, it's sort of a process. You have freedom at first, then if it doesn't pan out commercially, you start getting suggestions on what you might do to remedy that. Nobody ever belabored me with doing things, it was all pretty subtle. They would send someone around to say, "We were thinking the other day that if you did this or that . . ."[2]

In 1961, soon after Mose recorded his third album for Columbia Records, he asked for his release. This final record of vocal and piano pieces, *Mose Allison Takes to the Hills*, could easily have slid into oblivion since, at the time, Columbia had expressed no intention to release the tracks. Instead, certain tracks were subsequently subject to the "jumping on the bandwagon" mentality endemic to the record business. After Allison's release from Columbia and once Atlantic Records ballyhooed his vocal prowess, Columbia took the opportunity to capitalize on the now "hot" Allison, releasing a record of vocal tracks only. *Takes To the Hills* comprised six new tracks, vocal selections from the first two records, and avoided the piano material recorded specifically for the third album record date. The resulting album features standards from the blues, jazz and country repertoire leavened with Allison's increasingly musically and lyrically daring original tunes.

On this album, Mose continues his personalizing of the blues form, delivering Percy Mayfield's melancholic blues "Life Is Suicide" at a walking tempo, and performing the vitriolic Willie Love "V-8 Ford Blues" in a similar vein, making extensive use of the "smashed" device of minor seconds as a melodic motif in his improvisations. The irony in the former tune's lyric obviously attracted Allison to the song, written by one of his longtime singing heroes. Other tracks include "Please Don't Talk About Me When I'm Gone," a swinging jazz bounce, and a lively rendition of Hank Williams's country classic "Hey Good Lookin'," replete with Allison's stylistic hallmarks, namely his unique harmonic voicings and speaking style of singing.

The album's original songs, "Back on the Corner" and the sardonic "Ask Me Nice," with their blues motifs and pithy lyrics, continue Allison's progress from his allegorical "local color" texts to more accessible commentaries reflective of everyday life. The album is rounded off by "Baby Please Don't Go" and "'Deed I Do" from *Hiram Brown* and "I Love the Life I Live," "I Ain't Got Nobody," "You're a Sweetheart" and "Mad with You" from *I Love the Life I Live*. Mose still has mixed feelings about the resulting package:

> Some of the material from the third album, the instrumental stuff, that Columbia didn't release, I thought was pretty good. One of the instrumentals was "The Hills," an instrumental that they didn't release but ironically, they named the record of vocals after it. They ended up repackaging everything except those instrumentals. They wanted me to get more commercial, do something more accessible. They just kept suggesting songs for me to do, so I asked for a release and they gave it to me without a problem because they weren't selling any records of mine anyway.

As Allison's career on Atlantic Records flourished, however, Columbia continued to exploit his catalog, re-releasing and repackaging existing material to profit from his popularity. In 1966 Epic Records reissued the third record, *Mose Allison Takes to the Hills*, as *Mose Allison Sings and Plays the V-8 Ford Blues*. In 1968, a repackaged version of *The Transfiguration of Hiram Brown* wound up on record retailers' shelves as Columbia's Jazz Odyssey's *Mose Goes*. Another Columbia reissue in 1971, *Retrospective: The Best of Mose Allison*, is *Takes to the Hills/Sings and Plays the V-8 Ford Blues* resequenced and repackaged in a psychedelically designed Peter Max-style record jacket with liner notes imbued with hip 1960s jargon. Finally, in 1994 the unreleased tracks recorded from the *Takes to the Hills* sessions were released by Sony Special Products as an Allison compilation box set entitled *High Jinx*.

Mose Allison may not have adapted sufficiently to market demands to remain on the Columbia Records artist roster for the long term, but his *Transfiguration of Hiram Brown* and a handful of selected vocal tracks he recorded for Columbia can undoubtedly be counted among his significant works. A combination of factors may account for the low sales of Allison's Columbia records: the inconsistency of the musical material, and the poor quality of certain recordings. In addition to the poor sonic reproduction, an oversight on nearly all of the Columbia Records vocals is the open mike during Allison's piano improvisations. Two tunes in particular, "Baby Please Don't Go" and "Mad with You," feature the audible groans of the pianist during his solos. Like both the late jazz pianist Erroll Garner and the late pianist Glenn Gould, whose involuntary sounds accompanied his recorded performances of Bach and others, Allison's unconscious guttural throat noises are an irritating and distracting feature of much of his work for Columbia. Mose comments: "The groaning that I make is a completely involuntary response but it just happens and it's certainly not intentional. I've heard other piano players that do the same thing. It's something between a groan and a tone."

Al Kooper, however, views the groaning in a more positive light:

The thing we that we used to love about Mose's early records are the noises he used to make when he played. On the Prestige and Columbia stuff, they didn't pay much attention to it. They just left the mike open. He'd sing and then he'd play the solo and they'd leave the vocal mike open when they were recording. At Atlantic they used to shut it off. I used to point out to people the point where the engineer would shut off the mike. So, that was a goof, we'd laugh at that. And then we'd go see him just to see what that was about. I don't think you get that from anywhere. I think it's just one of those things that you just do—it's similar to guitar players who make faces when they hit the note. I mean, I do it totally unconsciously when I play. I immediately stopped doing it after I saw a video of myself playing . . . Maybe!

I don't really know if I stopped, because it's an unconscious thing, a passionate thing. With Mose's solos, after he stops singing, it's a comparatively intellectual thing, playing versus singing. Those noises are part of his legend, certainly among his admirers.

9

THE WORD FROM MOSE

"My philosophy is that you have to get a style and then you have to transcend it. You have to work on trying to rise above your style instead of getting trapped in it; you have to be able to take off from that style and get into other things."

Mose Allison

One of These Days

One of these days, I'm gonna get things right
I'm gonna do my business in the daylight
One of these days, I'm gonna get things right
I'm gonna do my business out in the broad daylight

One of these days, I'm gonna get things straight
I'm gonna stop hangin' out with jailbait
(I'm gonna stop acting like a reprobate)
One of these days, you know, I've got to get things straight
I'm gonna stop this foolin', hangin' out with jailhouse bait

One of these days, I've got to get in step
It won't be long before I'll be needing help
One of these days, you know, I've got to get in step
The way things goin' lately, I'll soon be needin' help

One of these days, I've got to go back home
Gonna sit out on my front porch and compose a poem
One of these days, you know, I've got to go back home

> You know, I'm gonna go sit out on my front porch, rock away, compose a poem
>
> Mose Allison

In 1961, Mose Allison found himself cast adrift into recording-company limbo, but he was artistically and spiritually undaunted by the experience. In four short years Allison's recording career had been tossed from one extreme—Prestige Records, the small independent label that launched him—to the other, in the shape of Columbia Records, a huge corporate conglomerate. Somewhere between the two on the American record-company graph lay Atlantic Records, then a fledgling independent label considered primarily as an R&B label with a jazz division.

Atlantic Records was a grass-roots company, both in operation and philosophy. Equipped with exceptional executives, producers and artists and repertoire staff, who often functioned simultaneously in all capacities, the company's initial and primary objective was to record and promote American music. Atlantic Records' stumbling upon Mose Allison seemed to be idyllic for the artist's career. Picking up where major-label Columbia had left off, the mid-sized independent could place him in the capable hands of their recording executives, who were experts in jazz and its history, who venerated the style and would nurture the individuality of Mose's music and further his career. No doubt Allison appreciated Atlantic's allegiance to the music, although, as is often the case in the artist–record-company relationship, their dealings were often fraught with creative disagreements.

As Columbia Records had done, the powers at Atlantic had mainstream objectives for the musically enigmatic Mose Allison. By the time Atlantic took over, Allison had developed into an internationally acclaimed artist with a sizeable following. But thus far, Mose had remained by and large an artistic oddity, his music a mélange of American musical styles, his songs teetering on the periphery of the blues/pop charts. His persona, however, remained uncertain, blurred by his simultaneous artistic allegiance to jazz, blues, pop and R&B. No music-industry wizard had yet been able to pigeonhole Allison's music, the first step towards achieving mass appeal for him. However, Atlantic's executives collectively seemed to be convinced that they could succeed where Columbia had failed. With the right record producers, marketing and promotions effort, the company decided it could produce the "crossover hit" that might catapult the cult figure Mose Allison out of his esoteric jazz/blues netherworld into the commercial music mainstream.

Nesuhi Ertegun, the renowned Turkish-born jazz producer, gambled on Mose Allison's signing to Atlantic Records in 1961. In 1947, his younger brother, Ahmet, had founded the label together with National Records recording director Herb Abramson. Ahmet Ertegun and Nesuhi eventually joined forces with Jerry Wexler, producer and ex-*Billboard* reviewer, and hiring producer/engineer Tom Dowd to build their empire in soul, pop and rock music in the 1960s, signing a roster of talent, including Otis Redding, Sam and Dave, Buffalo Springfield, Crosby, Stills and Nash and Aretha Franklin, most of whom have now been inducted into the Rock and Roll Hall of Fame. Nesuhi, the quieter, lesser known of the Ertegun brothers and an authority on American music, established a jazz division in 1956. His extensive knowledge of jazz and dedication to the music assisted in attracting some of the biggest names in the genre, such as John Coltrane, Charles Mingus, Ornette Coleman, and Herbie Mann to the Atlantic label. Nesuhi's goal was to expand and develop Allison's existing audience and as Allison's A&R man at Atlantic, he functioned as the artist's liaison with the label. In addition to his professional role at Atlantic, Nesuhi Ertegun was also an ardent fan and supporter of Allison. He personally supervised Mose's first Atlantic releases, and although the company's expansion cut his creative participation in Mose's later records on the label, Nesuhi continued to foster a cooperative relationship between artist and company. Consequently Mose Allison remained on the Atlantic roster for fifteen years, from 1961 to 1976, recording only eleven albums in that time, a relatively small number, especially considering that he had been contracted to produce six albums in his three-year stint at Prestige. Mose remembers:

> When I first signed with Atlantic, it was a small independent label with a small office on Broadway and 59th, I think. I just walked into Atlantic, met with Nesuhi Ertegun, and signed with him right there and that was it. Nesuhi was one of the people whom I admired and was friends with in the recording industry. I felt like I could rely on him. They had various producers there and some records I did myself. Nesuhi was in charge, though, and he came out to Hermosa Beach when we recorded *Mose Alive*. Whenever I needed anything, I dealt with Nesuhi and always had a good relationship with him.

Producer Tom Dowd recalls:

> Atlantic was still a privately-owned record company when we recorded Mose. The Erteguns were foreign-born, from a significant Turkish family. As children in Turkey in the 1930s, Ahmet and Nesuhi would hear the B.B.C. and they knew every jazz and blues record ever made. Of course, in those days, all the musicians were listed on the record and they were fans. So, when they came to the U.S., they were authorities on American music and it was their life. Nesuhi was a graduate of the Sorbonne and taught the history of American music at U.C.L.A. He knew a lot of musicians. I would travel to New Orleans with Nesuhi and people would pop out of doorways and call out, "Hey, cuz, how you doin'." He also supervised the sessions for a Dixieland label called Good Time while he was at U.C.L.A.
> Jerry Wexler was an aficionado of Harlem jazz because in those days the thing to do was to go up to the Piano Bar or Minton's. The three of them were brilliant because they were learned in blues and jazz and always trying to top each other with quizzes on who played on what records.
> Because Atlantic was an independent, successful record company, Ahmet, Nesuhi and Jerry would cater to some artists whom they thought were exceptional in technique,

unique in personality, or representative of an era they thought would never happen again. They knew that they weren't going to make gobs of money on John Coltrane but at the same time, they thought they would be betraying the artform if they didn't record him because if they didn't, who was going to? They were making money on Sonny and Cher and things like that, but they still had this affinity for wanting to preserve certain types of music. Whether it was going to recover somebody old time or somebody new, their mission was to try to capture vignettes of America—the way it was, the way it is, or what might be.

Whereas the Prestige and Columbia records had focused predominantly on Allison's piano compositions and playing, the Atlantic sessions concentrated on the artist as a singer/songwriter. Although Mose had always considered himself as much a singer as a pianist, because his original repertoire was limited, he was frequently short of songs when it came time to release a new record. During the Prestige and Columbia years, Allison typically selected tunes from the repertoire of jazz and blues standards to sit alongside his originals, particularly favoring songs from the Duke Ellington and country and western catalogs. However, as he made more records, it became increasingly difficult to choose appropriate songs from those lists, tunes that he actually felt strongly about laying down on tape. Thus, out of necessity, Allison was thrown on his own creative resources to generate new material for his recordings.

The record companies, Columbia, and now Atlantic, had also exerted pressure on Allison to write his own songs. Both record labels acknowledged "Parchman Farm" as a potential hit and recognized the fact that Mose Allison had the potential to write hit songs. In an effort to achieve the chart-topping success that had so far eluded Allison, both companies, especially Atlantic, strongly suggested he focus his efforts on producing more original material. The combination of Atlantic's coaxing and Allison's own decision to expand his vocal repertoire was timely in view of the fact that attention in the music industry was shifting from instrumental music to singer/songwriters.

When he signed to Atlantic Records, Allison's songwriting and piano style were in a state of development. His artistic life was evolving, steadily maturing fed by his life experiences. By 1962, the thirty-four-year-old cosmopolitan Mose Allison, seasoned by record releases, touring, and city life, was quickly shedding his Southern trappings. The worldly songwriter now turned more often to his serious side, expressing his observations in songs with sophisticated lyrics that dealt with more universal topics and breaking away from the provincial topics and "grits and gravy" persona which had established his career in 1959. Allison's debut recordings on Atlantic signaled this transition from Southern rustic observer to pithy social commentator. Ultimately, Allison eschewed his "sharecropper-type" songs, dropping tunes such as "Parchman Farm" and "If You Live" from his repertoire altogether. To those who wanted him to keep his classic songs alive, Allison would point to their anachronistic nature, commenting: "That era has gone by and you couldn't find a cotton sack in Mississippi today if you tried."

The updated style first heard on Allison's Atlantic records broadens his musical base yet remains tied to his Southern roots. He manages to strike a stylistic balance between his deeply imbedded Southern influences and his more sophisticated urban ones, explorations of social themes and experiments with disparate musical ideas. Allison's personal take on the spirit and irony of the country blues stays intact, however, his newer songs never stray far from the genre nor the Southern sardonicism that distinguishes his work:

> I feel the blues music is just as pertinent now as ever because it's survival music. It started as survival music and for the black country-blues singers, it was survival music. It helped them to survive the situation they were in and it was one over which they had no control. They had to find some way to put up with it. They used music, and irony and satire, to get through it. I think the world is pretty much in the same condition now. We're all faced with things we can't control.

So much of the country blues is innuendo and disguised comment. You have to really know the jargon to be able to get through. In other words, the plantation blues were the oppressed saying it right out in front of their tormentors and the tormentors didn't even pick it up.

Mose Allison's songwriting process originates with the text, his initial concept for a song typically springing from recurring phrases, words or feelings in a fashion directly traceable to his formal academic literary training. Although employing formal literary devices such as irony, satire, and metaphor in his lyrics, Mose's poetry is firmly rooted in American dialect, rich in colloquialisms, bombast, clever wordplays and aphorisms. His lyrics' informality notwithstanding, Allison has been known to research word choices for years before attaining the perfect text for his songs. He has a definite objective in this process: "I'm looking for basic, essential attitudes and attempting to get both ends of the thing, despair and elation," Allison explains of the goal of his poetry. He expands on this idea:

The poetry is based on intuition and instinct. I get ideas, they get into my subconscious and are reinforced. I choose phrases and lines that make a point and attempt to get a fresh line like any writer. I like to catch a phrase that sounds simple on the surface but that has some underlying meanings. I start with a fairly simple idea that most people are familiar with but try to work it in ways that you can get some deeper meaning out of.

It's a cryptic thing where you try to get a lot into a short phrase, and you use phrases that everybody can understand but on different levels. Words that have multiple connotations, that's what appeals to me. I think that I actually just get more out of the short song, trying to get a lot into a compact phrase than I would if I'd written fiction. I go for economy and conciseness. Actually, it turns out that the blues feeling and the blues structure, that lament and short structure, is what I'm really best at. I don't like to get too stretched out, too wordy, because I feel like the most touching things are actually simple, and they hit you. You don't have to have a lot of word power behind them if you just get the right thing, the right combination.[1]

The word choice is important and the melodic phrasing comes later. I write the songs when I can't sleep. I'll wake up too early in the morning or if I'm waiting for an airplane. I can come up with ideas for a song anytime, any place, and start working on them. But, it's very seldom I'll just do a whole song in one place.

A key consideration in crafting his texts is the accommodation of Allison's personal idiosyncrasies as a performer: his vocal range and diction, his ability to articulate certain words:

I'm also considering the sound of my voice, whether it's a good word when I'm singing it, whether it's good to hold on to or drop. I choose words I can sing and say comfortably, considering my accent. I don't take other singers into account when writing the lyrics, I use what's best for me.

I'm writing songs all the time, actually. I might write one in an afternoon, or I might mess around with one for two years before I get it in the shape I like. Sometimes it comes through all at once, sometimes very slow. But I don't just sit down and try to make up a song. It sort of comes little by little.[2]

In a manner similar to that employed by many art-song and opera composers who set music to existing libretti, Allison uses his music as a functional tool to set his poetry. Bearing this in mind, he crafts his blues-based melodic lines with the same subtlety, clarity and economy as he applies to his lyrics. After grounding a few word phrases, he shapes the melody line of the song organically, following no rigid compositional format, allowing word phrases and melodies to evolve simultaneously. Typically, Allison organizes vocal phrases in various lengths with a pattern of two- and the more regular four-bar phrasing predominating. The melodic lines are likely to follow a speech-like, asymmetrical phrasing reflective both of his conversational writing style and his vocal delivery of the lyrics. For example, one-measure phrases alternating with longer phrases is not an unusual scheme for him.

Characteristic of Allison's melodies are the rhythmic patterns in the phrase which facilitate his speech-like delivery. Allison's phrases also often include rhythmic disruptions or interruptions, where longer note durations or rests are placed at cadence points and mid-phrase. For example, Allison uses a half note after the second bar to break up the regular four-measure phrases in his word-heavy "Your Molecular Structure." A typical stylistic signature that creates a tension–resolution in both text and music is where Allison places a fermata, or an indefinite holding of the note at unanticipated points in the melodic line. His first recorded vocal, "Young Man Blues," and a modern version of "One of These Days," first heard on his third Atlantic album *The Word from Mose*, typify his use of a fermata as a key musical device.

Allison's melodies, especially in his early work, are predominantly based on the blues tonality. He describes his approach towards the blues tonality as "neither major nor minor, but an alternation of both," and his vacillation between major and minor intervals creates a naturally chromatic vocal line. Adhering to the traditional country-blues form, his melodies adopt the intervals of its blues scale, root, flat third, fourth, fifth, flatted fifth, fifth and flatted seventh, assuming a pentatonic, folk-like quality. Allison's mature work sometimes departs from the simpler folk framework, entertaining a larger spectrum of intervallic relationships while maintaining blues-like qualities. Once the melody and text have determined his song form, he finally moves to the piano to compose harmonic progressions and chord voicings, at this stage frequently discovering that the process of composing the chord changes might result in the altering of the song's melodic contour:

> If you listen to the very pure country-blues people, they don't play that minor blues sound that some of the jazz people started playing later. And also, they don't play strictly a major third thing, either. The tonality is more of a pentatonic tonality. So the way you get that is by using

the major third and the minor third together; you don't ever use just one of them by itself. So you never fall completely into a major or completely minor mode. That's the way I approach it.[3]

Allison's vocal range determines the key of the song:

The range of my voice designates a certain key depending on the harmonic relationship of the melodic line. So when I get the melody line, then I can tell pretty much what key it's gonna be in because if the melody line hangs on a fifth, or if it keeps returning to the fifth, the comfortable fifth for me would be B flat or in the neighborhood of B flat. So that means that the tune would be in E flat or F.[4]

Mose Allison composes the majority of his songs either in the standard twelve-bar blues form or in his own variation of the blues form, using blues-based harmonies and chord voicings. The earlier works, particularly the "cotton sack songs" stay within the traditional blues form or deviate slightly from it. Where the song does not adhere strictly to the straight twelve-bar blues, Allison's variation on the traditional form employs chords based on flatted thirds and sixths of the scale, substitutes for the IV and V chords, and stays predominantly within the blues tonality. Although he adheres to no particular formula on the blues-type variations, similar characteristics appear in each song. As one of his sidemen commented on Mose Allison's original repertoire: "None of them are the same but all of them are a little alike."

Because of Allison's blues base, chromaticism, which characterizes the contour of his melodies, also dominates his harmonic writing in chord progressions and voicings. His song "City Home" exemplifies Allison's use of a corresponding chromatic harmonic progression to accompany a chromatic vocal line. In the song, Allison's choice of a rather sophisticated, orthodox chord progression deceives the listener with its simple blues feel.

Allison uses terms such as "color" and "flavor" to describe

his choice of harmonic progressions and sound combinations. He made a stylistic imprint as a pianist using what he calls "smashed notes," in solos as well as placing the dissonant minor second inside the chord's outer tones in his chord voicings. Primarily a jazz pianist, Allison's sensibilities in this genre influence the tonality of his chord voicings as well as the progressions and harmonic rhythm of many of his songs. He favors the higher tertian sonorities found predominantly in jazz, dominant sevenths, raised and lowered ninths, elevenths and thirteenths in many of his voicings. His use of the fourth in chord voicings is novel and folk-influenced. The harmonic structure of his songs is also influenced by his use of the jazz-blues scale, intervals including the second, natural third and sixth degrees, which he adds to the country-blues scale in his piano solos and song melodies. Of the piano accompaniments to his songs Allison comments:

> My accompanying is sometimes slightly percussive. I'm an arranger and wrote band arrangements in college so I accompany myself from the point of view of an arranger. That is, I have certain techniques. I never play a note I'm singing. And I build the chord around the note but never repeat it. Effective accompanying doesn't double the note in the melody. As far as my style is concerned, when I sing a phrase and I have a certain amount of space left, I try to fill in the spaces the right way, depending on the tone of the tune. This is an arranger's approach that figures into it. I think that probably when I'm singing my piano playing maybe become simpler, more melodic and blueslike as the result of accompanying the vocal.

Mose Allison strives to attain a balance between music and poetry in his songwriting and the success of his songs depends crucially on the strength of both ingredients. His incisive texts, however, stand on their own literary merit, and they have enjoyed not only critical acclaim, but have attracted academic study for their literary value.

The all-pervading literary motif in Allison's song texts is

"ambivalence," for which his discerning postulate "Ambivalence plus interdependence equals contrariety" defines his key approach to lyric writing and also parallels his personal outlook on life. Ambivalence as a theme appears first in understated form in "Young Man Blues" from *Back Country Suite*, but he returns to the device in the lyrics of his Atlantic-years songs, fleshing out his ideas regarding the juxtapositions of contrary words and attitudes. He comments:

> Ambivalence is just where we are. The universe is built on the interaction of opposing forces. You've got to learn to live with that. You have to be able to entertain opposing ideas at the same time. I was reading a book on Zen, and I said to myself, "This is the way I've been thinking all along." But just staying open to these opposing forces, you accumulate some sort of direction.[5] Some of the parables have irony, twists, where everything is juxtaposed, or turned around or upside down. I've always had a tendency toward that kind of thing. After all the books I've read about Zen, I figure I'm a natural-born Zen master.

Ambivalence permeates both Allison's original material as well as the covers on his 1962 Atlantic debut *I Don't Worry 'bout a Thing*. Two songs, the title track and "Your Mind's on Vacation," exemplify his use of the device. Departing from the narratives of his "cotton sack" songs, Allison reinvents the text of the blues, adding an intelligent, sardonic twist to the lyric while maintaining the basic simplicity and integrity of the blues form. His cool delivery of the tunes, in his dry conversational singing style, imbues the wry lyrics with deadpan humor. In a song rife with ambivalence, Mose borrows the verses and inherently contrary hook "I don't worry 'bout a thing 'cause I known nothin's going to be alright" directly from the Southern idiom of farmers in the Mississippi Delta (see Chapter 7 epigraph). Here, he deviates from the AAB phrase pattern while maintaining the straight twelve-bar, medium-tempo traditional blues. He personalizes the modest structure by employing his signature IV-I vamp accompaniment (replacing the tonic chord in the straight blues) and easy-flowing but stylized melodic fillers between the IV and V chords. Mose himself acknowledges the song's deep ambivalence:

> I think "I don't worry 'bout a thing 'cause I known nothin's goin' to be alright" is just where we are. Nothing is cut and dried, nothing is completely black and white; all day long we're being pulled in one way and pushed in another. It's all a part of the interaction of opposing forces I'm trying to suggest in my songs. I think that people who are over-rewarded for their achievements accumulate some sort of psychic debt. And, if you're under-rewarded, then you have a psychic surplus. It took a few years for that song to catch on but it's true. No matter what, how good things get, there's always a new set of problems. No matter how many problems you solve, how much better things get, there's always a new set waiting around the corner.[6]

The text of Allison's vaudevillian-style lampoon "Your Mind's on Vacation" exudes the self-confidence of a satirist. Allison uses an epicurean approach to the simple twelve-bar blues in this chestnut. The idea for the song germinated in the late 1950s during his performance at the Showboat Lounge in Washington, D.C. Allison finished it later during an extended period of shows at the Village Vanguard in New York, the club atmosphere there continually reinforcing his original idea. Although initially inspired by the usual loquacious nightclub audience and the resultant challenge of playing music against such tumultuous conversation, the lyrics also have more general application, and Allison obviously intended them to have more than one meaning:

"Your Mind's on Vacation"

> You sittin' there yackin' right in my face
> I guess I'm going to have to put you in your place
> (You comin' on exactly like you own the place)
> If silence was golden, you couldn't raise a dime
> Because your mind is on vacation
> And your mouth is working overtime

You quotin' figures and droppin' names
You tellin' stories about the dames (and playing games)
You over laughing when things ain't funny
You tryin' to sound like the big money (you don't need money)
If talk were criminal, you'd lead a life of crime
Because your mind is on vacation
And your mouth is working overtime.

You know that life is short, talk is cheap
Don't be making promises that you can't keep
If you don't like this little song I'm singing
Just grin and bear it
All I can say is if the shoe fits wear it
If you must keep talking
Please try to make it rhyme
Because your mind is on vacation
and your mouth is working overtime

Mose Allison explains the lyrics:

Most musicians find out sooner or later that at first you play against the audience and if you play long enough, you acquire the audience and play with them. They will come to hear you. But when you're starting out, they don't know you and don't care, so there are a certain number of years where you have to put up with that.

But that song, like most of my songs, has other dimensions. It's not just what it seems to be about. It's also a comment about people who verbalize things, using empty words; myself included. You know I apply my songs to myself. I feel like if a song is a good song, it always applies to you as well as to other people.

A third Allison original, "It Didn't Turn Out That Way," also sets an ironic and ambivalent lyric to another blues-based tune:

When I was a schoolboy, my teacher said to me
Work hard, do right you can be what you want to be
But it didn't turn out that way
It just didn't turn out that way
No matter what that teacher had to say
It just didn't turn out that way

"Meet Me at No Particular Place (and I'll Be There at No Particular Time)," written by J. Russell Robinson, Arthur Terker and Harry Pyle, with lyrics such as "baby, it just ain't common sense, mixing up love with arguments," also conforms to the lyrical theme Allison establishes on his first Atlantic record. A tune popularized by the early Nat Cole trio, Mose continues to performs it in his live performances.

Mose Allison's Atlantic debut was supervised by Nesuhi Ertegun, engineered by Tom Dowd, and the singer accompanied by mainstay Addison Farmer on bass and Osie Johnson on drums. The two original vocals, "I Don't Worry 'bout a Thing" and "Your Mind's on Vacation," which he subsequently rerecorded on two later albums, remained in Allison's repertoire, eventually becoming synonymous with his classic style. Balanced with five piano compositions, and fleshed out with renditions of Basie's "Let Me See" and Adamson/Lane's "Everything I Have Is Yours," Allison's first Atlantic recording consolidated his mature piano style.

Swingin' Machine, Mose's second Atlantic album, was released in 1963, a year and a half after his debut on the label. The album offered a refreshing alternative to Allison's piano-trio instrumentation by featuring the trombone of Jimmy Knepper and the tenor saxophone of Jimmy Reider in horn accompaniments arranged by Allison himself. The lyrics of the two original twelve-bar blues, the medium-shuffle swing "If You're Goin' to the City," the slow blues "Stop This World" and his blues variation "Swingin' Machine" maintain Mose's urbane approach to lyric writing, characterized by pith and satire. Allison also quickly embraced Don George and Duke Ellington's "I Ain't Got Nothin' But the Blues," the song's wry, uptown lyrics and sultry blues-based melody instantly fitting into Allison's repertoire.

The piano instrumentals, "Saritha," first recorded on Prestige's *Ramblin' with Mose Allison*, and "Promenade" from Prestige's *Autumn Song*, enjoy the benefits of extended horn solos and exuberant horn accompaniments. By the time he had recorded *Swingin' Machine*, these two pieces were already staples of Allison's live performances.

The Word from Mose, Allison's third Atlantic album, released in 1964, proved another seminal and influential work in Allison's recording career. Already a legend in the U.K., where the country's love of American blues artists had assisted in amassing a sizeable European following for him, through the album Mose attracted an increasing number of docile British rockers, who became disciples of the cool, charismatic Mississippi hipster. Like *Back Country Suite*, *The Word from Mose* quickly entered the British rock vocabulary, establishing itself as the quintessential Mose Allison album of the mid-1960s. Stylistically, *The Word from Mose* leaps ahead of Allison's previous recorded work. An entire album of vocals, the variety of song subjects and his freer approach to the rhythmic feel and tempi of the songs themselves are significant advances in his style. This third Atlantic recording marks Allison's modern, free-form mature approach to rhythm and tempo, achieving a greater rhythmic independence and signaling his hard-won assurance in these critical areas.

A variation on the "swing shuffle" Allison had employed in his earlier work, he returns in full force on this album to his "rumboogie" uptempo dance groove on the Stephen Vincent Benet inspired track "Foolkiller." Even more pronounced on this song than in his earlier use of the groove in "Seventh Son" and "Baby Please Don't Go," the tempo and rhythmic sensibility are difficult to describe but easily felt. The song's groove is even more reminiscent of the free zydeco style, featuring a continuous, easy-flowing uptempo shuffle wedded to the accented rhythmic syncopations of the Latin and boogie-woogie styles. The buoyancy of the "rumboogie" groove, a style Mose later decided was better described as "Afro Cuban," has served Mose well over the years. Over an infectious dance beat that breathes vitality into his songs,

Allison's most ambitious and challenging piano improvisations are played out.

Another "rumboogie" is the rhythmically exuberant "I'm Not Talkin'," at first sight Allison's autobiographical comment on dealing with the media—or anyone else—circa 1964. Characteristically, however, multifarious interpretations are possible; any unambiguous autobiographical references in the lyrics of this song are impossible to discern. Set to one of Allison's blues variations, the wisecracking, ironic quips in the lyrics exemplify Allison's more refined authorship. Allison centers on the song's hook, "I'm not talkin'," in the vocal, using an extended three-bar duration of the closed consonant "n" to create a melodic/harmonic tension and emphasize the onomatopoeic "closed-lip" theme of the lyrics.

> "I'm Not Talkin'"
>
> I'm not talkin'
> Don't ask me what I have to say
> If I said things were splendid
> Some one would be offended
> If I said things were awful
> It might just be unlawful
> I'm not talkin'
> It just don't pay

The renowned English rock/R&B band, the Yardbirds, who were influenced largely by American bluesmen such as Sonny Boy Williamson, performed a pulsating 1960s cover version of Allison's "I'm Not Talkin'." Founded in 1963 by late vocalist/harmonica player Keith Relf, bassist Paul Samwell-Smith, and guitarists Chris Dreja and Tony "Top" Topham, the Yardbirds boasted a number of prestigious guitar virtuosi in their various line-ups, luminaries such as Eric Clapton, Jimmy Page and Jeff Beck having been associated with the band at one time or another. Jim McCarty, the band's longstanding drummer, recalls the genesis of the idea to cover Allison's tune:

We all had Mose's album that had "I'm Not Talkin'" on it and of course all of us liked jazz. I think it was Jeff Beck that came up with the idea of playing the song the way we did it, which was very different and unique. But that was just the way we played everything in those days. We played for excitement—it was all for the excitement—to get people jumping around. We interpreted other songs differently also. We were consciously trying to get people excited and that's how we did it. We covered all the blues stuff, especially a song like "I'm Not Talkin'" which was an ideal song to sing to put your own stamp on.

The "road to ruin" theme heard first in his successful cover of "Fool's Paradise" resurfaces in an original tune, the ruminating "One of These Days." In a masterful blues poem, written in four-line verses of symmetrical ABAB, Allison uses the straight twelve-bar blues form as a song structure, his piano accompaniment employing the signature IV-I vamp. In the 1970s, Mose recorded various versions of this tune, speeding up the tempo in its later renditions and, as discussed earlier, adding a fermata on the word "days" on the third phrase as a centering tone. His most contemporary version, which is not recorded, features a rewrite of the lyric's second verse: "One of these days I've got to get things straight, I've got to stop acting like a reprobate."

Also from *The Word from Mose*, "Look Here," Allison's flippant response to a bad attitude problem: "look here/ watchya think you gonna be doin' next year/no lie/how you know you not gonna up an die" was appropriately re-created in an anarchistic version by the British punk-rock group the Clash. By the time the Clash covered "Look Here," the British rock community had become adept at putting its own frenzied spin on Mose Allison's songs. Most of the covers appear almost generically performed, in that each band, regardless of the particular qualities of each song, raised the decibel level and accelerated the tempo to the speed of light. The Clash's contribution, although appearing some ten years after the onslaught of British covers of Allison's tunes, maintained the spirit of English rockers' interpretations of his songs. Although Allison himself may not have anticipated these rock reincarnations, in addition to carrying his message to a younger generation of musicians, they have also been instrumental in attracting fans to Mose Allison and increasing his popularity, particularly in the U.K.

Allison attributes the strains of his tune "Look Here" to a song composed by the great jazz piano master Thelonious Monk, whom Allison had met on several occasions. Later, Allison found the punk fate of his song oddly fitting since both Monk and Allison allegedly had trouble collecting their royalties for their respective tunes. And, although another songwriter might have regarded the Clash's somewhat offensive regurgitation of Allison's own reworking of a famous Monk tune as a sacrilege, Mose Allison deemed it part of the irony of life:

> Monk's manager, Harry Columby, a Long Island history teacher who took over Monk's career in the late fifties and ended up getting him on the *Time* magazine cover and record contracts, was also doing some things for me. He asked me if I would try to write some lyrics to Monk's tunes. So I picked one. Then I found out that Monk didn't even have the rights to that tune. It's his tune but somebody else had gotten the rights to it. I was going to perform the tune but I would give Monk the credit and I would get credit for the lyrics. I didn't think there was any need in doing it if Monk wasn't going to get the money. So, I just altered the tonal relations and melodic line, putting it in a different place.
>
> The first thing I heard about the Clash's version was that it was sped up about three times from my version. It's a lot faster and puts it into an entirely different thing. So, as it turns out "Look Here" is a reworking of a Monk tune with the Clash doing it. That sounds like Kurt Vonnegut or something.[7]

Another of Allison's medium-tempo blues variations is the anecdotal "Days Like This." The lyrics have his typical tongue-in-cheek humor, recounting the ironic events in one bad day, weaving threads of cosmic karma and phantasmagoria throughout. His piano solo on this tune foreshadows his mature piano improvisation style, featuring harmonica-like tremolos and linear melodic lines.

"Days Like This"

> There's something bad happening in the zodiac
> I gave money to a wino and he gave it back
> Sirens screaming, panic and disorder (panic in the street)
> I tried to get some whiskey but got salt water
> (My dancin' partner had two left feet)
> I must be on somebody's list
> A goblin tried to give me a kiss
> Excuse me while I slash my wrist
> They always told me there'd be days like this

Allison's covers of Richard M. Jones's "Your Red Wagon," Wild Man Willis's "Wild Man," Muddy Waters's "Rollin' Stone" and Percy Mayfield's "Lost Mind" also appear for the first time on *The Word from Mose*. These songs conformed to the direction of Allison's songwriting style, being intelligent but gritty, containing witty lyrics with plays on words, and interesting music that provided good settings for piano solo improvisation. The sophisticated rebukes in "Your Red Wagon" ("Well, you didn't have no love songs to fit my key, so don't come singin' your blues to me"), the lusty rebellion of the country blues "Rollin' Stone" ("She said you can come on in now honey, you know my husband just now left"), the colorful word schemes, playful metaphor and intricate mouthful of lyrics of "Wild Man" ("I'm just a wild man did a dance with Satan's grandma/I'm just a wild man cut a redwood with a handsaw") and Percy Mayfield's twist on unrequited love ("She was the devil with the face of an angel/sweet and cruel as home-made sin") remain as much a part of Allison's contemporary live repertoire as his original songs. He has rerecorded all of these covers except "Wild Man" on subsequent records; "Your Red Wagon" appears again on 1990's *My Backyard*, "Lost Mind" on his 1982 live performance at Montreux *Lessons in Living*, and "Rollin' Stone" on *Middle Class Whiteboy*, also released in 1982. Mose comments:

> Reality is the main thing I'm looking for when I add someone else's song to my repertoire. If there's something I can relate to, has some truth to it and expresses something that's real, or an attitude or feeling that I think is something we all feel, that's what I look for. I also like to keep my repertoire relevant to now.

The "road to ruin" theme found in songs like "One of These Days" resurfaces in his slow-tempo swing "Don't Forget to Smile." Its six quatrains exhibit Allison's affinity for rhyming the word "step" with "help," a combination he also uses in "One of These Days" and one that accommodates his Mississippi drawl. He later performs an uptempo version of the song in his 1972 live recorded performance, *Mose in Your Ear*:

"Don't Forget to Smile"

You don't know what you're doin'
You're on the road to ruin
You know you better watch your step
You're soon goin to be needin' help

A modern piano accompaniment and lyrics update the sequel to his famous "Parchman Farm" from *The Word from Mose* called "New Parchman." Allison retains the harmonic structure of the old "Parchman" but replaces the older version's lilting blues tempo and simple melodic ostinato in the right hand with a dynamic rhythmic impetus and a fresh, more engaging melodic ostinato. Dressed in new lyrics, the resultant song evokes an entirely new mood.

In addition to renovating the piano work of the first version of "Parchman Farm," Mose Allison imbues the piano solos on *The Word from Mose* with greater depth, variety and experimentation than he has shown before. His left hand assumes more independence and control, playing frequent double-octave melodic patterns which create a "thundering" effect in the bass. The antiphonal exchange of melodic and harmonic ideas between both right and left hands is also a marked change in his style. Allison's "rumboogie" groove is also more significant as a stylistic trait, enabling him to change the harmony of the chorus to sustained tonic chords, substituting most often for the IV chord. The sustained tonic provides the harmonic freedom to combine and create more complex repeating rhythmic figures and melodies and to develop interesting tonal relationships. Allison's improvisations also feature changing harmonic textures, where one-note monophonic melodic ideas alternate with dense homophonic chordal passages featuring repeated melodic/rhythmic figures, what he later terms his "Italian Section."

Although Mose's piano work showed signs of slow evolution throughout his career, it is most apparent on *The Word from Mose* and his next album, the live *Mose Allison Alive!*, that he has significantly departed from the early, simple piano improvisations. His continuing serious study of twentieth-century piano literature obviously yielded him new musical insights, ideas and techniques and through practice he was able to assimilate and incorporate those influences. The most obvious change is found in the independence in Allison's left hand. More sophisticated melodic patterns in the bass, a fluidity and technical dexterity add new color and dimension to both his improvisations and accompaniments. The musical ideas emerging in Allison's more aggressive improvisations reveal an artist challenging himself and his audience by taking substantial stylistic risks, departing from the contained style he favored just a few years earlier.

The advances in Allison's piano style are even more noticeable on *Mose Allison: Mose Allison Alive!*, recorded at his live engagements at the Lighthouse in Hermosa Beach, California from October 22 to 31, 1965. Always a skillful live performer, Allison excels in an intimate nightclub setting, where the confluence of audience, ambiance and musicians elicit his best work. These live sessions especially enable him to stretch out as a jazz piano improviser. The first of two live recordings, *Mose Allison Alive!* was reissued in 1985 by Demon Records, the independent record label owned by the English pop star Elvis Costello.

Mose Alive! the lodestar of Allison's modern piano style, reinterprets songs from his earlier recordings, adding two new original vocals and one new piano instrumental. Allison succeeds in refurbishing his old material in his modern style. A new version of "Parchman Farm" indicates that he prefers the more animated accompaniment found on Atlantic's "New Parchman" over the classic version, although the popular lyric from the first version is combined with his contemporary accompaniment from the second. "Seventh Son" and "Baby Please Don't Go" are performed with a new intensity; the technical panache Mose displays in "Seventh Son," particularly with its elongated, elaborate introduction and solos, exudes a studied appeal without violating the song's simple blues sensibilities. "I Love the Life I Live" is treated similarly, its trills and tremolos substituting for the once lucid single-note melody recorded previously on Columbia's *The Transfiguration of Hiram Brown*. "Love for Sale," however, from the same recording and performed once again as a piano instrumental, betrays no similarity at all with the version he recorded for Columbia. The altered melody, its elaborate introduction and solo could easily deceive the listener as to the pianist's identity. "The Chaser," an original piano instrumental, encapsulates Allison's modern piano style.

Two new originals also appear on this live recording, "I'm Smashed" and another classic "Tell Me Something I Don't Know." "I'm Smashed" debuts Mose's "personal crisis" song category, where the introspective text grapples with harsh reality or a state of turmoil. The song deals with the classic Mose Allison "down but not out" state, describing the singer's vulnerability and limitations, but showing him as a man prepared to get back into the race.

The song's musical setting is onomatopoeic. Allison "tone paints" the piano accompaniment between the first and second phrases with his classic "smashed notes." Mose rerecorded the number on his seventh Atlantic album, *Hello*

There Universe. Leon Russell, the American singer/songwriter famous for "This Masquerade" and "Tight Rope," also gives an exemplary performance of this idiosyncratic Allison tune, delivering an unbridled rendition of it in his own gravelly, wry style. Mose remembers writing the song:

> I was smashed when I wrote that song, but most of these songs have meanings that go beyond the surface meaning and that not only means boxed out on something, juice or whatever, but, it also means "smashed" psychologically, that you run up against things that you can't deal with. I think the thing that really gave me the idea for the song was being drunk one night.[8]

"I'm Smashed"

I'm smashed
Looks like I've gone and done it
Crashed
I think I stepped right on it
I'm tempting fate
It's gettin' late

And I'm ripped
You know my mind is spinnin'
Tripped
The other side is winnin'
Before you count me out
Let me tell you what it's all about

I always thought I was in control
I always thought I could play my role
But since I came to this town
My mind is upside down

I'm smashed
Just like a busted fender
Crashed
Where can a man surrender

Take me out coach I'm through
I'll get myself together in a day or two

I always thought that I was in control
I always thought I could reach my goal
Now I'm staring at my empty cup
Will the real me (world) please stand up

I'm smashed
Hello there operator
Crashed
You have to try me later
Just between me and you
I'll feel much better in a day or two

The epigrammatic "Tell Me Somethin' that I Don't Know" is a glib, stoic satire succinctly epitomizing Allison's unique style, perfectly capturing his attitude and featuring all the musical and poetic elements inherent in his songwriting. The song is heavy with hip-jazz vernacular, having one verse which repeats three times with different lyrics.

Allison's delivery of this song is the key to its success, his cool confidence and conversational tone elevating his musical stature almost to omniscient jazz sage. Additionally, Allison's sparse, simple piano work, in both accompaniment and improvisation, complement the mood of the piece while allowing ample room for the song's lyrics. Mose's subtle, intelligent piano solo is a fluid, evolving melody which he diversifies by alternating rhythmic and harmonic colors.

"Tell Me Somethin' that I Don't Know"

You say the world is mad
You say that you've been had
You don't like your part in the floor show
You say it's all a bust
There's no one you can trust
Well, tell me somethin' that I don't know

You say the world's a mess
It's anybody's guess
As to who will deliver that low blow
You suffer from the strain
You don't dig pain
Well, tell me something that I don't know

You say there's some mistake
You didn't get your break
You don't see the magic in the moonglow
Your life is incomplete
You're on a one-way street
Well, tell me something I don't know

You're uptight
It ain't right
Tell me something I don't know

Allison confirms his role of sagacious, hip observer in his fourth Atlantic release, *Wild Man on the Loose*, released in 1966. In "No Trouble Livin'," a jazz bounce with blues overtones, its hook: "I don't have no trouble livin'/It's just dyin' that bothers me," again captures the essence of Allison's lyric writing, the ambivalence, irony and profundity of its existential theme set forth in simple street vernacular.

"No Trouble Livin'"

Don't talk to me about life's problems
Or how you wish that things could be
'Cause I don't have no trouble livin'
It's just dyin' that bothers me

Don't offer me no sad story
Or tell me that you're all at sea
Cause I don't have no trouble livin'
It's just dyin' that bothers me

You lookin' great
You gettin' straight
You get your call
That's all

Allison's droll "Wild Man on the Loose," the album's title track, was written before he actually heard Wild Man Willis's "I'm Just a Wild Man" which Allison recorded on his previous album. Brimming with metaphor and colloquialism, Allison's aggressive piano accompaniment features more smashed notes, a ferocious rhythmic approach and a "rumboogie" groove, setting up the mischievous text. He recorded this song on 1971's *Hello There, Universe,* his seventh Atlantic release, and on Elektra/Musician *Lessons in Living* from 1982, rereleased on Discovery in the U.K. in 1994.

"Wild Man on the Loose"

Look out! Stand back!
Wild man on the loose!
Been in the country for thirty days
Saved up some money got some hell to raise
Soakin' up that juice,
Wild man on the loose!

Look out! Stand back!
Panther (Primate) on the prowl
Get yourself a cup of coffee and glass of water
Lock up your wife and hide your daughter
This is one man's night to howl
Panther on the prowl!

Look out! Stand back!
(Tiger) in the street
Gonna find a woman beg steal or borrow
Gonna wake up feelin' bad tomorrow
A fight would make the night complete
(Wild man) in the street
Look out! Stand back!

Two originals on *Wild Man on the Loose* contain texts that might enjoy many interpretations. "What's with You" is a professed response to music critics and is tonally reminiscent of "Don't Forget to Smile." "You Can Count on Me to Do My Part" serves as his answer to the itinerant *bon vivant* musician in a lively, straightahead twelve-bar blues.

"What's with You"

You told me what I was doin' wrong.
You told I wouldn't be here long,
You told me all the things that I didn't do
So now won't you tell me, baby
What's with you

"You Can Count on Me to Do My Part"

Let's talk it over, let's get it straight,
Don't let the situation escalate
You know there are always problems
When a man is wrapped in his art
So don't you worry baby
You can count on me to do my part

Mose Allison composed four significant jazz-piano pieces for *Wild Man on the Loose,* each of which remains in his current piano performance repertoire. At this stylistic juncture, the pianist concerns himself with achieving artistic balance in his piano playing, the more complex contradictory musical ideas, that are seemingly anathema to his artistic simplicity, fleshing out his newer style. A refined composer and an improved technician, Allison continues to incorporate disparate musical influences. New harmonic textures, dense homophony in progressive, unconventional voicings, alternate with the simple, flowing one-line melodies and short, succinct rhythmic ideas. Both his song structures and piano improvisations in the instrumentals reflect his overall approach; more sophisticated, developed musical ideas flesh out the simplicity of the melody and form.

The medium swing, meandering melodic direction and unusual harmonies of "Night Watch" conjure up a rather ominous mood, a departure from his previous piano pieces. The provocative "Power House" qualifies as one of two significant piano rampages in Allison's repertoire. His style here exhibits an almost maniacal rhythmic intensity, with its repeated, hypnotic rhythmic figure at a break tempo. The piece epitomizes Mose's balance of harmonic textures, the antiphonal exchange of thick chord and simple melodic lines. The rhapsodic, mellifluous "Never More" features lush chords under a languid melody and simple, fluent melodic phrases in the improvisation passages. "War Horse," also appropriately named, is delivered with the same drive and fervor as "Power House." This tune, however, relies more on the interesting voicing of the harmonies than on a repeated rhythmic pattern, and displays more left-handed melodic development in the improvisation section. Mose comments:

> So, it's like an accumulative thing. A real jazz player's style should always be in transition. It should never be changing radically—always gradually, I think—if you're really taking in new materials. What it amounts to is redistribution more than creation. You redistribute sounds in your own way. Every great jazz player has his own way of swinging—a pace that you can recognize as his, subtleties of tone and texture, and so forth. He might do different things from night to night—you hope he does—but he'll always have an approach that will be relatively consistent.[9]

10

WHEN YOU MEET YOUR DESTINY FACE TO FACE

In Order to

Apply for the position (I've forgotten now for what) I had to marry the Second Mayor's daughter by twelve noon. The order arrived at three minutes of.

I already had a wife; the Second Mayor was childless: but I did it.

Next they told me to shave off my father's beard. All right. No matter that he'd been a eunuch, and had succumbed in early childhood: I did it, I shaved him.

Then they told me to burn a village; next, a fair-sized town; then a city; a bigger city; a small, down-at-heels country; then one of "the great powers"; then another (another, another)—In fact, they went right on until they'd told me to burn up every man-made thing on the face of the earth! And I did it, I burned away every last trace, I left nothing, nothing of any kind whatever.

Then they told me to blow it all to hell and gone! And I blew it all to hell and gone (oh, didn't I) . . .

Now, they said, put it back together again; put it all back the way it was when you started.

Well . . . it was my turn to tell *them* something! Shucks, I didn't want any job that bad.[1]

Kenneth Patchen

"Everybody Cryin' Mercy"

I can't believe the things I'm seeing
I wonder 'bout some things I've heard
Everybody cryin' mercy
When they don't know the meaning of the word

A bad enough situation,
Is sure enough getting worse
Everybody cryin' justice
Just as long as there's business first

Toe to toe
Touch and go
Give a cheer
Get your souvenir

People running round in circles
Don't know what they're headed for
Everybody cryin' peace on earth
Just as soon as we win this war

Straight ahead
Knock 'em dead
Pack your kit
Choose your hypocrite

You don't have to go to off Broadway
To see something plain absurd
Everybody cryin' mercy
When they don't know the meaning of the word
Nobody knows the meaning of the word

Mose Allison

The year 1968 brought social upheaval to a rapidly changing world, and in the United States, the social malaise of the nation had intensified into a maelstrom. Public protest over an escalating war in Vietnam, the African-American fight for civil rights and the Women's Liberation Movement often resulted in bloodshed on city streets and college campuses, tearing the population into political and social factions. The social cataclysm had a profound effect on the thoughtful and observant Mose Allison, and his songwriting began to reflect the social revolution. His next three albums on Atlantic Records, *I've Been Doin' Some Thinkin'*, *Hello There, Universe*, and *Western Man*, served as cultural barometers, Allison's musical introspection gauging the social pressure of the times. The wry-humorist persona prevailed on these recordings, yet he delved deep into the state of the human condition circa 1968 with incisive, often disturbing texts underpinned by dramatic musical settings. At forty-one, a mature, pensive, and sometimes misanthropic Mose Allison grappled with new and relevant social issues, politics, spirituality and Eastern philosophy, personal conflicts and mid-life demons.

Always a voracious reader, Allison also publicly articulated the literary influences on his texts during this period of his writing. Earlier in his career, critics had quickly compared him to the noted American authors Mark Twain and especially William Faulkner, a fellow Mississippian and former janitor at the University of Mississippi, Oxford, who was already a successful writer during the years Allison studied there. The Southern connection in the minds of the critics notwithstanding Allison's relationship to Faulkner was quite remote. Although the two lived in Oxford at the same time, enjoying somewhat illustrious reputations simultaneously, Allison's work actually bore no literary similarities to Faulkner's prose, apart from its Southern themes and colloquialisms. Interestingly, though, their two paths did eventually cross and Allison has memories of the eccentric writer:

> I used to see Faulkner all the time, driving around Oxford in this old car with the top sawed off, like a do-it-yourself convertible. A friend of mine saw him go by on the square

in his overalls and suit coat and said, "That's the most distinguished looking tramp I ever saw." I never met him until later. I met him because my friend V.P. Ferguson, who is a writer in Paris, became friendly with him. This was after I had gotten out of school, probably the early fifties, 1952, or '53.

Allison's literary tastes gravitate more towards the surrealist school. He cites American author Kurt Vonnegut as one of his contemporary heroes. His favorite novelist, however, is the French surrealist Louis-Ferdinand Céline. Céline's novels, *Journey to the End of Night, Death on the Installment Plan, Guignol's Band, Castle to Castle, North*, and the posthumous *Rigandon* are all comical satires, written in a unique elliptical style in which the author explores the horror of a disordered, war-torn world. Curious and controversial, Céline focuses on the absurd in his satires, presenting his plots, characters and hallucinations in splintered sentences and stream-of-consciousness dialog.

Allison asserts that Céline's novel *Death on the Installment Plan* incorporates all the essential literary elements he attempts to capture and convey in his own song lyrics: irony, humor, satire, ambivalence and pathos. Yet, even if he was inspired chiefly by the French author's style, Allison was also clearly attracted by Céline's vision, since his own song texts are hardly as abstruse as Céline's prose. For example, Céline's book *Guignol's Band* includes one of Allison's favorite literary passages, the depiction of a musician and his piano performance in a London pawnshop. Oddly, Céline's description of the music parallels Allison's own musical style, particularly in his piano improvisations, where a bizarre eloquence emerges from the stammering text, sculpting explosive, percussive phrases out of simple yet colorful phrases and ideas.

In order to make room Boro would knock everything right and left . . . with big kicks . . . he'd pick at something in the pile, a saxophone, a piccolo, a mandolin . . . he'd fool around with the gadget for a while... just so... a bit of a prelude... a fantasy... nothing at all... he'd drop it... just a whim!... then, he'd yank out the piano, ferociously... clear away all the junk... whatever was in his way... the whole museum! ... Baraboom!... finally installed, stool, all ready... on with the waltz... Arpeggios, trills, gingerbread... you know... plugging it, street stuff... with the best possible variations for charm... plaintive, tinsel, sob-stuff, it could go on forever... it was irresistible... It would make a crocodile start daydreaming... But you've got to have the knack... It's the magic know-how... to turn on the charm anywhere, jolly place, dull occasion, smart salon, cuckold ball, gloomy lofts, sinister squares, hopeless streets, communions, country inns, All Saints' Day, low dives, July 14ths... a zim! bang! ding! and it starts... never meet resistance... I know what I'm talking about....[2]

In addition to Céline, Kenneth Patchen, the late American poet whose prophetic satires protest war and inhumanity, inspired Allison's textual style perhaps even more directly than the Frenchman's work did. Patchen examines his subjects in succinct, direct and simple verses, also a stylistic trait of Mose Allison, who comments: "Kenneth Patchen is my favorite poet. Even though I never got to meet him, I thought it was time to put his name out there. He gets so much *surprise* into lines. He knocks me out—especially the Patchen prose. Some of my songs were inspired by him."[3]

Of Patchen's novel, *The Journal of Albion Moonlight*, Allison says: "I've read that book about three times. It's a great book but it's so far out that it's the kind of thing that some people can't take. It's like an allegorical surreal diatribe by an outraged poet."

Mose Allison eventually realized that, as with Vonnegut, Céline and Patchen, addressing the human condition was of paramount thematic concern in his own song texts. Although the concern was less pronounced in his earlier work, Allison's lyrics increasingly and more deliberately evolved into translucent tableaux of human nature, dealing with topics derived from his own personal feelings and attitudes as well as his belief that all people share common experiences:

> Everybody's the same person, essentially. Different people exemplify different traits that essentially everybody has. All art, all communication and language is based on the assumption that all people are enough alike to understand each other. I try to get at the truth that is happening and express it in song form where it will be meaningful to me and accessible to others. There's some translating that goes on between me and the final song, but my attitude and outlook come through one way or another. It's important to give a truthful account of an attitude. If it applies to yourself, it generally will apply to others. I try to steer away from the trivial. I try to make some sort of point in each song. A lot of people tell me my songs help them to get through a bad period, they serve as a type of therapy. They've been therapeutic for me.

By 1968 and the release of his sixth Atlantic album, *I've Been Doin' Some Thinkin'*, Allison had composed enough songs for definite patterns to have emerged in his lyric/song writing style. He himself groups the songs into four distinct categories, classifying them according to their subject and lyrical content, using the terms "local color," "slapstick," "public service or social commentary," and "personal crisis/universal chants." With the exception of the "personal crisis/universal chants," whose sustained, chordal musical settings are most unlike Allison's earlier style, the twelve-bar blues song form, some variation thereof, or the more jazz-influenced popular song form ground his work.

"Local color" or "cotton sack" songs are his rural musical poetry, primarily written in twelve-bar country-blues style. These pieces include "Parchman Farm," "If You Live" (sixteen-bar blues), certain instrumental piano sketches from his Prestige years bearing pastoral titles, and covers of country-blues tunes such as "Eyesight to the Blind" and "One Room Country Shack." Allison undertakes a narrative style in his poetry, using the blues-song verse scheme AAB. The themes of these songs deal with the provincial Mississippi Delta lifestyle, such as that of sharecroppers, making the "local color" pieces instantly recognizable. This song category eventually became obsolete in Allison's repertoire.

"Slapstick" denotes the song category whose lyrics interweave humor, surprise and joke-like punchlines. These satirical pieces employ irony and wry descriptive language rich in aphorisms, colloquialisms, and metaphor in their texts. Although the "slapstick" tunes are effective in using humor to broach serious subjects, they just as often focus on whimsical topics. Allison's archetypal "slapstick" tune is "Your Mind's on Vacation" from his first Atlantic album, *I Don't Worry 'bout a Thing*, but other tunes from previous recordings qualifying as "slapstick" are "No Trouble Livin'," "Wild Man on the Loose," "Look Here," "I'm Not Talkin'" and "Swingin' Machine." Musically, "slapstick" songs most often employ variations of the twelve-bar blues form, i.e. thirty-two- or sixteen-bar verses. The composer notes that a subtle uniform thread of "slapstick," a phrase, word combination or attitude, weaves through most of these tunes. On his ideal audience response for "slapstick," Allison says: "The kind of reaction I'm trying to get is that Mona Lisa smile, not the big laugh, just that little smile."[4]

In "public service" or "social commentary" tunes, the text finds Mose speaking on behalf of humanity. Culled from universal observations and uniform life experiences, these pithy, thought-provoking lyrics perform a "public service" in that they offer unsolicited but necessary advice from a worldly jazz sage. Tunes such as "If You're Goin' to the City," "Foolkiller" and "Tell Me Somethin' that I Don't Know," which also draw upon the "slapstick" element, contain valuable adages and thus qualify as "public service" or "social commentary." The musical settings of these songs are often written in a variation of the blues form and may contain more complex jazz-based but unconventional harmonic progressions.

The texts of the poetic "personal crisis" songs or "universal chants" delve introspectively into the individual psyche during a state of self-conflict. Grappling for reason in the face of irrationality, the lyrics focus on individual humility, melancholy, and confusion. The sombre probes seethe with pathos, adroitly provoking common emotions and resolving the conflict in a positive dénouement, restoring faith in self and humanity. The dark, moody poetry is replete with symbolism and literary devices such as personification, allegory, irony and metaphor. Examples of the "personal crisis" tunes are "One of These Days," "Stop This World," and "I'm Smashed." Frequently realized in the straight twelve-bar-blues song form, these pieces often feature "tone painting" with lush musical settings. Allison comments: "Some people consider me an out and out cynic, but somebody once told me that he didn't think the songs were really downers because I never say, 'I'm dead.'"

The seminal *I've Been Doin' Some Thinkin'*, a poignant manifesto of Allison's state of mind in 1968, is a pivotal album in his career. Resurfacing after a three-year hiatus, the singer/songwriter exuded new confidence in his songwriting and studio performing. With a repertoire now crystallized into four thematic categories, Allison penned several significant additions to his vocal repertoire, and recorded four new signature pieces, three originals, "Everybody Cryin' Mercy," the quixotic "Feel So Good," a wordplay on hightech terminology in "Your Molecular Structure," and renovates the old American folk song "You Are My Sunshine" in a unique blues style. The youth having drained from his lighter baritone, Allison's late-1960s vocal timbre slips into the raspier, smokier, darker tone of middle age, where it convincingly delivers his new songs.

On this album Allison also established his own brand of love song, a "slapstick" crafted in his inimitable wry, literary style and sung with his compelling, cool delivery. The comedic attitude he espoused in "Your Mind's on Vacation" presides in these songs, which range, on the emotional spectrum, from edgy through petulant to endearing. Allison's lyrics to his singular jazz paean, "Your Molecular Structure," express physical attraction in high-tech jargon. Playful metaphors and witty, contrived word choices illustrate Allison's aplomb in turning the serious subject of love into a farcical valentine. The buoyant uptempo swing features cascading triplet melodic fillers between phrases, Allison's animated music perfectly realizing the text inspired by reading Marshall McLuhan.

"Your Molecular Structure"

Your molecular structure is really something fine
A first-rate example of functional design
That cosmic undulation is steady comin' through
Your molecular structure, baby, me and you

Your cellular organization is really something choice
Electromagnetism 'bout to make me lose my voice
Got all my circuits open, my systems reading go
Your cellular organization, baby, stop the show

Your molecular structure is really something swell
A high-frequency modulated jezebel
Thermodynamically you're getting to me
Your molecular structure, baby, ooo-wee

The introductory trills in Allison's blues "Look What You Made Me Do," executed in his Afro-American groove, anticipate Allison's modern piano style. An extended piano solo on this twelve-bar-blues progression shows more maturity in this new direction, and the lyric weaves together elements of both irony and slapstick:

I was leavin' the scene behind
I was workin on piece of mind
You strolled right down my avenue
You took me for a ride in your Subaru
Now look what you made me do

Allison treats the love theme of the blues-based "If You Really Loved Me Baby" with a similar slapstick and irony:

If you really loved me baby
You wouldn't come on that way
You turned cold, called me old
Said you gonna make me pay
I'm beginning to think that maybe
You don't really love me baby

"Feel So Good," a typical Allison "slapstick" love song, features a text anathema to the emotion itself. Allison considers this tune his masterpiece in textual writing, the lyrics brimming with contradictory phrases, words and attitudes, the text as a whole serving as the cornerstone of Allison's use of ambivalence. Strong blues overtones mark this medium-tempo swing. On his marked predilection for ambivalence, Mose comments:

> I consider myself a deadpan comedian. Life is beautiful and it's terrible, too. You got the beauty of life and the terror of life. You got to admit that they're both there and then, you have to deal with it in some way and humor is one way. A lot of the time it's a mixture. That's what we're confronted with and that's where you get ambivalence.

"Feel So Good"

I feel so good, it must be wrong
Feel like I might just come on strong
Guess I better knock on wood
I feel so good

You look so nice, you bring me down
Notice how you got me hanging around
Waiting for some bad advice
You look so nice

Well, now you got the wrong impression
Let me make a full confession
I feel so bad, it must be right

Have myself a nightmare every night
All of my friends are glad
I feel so bad

I been so far, I must be back
Airline, highway, railroad track
Won't you tell me where we are
I been so far

You lie so good, you think it's true
Funny how a man can count on you
I knew exactly where I stood
You lie so good

Well, go ahead and analyze me
I bet you that you can't surprise me

I know so much, I've lost my mind
Leaving this work-a-day world behind
Got myself a special crutch
I know so much
I been so far, I feel so good.

Mose's harmonic reworking, at a dirge-like tempo and in a minor key, of the American classic "You Are My Sunshine" transforms the traditionally bright tune into a heartfelt, sorrowful ballad, embossing the tune with his own stylistic imprint. In his performances, he jokingly prefaces the tune by commenting that a downtempo, melancholic version was probably the original intention of its composer, the former governor of the state of Louisiana, Jimmie Davis (who co-wrote the song with Charles Mitchell). Arguably, the lyrics support that contention: "You'll never know, dear, how much I love you; please don't take my sunshine away."

"Public service" or "social commentaries" from *I've Been Doin' Some Thinkin'* are "Jus' Like Livin'," "Now You See It," "If You're Goin' to the City," and a tune which eventually became an Allison classic, "Everybody Cryin' Mercy." Irony and ambivalence characterize these song texts, which explore serious issues, fundamental truths and realities. The humorous jazz bounce, "Jus' Like Livin'," includes the title of the album and also served as the title of a moderately successful off-Broadway revue of Allison's repertoire staged in 1983 by Murray Horwitz, the producer of the Fats Waller revue *Ain't Misbehavin'*. Mose comments on the nature of his "public service"/"social commentary" tunes:

> I try to put a fundamental idea or truth into something that strikes you or registers in a tune; most of it involves the ironies and humor in it. Most people say it's cynical but I feel as though it's positive too. The fact that the rhythm and the form I'm using make it positive. A lot of people get the idea that you're just exactly like your songs, which isn't true. I scuffle through everyday life just like everybody else and I have as much hysteria as everybody else.

> "Jus' Like Livin'"

> I've been doin' some thinkin'
> About the nature of the universe
> I found out things are gettin' better
> It's just people that are gettin' worse

> Ain't that jus' like livin'
> Just like family strife
> Ain't that jus' like livin'
> Whatever happened to real life?

The traditional twelve-bar blues "If You're Goin' to the City" incorporates Allison signature minor-second voicing, which here moves sequentially in a three-chord progression. Initially recorded on his second Atlantic recording, *Swingin' Machine*, the version from *I've Been Doin' Some Thinkin'* enjoys an uplift with an Afro-Cuban tempo. The song is thus the perfect vehicle for extensive piano improvisations. A "public service" tune, the lyric is rounded off with a slapstick punchline:

And if you stay up in the city
There's just two things I hope
I said, if you stay up in the city
There's just two things I hope
That you don't take money from a woman
And you don't start messin' 'round with dope

Irony and ambivalence are also present in the lyrics of another jazz "public service" tune, "Now You See It."

Now you're with it
Now you're not
Organized confusion
Find yourself right on the spot
Gonna have to draw your own conclusion

Mose Allison's best example of the "social commentary"/"public service" category is his classic, "Everybody Cryin' Mercy." Allison's observations decry with disquieting clarity the hypocrisy in the political and social system. Covered by singer/songwriters Bonnie Raitt and Elvis Costello, this tune is described by Mose as a rueful lament; "Sometimes I think that it should be the national anthem." The piece embodies all Allison's trademark textual elements in one phrase: "Everybody cryin' mercy when they don't know the meaning of the word."

Musically, like "City Home" which also appears on this recording in a faster tempo than previously recorded on *The Transfiguration of Hiram Brown*, "Everybody Cryin' Mercy" exemplifies the composer's technique of harmonizing a conventional blues melody with unorthodox harmony. Here, Allison uses the tonic and flat V, a substitute for the dominant in phrases one and two, creating an unusual tritone movement in the bass. Rather than use the subdominant, a more routine progression, he uses a whole-tone root movement in the third phrase, centering on the pentatonic scale and giving the tune a folk-like quality. The bridge is also typical of Mose Allison's harmonic affinities, the flatted VI and V alternating. Bonnie Raitt succinctly sums up the song's lyric qualities:

> Mose's ironic and sly world view, pointing out the hypocrisy and cruelty of the world around him, really sets him apart as a lyricist. As for his music, his amazingly soulful rhythmic style, combining blues, jazz, and wild improvisation is also completely unique. When he jabs at himself and the world, it's with a sense of humor and a certain sardonic weariness that's really so much hipper than just sitting around preaching about what's wrong. The only other person I can think of who's attempted that is Randy Newman, who's also from the South, by the way. There really is no separation between the musical counterculture that came out of the sixties and the political one; they're one and the same. I picked up the guitar so I could play Bob Dylan songs as well as the ones off the radio. And, in one song of Mose's "Everybody Cryin' Mercy," I can get the most pointed, concise and funky political message across I've ever found.

Mose adds:

That whole irony thing appeals to me, like "Everybody cryin' mercy when they don't know the meaning of the word." I don't know whether I have an irony hang-up or what, but irony has followed me like an albatross. I can find so many situations that are so completely ironical in my life. That's part of my movie—playing nightclubs. I'm not trying to write straight out poems that you write for recitation at literary teas or whatever. That whole thing doesn't appeal to me. I still dig the boogie-woogie and the feeling, the swing and rhythm. That's why I'm always surprised when people accuse me of being cynical. This has happened so much that I looked up "cynical" in the dictionary. It means "distrustful". When's the last time you left anything unlocked? The time, rhythm, and context of what I'm doing is a very positive life force, the rhythm of jazz and blues is a positive force.

As a poet, Allison excels at confronting complicated life issues in his "universal chants," personal crisis songs defined by chant-like vocals with free-form asymmetrical phrasing. The lyrics in these unique pieces are brooding, evocative and luminous in their imagery, metaphors and quirky word relationships. Most often, the poems contemplate destiny, showing an open-hearted respect for the spiritual forces that cast personal fate.

The corresponding musical beds of the "universal chants" are harmonically dense, with lush tone colors, giving the pieces a rhapsodic, languid, ethereal quality. Allison's term for the musical effect he seeks in these pieces is "texture." He references not only the conventional musicological definition of the term "texture," that is, the use of dense or sparse harmonies, but also the contrast in the single vocal line pitted against the thick, vertical harmony in the piano accompaniment. Perhaps more than in any other song category, Allison relies heavily on both the ambivalent components and their interdependence of musical and lyric schemes in the "universal chant," thus putting into effect his formula: "Ambivalence plus interdependence equals contrariety." For instance, the thick, lush sonorities he places in his piano accompaniments are juxtaposed with simple melodic lines; his lyrics, while crafted from plain language, are piercing in their profound philosophical content.

In composing piano accompaniments for the "universal chants" Allison asserts that twentieth-century classical composition inspired his choices of harmonies and voicings, in particular the compositional technique called "quartal harmony," a harmonic system based on the interval of the fourth. Quartal harmonies feature chords with intervals stacked in fourths creating spacial, ethereal tonal qualities. Allison readily identified with "quartal harmonies" not only because of the space he sought in the piano accompaniment but because the blues tonality hovers predominantly around the fourth degree of the scale.

Allison borrows from the twentieth-century classical harmonic vocabulary in these songs, using bichords or polychords and tone clusters in his "universal chant" accompaniments. Poly or bichords are thick chords that combine major or minor triads, or both, from different keys, often employing common tones as a unifier. Tone clusters feature two or more notes voiced in clusters of seconds. At certain points in his early stages of integrating certain twentieth-century compositional techniques, Allison actually reviewed a Hindemith score to determine what he was hearing. To the extent that he was able to integrate that information to his own work, Allison discovered that his musical affinity for modern music and his relationship to certain of its characteristics would enable him to evolve his piano style in both his accompaniments and improvisations. In general, though, he divides music into simple categories: "In fact, there's only three kinds of music: Bach, the blues, and Schoenberg. Bach is linear, melodic; Schoenberg is new sounds, twelve-tone harmony; and a universal blues is played in every country. Everything else is a mixture of those three elements to a certain degree."

Although in retrospect Allison cites his first vocal, "Young Man Blues," as a "universal chant," one of the first tunes in this category to flesh out his sophisticated musical concept is a song from *I've Been Doin' Some Thinkin'* which he rarely plays live, called "Let It Come Down." The appearance of this mood piece, the final track on the album, aptly prefigures Allison's poetic period. A mournful soliloquy, its meditative text laments failure and fate with forceful compassion. Allison imbues the vocal with a tender melancholia, setting the poem musically in a ruminating quartal chord accompaniment. Mose borrows the song title, the ending lines in the lyric and its destiny theme from the dialog in Shakespeare's drama *Macbeth*, Act III, Scene iii. It is in this scene that Banquo is murdered. Before his death, Banquo states, "It will be rain tonight." The first murderer replies, "Let it come down," a signal for the three murderers to ambush and kill Banquo.

The musical setting of "Let It Come Down" deftly explores Mose's reaction to the introspective poetic text, balancing opposing ideas in both lyrics and music. Using free-form verses of asymmetrical chant-like phrases, the song can be analyzed as a languid B flat blues tonality. Rhythmic variation highlights the melodic line, long pitch durations signal the importance of the key words and alternate with shorter, accented notes to emphasize other words. Melodic and harmonic suspensions, especially in the final notes of each verse, generate added musical and textual tension.

"Let It Come Down" is a brilliant example of Allison's use of piano accompaniment and its harmonic color to accentuate the power of his texts. Within the F minor blues melody centralized on the dominant in the first sixteen bars, the harmony concentrates on the F hovering around it from the D flat and its neighbors E, G flat, and E flat. Chord voicings alternate between the open, spacious quartal harmonies and closely voiced groupings of thirds and minor-second clusters. Sustained chords accompany text and melody. The chord tones are combined in an unconventional fashion, defying symbols typically used on jazz lead sheets, requiring Allison to write out the voicings in the notation of a piano score. He uses shorter note durations in the piano accompaniment when the vocal melody is sustained, thereby creating a rhythmic alternation between melody and accompaniment that engages the listener and provides musical impetus. Finally, his plaintive delivery in a rubato tempo dramatizes the text and tension-resolution in the music. Allison himself comments: "'Let It Come Down' is one of my most revolutionary songs, lyrically. It shows what it's like to be against the wall and having to act."

"Let It Come Down"

Frettin' 'bout what you're goin' through
Regrettin' the things you didn't do
Relyin' on compensations you found
Groanin'
beneath the weight of it
Bemoanin'
the fickle fate of it
Complyin' just to keep both feet on the ground

But that won't get you any place
Won't excuse you from the race
When you meet your destiny face to face
There'll be no more wrong or right
And no more wish I might
And if there's gonna be rain tonight
Let it come down

11

HELLO THERE, UNIVERSE

"I've always admired the phrase to 'instruct and entertain.' I like to think that if you analyze my songs, you'll get something out of it, other than just the surface swing.

Everything is autobiographical in a sense but it's repackaged so that it's not straight autobiography. It's transposed. I'm affected, and to start with, the song has to apply to me and I have to identify with it. But I don't want the songs to apply only just to me, therefore, I look for reinforcement in the experience of others, or the newspaper or T.V. set or whatever, to help you universalize your own experience."

Mose Allison

Hello there, Universe
Do you know what you're doin' to me?
You let me sample your treasure chest
Showed me how to choose the best
Then you gave me lessons in humility
Do you know what you're doin' to me?

Hello there, Universe
Am I doin' what you meant me to?
You let me feel your guiding (mystic) light
Showed me splendors of the night
Now you got me wondering if I missed my cue
Am I doin' what you meant me to?

I say there, Universe
I just thought I'd let you know
Though others doubt your good intent
Desecrate your sacrament
You can always count on me and even though
The good gets better
And the bad gets worse

Hello there, Universe

Mose Allison

Whatever commercial trappings the record executives at Atlantic Records had dreamed up for Mose Allison, by 1970 the artist himself had proscribed them. Having moved slowly into a ripening "poetic period" which commenced with "Let It Come Down" and to some degree, "Everybody Cryin' Mercy," a now unfettered Allison dismissed the idea of mainstream success. Instead, he concentrated on following his muse, whether it led him into areas visceral, intellectual, or spiritual, and he allowed his literary affinities and musical influences to surface in his music. In this new phase, Allison's music entered a fertile period characterized by catharsis, exploration and therapy, and he savored his new voice, dredged up from the soul searching and questioning of life, cosmos, and social milieu. Underpinning his ascetic contemplation were new tonal dimensions, sounds not readily familiar to most popular-music ears.

As Mose the artist dug deeper into himself, the young producer Joel Dorn took the helm for Allison's seventh album on Atlantic, entitled *Hello There, Universe*. Dorn was an aficionado of Mose Allison's music, which had permeated his language as a disc jockey from Philadelphia. Brought on board by the Erteguns to produce records, Dorn was assigned the arduous task of making blockbuster, Grammy-winning albums with Atlantic recording artists, a feat he did accomplish with songstresses Bette Midler and Roberta Flack. Dorn was thoroughly versed in the era's studio trends, ever observant of what worked at the time: string orchestrations and the Muscle Shoals and Memphis sounds, which had ostensibly generated the record sales of artists on the Atlantic roster. Yet the recalcitrant and reclusive Mose Allison shunned industry gimmickry, firmly resisting ephemeral faddishness, and Dorn, out of respect and admiration for his jazz hero, a taste he shared with Nesuhi Ertegun, deferred to the artist's vision. Dorn remembers:

> I was sad that I caught Mose at the time we worked together because just prior to that he was really cooking on an appealing level. By the time he and I hooked up he was going through some changes and was writing songs like "How Much Truth Can a Man Stand," "Western Man," and "Hello There, Universe." When I say I was a little sad that I caught him at that time, I mean that when I went in to record him, I was thinking what's the next "Parchman Farm," "Mind's on Vacation" or "Seventh Son." I was hoping to get those Mose Allison staples with him on his own terms. When these other heavy songs came in, I was taken by surprise. Not that I didn't like them or wasn't glad to be part of a body of Mose Allison's work, but I was caught short. Atlantic was pressuring me to make another "Seventh Son" or "Mind's on Vacation" and I was coming back with "How Much Truth Can a Man Stand" and "Hello There, Universe." They thought that I was pushing him in this direction because ultimately it's the producer's fault. The record sales were O.K. on these, though.

Hello There, Universe, released in 1970, was Allison's most colorful musical mélange on Atlantic to date and his first venture with full-blown horn arrangements. Entering the studio with a panoply of musical instruments, interesting orchestrations, and a stellar band of top-class jazzmen as sidemen, Mose experimented with his own brand of end-of-decade psychedelia arranged for jazzband. Allison's dense but intricate horn parts, replete with bursts, shakes, fall-offs and slow melodic descents and ascents, embellish his songs, finally bringing to the fore his formidable strength as a unique arranger. Featured on this date are tenor saxophonists Joe Henderson, Joe Farrell, and Seldon Powell and the celebrated baritone player Pepper Adams. Allison adds five new vocals, two new original instrumentals and a cover of the sultry Arlen/Mercer blues standard "Blues in the Night" to his repertoire. He also updates two older tunes, "I'm Smashed," which lends itself well to the horn arrangements, and "Wildman on the Loose," where the pianist switches to a Hammond B-3 organ.

The literary qualities of the text in the plodding blues "Monsters of the Id," and the title track "Hello There, Universe" are evidence of Allison's further movement into his "poetic" period. The peculiar text of "Monsters of the Id," which harkens back to songs like "Foolkiller," "Days Like This" and "Everybody Cryin' Mercy," is an example of Allison's lyric writing approaching downright erudition, its symbolism, Freudian references and phantasmagoria spinning out the themes of the "public service"/"social commentary" tune. Programmatic in nature, Allison's musical setting of the song features a typical science-fiction-movie musical theme in a connecting, repeated melodic motif. The horn parts in "Monsters of the Id" also evoke a horror-movie melodrama.

"Monsters of the Id"

Monsters of the Id
No longer staying hid
And terrors of the night
Are out in broad daylight

No need to knock on wood
Don't stop to say a prayer
It won't do any good
They're multiplying in the air

Creatures of the deep
Are goin' without sleep

TOP PHOTO:

LEFT TO RIGHT: Mose, Sr., and Maxine with Mose, Jr. and Joy, in Tippo, Mississippi, 1939.

BOTTOM PHOTO:

Mose, Sr., and Maxine Allison in Tippo, 1927.

The homestead of John Robert Allison (Mose's grandfather) on the island outside of Tippo, Mississippi. Mose was born here and it served as his earliest boyhood home.

A young Mose crooning at the summer resort at Lake Taneycomo, Rockaway Beach, Missouri, 1949. A trumpeter with Don Gilbert's band, he met his future wife Audre at the resort that summer.

Audre Mae Schwartz, age 17.

Mose and Audre in Baton Rouge, Louisiana, 1951.

Mose's band at Bill Bennett's club, 1952.
LEFT TO RIGHT: **Alto saxophonist Don Brooks, Taylor LaFargue, bass, Paul Logos, drums, Mose on pia**

The latecomers for "A Great Day in Harlem" photograph, 1958. LEFT TO RIGHT: Ronnie Free, Mose's sideman on drums, Mose Allison, tenor saxophonist Lester Young, pianist Mary Lou Williams, tenor saxophonist Charlie Rouse, bassist Oscar Pettiford. Young was one of Allison's jazz heroes.

Mose at the piano during his early years in New York, circa 1962.

Mose pictured with the late bluesman Willie Dixon, mid 1980s.

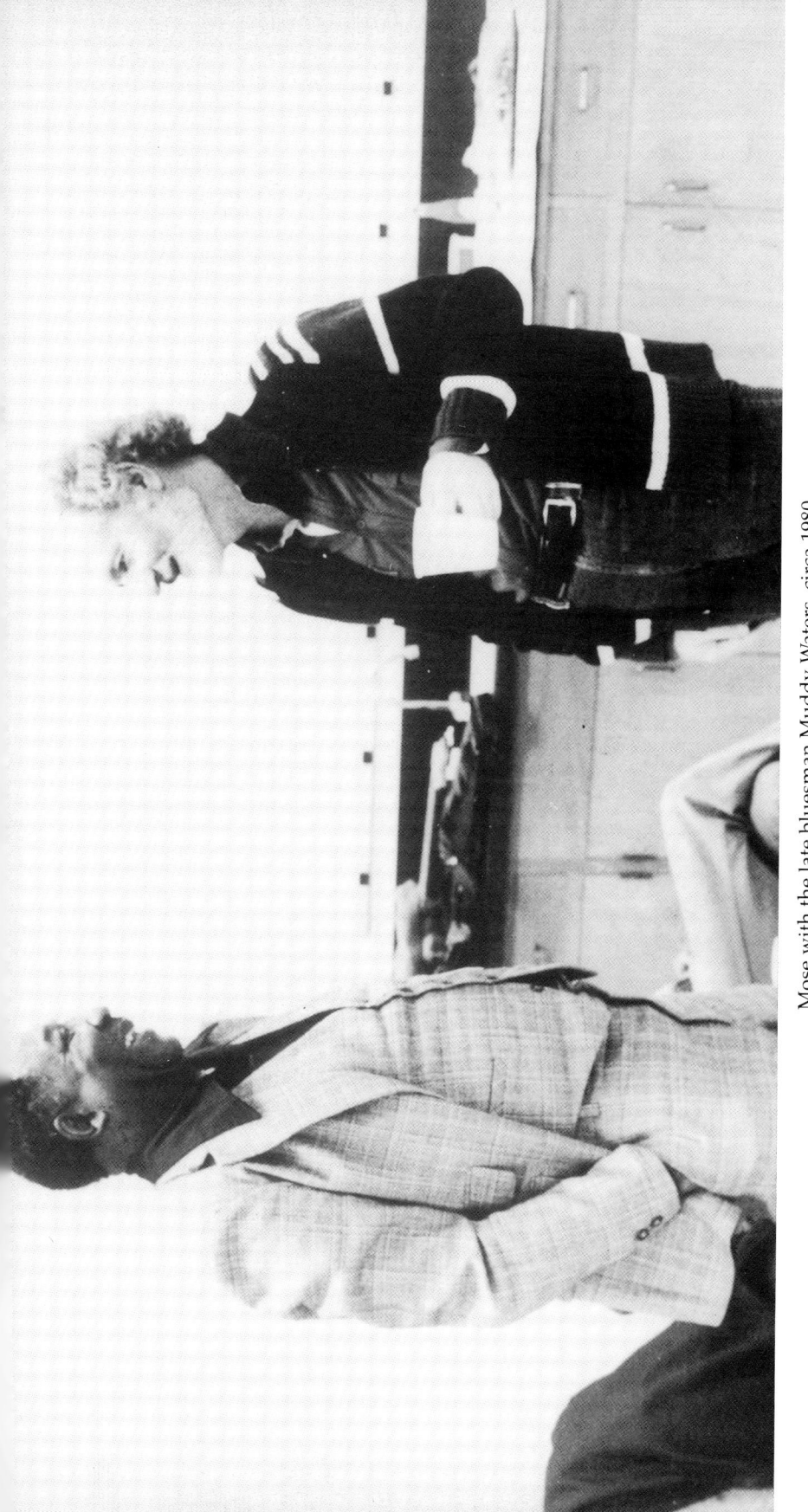

Mose with the late bluesman Muddy Waters, circa 1980.

Mose plays a show with bassist Milt Hinton in Hattiesburg, Mississippi, early 1980s.

And phantoms of the dark
Have their own place to park

No need to lock the door
They're sprouting through the cracks
They're making room for more
They're deputizing maniacs

Prehistoric ghouls
Are making their own rules
And resurrected Huns
Are passing out the guns

No need to cause a fuss
Don't go and make a scene
They know what's best for us
They're fighting fire with gasoline

Creatures from the swamp
Rewrite their own *Mein Kampf*
Neanderthal amok
Just trying to make a buck
Goblins and their hags
Are out there waving flags
When will we be rid
Of Monsters of the Id.

Jerry Granelli remembers:

I've known Mose since 1962 or '63 when I was in San Francisco working with Vince Garaldi. I was also playing drums with whomever came to town and Mose came to the Jazz Workshop and the owner, Art Auerbach, called me and asked me if I wanted to work two weeks with Mose. I met him on a Tuesday afternoon, the only rehearsal I ever had with the man, and we've been playing together ever since. I was around Mose when a lot of the tunes were being written. We laugh because of those songs from *Hello There, Universe* like "Monsters of the Id." Part of these songs came from this movie we love called *The Forbidden Planet*. Walter Pidgeon was in it and Robbie the Robot originally appeared in this movie. They had a machine called an "everything machine" where "the Krel" stored their consciousness. This was the "Monster of the Id" that depopulated the planet.

In the blues swing "On the Run" Allison alludes to past lyrics and foreshadows future ones, and refers to both literary and musical inspirations. "Seems like I've been there and back/I keep crossing my track" recalls lyrics from his tune "Feel So Good," whereas "On the move/Paranoid/Finger painting in the void" foreshadows the lyric "finger painting in the sand" from the 1971 album *Western Man*, the tune in question being "How Much Truth Can a Man Stand." The last verse "On the run/Traveling light/Journey to the end of night/Whatever happened to the Seventh Son/On the run" not only refers to his literary hero Céline in the third line, but also provides self-references, alluding to the Willie Dixon tune "Seventh Son" which gained Mose musical notoriety. "Somebody Gotta Move," with its flippant lyric: "'scuse me mister/Somethin' you should know/I don't look for trouble/But you're standin' on my toe," is composed in a similar blues swing vein to that of "On the Run."

"I Don't Want Much," another medium-tempo blues, appears first on this date, but Mose rerecorded it some ten years later, with a slightly altered lyric, on his first Elektra/Musician album *Middle Class White Boy*. The tune exudes the archetypal Allison irony and ambivalence also present in songs like "Feel So Good," and "I Don't Worry 'bout a Thing": "I don't want much in this life/Just the simple things I treasure/Till I die I would get by/On fame, riches, and sensual pleasure . . . All I want is plenty/But I will take more/Say please/I will take more."

The instrumentals on *Hello There, Universe* provide extended forums for Allison's modern piano style. He composed them as miniature jazz concertos, his solo piano alternating with extensive horn sections and accompanying horn improvisation sections. "No Exit," the more conservative of the two pieces, features interesting antiphonal exchanges between horns and piano. Allison gives each independent motifs; the horns short chromatic, melodic phrases, the piano parts replete with characteristics of Allison's piano style, trills in the right hand and double-octave scale-like melodies. "Hymn to Everything," the more virtuosic number, is closer stylistically to Allison's twentieth-century classical inspirations; in a rhapsodic introduction, he plants himself firmly in the sustained sonorities of thick chords with intriguing voicings borrowed from modern piano literature. The trills, tone clusters (smashed notes) and alternation between intricate melodies and simple block chords further distinguish Allison's style.

"Hello There, Universe," a cosmic prayer, is a "universal chant"/"personal crisis" song. Allison envelops the verses of the mystical dialectic in a simple, yet precise musical setting, the lush chord sonorities and the varied rhythms accentuating the quiet power of the introspective text. The last phrase of each verse is hymn-like, the blocked, sustained chords travelling with the rhythm of the vocal line. A cascading melodic motif bridges the gap between verses. Allison develops his coda even further in the phrase "The good gets better and the bad gets worse," using an unprecedented accented, ironical whimsical "carousel"-like rhythm to emphasize the seriousness of the text. Although this first version's horn arrangements deprive the song of some of its inherent intimacy, Allison is cautious with the brassy sounds, positioning them in supporting sections throughout the tune:

> I remember I was inspired to write "Hello There, Universe" when I was riding down the Pacific Coast Highway one night during a full moon. The idea and the way it's developed dictated its song form. It's one of my personal favorites and I think it's pretty basic. Everybody has to find some sort of working relationship beween themselves and the universe. Because if the universe knows what it's doing you can justify things by saying that it's part of a plan. If the universe doesn't know what it's doing, then we're really in trouble.[1]

Producer Joel Dorn recalls:

I've made a lot of records with a lot of people, and far-out people at that, Roland Kirk, jazz bagpipe people, Leon Redbone. The *Hello There, Universe* record stands out in terms of uniqueness as much as anything I've ever done. The arrangements, the lyrics, him playing the organ with all of the horns bunched around him. I did hundreds of albums in those years, but I remember that session vividly. We had Mose on B-3 organ and he had arrangements for five horns, and he asked that they be bunched around him to be close to him, but the sound problems were nightmares. But the look of it! I had never seen a recording studio look that way! Anything he would want, I would do.

Maybe *Hello There, Universe* is the most out-of-context record Mose Allison ever made. Basically, it's a trio record. The current records are mostly with saxophones. Rhythmically and melodically, most of the trio records are very similar. It's somewhat like Picasso's blue period where all the seventy-five pieces are blue and some of them are drastically different. The same with Mose, the difference of subject matters and subtleties distinguish the framework which could be very constricting or monotonous. Look at the cast of players on the *Hello, Universe* record. Richard Williams might be the unsung trumpet player of life; Jerome Richardson, there is not some reed instrument that he can't play and hasn't been playing in the studio for a hundred years; Joe Henderson is a real heavyweight, so is Joe Farrell and Pepper Adams is my favorite baritone player ... he and a guy named Hog Cooper, they really can play the baritone. At the time, I didn't realize how important those two records were. I also felt that I might have let him down by not producing records that would sell better. And catching any great artist, not necessarily in their blue period, I was just a kid and wanted to make a hit with Mose Allison.

The 1970s was a prosperous era for a new type of jazz. Apart from its integration into soul and rhythm and blues, inspired in part by the Muscle Shoals and Memphis sounds, jazz also commingled at this time with elements of rock and roll. The jazz fusion movement, led by young virtuosos like keyboardists Herbie Hancock and Chick Corea, both as familiar with the electric piano as with the acoustic instrument, and innovative trumpeter Freddie Hubbard, maintained the artistic purity of jazz, while rock bands with horn sections such as Blood, Sweat and Tears, Chicago and the Canadian band Chase flavored their vocal and guitar-oriented music with a stageband sound, further blurring the lines between musical categories.

Alert to the possibilities of the jazz fusion movement, Joel Dorn continued as producer on Allison's next Atlantic recording, 1971's *Western Man*. The sound quality of this record is noticeably different from that heard on Allison's previous albums, the unusually resonant vocals suggesting echo or reverb on the singer. In his attempt to keep Mose Allison in step with the evolution of jazz, at least in the United States, Dorn shifted the then forty-four-year-old jazz/bluesman to electric piano for certain songs on *Western Man* and hired one of the hippest young musicians of the decade to accompany him, drummer Billy Cobham. Cobham, a gifted soloist as well as a sideman, was a vital member of what was without doubt one of the decade's most progressive groups, the quintet founded by another virtuoso, guitarist John McLaughlin, called the Mahivishnu Orchestra. Cobham was also a sideman on many recordings released by Prestige as well as a leading independent jazz label of the 1970s, CTI Records, performing with the likes of trumpeters Lee Morgan and Freddie Hubbard. The drummer later also accompanied Mose at the Montreux Jazz Festival in Switzerland in 1982, a live performance released as Allison's second record on Bruce Lundvall's WEA label, Elektra/Musician. Cobham remembers:

> I knew Mose for the period of recording *Western Man*. The record date was the first time I'd met Mose and I knew very little about him, but I always respected him. My concept of him was that he was laying on the line of American folkloric

proletariat connection, and that's such a rich thing to investigate for me that I've just sort of put it off to the side to deal with because that's going to take a while. We didn't play long enough to do anything and I can't remember the tunes but I remember it jelled somehow. I have really good memories and positive feelings about the sessions but we never talked much. It could be that I never play the rim or the backbeat that I fit into Mose's music. It sounded more like we should be doing something from out of New Orleans, which is like a zydeco. That's how I hear Mose, more Mississippi River Delta feeling which has nothing to do with backbeat. He's definitely coming out of a tradition.

The esoteric, poetic content of part of Allison's song list in *Western Man* and the funereal tempo of most of the songs notwithstanding, the recording features a variety of themes and subjects, two covers, and two instrumentals. The lyrics of Lefty Frizzell's tongue-in-cheek "If You Got the Money (I've Got the Time)," another standard from the country/honky-tonk music catalog, clearly qualify for Allison's definition of "slapstick" and, consequently, inclusion in the Mose Allison repertoire. Mose also resurrects a Duke Ellington favorite, "Do Nothing Till You Hear From Me," which is closer to his current version, and presents a cleaner studio rendition of his wry "Tell Me Something that I Don't Know," although its dirge-like tempo diverges from the livelier version performed on *Mose Alive!* The instrumentals are even closer in their approach to Allison's current piano improvisation style. In "Mountains" he lays down his Afro-Cuban groove and sustains the tonic chord, two key musical ingredients for improvisation, providing extended melodic and rhythmic improvisational development and Cobham with ample space for sonic dynamic, tone-color and technical displays. The shorter, quieter and simpler "Meadows," played on electric piano with subdued bass and drums, is more of a jazz tune, with a defined melodic contour and a concise improvisation section.

The original songs on *Western Man* span Allison's song categories, from "personal crisis" to "slapstick," often containing elements of each, and continue the singer's appeal to the intelligentsia. A blues variation performed in his Afro-Cuban groove on electric piano, "If You Only Knew" is a "personal crisis" song but resembles the "public service" tune in its offering of conciliatory wisdom. Irish singer/songwriter Van Morrison, who has worked intermittently with Allison on stage over the years and who views him as an influence on his thinking, covered the song on his 1985 Polygram recording *A Sense of Wonder*.

"If You Only Knew"

If you only knew
All the problems that a man like me has to face
If you only knew
All the little things that keep a man from his place
I wouldn't want to bring you down
I just don't want to see you made a clown
Nobody's little dream came true
If you only knew

If you only knew
What can happen to a man for telling the truth
If you only knew
All the scruples that go down in gin and vermouth
I wouldn't want to steer you wrong
But if you really want to sing your own little song
You're gonna have to lose a few
If you only knew

The quirky two-minute blues "Benediction" or "Thank God for Self Love" is another "personal crisis" song which also carries a "public service" message with it: "My message this evening/Is simple indeed/Whenever you wander/Whatever your need/There's just one thing, baby/That comes from above/When push comes to shove/Thank God for self-love." The tune is one of two songs where Allison harmonizes with himself on another track (the other appeared in 1987 on his first Blue Note release, on a song called "I'm Alive"). Playing on the bill in a short tour with Van Morrison in 1990, Allison,

Morrison and English singer/songwriter and Hammond B-3 player Georgie Fame, the keyboardist and music director for Morrison, performed the song as a trio in live performance and in Morrison's video *Live at The Beacon Theatre*.

The autobiographical "Nightclub," one of Allison's "slapsticks," returns to the straight twelve-bar-blues song form with AAB form in the lyrics. The Afro-Cuban swing and simple structure again allow for an extended introduction and solo on electric piano, both evidence of Allison's evolution into his current style: "Been workin' in nightclubs so long/ Can hardly stand the break of day/Been workin' in nightclubs so long/Can hardly stand the break of day/Run-down rooms and bad pianos/But it's still the only way." First heard on Epic's *Takes to the Hills*, a more contemporary electric-piano version of the F minor blues "Ask Me Nice" might appear as a jeer at the record industry and media, and is lyrically reminiscent of "I'm Not Talking": "Don't try to make me what I'm not/I'm just trying to get by with what I've got/Live let live, that's my advice, if you've got questions/Ask me nice."

The "public service" tune and the title track "Western Man," Allison's wry look at modern Western civilization, advances the theme he put forward in "Everybody Cryin' Mercy." Through composed in an ABA song form, with A sections performed in a slow, rubato tempo and B in an uptempo Latin groove, Allison's chiding epic ends with a ray of optimism.

"Western Man"

Western man had a plan
And with his gun in his hand
Free from doubt, went right out
On the world

Western man with his cross
Meant to prove who was boss
In his pride he'd decide
For the world

Well at first he sailed right through
Seemed there's nothing that he couldn't do
Went right out and laid 'em low
Seemed there's nothing that he didn't know

Came up with crockets, sprockets, rockets, and jets
Two hundred million color T.V. sets
But when they added up the cost
Seems he'd played his ace and lost

Western man hung his head
Could be better off dead
Strong men wept, took a new concept
Turned around and got in step
With the world

"How Much Truth Can a Man Stand," another meditative "personal crisis" song/"universal chant," composed after the manner of "Hello There, Universe," also demonstrates Mose Allison's genius as a songwriter, the words and music working perfectly together, creating a contemplative ambiance. In this text, Allison transcends the personal questioning and destiny themes, distilling his astute observations as a "public servant." Allison's version of "The Unanswered Question," the apocalyptic piece displays his gift for social critique; the images and metaphor he evokes in the text, for example "just another lamb for slaughter," although humorous in the context, are none the less vivid and startling. The song's piano accompaniment is appropriately more pared down and sustained than in the more animated "Hello There, Universe."

"How Much Truth Can a Man Stand"

How much truth can a man stand
Sittin' by the ocean
Nothin' but perpetual motion
Finger paintin' in the sand
How much truth can a man stand

How much truth can a woman stand
Lookin' at a teenage daughter
Just another lamb for slaughter
Fifteen years with a lying man
How much truth can a woman stand

How much truth can a world stand
Left without its daydreams
One in a million so it seems
Wondering how it all began
Threatened by the works of man
Destined for the fryin' pan

How much truth can a world stand
How much truth can this world stand

Mose Allison comments: "I got the idea for the fryin' pan line of the song when I was in Boston at the Planetarium. They showed what would happen when the sun began to swell because that's a property of all of stars. Then the earth would be burnt to a crisp."

Mose in Your Ear, Allison's tenth Atlantic album, recorded in 1972 during his live performances at In Your Ear, a jazz club in Palo Alto, California, stands out as one of the most representative of the artist's work because it features Allison in his native element, live performance. Presenting a diverse group of songs from his repertoire, both originals and covers, and extensive passages that display his modern and current piano style, this is clearly the strongest of Allison's three live recordings and stands out as a significant record in his discography. It is important to note that Allison is primarily a live performer who excels on stage but who has never felt completely comfortable recording in a studio, where the sterile, clinical environment, time and finances all limit his creativity. Because the performances during the live sets at In Your Ear come closer to capturing his style and its essence than any of his other work on record, this album is also one of Mose Allison's personal favorites. The only drawback to the 1972 recording is its lack of songs from the "personal crisis"/

"universal chant" category, although Allison's ruminating slow-drag rendition of the traditional "You Are My Sunshine" might qualify as such.

The songs Allison played during his In Your Ear sets have stood the test of time, most having been included in his repertoire for at least fifteen years. The performances on this recording find the singer in good voice as well as both technically fluent and artistically dynamic on the piano. The piano work demonstrates that Allison's modern style has finally reached maturity, and he renovates the older but ageless tunes, playing them with new panache, grace and excitement.

"I Don't Worry 'bout a Thing" and Johnny Fuller's "Fool's Paradise" are injected with faster tempos and right-hand trills, the mark of his later piano style. The Hank Williams classic, "Hey, Good Lookin'," the conventional prototype for Allison's "Your Molecular Structure," is added to the live repertoire, having first appeared on the Epic album *Takes to the Hills*, its interpretation heavy with Allison stylistic signatures in the piano accompaniment, with minor-second, smashed notes in the chord voicings, chords rhythmically displaced, and a piano solo indicative of Allison's innovative spirit. Duke Ellington's masterful "I Ain't Got Nothing But the Blues" enjoys a similar Allison facelift, its medium tempo and changes in the piano accompaniment, especially in the dramatic, animated eighth-note coda, providing a livelier rendition of the song that Allison first covered ten years earlier.

The most progressive piano enhancements of the songs are in Willie Dixon's blues "Seventh Son," recorded first in 1958 on his fourth Prestige album *Creek Bank*, the longest to remain in his repertoire, and two newer tunes, "Look What You Made Me Do" from Atlantic's 1968 release *Swingin' Machine* and the instrumental "Power House" from *Wildman on the Loose*, recorded first in 1965. The simple harmonic structures of these songs allow Allison to run rampant with color and texture on piano, and the Afro-Cuban groove facilitates his communication with the rhythm section, which is integral in his stretching out in his avant-garde style. Allison uses lengthy introductions and solos to integrate his fleshed-out ideas on piano. A fully independent left hand emerges, with fluid melodies and doubled octaves in the bass, chromatic melodies in the right hand, scale-like passages frequently voiced in parallel thirds and fourths which alternate with blocked chords voiced with the minor-second "smashed note" played in abrupt rhythms creating a rather maniacal, hammering effect. Chromatic passages in both chords and single-line melodies dominate in both treble and bass. Another idiosyncrasy is Allison's frequent use of the pedal to blur his ideas. At this juncture of his artistic evolution, Allison's novel, holistic, and frenzied approach to his piano playing has gained wide recognition, and critics have either embraced the new style as unique or rejected it as arcane, even as "a mad scientist experimenting with tinker toys."

Although extensive examples of the new piano style were absent on his eleventh and final recording for Atlantic, his poetic material was plentiful and vibrant. Four years had passed between records, the longest period of time that Allison had gone without releasing material, and Mose continued to resist record-company pressure as regarded his artistic direction. It appeared to the corporate mind that Allison was plunging even further into the deep end artistically, and that his sophisticated style and poetic aspirations had deleterious results on record sales. Atlantic executives did not view Allison's resistance favorably and the fledgling independent, which had now turned into a major label record company and had become part of the Warner Brothers Entertainment family, began to carefully scrutinize Allison's bottom line. Nevertheless, the company, now preoccupied with its rock-and-roll roster, put him in the studio in 1976 to record *Your Mind's on Vacation*, another seminal work which would be both a minor comeback and his final date for Atlantic Records.

At another artistic peak of his career, Mose Allison's last effort on Atlantic Records produced a performance full of renewed artistic confidence. His clear baritone, in a mature stage of vocal development, is in its fittest form, and Allison's perfect diction, and his laid-back, impassioned vocal delivery demonstrate that as a singer Mose Allison had never sounded better nor exuded such honesty as on this record. The recording combines his vocal prowess with the aggressive, multi-dimensional, colorful piano style which, at this juncture, had also evolved into maturity. Where *In Your Ear* had signaled the complete arrival of Allison's modern piano style, four years later, *Your Mind Is on Vacation* marks the complete assimilation of Mose's stylistic influences and establishes a style still intact today.

Your Mind Is on Vacation is also momentous in its artistic equilibrium; the mood and subject of the songs, the diversity of the orchestration and the superior level of the sidemen's musicianship make this a significant album in Allison's discography. Re-recording six tunes from his standard repertoire, adding two new covers, and four new originals, the song list combines enough old and new to engage old and attract new listeners. Of the new songs, three are "personal crisis"/"universal chants," one, "The Fires of Spring" inspired by Allison's profound interest in ethnic music. In fleshing out his songs, Mose employs the intimate trio format for some, adds horn parts to others, and features a lone solo tenor saxophone in just two tunes. Probably the strongest team Allison has assembled, the sideman line-up on the record is particularly noteworthy. His rhythm section of veteran Jack Hannah on bass and long-time colleague and friend Jerry Granelli on drums, have a firm grasp of Allison's style and songs, driving Allison's music forward while adding the requisite sensitivity, nuance and tone color to the older standards as well as to the poetic, more esoteric material. The horn section is no less talented in interpreting Allison's scores, and includes a combination of young and former Allison sidemen, the young alto saxophonist David Sanborn joining with trumpeter Al Porcino and tenor player Joe Farrell, whom Allison invited back after the *Hello There, Universe* dates. A highlight of the recording is the solo work of swing tenor great Al Cohn, who turns in a poignant performance on two swing-style covers that Allison mined from the jazz standard repertoire. The ironic lyrics in both songs, the Lawrence/Tinturin tune "I'm Just Foolin' Myself" and the

Robinson/Stanford tune "I Can't See For Lookin'," conform neatly to Allison's song criteria, and on the latter tune, the depth and warmth of Al Cohn's subtle tenor sax merges perfectly with Allison's relaxed vocal.

Alto saxophonist David Sanborn's ornate, poppish horn solos can be heard on Mose's new version of his "personal crisis" song, the blues tune "One of These Days." By 1976, Allison had altered the phrasing and dynamics of the tune, placing a fermata over the word "days" in the second phrase, using it as a centering tone to concentrate and reclaim audience attention. "Feel So Good," his classic in ambivalent lyrics, is also taken at a faster tempo and, thanks in large part to the impetus of the Hannah-Granelli rhythm section, receives its most musical delivery to date. Updated renditions of "slapstick" blues numbers "Your Molecular Structure," "Your Mind Is on Vacation" and "If You Only Knew," all set in Allison's Afro-Cuban groove, feature horn arrangements as well as the pianist's contemporary style, elongated piano introductions and flamboyant solos. Two tunes, the familiar "Swingin' Machine" and especially a new original "No Matter," boast piano solos with extensive improvisations on the tonic chord and best exemplify the pianist's contemporary approach. The latter song's improvisation section is closest to how Allison might treat the sustained tonic passages today, its parallel octaves and antiphonal melodies in both bass and treble, chords alternating with blurred sequential scale-like melodies in the higher register followed by rapid tremolos creating the effect of a bell ringing, characterizing the "hammering" style Allison favors on stage.

Three "personal crisis"/"universal chants" round off *Your Mind's on Vacation*. Mose poses another unanswered question in his doleful tune "What Do You Do After You've Ruined Your Life." The melancholic lyrics savor sadness as a natural impulse that seems to give moral guidance. In wrestling with the dilemma, he turns to an enigmatic twist in the Humphrey Bogart coda: "What do you do/Here's lookin' at you." In these songs, Allison's primary goal in his musical settings is to evoke the mood of the piece and here he accompanies the asymmetrical phrases of this blues-based melody with his trademark blocked sustained chords to emphasize the lyric. In this tune, however, the dynamics of the piano accompaniment are toned down and the vocal is heard unaccompanied in certain phrases. As with other songs in this category, Mose contrasts the sobriety of the verses with a louder, animated tag or bridging section.

"What Do You Do After You've Ruined Your Life"

What do you do after you've ruined your life
Where do you go, who do you know
That will give you anything to go with
Good advice
Do you tell your friends
Can you face your wife
What do you do after you've ruined your life

What do you do after you've blown the game
Cut down to size, no alibis
And you know that nothing's ever gonna
Be the same
Do you change your ways
Or just go down in flame
What do you do after you've blown the game

What do you do after you've been found out
No place to hide, no friendly guide
Who will lead you on your little psychic
Walkabout
Do you face the truth
In times when lies are rife
What do you do
Here's lookin at you
What do you do after you've ruined your life

Reminiscent of his cosmic hymn, "Hello There, Universe," the sentimental musical portrait "Perfect Moment" is Allison's ode to the beauty of nature. The frail simplicity of the phrase "sunset glow from a hill" and the metaphor "such a perfect moment, Mona Lisa smile" find the poet humbly grateful for natural wonders, seeing in them the reward and sustenance necessary to endure the tedium and tribulations of twentieth-century life. "Perfect Moment" is appropriately short and concise; its simple plaintive melody of short phrases comprises only a thirteen-bar verse. Played rubato, Allison accompanies the "universal chant" in his familiar fashion, blocked chords with shorter rhythms at phrase endings. In the short homophonic piano solo, Allison elegantly repeats the melody in the top voice, illuminating it with lavish sonorities underneath. The rhythm section of Hannah and Granelli excel in painting tone color on the romantic text and the lyrical piano solo. Jerry Granelli, who obviously understands tune, text and texture equally thoroughly, renders an exceptionally expressive and musical performance. He remembers:

> When Mose was hunting for the words for "Perfect Moment" he was looking for this one word to describe "valentine" and it took him months to find the right word, which turned out to be "miocene," a geological term pertaining to the epoch of the earth's development where mountains, apes and whales first appeared. He was looking for this one word to make the right rhyme and he looked everywhere, like in the Library of Congress. I've seen him wait months for the right words to songs or try words to see if they work.

Finally, one "universal chant" that has received little notice is the intriguing, exotic short piece "Fires of Spring," a chant-like tune that probably assisted Allison in coining the name for the song category. Several years before composing the tune, and about the same period that he had seriously undertaken his study and integration of twentieth-century classical music into his style, Mose had also developed an ardent interest in ethnomusicology. Listening to music from around the world altered his own musical frame of reference, and Allison began to discover the correlations between the music of his own background and the folk music from Eastern Europe and China as well as other countries. Early on, Allison openly voiced his well-researched opinion that every country celebrated its own form of blues:

> There's a world blues, you know. All societies have something akin to the blues. There's a universal lament that's interchangeable with country blues, and I'm real interested in that. Blues is just one of those basic ingredients.
> I'm interested in ethnic music and music from other cultures. I like to hear stuff from Asia, China or Africa. I went to a Chinese opera one time in San Francisco and there was an old guy who sounded just like Lightin' Hopkins to me. They were essentially singing blues harmonies. One of my daughters gave me a recording of the gamelan from Java that is like pure blues. There are people outdoors singing the blues and there are mostly string instruments accompanying. The major theme was being carried out by voices and underneath it and around it, there were xylophones and other instruments that were playing completely counter, which is exactly what is happening in jazz and modern music. So, I see that thread, that universal thread all over. I've seen it in the pentatonic, the five-note scale in Irish and Chinese music. It's all related. The music that's passed down, the so-called folk music, has a worldwide basic thread there. And I'm interested in that because that's the same reason I'm interested in the blues. That's what blues is.[2]

Mose based the mournful chant "Fires of Spring" on a Rumanian love song written by a widow grieving for her dead husband, a tune he believes he first heard on a Nonesuch/Folkways recording of folk songs from Eastern Europe. Inspired by the Rumanian folk melody, a pentatonic blues-like chant with a "wailing" motif, Allison altered little of the tune itself, writing new lyrics, composing the piano accompaniment and, for at least this version, adding horn arrangements. One of his most brilliant poems, "Fires of

Spring" combines cosmic themes from "Hello There, Universe" with the natural-wonder motif he created in "Perfect Moment." As with those poems, the metaphorical text in "Fires of Spring" elicits powerful images of pagan rituals and natural phenomena. The last verse broods with unknowing, resting on an existential premise, the resurgence of the fires of spring, its figurative last line presenting one of his most dramatic closures since "Parchman Farm."

Allison's tonal concept of the blues as neither major nor minor, but as weaving in and out of both, dictates the tonal framework in this piece, which commences as an E flat minor blues, but where G major becomes a tonal center as well. His piano accompaniment adheres to the pattern he has developed for these songs, with lush voicings for sustained chords that are played in shorter rhythms when the vocal line is sustained, offsetting the text. The chant here is again heard almost acapella, Allison singing the dramatic last line entirely alone, emphasizing the starkness of the image. The horns are effectively brought in as ornaments to the text on the last two verses, decorating words such as "galactic swirl," "rampaging sun" and "crucifying" with frenetic saxophone flurries. Otherwise, as he established in other songs, Allison arranges adjoining melodies for the horns, using them as fillers between phrases and verse.

"The Fires of Spring"

The fires of spring
Bring forth their wondrous light
Returning spring
The fires admiring
The spinning suns
Traverse the endless night
Each raging sun
In time expiring

Galactic swirl
Proceeding on your way
Fantastic swirl

Beyond decoding
The spinning suns
Bring back another day
Rampaging suns
In time exploding

No man can say
He's made the most of life
No man can tell
What comes with dying
The fires of spring
Remain the toast of life
Each man in time
A crucifying

Each man in time
A crucifying

Mose Allison comments:

> Someone said truth is associated with blows. It looks like you have to go through something bad to learn anything. In the process you try to come up with a comment that crystallizes your feelings about it. It forces you into new ways of thinking about yourself, a self-realization process. As long as you don't let it get you down, you can learn something.

12

STILL NO TOP FORTY RECORD

"One of the most memorable road things that happened when I was playing with Mose was when we were on a plane flying someplace out of Los Angeles. I guess this lady had seen the instruments and she came up to us on the plane and asked, 'Are you a band?' And Mose said, 'NO NO, we're not a band, no.' She said, 'Well, should I know you?' And Mose said, 'Ah, no, look, we're relatively obscure jazz figures.' Or sometimes we'd be in one of those situations where he'd just turn to me and say, 'Another humiliation . . . just to keep you humble, man, just to keep us humble'."

Jerry Granelli

"Middle Class White Boy"

I never did a damn thing my way
I wouldn't die for love
The only time I take control
Is when push comes to shove
I'm not your hootchie-cootchie man
I'm not the seventh son
Just another (little) middle-class white boy
Out tryin' to have some fun

I got myself some costumes
That scandalize my folks
The mountain man
The Fu Manchu

And the renegade cowpokes
And when I ride my motorbike
It's pure Attila the Hun
Just another (little) middle-class white boy
Out tryin' to have some fun

I'll never be a hero
Unless it's in disguise
I just want to do everything wrong
And still pick up first prize
I even got in trouble
And left town on the run
Just another (little) middle-class white boy
Out tryin' to have some fun

I got myself a brand-new name
A new religion too
I went halfway around the world
To find the right guru
When he tried to steal my girlfriend
The whole thing came undone
Just another middle-class white boy
Out tryin' to have some fun

Just another middle-class white boy
Out tryin' to have some fun

Mose Allison

An implacable Mose Allison continued to resist the mounting pressure put on him by Atlantic Records to commercialize his music. After the last recording session in 1976, and the disappointing sales performance of the album from those sessions, ironically one of his best, the company reiterated its suggestions that Mose should conform to the pop-music formula, this time in a louder and stronger voice. Up until that point, Allison had been successful in retaining creative control, deflecting Atlantic's proposals while hanging on to his recording contract. However, when he was approached with creative suggestions that would actually compromise his musical integrity, the addition of female back-up singers and the request to make a disco album when the style was *en vogue* during the late 1970s, Allison began seriously to doubt whether he had any artistic ideals in common with Atlantic's A&R department. With Warner Brothers Entertainment in control, Nesuhi Ertegun was no longer looking after Allison as he had in previous years, and as the power of his long-time ally and advocate diminished, Jerry Wexler assumed the helm of Atlantic A&R operations and took control of the label's roster. Wexler was a rock-and-roll mogul who had started the careers of many Atlantic recording stars, transforming raw talent into commercial commodity. From the outset, it was Wexler who recommended Allison's pop makeover, suggesting for instance that a Muscle Shoals sound might help Allison as it had other Atlantic artists. Although Wexler's position was understandable, given the financial and celebrity possibilities it conjured up, his suggestions exhibited no obvious sensitivity towards Mose Allison nor to the artistic purity of Allison's approach to his music.

An eloquent Jerry Wexler, on the other hand, heaps praise on Mose Allison, calling him "one of the greatest artists of the century, the incarnation of Southern reconstructive intelligent blues/funk . . . the William Faulkner of white funk and jazz . . . the Caucasian analog of Percy Mayfield." He further asserts that since Mose Allison was a cult artist with a small but devoted following, his contract was always a losing economic proposition for Atlantic Records. His company, Wexler insists, recorded Mose Allison "out of love" and "out of respect" for his work, not necessarily for financial gain: "The great mystery of the great Percy Mayfield is akin to the great mystery of the great Mose Allison."

Whether Allison's was in fact the case of a disgruntled artist who in record-company terms was "recounting the official heresy of the untouchable artist who believes the record company will dilute and commercialize his music" is a moot point. From the outset of his career, Allison had always stood by his artistic integrity and conscience, fiercely maintaining his position against commercialism. For fifteen years and eleven records on Atlantic, and before that on Columbia, he had resisted his record company's efforts to record his music differently. Atlantic may have kept him on the roster out of respect or as a status artist but, according to Allison, his records were not only not well received by the company, they were not supported.

Allison's relationship with Atlantic, which had never been good, began to deteriorate dramatically a few years prior to the release of *Your Mind's on Vacation* in 1976. In 1974, the *Chicago Reader* wrote: "Probably no more than 20,000 people ever owned the song ["Your Mind's On Vacation"], even though it's on two of his albums, and that's why Mose and, more accurately, Jerry Wexler and the company he represents, are now in the estranged-bedfellows category." Allison commented in the same article:

> Well, there's always problems with record companies, unless you're selling a million copies. If you're selling a lot of records, there's no problem. But I'm not selling a lot of records, so there's a problem.
>
> I think it's their fault I'm not selling more and they think it's my fault. I think it's because they're not promoting me, not spending any money, and they think it's because I won't do a record like they want, which is like, the kind of thing that sold last year.[1]

In a later interview, Mose expanded on this point:

> Atlantic offices around the country, a lot of them don't even know that I'm still with Atlantic. I go to a town a lot of times and people will call up and try to get a couple of albums from Atlantic and they won't even know I'm with them. That's happened in several places. So certainly I haven't gotten where I am as a result of record promotion. What I try to put across is that if I'm doing well with what I do, why can't they just record that and promote it? But they can't see it that way, you know. The idea is to persuade you to do what they think is most accessible based on what sold best last year. They have their assembly line, and they have

their routines and their charts and graphs from last year. We're going to make you into a star sort of thing. They're always trying to get you to do what they think is gonna be most successful, most commercial.[2]

The scenario to which Allison alluded in the *Chicago Reader* is a typical misfortune in the record industry and one which is certain to occur if an artist delivers a recording that fails to meet the acceptable criteria of an A&R department whose duty is to champion that record to the company infrastructure. Without A&R backing and direction from a higher corporate entity, it is improbable that the departments in the organization, promotion, marketing, sales and artist development, will support the artist's projects. Without the assistance of these vital departments, failure of an artist's record is almost always guaranteed, since the hefty financial support of each department generates sales. However, Allison did enjoy something of an advantage even throughout his falling out with his record company. Generally, when a record company determines a record is commercially unsatisfactory, it is never released to the public and the artist is finally dropped from the roster. At least in Mose Allison's case, the polarization of the creative differences between record company and artist notwithstanding, he stayed on the roster and his records made their way to the stores.

Interestingly, Atlantic consistently alleged that none of Allison's recordings had recouped; in other words, that all eleven of his albums, recorded and released in fifteen years, from 1962 to 1976, had been financial losses to the corporation. Thus, the celebrated blues and jazz man, once a status artist on the Atlantic jazz roster, had become a rather insignificant figure to the label and an increasing liability to the corporation. And, worst of all, as far as the label was concerned, Allison had often been perceived as an uncooperative artist, refusing to budge his position, adhering instead to his aesthetic dogma, when his pliancy could have resulted in both the record company and artist being better off financially. About the time of his serious disagreements over creative control, Allison also discovered that Atlantic had increased its monetary advances to its artists. In 1979, when Allison was due to deliver his next record, he argued for equal financial treatment. The company denied his request. At that juncture, Atlantic offered Allison an ultimatum, that he should accept his usual advance or elect to be released from his recording contract. With this financial squabble compounding the ongoing artistic disagreements, Mose Allison opted for the release. Atlantic readily complied.

The stalemate between Atlantic and Mose Allison was not in vain. Rather, Allison was inspired to write the perfect tongue-in-cheek jab at the record industry, an anthem for the struggling recording artist, a satire called "Top 40 Record": "When I make my top forty big beat rock and roll record/ Everything is gonna be just fine/When I make my top forty big beat rock and roll disc/I'll be the record company's valentine." Some fourteen years later, Mose finally recorded the tune with a big-band arrangement for his first Blue Note album, *Ever Since the World Ended*, a recording subsequently nominated for a Grammy award. British R&B/pop superstar Robert Palmer later covered "Top 40 Record."

Tom Dowd comments about Mose's situation with Atlantic:

> Jerry was the one who stayed home and was probably turning over readouts. By then we were probably a part of Warner Communications, by August of 1967 or '68, we were answering to another power. With that, you weren't a dilettante of the arts anymore but unfortunately, were responsible to the corporate readout thing. In the initial Mose concept, the corporate thing probably didn't fit. He was in that pocket where the record company could capture his thing at the time when it would turn heads but they didn't want to groom him into something he wasn't. They just wanted to get a bigger audience for him. Then, when the corporate thing hit, it was no longer up to Nesuhi or Jerry or any of us involved because someone was sitting up there at the end of the quarter knowing that he has an SEC examiner coming in and asking him his prognosis. He only sees a red line and doesn't even see the name of the artist. He might ask questions like, is he recording? If not, drop

him. Does he have a hit record? If not, then drop him. It's that cold and calculating—here is the guy who doesn't know the note on the staff from a bank note. It wasn't anything personal to Mose.

Freedom from Atlantic posed a new challenge for the aging hipster: securing a new record label. At first Allison thought he would be able to obtain a new record deal relatively quickly. But after 1978 was hailed as one of the most profitable years in the recording industry, 1979 followed as one of the most financially disastrous. One of his sidemen, drummer George Marsh, coined the phrase that a "record for a jazz player is nothing more than an expensive business card" and Allison believed it. But, as a veteran recording artist, he realized the importance of keeping current records in the stacks to keep his work viable and boost attendances at his live shows.

Allison therefore began to contact record companies, informing them of his free-agent status, but he soon realized that securing a new deal would take longer than he had imagined. A younger generation had taken over the industry. Mose recalls that his solicitations were often met by novice A&R staffers unfamiliar with his name and work. The legendary Allison, who had written the anthem of a generation in "Young Man Blues," found himself in the humiliating position of being asked to send demonstration tapes. Three years elapsed, six since he had released a record, but Mose, far from being acrimonious, simply proceeded with the career that he had always considered "on the job training"; he stayed out on the road and composed new material.

Fortunately, by 1981, one of Mose Allison's most ardent fans in the record business, the former Columbia Records senior executive Bruce Lundvall, founded a new jazz label under the auspices of Elektra/Warner Brothers called Elektra/ Musician. He immediately signed Allison to his new label, rescuing him from a second bout of record-company limbo. Lundvall released two solid Mose Allison records on Elektra/ Musician in the early 1980s. And, although the initial label was short-lived, Lundvall subsequently went on to preside over the prestigious jazz label Blue Note, taking Mose Allison with him for its roster.

Middle Class White Boy, released in 1982, marked Mose's debut on the new Elektra/Musician label. Recorded in Los Angeles, where he had recorded only one other date in 1968, *I've Been Doin' Some Thinkin'*, the album contained the new material Mose had accumulated while between record companies. However, as optimistic as Allison was about his new material and what he anticipated as an important record date, his own perception of the date was one of disappointment:

> In this case, I had played most of the material on the record in clubs for quite a while, at least a few months, which is something I hadn't done a lot before. In some of my earlier studio dates, I would be playing or singing tunes for practically the first time when I recorded them. At least here, I had the chance to work some of this material through. I had a few more songs to record but the album was done in about ten hours or less, so it was a pretty rushed-up affair.[3]

Esmond Edwards, noted for his work with Chuck Berry and jazz pianist Keith Jarrett, produced the sessions. Mose remembers that Edwards had worked at diverse jobs and was employed at Prestige Records while he was signed to that label. In fact, Edwards had photographed Allison for the album *Young Man Mose*. As a record producer, Edwards assembled an interesting jazz combo for the *Middle Class White Boy* dates; tenor saxophonist Joe Farrell, bassist Putter Smith and drummer John Dentz, who had accompanied Allison for several years and knew the repertoire for this recording. Two instruments appear for the first time with Allison, adding new color to Allison's music: conga, played by percussionist Ron Powell, and guitar, performed by jazzman Phil Upchurch, who achieves a bright tone on the instrument, creating a refined blend with Allison's deeper timbre on vocals and brighter piano.

Compared with his prior album *Your Mind Is on Vacation* and the live sessions recorded in Montreux a few months later for *Lessons in Living*, Mose's own piano work during the 1982 *Middle Class White Boy* sessions is reserved, attributable, perhaps in part, to the limitations of the electric piano he plays on this recording. Although it allows for technical proficiency, the instrument is incapable of providing the texture and subtlety of the acoustic model, muting the pianist's virtuosity. Allison had been experimenting with and playing on electric pianos since 1968, starting on the classic Fender Rhodes, and he had finally found an electric piano that played more like an acoustic, the Yamaha CP30. Here, although he plays the Yamaha, it produces a peculiar, unique plucked sound, an effect that Allison asserts was accidental, owing in part to equipment failures in the studio. Overall, the resulting sound is mixed and inconsistent, either intriguing and novel, or simply bland, depending on the tune. For example, where color is lacking in the Muddy Waters classic "Rolling Stone," the instrument compensates in achieving an innovative tenor to "How Does It Feel? (To Be Good Lookin')." Mose comments:

> Over the last few years, I've had occasion to play a Yamaha CP30 electric several times and it's my favorite among the electric pianos I tried. So, I started to tell people if they couldn't get a good acoustic piano for a one-nighter somewhere, to get a CP30 if they could. I liked the way it sounded and felt. It's a lighter touch and like a toy piano almost. It sustains notes and has a more uniform sound and plays more like a real piano. I wanted to use one on my new record date because some of those tunes I felt would sound better with a piano where you could have a long tone. I asked for a CP30 Yamaha and they got a long tone but they didn't get the amp to it, so they wanted to run it through the studio equipment. I don't know what happened, man, but the sound of that piano was a complete surprise to me as well as everybody else. All of the Yamaha CP30s I'd played over the years never even remotely sounded like the one I played on this record date. I guess a technician or

Yamaha person can tell you what happened. It's certainly different from what I expected.

Afterwards, I was worried that it was not going to come through on the tape, stand out enough. By that time, the people in the studio had decided, "Hey, this is a new sound we've got here." They were all enthused about it, so I decided to go along with it. It sounds like a banjo or a stringed instrument.[4]

The uptempo, almost rock-and-roll swing of "How Does It Feel to Be Good Lookin'" evokes the "1970s Me Era" through Allison's sarcasm and wry wit, transporting the song into the age of Ronald Reagan: "How does it feel to be good lookin'/To go around spreading that old sex appeal/Never any problem gettin' a bookin'/How does it feel? How does it feel to be born lucky/Always goin' to get the best of the deal/The world is just your rubber ducky/Born lucky/How does it feel?" With Upchurch's guitar filling in between phrases and verses, the chromatic chord changes in certain passages lend both a jazz and blues feeling to the spirited tune, and a certain panache to Mose's sophistication. Upchurch's lyrical guitar work also exudes a soulful blues and a seemingly flawless synchronization with Allison's urban take on Muddy Waters's "Rolling Stone." Mose first recorded the song in 1964 and it exudes newfound confidence nearly twenty years later, settling into the faster tempo on this recording.

"I Don't Want Much," first released in 1968, receives the same enthusiastic interpretation. With Mose on electric piano and Joe Farrell soloing on tenor, Allison updates the political reference on the second verse of the text: "I don't want much in this life/No special consideration/Just treat me like his majesty/Of a friendly OPEC nation."

Irony and ambivalence also characterize the lyrics of "I'm Nobody Today," written by Ron Creagh, and Allison's own "Kiddin' on the Square." Mose unearthed "I'm Nobody Today (but I was somebody last night)" from the country-music repertoire, its hard-living, barroom theme making the tune a 1980s version of Willie Dixon's "I Love the Life I Live" or Johnny Fuller's "Fool's Paradise": "It's the same old morning after/From the usual night before/Same old crowd of misfits/ Just hanging out trying to score/How can some folks lead the simple life/When I need city light/I'm nobody today/But I was somebody last night." Allison based his bluesy "Kiddin' on the Square" on a recurring colloquialism that he frequently uses in conversation; the inherent ambivalence and irony in the song hook also filters through the text: "I'm not yo' Prince Charming/You're not Juliet/Even if we break up/Not much to regret/You know I'm only kiddin'/Fightin' off despair/I'm only kiddin' you, babe/I'm kiddin' on the square."

Middle Class White Boy is not without Allison's traditional cover of a ballad, his practice in the Prestige and Columbia years. Although he focused more on his own compositions during his Atlantic years, he sporadically included songs from the country and popular-music repertoire, typically more obscure tunes that received little recognition. Duke Ellington/David Mack's "I'm Just a Lucky So and So" classifies for this genre, its relaxed phrasing and jazz swing harking back to the mood of an album like *Creek Bank*: "And when the day is through/I hurry to/A place where love waits I know/I guess I'm just a lucky so and so."

Mose designates the sentimental World War II ballad/ serenade "When My Dreamboat Comes Home" as his next "national anthem" or "rhapsodic mirage," a new song category he created in the 1980s. To qualify as this song type, the text must emote a fantasy-like truth in a concise lyric with strong literary overtones. He cites his own composition, "Everybody Cryin' Mercy," as his first national anthem, but Mose typically uncovers these gems he calls "rhapsodic mirages" from a large body of existing pop-tune standards. In "When My Dreamboat Comes Home," Allison switches to acoustic piano and sculpts the song in his own inimitable style, couching the delicate melody with underlying voluptuous blues sonorities in the piano accompaniment, illuminating the text in much the same fashion as he would one of his "universal chants." A double-time swing tempo on the second verse and various degrees of rhythmic and dynamic intensity and harmonic density tone paint the piece, changing the mood with the changes of rhythm and harmony. In what is clearly one of his most dynamic renditions of a cover, Mose savors his favorite song lyrics of the moment, "moonlit waters will sing," musically enveloping the literary image with thick, descending dense chords, trills and tremolos. He comments:

> The thing I like about "When My Dreamboat Comes Home," which is my current favorite for the national anthem, is that the song's harmony is like a bugle call. It's also the pervasive fantasy of all Americans. Everybody's waiting for the "Dreamboat," the big score or the big romantic thing, or something. The whole society is directed with that in mind. I think that fantasy keeps the whole United States going. There are also a couple of lines in there that I really like, for example "moonlit waters will sing" really tears me up. That's the whole romantic fantasy thing all wrapped up in one little line.[5]

"Hello There, Universe," a remake of the classic he recorded on Atlantic, enjoys a different interpretation on *Middle Class White Boy*. Departing from the horn-orchestrated version first heard in 1968, Allison swathes the piece in acoustic piano, subtle timbres in the rhythm section and a fluid flute part that realizes the intimate reverie without sacrificing texture, color and nuance. He remembers:

> I wasn't completely satisfied with the first version of "Hello There, Universe" with the horns. I didn't have a chance to play with the people on that record long enough to really get it the way I wanted it. The other reason I recorded it again is that I think it's one of my better songs, I get a lot of requests for it. The album it was on was like a complete mystery and didn't get around too much; hardly anybody heard the song. Also, I just really like the song and felt I could do a better job with it now. I wanted to do it scaled down with a small group. I liked the idea of a flute and I knew Joe Farrell was a good flute player.[6]

The satire "Back Down South" and folk/country standard

"Tennessee Waltz" return the middle-aged Allison to the themes of Southern culture and provincialism. His satirical "Back Down South," a blues bounce, is redolent with autobiographical references, fitting into the "public service" song category: "Well, I'm back down South/Where they smile and say hello/Then they look into your background/See if your family's got some dough." Mose offers an original take on the standard "Tennessee Waltz," playing it in 4/4 time instead of in traditional waltz tempo. He recalls: "I got the inspiration to do 'Back Down South' when I was in Austin, Texas. I was sitting in a motel down there looking out the window at the franchise ghetto which is all over now but had just recently gotten to the South."[7]

The self-effacing irony of the title track "Middle Class White Boy" was instantly recognized as classic Mose Allison. The lighthearted narrative resounds in Allisonian slapstick, replete with events, attitudes and real-life statements on pop culture. The self-deprecating text parodies the issue of race and class, the first time the lyricist has explored these two themes together. Performed in an uptempo bounce, with a musical feel and structure similar to "How Does It Feel to Be Good Lookin'," the electric piano and guitar enliven this first version of a song that is as identifiable to Mose Allison as his earlier chestnuts "Your Mind's on Vacation" or "Parchman Farm."

Mose acknowledged the popularity of his song "Middle Class White Boy" when he added it to his setlist at the Montreux Jazz Festival in Switzerland in July, 1982. Taping the show at Montreux was the idea of record-label president Bruce Lundvall and French producer Philippe Rault was enlisted to record the sessions. The performances were subsequently released as Mose Allison's second Elektra/Musician album, entitled *Lessons in Living*. Drummer Billy Cobham returns to the stage as Mose's sideman and another legend, this time from the world of rock and roll, former Cream bassist/vocalist, Jack Bruce, joins the Montreux trio. Although a proficient performance, capturing what Allison calls in his liner notes "the immediacy and excitement unique to the occasion," the Montreux live set is plagued by a clear lack of communication between Allison's formidable piano improvisations and his somewhat bewildered trio. Without the contribution of a knowledgeable rhythm section on the solos, the record falls short of what might have been a superlative live documentation of Mose Allison music. Obviously unprepared for the highly evolved pianist Mose Allison had become, Bruce and Cobham, through no fault of their own, approached the set in Switzerland without a rehearsal. Following the simplicity of Allison's song structures posed no problem for the two great players, but accompanying the current Allison is no small task. Allison's piano solos are intimidating and unpredictable for even the most experienced jazz sidemen, players who have accompanied him extensively. Of the two sidemen, Cobham had the obvious advantage of having recorded sessions with Allison some fifteen years earlier and he thus had some exposure to the repertoire and Allison's basic style; Jack Bruce, meanwhile, although a gifted bassist in his own right, with a solid background in jazz and blues, came to the stage with no firm idea of what to expect from Allison. Although putting forth their best efforts, the performers later expressed their disappointment with the results. The participants' own personal misgivings notwithstanding, *Lessons in Living* met with critical acclaim and was even nominated for a 1982 Grammy award.

The setlist from *Lessons in Living* is a Mose Allison "Best of" for the 1980s, a mélange of the standards in his repertoire, representing the peaks in his recording career. Saxophonist Lou Donaldson breaks up the monotony of the trio format, his gutsy horn solos highlighting the power of the Allison standards, particularly the blues "I Don't Worry 'bout a Thing." Blues guitarist Eric Gale also joins the set for "Nightclub" and "I Don't Worry 'bout a Thing."

Mose's impressive piano work in an up-to-date documentation of his improvisation style, is the outstanding ingredient of the album. Obviously, in some instances, the lack of rehearsal and experience with Allison's repertoire in the rhythm section appears to constrain Allison's solos. He does, however, aggressively work the twelve-bar blues and Afro-Cuban grooves of "Your Mind Is on Vacation," "Seventh

Son," and "I Don't Worry 'bout a Thing," performed as a conventional blues with sax and guitar, and on one of his variations on the blues "Wildman on the Loose." The more conservative Percy Mayfield tune "Lost Mind" also enjoys a more extended treatment in the piano solo while the twelve-bar blues "Nightclub," performed here in a type of New Orleans second-line shuffle, appears more constricted by the beat; his routine rendition set in the looser Afro-Cuban groove allows for an elaborate fleshing out in the solo.

Varying the set, Allison departs from the extensive soloing in other tunes. The tempo is slower in Allison's classic "Everybody's Cryin' Mercy" but the song is no less effective, a melancholy and stronger blues feeling saturating the tune. Conversely, the slower tempo in the line rendition of "Middle Class White Boy" finds Allison in the frustrating position of attempting to drive his rhythm section up to his speed. In another slow number, "You Are My Sunshine," Lou Donaldson's sultry solo in Allison's ballad version of the standard adds new dimension to the tune. The song receives an honorable response from the European audience, as does the familiar blues "I Don't Worry 'bout a Thing," where an appreciative crowd participates on the recording with steady hand-clapping. Mose comments:

> Sometimes when I do a song, I notice that people are sort of puzzled, sometimes for two or three years. Then, all of the sudden they'll start responding to it. So, either something has happened, or else I'm learning to put it over better or else something is happening in the interim that made them understand the song. That's happened with several songs. And some of the new ones I'm doing, they initially got that same reaction and now they're beginning to get across.
>
> People used to ask me about idioms in my tunes, like if they would be hard to transfer in foreign places. I would always respond that it took ten years before they started picking up on them here. I can remember I had been playing all over the country for maybe ten years and I played a job in Berkeley, California and for the first time in my life, I noticed that people were singing along. That was the first

time I ever had the feeling that it was coming through and people were picking up on it.

The Grammy award nomination and the enthusiastic audience response notwithstanding, Allison's set at Montreux was a somewhat unrepresentative example of the artist's live performances. It failed to capture a dynamic pianist whose singular style on the instrument was coming of age, the musician in Mose now comfortably merged with the mature songwriter.

13

ALMOST SUCCESSFUL

"There's a certain retrospective element in my recent songs. I'm going to continue to write songs about where I am rather than where I wish I was."

> Mose Allison

"Gettin' There"

People ask me questions
'bout the way I've spent my life
Thirty years in showbiz
Only had one wife
Limousines and swimming pools
I didn't get my share
But I'm not downhearted
I am not downhearted
I'm not downhearted
But, I'm gettin' there

Did you ever get the feeling
You've been taken for a ride
The big ones eat the little ones
And there's no place left to hide
Just don't drink the water
Try not to breathe the air
But I'm not discouraged
I am not discouraged
I'm not discouraged
But, I'm gettin' there

No matter how I'm feelin'
I still propose a toast
If you're almost successful
You're better off than most
If I was selling fantasy
I'd be a millionaire
But I'm not disillusioned
I am not disillusioned
I'm not disillusioned
But, I'm gettin' there

Mose Allison had weathered the storm of Atlantic Records and would also survive the demise of his most recent record label, Elektra/Musician, disbanded when his industry ally, Bruce Lundvall assumed the presidency of the prestigious jazz label of Capitol/EMI, Blue Note Records. Allison accompanied Lundvall to Blue Note but it was five years before the artist released a debut record on his new label. During this five-year respite, business went on as usual for the persevering Mose Allison; his usual "on-the-job training" involved constant touring and composing. Allison had last released new material on his 1982 salute to the bourgeoisie, *Middle Class White Boy*, so these five years proved productive for Allison as a songwriter, enabling him to add substantial and significant songs to his catalogue, pieces that showed signs of some shift in his thematic concerns.

In retrospect, if the Prestige and Columbia years are regarded as Mose Allison's first style period, Atlantic and Elektra/Musician his second, then the Blue Note years certainly chronicle on record Allison's third style period. Now on the verge of senior citizenship, he had finally grown into his philosophic-sage persona, personifying a species of avuncular hipness and earning a credibility that only advancing years can bring. In this style period, Allison's music dramatized a head-on confrontation with an inescapable aspect of his new reality: aging. Long regarded as a thematic taboo or else delivered in the shrink-wrapped mawkishness of a Frank Sinatra, this sensitive theme is treated with panache by Allison. He treats the subject with his classic wit and self-effacing humor, but his lyrics are firmly grounded in universal truths.

In 1987, as Mose Allison entered his thirty-seventh year in show business and celebrated his sixtieth birthday, he released his first Blue Note effort, his thirtieth album, *Ever Since the World Ended*. He achieves a cohesive, jazz-band flavor on this album, arranging unobtrusive parts for saxophones and guitar, instruments that have adapted well to his intimate, simpler style. He also provides space in his music for the virtuoso players accompanying him: Bob Malach, who alternates tenor and alto saxophone; tenor player Bennie Wallace; alto saxophonist Arthur Blythe; guitarist Kenny Burrell. Drummer Tom Whaley and Dennis Irwin on bass, his New York sidemen at the time, comprise the rhythm section for this date. Featuring a diversity of orchestrations, these outstanding sessions reveal that the subtle mélange of the cool emotionalism of jazz and the down-home realism of the blues which had always characterized Mose Allison's unique style, has matured gracefully along with the aging songwriter.

Two covers, "Josephine," and "Trouble in Mind," and an older original never before recorded, "Top Forty," composed some fifteen years earlier, aside, the material is new, crisp and quintessential Mose Allison. In keeping with his maturity, Allison's "slapstick", "personal crisis" and "public service" tunes on this album take on a nostalgia, even a sentimentality, rooted in the winter of life. Themes of aging predominate on *Ever Since the World Ended*, four of the album's ten songs, "Gettin' There," "Puttin' up with Me," "I'm Alive," and "I Looked in the Mirror" addressing sentiments or situations contemplated, in the main, in retrospection. As usual, however, Allison is keen to ensure that his themes remain generally applicable to all, transcending the narrow scope of age. Musically, Allison's song structures continue in the style of sophisticated composing he established in *Middle Class White Boy*. He embellishes the simple twelve-bar-blues form and variations of it with harmonic diversity as he demonstrated previously in songs like "Middle Class White Boy" and "How Does It Feel to Be Good Lookin'." Here, as well, he favors shorter harmonic rhythms and increased chromatic movement in the chord progressions, often lending ambiguous tonal centers to his tunes.

"Gettin' There" exemplifies Mose Allison's lyrical and musical objectives at this style period. Centering on the strong IV-I progression indigenous to the blues, the song begins in a type of tonal fluctuation, a first bar of chromatic chord progressions and a second of whole-tone movement ensuing before the song settles into the strong feeling of a blues in B flat. The subtle horn parts and an elaborate alto saxophone solo by Arthur Blythe round out the tune.

Lyrically, the autobiographical "Gettin' There" is the paradigm of Mose Allison's poetic ambivalence in his senior years. The inherent ambivalence in the concise hook, "I'm not discouraged but I'm getting there" also balances the theme of pessimism remaining in each verse. With phrases such as "if you're almost successful/you're better off than most" and "if I was selling fantasy/I'd be a millionaire," the song instantly became a Mose Allison classic.

"Puttin' up with Me," a self-deprecating blues ode to marriage, is written in the typical style of the "slapstick" love song of the elder Allison: "For so many years we have shared this bed/We grew up together after we were wed/We moved around the country from Maine to Tennessee/But I still can't forgive you for puttin' up with me." Recalling his cover of Muddy Waters's "Rolling Stone," Allison borrows from himself in the song's introductory vamp, slowing down the I-IV-I medium walking blues as the song's introduction. On the way out of the tune, Mose adds a descending chromatic twist on this variation of the blues.

Descending chromatic chord flourishes also characterize the song "I'm Alive." A contemporary version of the "personal crisis" tune that confronts the aging issue. "I'm Alive" also harks back musically to the "personal crisis" song of the 1960s and 1970s, commencing a capella in a rubato tempo with big, dramatic blocked chords subsequently answering the call of the lyric. Here, however, the song settles to a steady medium tempo and is unique in its use of backup vocals, being one of two songs where Allison harmonizes with his lead vocal on another track. The lyrics, although as profound, disturbing and resilient as the type of "personal crisis" tune Allison authored in the 1960s and 1970s, also contain the important element of slapstick, which in Allison's later years infiltrates virtually every new song: "I'm alive/Just survived a near disaster/Thought that I had met my master/Some folks think I'm jive/But I'm alive. I'm still here/I ain't had but one little cancer/Never thought I knew the answer/Bringing up the rear/I'm still here."

Another "personal crisis" tune, the nostalgic "I Looked in the Mirror," is a life flashback: "I looked in the mirror this morning/And what did I see?/Grey a plenty/Could be the reason I'm not getting any/I looked in the mirror today." The positive resolution in the dénouement appears autobiographical, particularly in the musical references, although the lyric is also the motto of any survivor: "One more look in the mirror/And on with the show/Believe I still got a way to go/Not too fast and not too slow/Mixing up the boogie with the do si do/I looked in the mirror today."

More overtly autobiographical, however, is the tune "Tai Chi Life." Allison is practiced in this ancient Chinese form of physical exercise and martial art, used for meditation as well as self-defense. Mose learned the Tai Chi positions to help him with his balance while in therapy after inner-ear surgery. More a jazz bounce than a blues variation, with well-crafted horn parts, the verses describe the state of being in Tai Chi and flow into each other without a break until Bennie Wallace's colorful tenor sax solo: "Gimme that Tai Chi life/With the gently flowing motion/For every move, the same devotion/Oriental magic potion/It's that Tai Chi life/My mind is in position/Place to place in smooth transition/You can even do your own rendition."

"What's Your Movie" was constructed around another recurring phrase that Allison had heard for several years. Posing a fundamental human question in the simple metaphor in the hook, "what's your movie," Allison assumes that since all people aspire to grandiose ideas of social purpose and relevance, each should be able to define his or her role. In attempting to separate fact from fantasy, reality from self-deception, Allison's lyrics continue in suggesting a few prototype roles: "What's your movie/Are you playing the Talk of the Town/The prince who gave up a crown/Or are you standing up singing as the ship goes down/What's your movie?"

Of all the songs in Allison's repertoire, "What's Your Movie" is undoubtedly the most chromatic, the underlying piano accompaniment to the lyric hook forged from a descending chromatic melodic phrase. Both hooks, the chromatic line in the piano and the song phrase, make the tune instantly memorable. Guitarist Kenny Burrell handles the chromaticism with ease, spinning a lyrical solo out of the simple progression.

Allison's two covers for this date are the Great Depression favorite "Josephine," written by Gus Kahn, Wayne King and Birk Bivens, and a favorite tune, Richard M. Jones's "Trouble in Mind." A third, "Tumblin' Tumbleweed," whose lyrics typify the retrospection theme in Allison's newer approach, was popularized by Bob Nolan and the Sons of the Pioneers and by Roy Rogers. It appears as a bonus track only on the compact-disc version of *Ever Since the World Ended*.

Mose comments on the 1930's chestnut "Josephine,":

One of my favorite things is to find an old tune that I get something out of. These tunes usually represent the "rhapsodic mirage" which is one of the main things in American culture—all the love songs. I do these songs as a sort of counter to the tunes that I myself would write, which are a little more tortured.

These songs sort of come to me; they're buried there. They're usually something that I've had in there all along. "Josephine" is a song that I used to hear as a kid in Mississippi. It was a hit in the 1930s and one of those tunes that you heard everywhere you went for a couple of years.

Mose Allison's thirtieth solo album would not be complete without a classic blues and Mose recorded a contemporary version of "Trouble in Mind." Allison's first rendition of the tune was for solo trumpet, but his update offers a gritty vocal.

Horn arrangements flesh out the medium-tempo blues, the airy, loose tenor of Bennie Wallace and lucid lines of Bob Malach surrounding a chromatic walking bass line midway through the tune. Mose continues to includes this version in his live repertoire and adds his own coda, a final comical throwaway line: "I ain't no fool" which responds to Jones's last line: "And when I hear that whistle blowing/You know I'm going to jump right back."

The clever, highbrow sarcasm in Allison's 1970s "slapstick" satire on the record industry, "Top Forty," reverberates with relevance today: "When I make my top forty, big beat rock and roll record, everything is gonna be just fine." Originally penned as a professional rebuttal to the querulous A&R department at Altantic Records, this gem is set in a jazzband-style horn arrangement which conjures up a suitable mood for the text. R&B/pop icon Robert Palmer was inspired to cover this tune on his first release on EMI records, *Aeroplane*. Mose recalls:

> I wrote "Top Forty" in the late sixties and never did it because I thought it was a little too cute. Then I decided to use it because I had too many slow songs and needed a bouncy song on this record date. The chord progression is perfect for two horns. The way the chords move, it's easy to write two-part harmony for horns and it's excellent for good players to play on.

"Top Forty (Big Beat, Rock and Roll Record)"

When I make my top forty, big beat rock and roll record
    everything is gonna be just fine
When I make my top forty big beat rock and roll disc
    I'll be the record company's valentine
No more philosophic melancholia, eight hundred pounds
    of electric genitalia
When I make my top forty, big beat rock and roll record
    everything is gonna be just fine

When I make my fuzz tone, wah wah, synthesized record
    everything is gonna be just grand

When I make my fuzz tone, wah wah, synthesized disc
    I'll have to get myself a moving van
Costume, hairdo, made up cute
    A personal connection in a business suit
When I make my fuzz tone, wah wah synthesized record
    everything is gonna be just grand.

When I make my dynamite, heavy soul, freaked out record
    everything is gonna be just swell
When I make my dynamite, heavy soul, freaked out disc,
    I'll be living it up pell mell
Mountaintop hideaway, three-car garage, out there
    hustling that sonic massage
When I make my top forty, big beat, heavy soul, solid gold,
    freaked out, synthesized, rock and roll record
Everything is gonna be just fine

    Finally, the eponymous track, "Ever Since the World Ended" is perhaps one of Mose Allison's two literary masterpieces of the decade. Harking back to the social commentary of "Everybody Cryin' Mercy," and reminiscent of the introspective, spiritual and science-fiction themes of "Hello There, Universe," Allison imbues this end-of-the-millennium "public service" tune with allegory, metaphor and phlegmatic emotion. In the song, Mose again reveals his remarkable gift for social critique. He treats the horrifying truth of the apocalypse in a typically offhand, deadpan manner, and describes life without the world as we know it with disturbing clarity.
    Allison's vocal delivery, in his cool, conversational matter-of-fact style cements the message of the poem. A blues variation, the rubato tempo on the first verse of "Ever Since the World Ended" with solo piano accompaniment, sets up the lyric, yielding to horn arrangements on the additional verses. Saxophone solos add contrast and diversity to the song; alto player Arthur Blythe lends a blues feel, while Bennie Wallace's interpretation of the tune is enunciated in angular and disjointed lines. A dramatic coda, with blocked chords in

piano and horn, sets up Allison's punchline: "Ever since the world ended, I face the future with a smile."

"Ever Since the World Ended"

Ever since the world ended
I don't go out as much
People that I once befriended
Just don't bother to stay in touch
Things that used to seem so splendid
Don't really matter today
It's just as well the world ended
It wasn't working anyway

Ever since the world ended
There's no more bible belt
Remember how we all pretended
Going round lyin' about the way we felt
Every rule has been amended
There's no one keeping score
It's just as well the world ended
We couldn't have taken much more

Ever since the world ended
There's no more black or white
Ever since we all got blended
There's no more reason to fuss and fight
Dogmas that we once defended
No longer seem worthwhile
Ever since the world ended
I face the future with a smile.

Mose Allison remembers:

I got the idea for "Ever Since the World Ended" when a few years ago all of the planets lined up and the astrologists were saying something was going to happen. When it happened and there were no recognizable after-effects, everybody sort of laughed it off. The thing I thought of was, what if the world really did end then and we just don't know it? What if something happened then that we won't find out about for another few years? What if that was the beginning of it? That's what gave me the idea, that the world may have ended that day but we don't even know about it. We'll find out later.

Altogether, *Ever Since the World Ended* provides further testimony to Allison's unique talent as a songwriter, vocalist and arranger. With a wealth of strong new songs, these sessions also showcase Allison's ability to drench his compositions in the appropriate texture and tone color. His style as an arranger is less distracting and glaring than on previous recordings, the horn parts flowing organically from the melody, commenting and collaborating rather than simply ornamenting. Allison also stands out as a singer on this album, his solid vocal deliveries evidence that age has added charm rather than diminishing his prowess. Although the weathered baritone appears to stumble on certain phrases, it is not as much a problem with intonation as with a gravel throat, no doubt a by-product of his mature years. This quality adds a new genuineness and character to his singing, particularly on the one note that closes the album. Allison's finish to "I'm Alive" is typically ironic; as he reaches to his falsetto for the final note, his voice struggles for a moment, cracking through the break in his voice to the higher octave. He then surmounts the hesitation with relative ease, proceeding to the high note on the word "alive" perfectly in tune.

If *Ever Since the World Ended* falters in one critical area, it is in the fact that Allison's unique and flamboyant piano style is completely absent from it. There is simply no outlet for Allison's leggy piano work to stretch out on this material, since each song is a succinct, self-contained unit that can accommodate only concise post-bop-style solos, recalling those of his Prestige years. The reason behind this omission could have been the economics and political mechanics of the record date itself. Along with time constraints in the studio, Allison is also conscious of the star quality of his sidemen and so, providing the horns with the opportunity to play makes good musical and economical sense.

Conversely, no doubt Mose Allison cognoscenti were disappointed with his subdued piano work on *Ever Since the World Ended*. With not one solo exhibiting the colorful piano style which is now synonymous with Mose Allison, the Blue Note recording sharply contrasts with Mose's previous three records, which emphasized this facet of his music. Nevertheless, it should be noted that *Ever Since the World Ended* had great commercial appeal; indeed Allison was deservedly nominated for a Grammy award in the Best Jazz Vocalist (Male) category for the record in 1987, an accolade which he almost won, losing in the end to jazz singer Bobby McFerrin. The record is also important in that several of the tunes from it quickly escaped the sterility of the recording studio, making a successful transition into his live-performance repertoire, these including "Gettin' There," "What's Your Movie," "Josephine" and "Ever Since the World Ended."

My Backyard, recorded in December 1989 and released in 1990, is as close to a "concept record" as Allison has come. Not bewitched by the Muscle Shoals or Memphis sounds when they were fashionable during his Atlantic years, Allison was encouraged to record the date in New Orleans after a conversation with the record's producer, jazzman Ben Sidran, who also successfully oversaw Mose's debut on Blue Note. Allison and Sidran went to the "Big Easy" to capitalize on the talents of some extraordinary native musicians, interested in particular by the work of New Orleans drummer John Vidacovich, whose free-form playing synchronized with the shuffle feel in Allison's music. Bassist Bill Huntington, guitarist Steve Masakowski and tenor saxophonist Tony Dagradi, other sidemen on the date, are no less sympathetic to Allison, and in their own right enjoy legendary reputations in the New Orleans region. As natives, their innate sensibility to the New Orleans musical tradition created a distinct dynamic in the recording studio. Thanks to the talent on this recording, as with its predecessor and to some extent *Middle Class White Boy*, the results are very much a joint musical venture between Allison and his sidemen.

The opening track, "Ever Since I Stole the Blues," features Masakowski's smooth phrasing on guitar, weaving throughout the blues variation whose introductory vamp, recalling "Puttin' up with Me," has become an instantly recognizable Allison stylistic trait. An outstanding satirical "slapstick" from Allison's later repertoire, the song's lyrics continue his "ever since" motif. He explains that he was inspired to write the tune as a musical retort to a British interviewer:

> "Ever Since I Stole the Blues" came from an interview in London where the lady asked me if I ever had any problems when I was stealing black music. When she said that, I got this vision of what would really happen if somebody stole the blues in the 1940s. There wouldn't have been any Muddy Waters. There wouldn't have been any blues revival in England—they would have been broke by now. Anyhow, I thought the whole idea was kind of funny and sort of like a fantasy. After the original mirage, it was easy to write; I wrote it out in about thirty minutes. I was trying to decide whether to get indignant or not, but that idea about stealing the blues has been around so long and it's part of what I do. It always has been and it always will be. So, I think I told her I'm not a black impersonator, there's plenty of those right here in London. At first, I thought I was joking. But, a lot of times when I say something like that, it turns into a song, like "Middle Class White Boy" and "Kiddin' on the Square."

"The Gettin' Paid Waltz," like his earlier "Nightclub," parodies the routine of a musician's life. Here, Mose satirizes the common situation of trying to collect his share of the night's takings when the club is about to close, a standard practice in playing club gigs: "I'm doing the gettin' paid waltz/I'm doing the gettin' paid waltz/All night long he was hanging around/Now that I need him he's not to be found/All of the people are homeward bound/And I'm doing the gettin' paid waltz." Written in an uptempo blues waltz swing, the song features Vidacovich's drums, which are clearly the musical focal point of the piece, his loose groove allowing both Allison's piano vocals and Dagradi's tenor to play around and against his shuffle time.

"Big Brother" focuses again on Vidacovich's virtuosity, this time showcasing his rendition of the classic New Orleans "second line" beat, the dance groove associated most frequently with the black funeral processions or the parades, such as those on Mardi Gras in particular, where the marchers dance following the band procession. The second line beat notwithstanding, the entire tune illustrates the magical musical personality of New Orleans. Allison's comping in the New Orleans style of delayed back phrasing combines with the halting phrasing of Dagradi's tenor, which has a squawking timbre. Allison's vocals are not lost in the dense texture of the instruments; rather, he imparts a serious message in the simple blues. Composed years earlier and revived for this second date, "Big Brother" has an important Orwellian theme, with science-fiction and social-commentary overtones: "Just let me give you some good advice/Don't get caught in the same trap twice/Every little thing you do/Big Brother is watching you."

Another social commentary, the literary blues "Dr. Jekyll and Mr. Hyde," addresses the fundamental theme that Allison posed in "What's Your Movie," regarding human purpose and life roles. Here, however, Allison uses the literary allusion to Robert Louis Stevenson's fictional character, Dr. Jekyll and his alter ego Mr. Hyde, and the cinematic reference to Spencer Tracy (who famously played the role in 1941), to beg the question in his lyric. The text depicts the two faces of human beings, the good, desiring to save the world, and the evil, self-serving philistine:

"Am I trying to serve the human race
Or am I just along for the ride
I guess I'm just a classic case of
Dr. Jekyll and Mr. Hyde
Do I show my concern for the needy
For the folks who are living outside
Or am I just plain greedy
Dr. Jekyll and Mr. Hyde

Am I seeking a new morality
Or am I just self-satisfied
Welcome to reality
Dr. Jekyll and Mr Hyde."

Mose comments:

> Everybody has in them the desire to be or the fantasy of being socially relevant, to try to better things and make a positive contribution. It takes some people a while to get down to it. I'm officially a senior citizen now and I've been through a lot of phases. I believe that everybody, whether they realize it or not, would like to save the world and have a lot of fun. That line in Dr. Jekyll and Mr. Hyde "am I trying to serve the human race or am I here for the ride" relates to that idea.

Mose performs four cover songs on *My Backyard*, all blues of the sophisticated variety, or blues-based jazz tunes. A buoyant version of a favorite blues standard, Richard M. Jones's "That's Your Red Wagon," features Steve Masakowski's sanguine guitar filling in between vocal phrases and stretching out in a blues solo, a genre which is clearly the guitarist's forte. Allison's piano solo is more avant-garde in this selection, departing from the constriction imposed by most of the tunes.

The simple, straight twelve-bar blues, "Stranger in My Own Hometown," also facilitates Allison's elaborate soloing on piano. Written by one of Mose's singing heroes, Louisiana bluesman Percy Mayfield, the text has autobiographical overtones for the Mississippi singer and enunciates a theme popularized by another Southern writer, author Thomas Wolfe, in his novel *You Can't Go Home Again*.

Mose rewrote part of the text to John D. Loudermilk's farcical blues-based "You Call It Joggin'," a wry "slapstick" on an extramarital affair. Its twin subjects, adultery and physical fitness, spun together in an ironic, humorous narrative, instantly catapulted this tune into the standard Mose Allison repertoire as an audience favorite: "You say it's the best release that you ever found/You say that you're trying to lose weight but you ain't lost a pound/While you're out there with your friend/I'm home feeding the kids again/You call it jogging/But I call it running around."

"Sleepy Lagoon," Allison's selection for the album's "rhapsodic mirage," closes the first side of the album (LP) and the CD of *My Backyard*. The song, popularized by Harry James and by singers Vaughn Monroe and Dinan Shore during World War II, includes all the essential elements of Allison's musical and lyrical criteria for the sub-genre, the romantic fantasy in Jack Lawrence's popular song lyric: "Sleepy lagoon, a tropical moon and two on an island/A sleepy lagoon and two hearts in tune in some lullaby land/The fireflies gleam, reflects in the stream/They sparkle and shimmer/A star from on high/Falls out of the sky and slowly grows dimmer." Allison explains the song's appeal:

> The "rhapsodic mirages" have good changes and lend themselves well to improvisation. Sometimes I do change the phrase to get it into the shape I want it in. In view of the way things are today, I enjoy the irony of the lyric and almost break up laughing everytime I do it. "When My Dreamboat Comes Home" is the same thing. "Sleepy Lagoon" was a popular song, and even though it's considered obscure here, in England somebody's been using it as a theme song for a program over there ["Desert Island Discs"] for thirty years. In England they couldn't understand why the reviewers consider it an obscure song.

In "Long Song" Allison parodies the sentimentality in the archetypal love song, referencing trite clichés found in many Broadway and movie-theme lyrics: "I'll have to come up with a line or two/On how I just can't go on without you/Or maybe that ole stand-by/I'm gonna love you till the day I die/If that ain't long enough/I may have to forget all that stuff/And tell them how you did me wrong/What this show needs is a long song." Here, Vidacovich once again lends a second line feel to this blues, and a musical quote from Allison's "What's Your Movie," the descending chromatic hook in the accompaniment, filters in by way of the tenor-saxophone line.

Saxophone solos also add contrasting tone color and texture to the album's title track, the introspective "My Backyard" and the self-analytical "Sentimental Fool." The two songs have thematic similarities in their texts, both being written in a loose type of the "personal crisis" tune, their contemplative lyrics culminating in a personal truth or reality. "Sentimental Fool" is the more relaxed with its colloquialisms: "I fooled around and got to feeling good/I was considerably misunderstood/I had my doubts about brotherhood/I didn't know if I still could/I have fooled around and got to feelin' good." The lyrics in his reverie, "My Backyard," are more pensive and self-effacing, recalling the ambiance and emphasis on nature in "Perfect Moment": "My backyard is a feature/Where a creature like me/Can have a look see/At the trees in the wind/. . . My backyard in the moonlight/A buffoon might relax/Dispense with wisecracks/Start over again."

"Was," a poignant ballad that closes the album, has yet to be recognized as this album's standout and, more generally, as a Mose Allison masterpiece. The poem deals with the sensitive subject of death, too often treated with maudlin texts. Instead, as he contemplates the state of non-existence, Allison again assumes the role of droll raconteur. His clever word choices, metaphors and imagery elicit a nostalgia and grace that elevate the text close to poetic genius in the jazz songwriting genre. Crafting a simple song around this profound text, Allison creates a memorable melody unlike any he had heretofore produced, and uses chord changes that resemble those of a standard jazz ballad rather than the blues or a variation thereof. In fact, "Was" could almost be considered something of an anomaly in Mose Allison's catalog, his songwriting here almost reminiscent of the Rodgers and Hammerstein tradition. Dagradi's saxophone helps to evoke the mood as well, as he turns from the squawking timbre and aggressive phrasing that characterized much of his playing on the album to a beautiful legato lyricism. The final verse features a stunning duet of vocal line and saxophone, documenting some of the finest music Mose Allison has recorded to date.

"Was"

When I become was
And we become were
Will there be any sign or a trace
Of the lovely contour of your face
And will there be someone around
With essentially my kind of sound

When am turns to was
And now is back when
Will someone have moments like this
Moments of unspoken bliss
And will there be heroes and saints
Or just a dark new age of complaints

When I become was
And we become were
Will there be any Susans and Ralphs
Looking at old photographs
And wondering aloud to a friend
What was it like to be then

Mose Allison remembers:

I had the idea for the first verse of "Was" for a long time, several years. I didn't think I'd make a song out of it. Then, several years later, I got the idea for the next two verses and started playing it at home. I thought it was kind of lugubrious and odd for what I normally do. I don't know where the melody came from; it's probably an old Irish folk tune or something. I'm sure there's a song like that in folklore somewhere.

14

TOWARDS A PIANO STYLE

"One day Mose Allison the songwriter and Mose Allison the singer got together and said, 'If we got rid of this piano player we could make some money.' Then the piano player says, 'Yeah, but neither of you guys would even be around it if wasn't for me.'"[1]

"I think that if a person's got any talent for it or any capacity for doing it, he can make it if he can put things together in a way that gives an illusion of originality. In fact, sometimes when people ask me what I am, I say I'm an illusionist because I create an illusion of originality by putting things together in a way that haven't been done exactly in that way before.

"What I do is a conglomeration of everything. But I have the stigma of being a jazz player. That's one of the ways I've been cubbyholed. I was always regarded by everybody as a jazz player *except* by the jazz establishment.

"I don't think all of this is as complicated as people like to make it. I see what I do as the New Orleans tradition, an ironic realism, as opposed to the old romantic myths."

Mose Allison

"Who's In Who's Out"

Who's in, who's out,
Who's gonna tell us what it's all about
Who's hot, who's not
Who's really happy 'bout what they got

Let's all get excited
About th' party to which we're uninvited
Who's out, who's in
Who's real now and who has been

Who's hot, who's cold
Who's turning garbage into gold
Let's all go play hide and seek
Here's to the victim of the week

Who's neat, who's yuck
Who's in the fast lane pressing their luck
Who's real, who's jive
Who is the sexiest thing alive
Tell me what they're wearing
Whose outfit is the most daring

Who's thin, who's fat
Who's gonna raise your thermostat
Who's cool, who's not,
Who went to bed with a bigshot
Who needs better things to do
Could be me, and it could be you

Mose Allison

The duality of Mose Allison, the downhome blues singer/Will Rogers-style wordsmith and sophisticated jazz pianist, has been evident since 1957's *Back Country Suite* and has remained a stylistic enigma over the years. Initially celebrated predominantly as a jazz pianist who subtly fused elements of the post-bepop tradition with the blues, Allison's stature as a pianist was gradually overshadowed by his accomplishments as a unique songwriter and colorful vocal stylist. He nevertheless concentrated on developing a singular artistry on piano, assimilating stylistic traits of twentieth-century piano literature and ethnic music into his distinctive approach to blues and jazz.

As with his songs, economy and clarity characterized Allison's earliest piano work. Primarily versed in the swing school as a player, he drew his influences from a diverse group, citing pianists such as Nat Cole, Erroll Garner, and Al Haig, saxophonist Lester Young and trumpeter Louis Armstrong as formulative in his early style. While maintaining his swing sensibilities, Mose Allison defined his overall musical approach as first and foremost cast in the New Orleans tradition, a type of "boogie-woogie," laying claim to what he terms "the neo-New Orleans classic jazz style." He describes this as a "type of free-form funk with rhythmic bounce and buoyancy, where playing behind the beat or pushing it ahead a little, dictates the sensibility of the music." He expands on this:

> The traditional New Orleans style messed with the time. They played behind and ahead of time. This is a traditional element and people can take it further, as long as they don't take it too far. The idea is to achieve a balance between novelty and tradition. I always like to preserve the rhythmic shuffle; that's the basic ingredient. Everything else I do is put on top of it but not to the point of overloading or disrupting it. I heard one great jazz player, Max Roach, say, "The thing about jazz is the way you play a quarter note."

Allison merged the rhythmic spirit of the New Orleans style with the form and tonality of its exotic musical neighbor, the blues. Later, he blended Southern exuberance with the modern piano school, adding ingredients of the moderns, Bud Powell and Lennie Tristano. Particularly in Tristano, Allison discovered a significant role model who inspired his attitude towards a fresh approach to the instrument. A lesser-known pianist by commercial standards, Tristano was a jazz pedagogue, a musician's musician who had successfully merged music from the concert hall with jazz-piano style. Allison considered Lennie Tristano one of the founders of modern jazz piano and commented in 1967 in *Crescendo* magazine:

The one who has had the most results so far in integrating the techniques and devices of academic music is Lennie Tristano. He still plays "Melancholy Baby" but he applies all the most advanced concepts of counter-melody and everything. It's as modern as you can get and still has the basic qualities. Lennie hasn't had as much effect on people as Bud has, but he's just as important as an innovator.[2]

Mose Allison had laid the groundwork in his style for the musical evolution that would take place. Before arriving on the New York jazz scene in the late 1950s, he built solid credentials on the road in the South, his experience accompanying horn players on piano yielding skills in both comping and soloing. His Southern-swing approach to the groove, combined with the modern technique and a talent for spinning a simple melodious solo line, made him a sought-after sideman for many jazz stars of the time, such as Stan Getz, Al Cohn, Zoot Sims and Chet Baker. Although Allison's solo debut *Back Country Suite* established him as an artist in his own right, he continued as an accompanist on many recordings throughout the 1950s and early 1960s, valuable work which assisted in developing his artistry and provided financial security for the father of four.

Allison's trio albums on the Prestige and Columbia labels and at least his first three Atlantic records were marked by a conservative approach to the piano. A more intrepid departure in style appears at an embryonic stage on the 1959 Columbia masterpiece *The Transfiguration of Hiram Brown*, which audibly foreshadowed Allison's predilection for the music of the twentieth-century piano repertoire. Drawn to this genre while a student at Louisiana State University in Baton Rouge about the time he composed *Back Country Suite*, the distinctive stylistic elements of the twentieth-century piano school emerged years later in Allison's musical vocabulary when, stifled creatively by the trappings of his post-bebop style, he deliberately sought new vistas in his piano playing. The evolution of Allison's piano style was thus organic and gradual.

By 1965, however, Mose Allison's piano style had turned a radical corner. His live sessions recorded at the nightclub the Lighthouse in Hermosa Beach, California, revealed a pianist navigating into uncharted musical territory. Allison's piano on *Mose Alive!* evidenced a stylistic metamorphosis, with dramatic and frequent departures from the clean-cut style that had initially defined his artistic persona. Subsequent recordings throughout the mid-1960s and 1970s, such as 1966's *Wild Man on the Loose*, and 1968's *I've Been Doin' Some Thinkin'* delved deeper stylistically, often featuring an unbridled pianist confidently reigning over the full range of the instrument.

On his crusade for greater color and artistic expression, Allison's passion for the blues had also spawned an interest in ethnic music. He renewed his fascination with folk music, acquiring recordings, listening to radio broadcasts and sometimes attending concerts by musicians from other countries. Allison often commented on the blues echoes he heard in this music from around the world and he would categorize music simply, asserting semi-facetiously that what was not either Bach or Schoenberg must be the blues.

The Baroque school of J.S. Bach and the esoteric twelve-tone serialism of Arnold Schoenberg were significant musical models for Allison but stylistically not as accessible technically nor, perhaps, artistically, as the body of work from the twentieth-century piano repertoire, and so the notion that Mose Allison would turn to "serious music" for creative inspiration was unsurprising. While Allison's jazz colleagues delved into the avant-garde and free-form approach for new expression, Allison returned to what was familiar. In the works of Béla Bartók, who merged folk motifs with contemporary sonorities, Allison had heard his own musical voice as a college student. Enrolled in a music course at LSU, Allison heard Bartók's piano suite Hungarian Sketches, which directly inspired his *Back Country Suite*. A threshold composer, it made perfect sense to explore the music of Bartók's contemporaries, bearing in mind that Allison was naturally inquisitive about the music itself and was simultaneously searching to incorporate new, meaningful ideas into his artistry. Mose himself comments:

> I guess I went backwards in my listening. I started listening to the contemporary people, went through the Romantic era and then to the Baroque as far as listening to classical music goes. I like all sorts of music, but at this point, I can listen to Bach all day long. I get the most pleasure out of those composers who know the modern stuff but who are also melodic. For example, in one of Prokofiev's sonatas, he used what sounded like drinking songs. Bartók also used something like drinking songs in his Concerto for Orchestra. What I like are people who combine the modern techniques with the basic, universal melodic ideas.

Apart from Béla Bartók, Mose Allison's record collection included the piano concertos and sonatas of two Russian composers, Sergei Prokofiev (whose compositions were pivotal and considered neo-classical, bridging the Romantic period and the twentieth century) and the less celebrated Alexander Scriabin. The piano sonata of American Samuel Barber, a composer most recognized for his contributions to the vocal-music and orchestral repertoires, and the piano works of another American, Carl Ruggles, were also influential. The two guiding musical forces that precipitated the most dramatic stylistic changes, however, were the German composer/musicologist Paul Hindemith and the idiosyncratic New Englander Charles Ives.

Like Mose Allison, Charles Ives was a stylistic enigma who drew ideas from the American musical landscape indigenous to him. A quirky, opinionated and controversial composer, his musical voice personified New England, quoting motifs from the Protestant hymns, anthems, and folk songs which he heard growing up in Connecticut. The son of a Civil War bandleader, as a youth Ives also marvelled at the polyphony and polyrhythms he heard in parading marching bands. Eventually, he mastered these techniques, found strewn throughout his compositions, works which he wrote primarily for orchestra, chamber ensembles, and the voice.

Interestingly, Ives was also isolated from the American musical mainstream, which may have contributed to his fiercely independent musical spirit and unique compositional style. Although he had majored in musical composition at Yale University, where his teacher, Horatio Parker, was horrified at his originality, Ives's family had insisted music was an "emasculated endeavor," and he was pressed to enter the insurance field, where he became an executive and a millionaire. Thus Ives composed only on a part-time basis, but did so voraciously and prolifically, though befriending few in serious music circles. Dismissing composers such as Mozart as authors of "pretty sounds", Ives undertook what he perceived as a masculine "tough" approach, gorging intentionally on texture and musical density, angular lines, intertwining American motifs into aurally challenging juxtapositions of keys and orchestral color. Ives's piano repertoire is sparse albeit flamboyant and often difficult to execute. Apart from the colorful piano accompaniments to his songs, he wrote only two full piano sonatas. His second, the gargantuan, programatic Concord Sonata, based on the four New England Transcendentalists, Emerson, Hawthorne, the Alcotts and Thoreau, is probably the more noteworthy.

Charles Ives trades on musical drama in his works. Characteristic of Ives piano compositions are contrapuntal textures, dissonance, and an unorthodox use of the entire range of the piano keyboard. A predominant stylistic trait in Ives is the use of alternating textures, where dense, lugubrious chordal passages alternate with simpler passages of runs and flourishes. Tone clusters abound in Ives's works, sonorities which offer density and color. Allison listened to these elements and, by osmosis, gradually began to incorporate them into his piano improvisation style. Key aspects of Allison's improvisational style are thus borrowed from the vocabulary of Charles Ives's piano sonatas and feature alternating texture; chordal passages with parallel runs, trills and the frequent use of tone clusters. Inspired by the Ives approach to the instrument, Allison continues to develop his use of the entire piano keyboard in his improvisation sections. And, like Ives, Allison revels in dissonance when an improvised passage leads him to it.

Probably the most pronounced stylistic trait that Allison attributes to Ives, as well as to the Russian pianist Alexander Scriabin and other twentieth-century composers, is left-hand independence. Ives's compositions feature melodic motifs played in parallel octaves in the left hand with thematic answers in the right hand. Similarly, Allison's use of melodies played in parallel octaves in the left hand are pitted against right-handed ostinati, what he calls "automatic figures." He comments:

> I got bored with the right-hand, single-note, bop style where the right hand does all the work and the left hand just plays chords. I felt like that style had gone about as far as it could go and I needed to get something else happening. I started listening to piano sonatas to see how the two hands were integrated and to see what was possible for improvising. I just listened. I'm not a good sightreader, I just got the basic idea of what these composers were doing. In addition to the general influence, I found techniques I could use. For instance, if I heard a single-note run in the left hand against three chords in the right, that would register. I'd realize that was something I could do when I'm improvising. When I started thinking in those terms, it opened me up a lot.
>
> The two Ives piano sonatas contain precedents for everything that has happened since in American music. Ives does something with "Bringing in the Sheaves" in the First Sonata that sounds exactly like Thelonious Monk.

By 1967, Allison had immersed himself in the left-handed direction his piano style had taken. In *Crescendo* he commented:

> I'm trying to learn how to play with more facility with the left hand so I practice left-handed things. You have to think

two-handed, though I don't know anybody who can think two separate lines at once. One has got to dominate. So, I'm trying to concentrate on what I'm playing with my left hand sometimes.[3]

In focusing on the left hand, Allison's objective was not only to strengthen his technique but to integrate left-handed elements into the scope of the improvisation, thus providing for equal creative freedom in both right and left hands. To acquire manual dexterity and flexibility, he set himself to practicing the exercises of Schmidt, a series of finger patterns and repetitions used to develop the technique necessary to play the classical repertoire. He supplemented Schmidt with his own system of piano exercises to reinforce the musical devices he wanted to incorporate into his playing. Allison remarked that developing two-handed improvisation was a slow process that could take a lifetime, "keeping him interested and changing up his style a little":

> To try to improvise with both hands is a pretty big order. There have been a few people who could do it, I'm sure. But, I was never a real accomplished technician. My style is pretty much the self-taught, primitive type, so I had to develop facility with my left hand and even the real technical wizards will tell you that you have to work to keep that left hand up, to keep it sharp. Ideally, what I try to get into is to be able to have the freedom to use both hands in improvising, playing against each other, parallel lines, octaves in one hand, harmonies in another. You can find these types of techniques in the classical composers.

Paul Hindemith, the other twentieth-century composer with whom Allison shared a musical kinship, was quite the opposite of the bombastic Charles Ives. Probably one of the most underrated composers of the century, Hindemith was also a musicologist and pedagogue. His four piano sonatas were defined by a musical mood of "repose," and Allison had a special reverence for their harmonic richness and melodic subtlety. Intrigued by Hindemith's use of quartal harmonies and voicings, Allison's modern style borrowed freely from Hindemith's quartal technique:

> I finally bought a piece of music by Hindemith and found it interesting because of the way he voiced things. I noticed he never voiced the tonic on the bottom, or very seldom. It was usually the fourth. The spacing of the chords was completely different from anything I'd ever done. I always had the tonic on the bottom. I'm not well enough versed in music to get everything out of it; I depend on my ear to do it.

The 1970s found Allison in the throes of an evolution of style on the piano. In 1975 he commented on the influence the twentieth-century composers had on his work and the antithetical nature of the two styles:

> Every now and then I'll hear someone and I'll go buy the record and listen to it. I don't try to analyze anything. I just listen to it over and over and get the feeling of what he's doing and maybe pick up some pointers on some of the techniques he employs.
> A jazz player doesn't exactly take anything straight from anything. For instance, by listening to Charles Ives, I might have picked up two or three little tricks which I employ that aren't exactly the way he did it at all. When it comes out it's not Charles Ives, it's what I got from Charles Ives. I don't adopt things straight. It's a matter of getting more things at your disposal. It's like collecting data.[4]

Although his catalogue is extensive and impressive, Mose Allison's recordings only hint at his true artistry on piano. Certain albums recorded in the 1960s and 1970s, when Allison was developing his modern approach to piano improvisation, capture the pianist only in a transitory state. Atlantic's *Your Mind's on Vacation*, released in 1976, documents glimpses of Mose Allison's neophyte piano style in what could be considered a final representation on record. Subdued performances on subsequent recordings throughout later decades are glaringly lacking in Allison's singular live-piano style. Only one live recording in the 1980s, Elektra/Musician's *Lessons in Living*, recorded live at the Montreux Jazz Festival, presents Allison's change in pianistic direction. The performance on this record, however, is marred by the lack of preparation for the session and thus fails accurately to depict Allison's music at that time. Suffice it to say that to date, Allison's later records present only half the contemporary Mose Allison. The neglect of the modern style of his piano solos and what he calls his "piano instrumentals" is startling, since Allison's live performances now reveal a mature, incomparable artist at the height of his creative and technical abilities on the instrument. Allison has always been at his artistic peak in live performance; he has evolved into a master of an original piano style in his twilight years. Allison's live sets offer the opportunity to experience the breadth of his work on the instrument. He acknowledges this:

> My piano style is always going through a process of evolution and also, the record companies have not been too interested in my piano style. They're interested more in my vocal stuff and songs. The record companies don't mind me playing on those new songs but they're not interested in any extended instrumental pieces. In fact, even on some of the live dates where there were instrumental tracks, they didn't get on the records. People are surprised a lot of the times when they come to hear me for the first time because I'm playing a different piano style than I was on the records thirty years ago.[5]

Mose's live performances feature a trio, the pianist and rhythm section with a horn player sitting in on rare occasions. Allison plays an average of 130 dates a year. After years of touring different venues in the United States and abroad, Allison generally prefers to book the dates himself, having developed relationships with many club owners and promoters. Rather than travel with the same band night after night, Allison is best known in jazz circles for his anomalous routine of selecting local sidemen on the road. His tight travel schedule affords no rehearsal time for newcomers and Allison thrives on the potential musical spontaneity:

> There is no preparation, really, no rehearsal for my shows. But you allow for certain variables. And you allow for the personalities of the other players. I have different players I play with in each place. If they can't make it, they recommend somebody. So, sometimes, I go to places and play with somebody I've never played with before. I try to have at least one person that I've played with before. It's always a question mark if the new person can do it. Most guys are familiar with what I'm doing, so usually if there is one player, I can rely on him to get somebody who will at least fill in pretty good. I actually like to play with different people sometimes. It gives you a little different point of view on what you're doing and it throws you into a little different gear. And just making allowances for different personalities, their strengths and weaknesses, it keeps it interesting.

Paul Motian, one of Mose's most celebrated drummers, comments:

> I was playing with Mose at Birdland one time in New York in the mid-sixties. We were playing opposite John Coltrane. I got to play with Coltrane a little bit during those weeks because his drummer Elvin Jones was late sometimes. In those days, they wanted one band and as soon as one came off the next was supposed to go right on with almost no break in between. With John's drummer missing, as I was coming off the bandstand with Mose, they would talk me into doing it. I was lucky to play with Coltrane a little bit. I remember having a conversation with John Coltrane at Birdland and he said to me, "Where you guys going next?" I said, "Well, I don't travel with Mose. Mose travels by himself and uses local rhythm sections wherever he goes." John said to me, "Wow, isn't that something, I wish I could do that." At the time I thought to myself, this man must be

crazy. He's got this incredible band—Jimmy Garrison, McCoy Tyner, Elvin Jones—and he's talking about wishing he could be like Mose Allison and go out and play with other people. I didn't understand it until I got my own band and started playing my own music. Then, I finally realized what Coltrane meant. What he meant was that you could be so independent that you could play *your* music no matter who you played with. Your stuff is so together that no matter who plays with you, it's going to be just as great whether it's with Joe Schmo or Jim Smith.

Allison's live sets generally distribute the simpler, straight-ahead vocals equally with piano instrumentals/vocals featuring extensive solos. Fundamental to Allison's success with his improvised material is establishing an uninterrupted, even-flowing groove with his rhythm section; he acknowledges this:

The purpose of any musical performance is to get off the ground. The time, the rhythm is the central most important thing in this music. The rhythmic feeling, the trance of getting the rhythm to flow right is important and your body gets set for that (my version of this is to get into the "spime"—my word for space-time). It affects the vocal style as well. The basic proposition is from the jazz tradition, to capture the exuberance of jazz. The approach should be a movement of exhilaration. You start there and go further depending on what you concoct.

George Marsh, a veteran drummer in Allison's California line-ups, elaborates on Mose's approach to phrasing, relating this directly to Allison's unique approach to the time:

The way Mose phrases is different. A lot of blues players might be playing shuffles with triplet feel. Mose might play a triplet feel for a half measure and a straight feel for another half measure and something else you can't write down for the next four measures. So, that feel has to be based upon an internal sense. 8/8 is what he seems to play, the boogie-woogie, eight to the bar. But Mose doesn't really play straight eighth notes; they're rounded off and if you actually wrote them down, they'd be very complex like quintuplets instead of triplets. He plays in the cracks like people like Parker, Tatum and Armstrong. I suppose one could write it down in groups of five or something. Mose has a wide range of those feels and it took me a couple of years to realize just how subtle it was.

It's really important to understand Mose's phrasing, not to interrupt the momentum he creates. He uses a lot of 3-2-2 phrases as a core. This is the New Orleans, second line beat. This is something that he's internally familiar with and he plays phrases with this as an underlying feeling and superimposes over it. When I figured this out, everything started to make sense for me. Players who aren't familiar with this can really get lost because Mose is not traditional in this sense at all.

Invariably, sidemen view their performances with Mose Allison as a challenging test of their technical and artistic mettle. Before he begins the live performance, Mose briefly instructs members of his rhythm section who have not previously played with him on specific requirements of the music. For bassists, Allison asks for the avoidance of the third of the triad because it defines the tonality of tune. The tonal ambiguity allows Allison the flexibility to traverse major and minor keys while improvising and maintains the blues sensibility to the tune. Drummers might be slightly more challenged. Allison is adamant about their avoiding heavy backbeats; no hi-hats on the second and fourth beats, no rim shots. Rather, he seeks a free-form, shuffle feel devoid of the pointed beats that define most popular music:

The backbeat has become so annoying. It's become the commercial, rock-and-roll beat as far as I'm concerned. You don't find the backbeat in any of the African drumming, or Afro-Cuban drumming, or in the Asian drumming, any drumming of the world that was the bedrock for the evolution of jazz. So, my idea is that somebody said, "We've got to play this backbeat and make it so strong so they'll know where two is." If you isolate the drum part from the average rock-and-roll track you'll hear mmm-BAM-mmm-BAM incessantly. Is there any musical value in that? To me, that's more related to construction work than to music . . .

And, every jazz player is his own timekeeper. I have a friend who saw Lester Young play a dance by himself. So the whole idea of having a drummer going back there, BAM, BAM, BAM, as a timekeeper, that's completely superfluous. That's part of swinging, having time . . .

To me, the backbeat is another form of pollution, bad air. It makes some drummers uncomfortable because they've been playing it for so long. But, some that I run across say, "Thank God somebody's come along and I don't have to do that all night."[6]

George Marsh and Jerry Granelli, both drummers who often have worked with Allison, respond readily to Mose's instructions to them. Marsh says:

I relate to Mose's directions as a challenge, forcing me to be right in the moment in a particular way. It's actually harder to do this because most jazz drumming does have two and four on the hi-hat and even though that's not very loud, it's still the backbeat. If you listen to Mose's earlier records, the drummers did play the backbeat. Later on he decided he didn't want that because it frees up his rhythmic approach. He may be playing some complex rhythms that cross over with a particular energy and the backbeat just doesn't work for him. Sometimes I'll use it, though, because it just sounds right to me. The backbeat has to be there, that's the interesting thing. If you don't feel it, the other thing isn't there either. You have to play the backbeat internally. Without that, it really doesn't work.

Granelli comments:

Mose wasn't always playing quite as out as he does now, but he was still playing out. His playing is a combination of blues and jazz and Mose, all coming together. He plays the blues in what you think is formless 99 percent of the time. He was doing this in 1962 when I first met him. One of the most refreshing things Mose said to me in 1962 was to not play the hi-hat on two and four. At the time, I didn't want to either. I will though, if the music requires it. What Mose doesn't want is for that to be habitual. He's not a habitual player.

Allison begins his performances with one, often two piano instrumentals, pieces he hears as "boogie-woogie sonatas." He selects the piano instrumentals either from his older repertoire, such as "Saritha" or "Powerhouse" ("charts") or bases them on a various chord progressions, referring to these as "schemes." The melodic ideas he develops from the schemes serve as a point of departure for his improvisations:

I start out with instrumentals because I like to get loosened up. I feel like playing a medium swing to get the excess off. In other words, you work the tension out to start with or else if you don't have any you get some going. You can either start off down and work up or vice versa. Having an extended improvisational instrumental at the front is good because I want to continue to utilize that part of what I do. Commercially speaking, a lot of people would just as soon I quit playing the piano, but I'm not willing to give that part up. It's one of the most challenging things I do and the opening of the sets is the best place for it. It's like the overture.

I start out with a chart. Now I usually play the schemes. Sometimes I begin playing a simple figure based on the seventh chord and develop that to see how it will turn out. You never really know. Sometimes I'm surprised. The whole idea is developing and completing ideas. It's a test of your ability. The scheme underlies it but the improvisation comes from the air.

After laying out the scheme, Allison embarks on a lengthy improvisation that assumes an ABA form. The ternary form serves as a structural guideline and boundary for the exploration of extemporaneous musical ideas. Generally, the A section is primarily linear in character, consisting of modal melodies based on the pentatonic scale. Here, Allison will typically use a minor-seventh chord as the harmonic foundation and develop his melodies around the indefinite duration of the tonic chord.

The B section contrasts with the horizontal nature of the preceding material. A dense harmonic texture fills this section, which is organized in what Allison terms "suspended chords." These are chords which blur the tonal definition of the piece and do not immediately resolve. Allison's suspended chords are voiced with his signature minor second middle of the spacing. He builds suspense by "planing" the suspended chord on different notes in either direction, using its top note for a melody line. He also frequently uses the chord as a drone, changing its character by developing a melodic line in the bass in what Allison describes as "alternating tonics." With the suspended chord on top, Allison is also able to create various contrapuntal melodic phrases, such as with parallel lines in oblique motion, "alternate tonics" in the bass and top note of the chords serving as the opposing lines. Allison complicates the dense vertical chordal movement using abrupt changes in tempo and rhythm and emphasizes its thicker texture and tone color with percussive, rhythmic effects. The sudden mood change in this section adds to the musical drama and he describes it as the "Italian Section," since he believes it to be "operatic" in nature.

Allison concludes the improvisation returning to the A section, recapitulating the linear motif and resolving the "suspended chords." The return to the simpler musical idea has its roots in the jazz aesthetic. Additionally, Allison views the contrasting sections as a type of "east meets west" musical balance, the simple pentatonic melodic themes juxtaposed with the complexity of dense tonal material:

> One of the things I learned about from the great jazz players was alternation. If they played something real complex, they'd play something simple next. Charlie

Parker did that a lot. He would go into a pyrotechnic display and then come out by playing a hymn, a lick or a riff. It gets boring to play just licks all night or to play just virtuoso material all night. The idea is to get different tonal colors, to get different tonal effects.

Apart from his piano instrumentals, the eight-to-the-bar blues tunes, both original compositions and covers, provide the best vehicles for Allison's extended solo piano improvisations. The straight twelve-bar blues or a variation played in the Afro-Cuban (rumboogie) grooves, such as "If You're Goin' to the City," "Wild Man on the Loose," and Willie Dixon's "Seventh Son," feature a simple structure and rhythmic intensity that encourage the freedom to develop musical ideas. Over the years, Allison has manipulated the time and tempo in these eight-to-the-bar songs, reinventing them with new treatments and changing the character of the tune itself. These tunes have undergone the most drastic overhaul during the evolution of his piano style.

In approaching the songs with a fresh perspective, Mose contends that playing the blues is not as simple as it appears:

The thing is, you can get an infinite variety out of playing the blues, actually, if you've got the imagination to do it. There are blues clichés. There are some very revealing records around, if someone wants to dig them up, where you have an all-star line-up of jazzmen playing the blues with blues clichés. Just the standard clichés like reciting the Gettysburg Address, things that have become public domain and anybody who wants to can learn those licks. But, then there will be somebody who will really try to invent something and use some imagination on the twelve-bar blues. And you know, it's still there to be done. I always offer up, as a model for what can be done with a twelve-bar blues, Charlie Parker's "Parker's Mood." If you want to hear what someone with imagination and energy, what a genius can do, with twelve-bar blues, listen to that. He doesn't play anything that even resembles a blues cliché.

> That's why I'm trying to keep my blues fresh. I don't want to fall into the old hackneyed licks.[7]

Over the last three decades, Allison has eschewed blues clichés, using his musical imagination in synthesizing elements derived, by and large, from twentieth-century piano literature and blues-folk elements into his piano improvisations. Definite patterns emerge and recur during extended solo passages on the blues tunes. Allison considers his improvisational style as predominantly chromatic and linear, referring to it as "chromatic funk," a term that critic Phillip Elwood first used to describe his music. The chromaticism in his melodies arises in Allison's traversing of major and minor keys. Juxtaposing pentatonic, modal melodies with diatonic melodies based on the dominant seventh chord, Allison improvises patterns using parallel octaves and lines that have various intervallic relationships, such as parallel fourths or thirds. His mature piano style during improvisational sections is characterized mostly by the following devices: 1) melodies which develop contrapuntally; 2) melodic ideas that develop in parallel octaves or lines; 3) a series of chords in the bass that are pitted against a right-hand improvised melody or vice versa; 4) identical repetitious ideas in both hands that alternate consecutively or the use of a pivotal pedal to connect them; 5) contrapuntal lines that become parallel ones; 6) brief ostinati in the right hand ("automatic figures") and an improvised melody in the left; 7) parallel lines that develop in thirds, fourths or in polytonality so that for example, the left hand plays in the key of F, the right in the key of G flat. Additionally, Allison frequently uses trills, either in both hands for a "harmonica effect" or separately, playing an improvised melody in the other. Allison refers to these as his "sound effects," or the familiar homing devices that recur during his musical excursions:

> All jazz musicians use what I would describe as "sound effects." This is something that you've done before and know how it will go and you use it to break up the melodic line. Sound effects are things I do every night, like say, a

run with a trill at the top. You stick these in the flow to break up the melodic line. Sound effects are the things you've acquired along the way. Every great jazz player, if you listen to them, you'll find sound effects; Lester Young, Charlie Parker, and others had certain things that they did all the time, certain devices in their style.

Harmonically, Allison's improvisations on the eight-to-the-bar tunes stray from the standard twelve-bar structure. Where the standard solo section in blues will employ the traditional form on the tonic, sub-dominant and dominant seventh chords, Allison's approach is similar to the A section of his piano instrumentals. Here, Allison establishes the tonic (I) chord as a drone or pedal tone, continues the harmony indefinitely and occasionally alternates the tonic with a flatted VI chord. Over this extended, indefinite period of the tonic chord, he then weaves his "sound effects" with freely improvisational, spontaneously created musical ideas. The "extended tonic" affords the freedom and flexibility to flesh out various melodies and textures. He then uses the flatted VI chord–dominant (flat VI-I) as a cadencial progression, repeating it up to three times, as a cue to the rhythm section that he is returning to the original song form or "head of the tune." He comments:

What you have is an alternation between melodic invention and sound effects. You create the melodic invention spontaneously but the sound effects you have at your disposal, you're just scattering those around. For example, with the octaves I use, those might be melodic lines or I might use them as sound effects. Nobody can get up and improvise a completely original melody line for three hours every night. People can't even write original melody lines. To do that while you're playing and trying to swing with a rhythmic momentum going—you're depending on intuitive knowledge. So, what you're trying to achieve is a balance between what you know and what you don't know.

Mose verbalizes his basic approach to improvisation, a

process which musicians find difficult to articulate:

> You got a key, a tempo and you got the space. You start off with a vocabulary, an approach and develop things off of the approach. It depends on the tune. What you're trying to do is invent some sort of melodic line. It's usually in the right hand but sometimes I try to develop some sort of melodic line in the left hand. When you do a melodic line in the left hand, you have to do something fairly automatic in the right because it's impossible to concentrate on two different lines at the same time.
>   Sometimes I'm doing this two handed—sometimes it's octaves or fourths. Sometimes I don't know what it is—I play different things with each hand just to see how it comes out. There's a lot of hit and miss involved. Of course, the better you get at it, the fewer misses there are. The misses are usually not that glaring; nobody knows but you when you play something you didn't expect to play or it comes out the way you weren't expecting. Then, you have to play something else that makes that unexpected thing sound reasonable. The idea is to try to make something out of whatever's happening. I'm trying to achieve a 'linear' continuity melodically.

Manipulation of time, rhythm, tempo and meter is another means of stimulating Allison's creative faculties in playing a conventional blues pattern. In more recent years, Allison has articulated his concept about his treatment of "time" in what he calls "anti-time." These "free-form" passages, occurring during the solo sections in the eight-to-the-bar tunes and the piano instrumentals, completely digress from the established tempo, meter and rhythm of the piece. Allison explains that in his "anti-time" the radical, almost rebellious departure in time erupting instantaneously from melodic ideas differs from the conventional jazz concept of "out of time" (a device that Allison might also use in the instrumentals) where brief rubato sections or clear contrasting meters define the overall passage. In his anti-time section, Allison seeks to convey the impact and disruption of the time change, an antithetical feeling, whereas "out of time" sequences are probably less threatening to the overall time sensibility. In the non-verbal language of music, Allison invites the rhythm section to join him on his anti-time sojourn. Frequently, however, the bass and drums retain the original time while Allison takes the improvisation out. As in the instrumentals, Allison returns to the flatted VI–V cadence, playing it two or three times, signaling the rhythm section on the conclusion of his solo and immediate return to the original song form:

> One of my goals is to maintain the rhythmic impact, feeling, tonality and tonal color of the blues and still invent and use imagination without using blues clichés. A lot depends on how you get started, the first notes you play. The simple tunes have a nice comfortable beat. Sometimes I go into what I refer to as anti-time. It's hard to explain because I'm just getting into it myself. If the rhythm section stays in the right place, I get out of time and come back in. I'm able to come out of it and it becomes time. For example, say you're walking along and you decide to do something different that breaks the rhythm of that completely. The idea is to go against, to break, or go out of the time but to get back into it too. The other players are important. The more confidence you have in them, the more chances you can take.

George Marsh comments:

> There's this thing that Mose calls anti-time. What it feels like, from my viewpoint, is that he's throwing the phrases right out. They don't have to be right in the time feel yet there's a larger energy that keeps going simultaneously. Overall, it sounds like you left the time feel behind, like anti-time, dismantling it or rebelling against it—he's just pushing these other phrases out. If you're real calm about it, the time keeps on going, so you can come back in. Most of the time we land together when we go out into that space. If you analyzed it, you could come up with long groups of

seven or long groups of five superimposed. From my viewpoint, even though it's called anti-time, it's very much integrated into the time and it's just more complex phrasing. There is a definite feeling of opposition against the established time and the creation of the maximum amount of tension. But, if a player just totally gives the time up while he's doing this, then it loses the opposition. Often, I'll just keep playing straight time, barely straight time, while he goes way out. Or, I'll play straight time with one hand and get free with some other limb.

Bassist Tommy Cecil has accompanied Mose in the Washington, D.C. region for over a decade:

A lot of times when we play on a solo, I'll play completely out of time and feel the length of the phrase not in terms of numbers of bars but just the phrase—it might be floating for an extended period, then he'll play something that will bring it back to the tempo we started with or a tempo from a certain section of the tune.

Playing with Mose is like when you're learning how to drive a stick shift. When you first learn how to drive and you're making a turn, you have to learn how to downshift, using the clutch, the wheel and the brake, you have to think of all of these things at once. But in time, it makes perfect sense as to why you're doing all these. With Mose, you have to think about this or that and stalling out. After a while you get used to the actual sound that he's going for, then all of the sudden all of those things that make it up come together and it makes sense. Playing with Mose is also very physically demanding.

Mose comments:

Sometimes you throw in something new that you didn't expect. On any good night, you'll run across passages that you've never played before—and you can't figure out why you didn't play them that way before. But you never remember it later. It's possible that you might have played it that way in the past but forgot it. I'll be playing and I'll notice that I never played a passage that way but I don't try to make a note of it. It's one of the things that goes by.

Allison recognizes the evolutionary process of his piano improvisation style:

Generally, you go from one extreme to another in your playing. I went from a real economical style, playing with no excess. Then, I went through a thing when I was trying to play more—that's when I was listening to a lot of the classical sonatas and trying to emulate those to a certain degree, using both hands and figures with octaves. So, you go through a phase where you do something a little too much. Then, that element gradually works its way into the overall thing. So, the development is never-ending, a process of refinement and self-revelation that continues.

After several decades of the physical, emotional and intellectual demands of concocting new improvised material, performance after performance, Mose Allison contends he has no particular formula for staying in shape creatively. Physical exercise, such as running and swimming, has always been a part of his daily routine, on and off the road, and like many musicians, the athletic activity helps to prepare him for performances:

I look at a set as an hour, or an hour and ten minutes of music. I try to get everything I'm interested in doing in that hour and ten minutes. Every night's a challenge on what you can get going. There's no set direction other than the harmonic progression and what you play depends on how you start out, your hand position, whether or not you can develop and complete the ideas. Some nights you feel like you can do it. Other nights, you struggle to try and make it happen. Every night is quite different. It's having the clarity of just seeing the music happen underneath your fingers. Sometimes it pours out without much effort. It has to do a lot with whether the rhythm is happening. You can recognize it but not describe it. I like the quote from *Zen and the Art of Motorcycle Maintenance*, "Quality can be recognized but not described." I can approximate what I'm doing, but I really can't describe it.

You don't know what's going to make you play well. One night it's like you're Superman or the Seventh Son. Other nights it's hard labor, man. You wish you were somewhere else. The irony is that sometimes when you felt terrible playing, you listen back to it three weeks later and it might sound better to you than one of the nights when you thought you were playing great. So, it's very subtle. I've always said that it never sounded as good to me as it felt.[8]

15

MOSE ALLISON: A SOURCE

"I get a lot of insights from the things fans say. Somebody once said to me, 'You were socially relevant before Dylan, you were satirical before Newman, you were mean before Jagger, why aren't you a big star?' My answer to that is, 'Just lucky, I guess.'"

Mose Allison

"The British blues purists were desperately serious; fun was counter-revolutionary. Their music had been derived exclusively from records, and from encounters with touring American bluesmen who were most likely to be older musicians like Muddy Waters, Sonny Boy Williamson and Jimmy Reed."[1]

Charles Shaar Murray (author)

"I think Mose Allison is one of the most original artists that I have had the pleasure to work with. He is uniquely an American artist. He doesn't sing like anyone else. He doesn't write like anyone else. A lot of people call him the William Faulkner of jazz. He is one of these very literary and gifted individuals who influenced a lot of other people in music."

Bruce Lundvall

"If you were British playing the blues in the 1960s, you were influenced by Mose Allison."

Mick Taylor (guitarist)

"Ever Since I Stole the Blues"

Have you heard the latest?
Are you in the know?
It's in the morning paper
And it's on the radio
It's even going to make the TV news
White boy steals the blues

Well you can wake up in the morning
And they won't come tumbling down
Your woman can leave you
And they won't be coming round
Don't even have to pay those dues
Ever since I stole the blues

Well down in the Delta
And on the South side
All of the players diggin' Charlie Pride
They even closing down the barbecue
Ever since I stole the blues

Well the blues police from down in Dixieland
Tried to catch me with the goods on hand
They broke down my door but I was all smiles
I had already shipped them to the British Isles
Did wonders for their revenue
Ever since I stole the blues

Since the white boy stole the blues

Mose Allison

Mose Allison's oeuvre, combining unique songwriting,

literary lyrics, and a singular style of piano improvisation, is as far-reaching in its influence as it is significant in a historical and musicological sense. An American original, Mose Allison is a jazz/blues hybrid who never committed himself exclusively to either genre. A musical enigma for some, Allison has often found himself falling into a categorical chasm. At one point in his career, one of his promoters even created a special Mose Allison category, informing clubs that he represented blues artists, jazz artists and Mose Allison. As both a distinct bluesman and a distinct jazzer, Allison has carved out an individual niche, one that has influenced many musicians in various genres.

Mose Allison's early work was celebrated at a crucial time in the evolution of popular music. In the early 1960s, when his music had made its way overseas, the influence of American blues, jazz and rock and roll permeated European culture. Allison's own work was immediately associated with other American bluesmen such as Muddy Waters, Howlin' Wolf, and Big Bill Broonzy, who inspired the British blues revival, British R&B and rock and roll, but his jazz style also appealed to young devotees of that genre whose own talents also spilled over into those media. Thus, Allison quickly became a source of inspiration for the various popular-music tributaries and a formative influence on legions of young people around the world. And Allison continues as a source. His work's intrinsic artistic worth aside, Mose Allison also enters the lexicon of popular music as an influential stylist and one of the imprinteurs of a new music. An unassuming Mose Allison, consistently modest about the legendary status bestowed upon him by rock-and-roll stars and jazz vocalists, simply passes it off, more interested in going about his business as a songwriter, singer/pianist, arranger and performer.

It is not as if the American recording industry, the starmaking machinery, rallied to the artist's cause. Allison's is the typical case of an artist falling through the proverbial cracks into the netherworld between art and commercialism. Off to a good start on Prestige, Allison stood at the nexus of art and commercialism at a time when the public appetite for jazz was high. The tides were beginning to change when Allison moved to Columbia Records and his records for the label faltered, despite record-company support. Once Atlantic took the reins, Allison's artistic direction began to digress and mass consumption for jazz became a thing of the past. There, because Allison was unwilling to submit himself to some type of popular formula, any plans for commercial success the company had for him were dashed. Allison therefore found himself, at the height of his creative and aesthetic powers, suffering relegation to the bottom of the Atlantic Records heap. Where some modicum of commercial support might have perpetuated and distinguished his career, as it were, Allison limped along alone, continuing almost singlehandedly to develop his fan base. Thus, even though the record company continued to release his material, most of his followers, especially throughout the 1970s, discovered Mose Allison by word of mouth, in the record bin, or out of curiosity when he rolled into town alone to play a local club with his regional, hand-picked sidemen.

The reasons Mose Allison remains a cult figure in American music are complicated, but Atlantic Records must bear some of the blame for not using its heavyweight publicists, promoters and sales force continually to thrust his name out into the spotlight. Their artistic differences notwithstanding, Allison spent fifteen years on Atlantic and should have been afforded the same treatment as artists on the label's jazz roster, many of whom, with the requisite attention, sold records. Mose Allison already had an audience, but Atlantic, at some point, simply gave up on him.

On the other hand, Mose Allison was also responsible for his choices, and must bear his share of the blame. An independent artist, fiercely loyal to his perception of his music as art, Allison regarded as an absolute truth a view held more often by those working in a classical-music milieu: art thrust into the world by commerce inevitably dies. To fault Allison for following his artistic soul would be unfair, since he chose and continues to choose his own path, fearless and accepting of the results of his choice. Other artists and colleagues marvel at his integrity, at his not sacrificing, not "selling out."

In part, Mose's resistance might be attributable simply to his discomfort with many aspects of celebrity. Although always accessible to the media for interviews to discuss his work, Mose has shied away from the hype and staged publicity generally required of artists by record companies and publicists, the personal "meet and greet" appearances, record autograph sessions, the type of press that many celebrities hire public-relations firms to garner. Allison has always believed in the artistic integrity of his work, that the music speaks for itself and that his fans are the sort of music lovers most likely to attend his performances, not wait in line for his autograph at a record store.

Allison, therefore, made some choices that might have been detrimental to his career. In the final analysis, as it happens, fate may have played him a good hand, for in remaining truthful to his aesthetic conscience, his work has developed organically, without outside interference. Although more public recognition and financial success is well deserved for an artist of his artistic caliber and longevity, Mose Allison is no less significant as an artist today, his work as vital and meaningful as it was in 1959.

Since commercial support had been virtually non-existent during most of his career, Mose Allison's fans have discovered him through unconventional means. Historically, Mose Allison's musical impact was felt most strongly in England, where young, eager British musicians, who had grasped the blues vocabulary of the American masters, distilled it, combined it with an embryonic form of rock, and developed the sound, reinventing it as a forceful form of musical expression. Georgie Fame, the bandleader at the famous Flamingo Club and a singer whose style, as he would be the first to admit, owes a great deal to Allison, was the American's primary advocate in the U.K., spreading the Allison gospel to the horde patronizing the club. Other British musicians followed suit and Mose Allison became a household name among them.

A white man playing in what had traditionally been an African-American musical genre, Mose Allison, as part bluesman, was particularly important to English teenagers who were experiencing social oppression in their own country, much as their black counterparts had in America. An American white man singing black music broke down racial barriers and tradition, supporting the notion that music is a universal expression, without race. Further, it immediately justified British euphoria over the blues and remedied the notion that music was national, paving the way for a legitimate British contribution.

Today, the British music community stands accused of plagiarizing the blues from the Americans and sending it back in regurgitated form to the land of its birth. That argument might hold some water as regards the music of disingenuous copycats such as Led Zeppelin and, to some extent, the Rolling Stones. Others, however, argue that certain British followers venerated the style, internalized the blues as an artform, and synthesized their ideas, eventually producing their own medium. These artists had turned their oppression into anger, venting their rage through a music that in large part incorporated the blues, or at least some of its elements. This argument also has some truth in it, evidenced in the music of the Who, the Yardbirds, and Cream, who rendered original, often innovative interpretations of the blues repertoire as well as concocting their own style. If it is a fact that the blues provided the impetus for this musical innovation, Mose Allison's music played a major role in the process.

On the other side of the Atlantic, a myriad of factors contributed to the lack of recognition of the blues in its own country. For the most part, American teenagers were lulled by the sounds of British pop imports and the milquetoast teen idols fed to them by the American mass media. The war in Vietnam, however, soon swept away their complacency, and a gradual social movement sparked an angry counter-culture. At the point of combustion, the Americans and British met each other on equal footing, the rage expressed by their British contemporaries now matching that of the angry, mobilized young Americans. If the blues returned to American shores mainly through British voices, it mattered little to the fresh young Americans who welcomed it home, identifying with both the message and its fresh, loud, frenzied, often drug-induced power.

Unfortunate as it seems, at the time English kids were discovering it on the B.B.C., the blues might have simply been too close to home to garner the necessary attention in the U.S.A. At the time, in the mainstream, black musicians attained celebrity first and foremost as entertainers, as the purveyors of music such as "doo wop" or dance crazes such as "the twist." Blues, a subtle, sensitive, art music, was generally considered too esoteric to attract mass attention, unless diffused through a figure popular to white audiences such as Count Basie, Duke Ellington or later, Nat King Cole. Race records, as they were called, did not exist in every American's record collection.

That is not to say that the United States repudiated the music altogether. Sam Phillips of Sun Records in Memphis, where the blues had a strong foothold, realized the power inherent in the music with one statement: "If I could find a white boy with a Negro sound I could make a million dollars." And the form has not been without its own young American disciples. Various periods in the 1960s yielded blues booms and the genre boasted an elite following of celebrated blues purists, such as the late Mike Bloomfield's band in Chicago, the Paul Butterfield Blues Band and Al Kooper's Blues Project in New York. American musicians such as Jimi Hendrix, Janis Joplin, and Bonnie Raitt found their own voices through the genre in much the same fashion as the British rock community had. Like Mose Allison, each embraced the blues primarily as a point of departure, as an ingredient of their style, and a form of meaningful, musical self-expression. In America, whether or not cognizant of it, Mose Allison was revered by many as a counter-culture hero, his music appealing to the bohemians and politically recalcitrant "Woodstock generation" because of its intelligent, "telling it how it is" message and grass-roots musical feel.

Both British and American musicians held Mose Allison up as a musical icon. In covering his songs, they found their own musical voices as well. Mose Allison attributes this to their "common denominator," the blues:

There are elements that are common to music all over the world. If it's based on the blues, which it all is, it comes out of the Southern Afro-American blues and rhythm and blues. That's where it all comes from, so it carries over in all categories of music. The first English musician to do my material was Georgie Fame in about 1960. Then there was Brian Auger, the Yardbirds, John Mayall, the Who and then the Clash. Van Morrison did a few things. Robert Palmer did Top 40 . . .

Sometimes it surprises me to hear those versions of my songs, but I've always said that I do my own job on other people's songs so I don't really care what people do with my songs. All I want them to do is be sure they give me credit for it. I'm not that finicky about what people do with them—I am sometimes surprised by the tempo or approach used, but it doesn't bug me or anything. Every time someone does one of my tunes, it gives me a little push.[1]

APPENDIX: ARTISTS ON ALLISON

Bonnie Raitt: Singer/Songwriter

When I was growing up in California in the 1950s and 1960s, like most kids, I was influenced by what I heard on the radio. For the first time you could hear black and white music together—a Doris Day or Connie Francis record right next to Little Richard and Chuck Berry. I got a box of Ray Charles records from a family friend when I was eleven or twelve and used to listen to them over and over as well as a jazz radio show I used to tune into. That was probably my only exposure to jazz early on. Then, of course, came the golden era of Motown, Stax and Atlantic, coupled with the British invasion of the Beatles, and the Stones. Added to that pop-radio culture was my growing adoration of folk music, which I had been exposed to at a progressive summer camp all during that time. College kids who were counselors there were going crazy for Odetta, Joan Baez, Pete Seeger, and I picked up the guitar at around eight so I could teach myself all the songs they used to sing. The whole mystique about coffee houses and beatniks as well as the growing peace and civil-rights movements became lumped together in my eager adolescent mind. I became obsessed with anything *not* Los Angeles: Liverpool, London, Mississippi, Scotland and, of course, all of Greenwich Village. I think that whole cultural mix came together in the 1960s in the village and that's partly what made my first listening to Mose Allison so powerful.

I never really heard anyone as cool as him. He just seemed to be the epitome of everything I wanted to get into and the opposite of everything in L.A. that I couldn't stand. He played Greenwich Village, he looked like a beatnik. He had this really cool laid-back style. His music was not only bluesy, he was covering blues songs which I already knew, he was also singing about social issues that were really important to me, having been raised in the peace and civil-rights movements. He was basically "it" as far as I was concerned.

I had no idea where his style had come from except reading a little bit about him on his album notes that he was from Mississippi made him even more intriguing. The fact that a white guy could come out of that racist situation in the South and, having never been there, only knowing it from television and civil-rights marches and all that brutality down there, he seemed to me as a kindred spirit in terms of loving black music. As someone who also had a sense of conscience and justice about the civil-rights situation, he was just an immediate soulmate and somebody I idolized and couldn't wait to meet.

Although I took five years of piano lessons, I taught myself to play guitar by ear so I could sing my favorite songs for my own enjoyment. I was never expecting to do it for a living; it was more just for the love of it. The process by which you're influenced is more osmosis than anything else. You've either got the ability to absorb it and make it your own or you don't. You can't really imitate someone as original as Mose Allison without being obvious—that's how it is with all distinctive stylists. You know that John Lee Hooker heard some local blues player growing up in Mississippi and made those licks his own. Mose grew up in a hotbed of great music—white and black—and is one of the first white artists to incorporate the Delta blues into their music. And yet, he absorbed it and created something new out of it. That's one of the ways he's inspired me the most. When I'm singing a song by someone I love, Aretha, Charles Brown (or Jackson Browne for that matter) or Mose, I don't think about the original, I just get into it. The influence is already absorbed and it's pure emotion and connection with the song. Thank God there's nothing intellectual about it.

Mose and I did a double-bill tour for about a month in the 1970s including a great P.B.S. special called "Performance" at Wolftrap, outside of Washington, D.C., always my largest audience. As I had spent my early career opening for my heroes—James Taylor, Jackson Browne, Muddy Waters, Mississippi Fred McDowell—I thought it would be great to expose my growing, mostly college audience to someone I idolized whom they might not have heard. And, of course, there were his fans who hadn't seen me. It will always be one of my fondest memories—that time we got to play together, as well as the other times we've gone to see each other play or shared the bill. To be able to have a mutually affectionate and long-term friendship with one of my heroes has been a wonderful thing.

I don't know any musicians who don't love Mose Allison. Like Ray Charles or the Staples Singers or the great blues and jazz artists who've stood the test of time, his appeal cuts across all musical boundaries. In the over twenty years I've been going to see him live, he's blown me away every time. I think musicians are in a unique position to appreciate the consistent risk-taking in his work because we all have that drive. We became musicians because we had that fever. And, when you have that, someone who's obviously so deep into it also will inspire you to get even more immersed. That's the effect Mose will always have.

Bruce Lundvall: Record-company Executive

The day we were signing Robert Palmer here on EMI Records we were taking photographs of the signing and drinking champagne, which is the usual thing when you sign artists. I was sitting there on the couch with Robert Palmer, who I really didn't know well, and was talking to him and said, "Gee, do you like Mose Allison?" And he said, "Mose is one of my heroes." So, I gave him a cassette of Mose's first album on Blue Note: "You'll probably want to hear this; he just finished this album." I gave him *Ever Since the World Ended*. Then, a year later, in the summer of 1989, I ran into him in a restaurant and he said, "I got to talk to you." I went over and sat down at his table. He said, "Do you remember when you gave me Mose Allison's tape? I just recorded 'Top Forty.'"

Robert Palmer: Singer/Songwriter

I guess I first heard of Mose Allison through songs like "Do

Nothin' 'Till You Hear from Me" and "Lost Mind"—his versions of those songs. I picked the album up that had those two songs on it probably in 1968. He's so distinctive, his phrasing and everything, that I'd probably heard him on American Forces Network when I was a youngster in Malta. My parents always played a lot of music so I knew those songs from my childhood or at least from an early age. Then, it was a matter of me putting the name to the voice. The next thing that came up that I remember was that he opened for me in Atlanta, that was 1976 maybe—which I couldn't believe; it was like, "Geez—there's something wrong here." I also recorded my first album with a group from New Orleans called the Meters and a couple of years after the release of the album I showed up in New Orleans and the Meters were the opening act. Very embarrassing. Mose didn't sing a lot that night. It was the first time I'd seen him, actually, because the album I had didn't have his picture on it. I didn't think he was black though. Not at all.

Mose sings very ahead of the beat, almost like triplets ahead of the beat, which is a great way to get a story over because the words are coming at you before the groove—especially in a tune like "Lost Mind." And the noises that he makes, that business, you can hear him punching a hole in the music to where the word has to go. To a certain extent I incorporated this. I was aware when I was doing his material that I may have been doing that—I sort of tried to avoid doing it. It's difficult to avoid it because it's part of the structure of the tune.

The thing that I find most attractive about his stuff is his lyrics. My lyrics are a lot like Mose's, particularly in one song that I do called "Pride." It has a line in it "anorexia nervosa mannequin." It's like that line of Mose's, "no more philosophic melancholia, 800 pounds of electric genitalia." Also, there's another classic line of his that I love; it's from that song "If You Only Knew." "You gonna have to have your own breakthrough—if you only knew." That kind of laconic, wry thing is an influence. Even Randy Newman. Mose tends to be a bit darker than Randy Newman, I guess. The lyrics come across as bitter sometimes but mostly they come across in a self-effacing intelligence like "Ever Since I Stole the Blues" and "Jogging," although those two are more recent.

I use seconds and fourths in my vocal harmonies and never thirds, which are structural musical similarities to Mose. If you can hear a third in there, it's an accident. I've been working with Teo Macero, a producer, lately and we'll go over the music at lunchtime when the musicians are all out, go through all the charts and scrub out all the thirds. Thirds are sick. They limit the melody. There's no need to have them there. They're vile hangovers from some Christian dogma. There are no thirds in R&B anyway because otherwise you immediately depict if you're in a major or minor key, which hangs up your melody. For instance, when you depict it—the change from major to minor is gorgeous. There's a song on my album *Aeroplane* which starts off in B flat and resolves to an E minor 9 with a big third in the middle of it. That minor in the E chord relates to the thing working at the top. But then it immediately drops it again and goes to a second in the next chord. I'll use the third as an effect. As soon as I hear thirds, I tend to switch off. In country and western, it's O.K. Part of the reason I find Mose's music attractive is because he doesn't use the third, I guess.

Come to think of it, I suppose his soloing on piano is very much the same—the way he anticipates in his singing. When you hear one of his songs, though, you never can guess what is going to happen musically—you don't know where he's going to go.

I grew up listening to Nat Cole, Billie Holiday and Lebanese singers. For me, they're perfect. The music of the 1950s, that was my parents' thing—when I heard soul music like Otis Redding, for instance, that was my rock and roll, my music. I've been singing into my father's tape recorder since I was five, things like Ketty Lester—she had a wonderful song called "Love Letters."

Like Mose, I don't really fall into a musical category. In fact, the other night a critic wrote that I was a cross between Harry Connick, Motorhead, and Marvin Gaye. I studied with a couple of African musicians in the early seventies who taught me about syncopation. Since then, I've been into ethnic music—when I discovered the African syncopation, that was a huge change for me, I suddenly understood a lot about all the music that I heard. I'm also fond of Pakistani and Lebanese singers.

Jack Bruce: Singer/Songwriter/Bassist

I first heard of Mose from his first record, *Back Country Suite*, when I got to London in the early 1960s, because it was definitely around then. But, I wasn't really tremendously aware of him—he wasn't as well known as other people like Ray Charles—Mose was more underground. I was exposed to him through Georgie Fame.

I came more from the jazz community—there were no R&B clubs. There were only two or three clubs in London when I arrived there. I left Glasgow when I was seventeen and traveled around Europe a lot and ended up in London. But at that time, there wasn't a scene that differentiated R&B and all of that. I was in bands that opened up the R&B scene around 1962 with Alexis Korner and Graham Bond. You would get a club like the Flamingo, which was probably, for the kind of music we're talking about, the most important club; there was also Ronnie Scott's, which was a jazz club. The Flamingo had a big American influence—I don't mean from musicians coming in, although that happened a lot. I got to play with a lot of great American musicians, people who came in with Duke Ellington and Count Basie, people who were playing in London would come by and jam. I played with Cat Anderson and all types of different people with Ginger Baker on drums, because we were kind of a rhythm section. The Flamingo was important because the American influence was a local one through the, mainly black, American servicemen who were stationed in Britain. They would go to the Flamingo to hang out. I played with a guy called Ronnie Jones, who was a serviceman and became quite a well-known singer. He played with Alexis Korner. Unfortunately, while I was there, there was some type of a problem, a stabbing or something, and they put it off limits for the servicemen. After that, the club died. But it was *the* club for the meeting of ideas for me. I was a teenaged Scotsman with wide-open eyes to all of the stuff that was happening—very enthralled with it all, meeting people like Phil Seamen and all of the great British jazz musicians from the generation in front of me. The bandroom at the Flamingo was the center of the universe. You would meet everybody there. I was allowed to be there because I was one of the bass players in the band. Georgie's was the house band and I was in Friday- and Saturday-night all nighters. We used to do the interval spots sometimes with the Johnny Birch Band, sometimes with Graham Bond, sometimes with Dick Hextall-Smith, but always with Ginger because we were the rhythm section. We got £2 a night and we would be there from midnight until the sun came up. That was big money in those days.

Basically, there were certain aspects in that scene that were mandatory. Mose was one of them. There were certain things at the time that you had to be aware of, like Eric Dolphy, certain things that were the vibe at the time, and Mose was one of them. I'm not saying that he was as important as certain figures in music at that time in jazz. But he was part of that vibe that was going on at the time, the Ornette Coleman, Miles Davis thing—he certainly was very much a part of it and I was aware of it. Of course, after you heard "Parchman Farm," you wanted to hear the other stuff. It was just like a voice. We were all so open-minded. We didn't label things, we didn't even particularly care about names—we just wanted to hear more.

With me, I was very open to the musical ideas he had to offer. I was such a purist with a tight ass that the more things that could open my ears, the better. It was only at the same time that I heard Mose that I heard Muddy Waters, Howlin' Wolf, and Willie Dixon. Only then was I just beginning to hear that there was more than just bebop and straightahead jazz. This is what's happened to me—my life has been a process of breaking down barriers and opening my mind. Before I heard things like Mose, I wouldn't allow myself to appreciate certain things like the blues, so I think that Mose was very important to me. He helped me to open my ears to the blues. It's not necessarily about technique, although he does employ a lot of it to do what he does. To hear this purity, this openness, in my mind, it enabled me, for better or worse—because maybe it's not always for the better—to change my sights, not to lower them, but to change them—to listen to Buddy Guy and all of the different stuff that I've now come to love which I might not have done if it hadn't been because of that time. Not for Mose, but for that time, because Mose was a part of that time. Thank God for it.

The important thing to me about influence is not so much selling millions of records, although that might be important to some people, but the things that count to me are the things that even if you didn't write about them would still be important. These things enter the currency, the language of music. Many people may not know Mose's name, they maybe don't even know his songs or have just heard them for the first time, but that stuff has gone in to enrich the musical language. Like James Jamerson, who is the bass player of Motown. Nobody knows him, and he's dead now, but his playing has just gone into the language.

On the Montreux record I did with Mose, for me, it was kind of nerve-racking because I wasn't expecting to do it and there were no rehearsals, but only maybe a little run-through, or something. But, I think it worked out all right. Those things are so weird anyway. For me, it was joy to stand close to Mose on stage and he was playing his ass off. His solos were going way out. I would have liked to have felt more comfortable so that I could have given more. But in another way, the bass has never been that important in his stuff. He always had kind of fairly weedy bass players. He told me not to play the thirds but I played them anyway. Whenever anyone tells me that, I agree, and play what I hear. Maybe I didn't play any but I didn't *deliberately* not play any!

My musical influences are much, much older—Scottish music—in the music of my country. I would never want to be a "Scottish musician," though. I don't respect people who consciously use those things. They are the things that just exist in me because of who I happen to be, as Mose has brought the elements of who he is to his music. There's more calculation than that. My first solo record, the horn parts were influenced by Stravinsky. All of this stuff when you talk about it sounds so self-conscious and ego-tripping, but I think there is this thing that people always say, like Louis Armstrong, he didn't know what he was doing, it was just him. But, he knew very well what he was doing and he worked very hard at it. And I think we all do. Listening to Mose, he definitely knows what he's doing. It's not just something that just comes easily—it might after several years of hard work—but the work and the thought is there initially.

I've always been a singer. I started off as a singer in a church. Funnily enough, I always had this vibrato as a boy soprano which was used because I used to sing Benjamin Britten pieces and so on. I would sing more like a female soprano as opposed to a boy soprano, which is more of a straight tone. Hearing Mose, with his lack of vibrato, I thought, "That's amazing—he's either got that or he's decided consciously not to have one, which is quite a choice because a vibrato is the 'warmth.'" I think the influence of that was quite deep—that non-vibrato—much deeper than Mose or anyone else probably realizes. When I listen to people like the Beatles—their classic records, not the early ones—where they got into their studio techniques and sang close-miked, they would deliberately not use vibrato, particularly John Lennon. I imagine it must have been a big influence on them, hearing Mose, unless it was just a feeling. I imagine, rightly or wrongly, that Mose made a choice to get more of an instrumental sound and feeling with his voice and not to use a vibrato. Whether or not he did that, I think that it really had a big influence on singers of slightly later. Also, it's quite a "white" approach to do that... maybe it's even got something to do with that because the black way of singing, the gospel thing, is very much a vibrato way of singing. Maybe it was Mose's way of saying, "Yeah, I'm a white boy, so my voice is like this," but that's getting very analytical about it and I don't know how deeply performers think in that way—I know I don't.

I don't think there is any need to make an analysis that

Mose was a bridge between black music and white rock and roll. That kind of talk upsets me. I don't see it. I mean about links—I just meant that if you've got something, you'll want to use it to the best advantage, if that's your instrument. The point about music is that you don't have to talk about race or country to make music. I've never been a part of that "British" group—even when I was a part of it, I was never a part of it. I don't play the way they do—I do have a different rhythmical approach and a classical background and I'm not really a joiner. I guess I'm the Anthony Hopkins of rock music. I think Mose is like that, also. There are a few people who are so out that those labels don't apply anymore. It's fun to sort of talk about it but they don't apply. If you want to talk about Indonesian gamelan music, I'm your man.

Pete Brown: Lyricist, Poet, Writer, Singer/Songwriter

I've been aware of Mose's stuff probably since it's been available in the U.K.—on record. I've always searched for people who were hip, to try to find kindred spirits—people like Screaming Jay Hawkins and Wynonie Harris, although he didn't write most of his own songs; some people like Slim Gaillard, who crossed barriers and were out of the ordinary. I was probably first aware of Mose's piano playing on bebop records, just as a sideman. I listened to him first as a pianist only. Basically, I'm a jazz nut but I wasn't writing songs, although I was a poet. I must have been aware of Mose since the 1950s, because I was getting into jazz when I was like fourteen and that would have been around 1955. By the late 1950s I certainly would have been aware of him on record since Al Cohn, Zoot Sims and Stan Getz were pretty important over here and had a big influence on people at that time. Zoot Sims was also one of the first Americans to tour over here after the Musicians' Union ban got relaxed.

Then, in the early sixties, with the British blues thing, radio programs played him—any programs that were at all hip at the time were playing him. At that point, a very strange thing was happening in Britain. There used to be strict barriers between Dixieland revival jazz and modern jazz. Then there was another barrier. There were about ten or twelve people playing jazz at that time, the rest of them did other gigs. They were professional musicians, but played other gigs. When the R&B thing happened, Alexis Korner, a guitarist who was the father of British blues, and various people, those guys realized that they wanted to employ jazz musicians of the younger and progressive type who were into the blues and that. There was quite a snobbery about those guys, those young musicians. In fact, Alexis Korner asked Graham Bond, who was one of the first musicians to cover Mose Allison (he started off playing saxophone but was also a good pianist) to do a radio broadcast gig with him and Graham agreed because he loved the blues and everything but asked Alexis not to mention his name because he'd just been voted new jazz star of that year and was scared it would get him prejudice. As the blues scene grew, the R&B scene was happening at the Flamingo. The Flamingo was kind of a mixture of jazz and blues and so was the Marquee. The Marquee was started off by people who did jazz and they were fairly liberal in the sense that they came from promoting Dixieland jazz and had contacts with Chris Barber who was the first person to bring Muddy Waters over here. That turned people on to the blues. Alexis Korner's first band had a lot of amateurs in it like Mick Jagger. They were all in it and sat in and did bits. Eventually, Alexis realized that there were these very fine jazz musicians around like Dick Hextall-Smith, Ginger Baker, and Jack Bruce and Graham Bond, who needed the work and he would pay them in a very small way. And these musicians were attracted to the blues, they were much more open than the previous generation. In Manchester, John Mayall was also using jazz musicians.

These musicians felt a tremendous affinity for Mose because he was a jazz musician who also sang the blues. He also sang original, quirky, hip-type songs. So, those people were attracted to Mose because he combined these three elements: the jazz, the blues, and the sort of hip attitude. To me, it was great because it felt like another ally out there. The other thing that Mose and I have in common is a sort of cynicism; we exploit our world-weariness in a similar way.

Then, you did hear a lot of his songs around—the disc jockeys and the musicians were playing them. "Seventh Son," "I Love the Life I Live" and "Parchman Farm." In the early sixties, I was a starving poet so I didn't have a large record collection, but I did go to gigs and hung out with the guys from the Alexis Korner band, so I was aware of all that material. I didn't start buying records again until I started making money from songs and having a permanent place to live. Everyone was aware of the way of combining jazz with blues so that it would be accessible, interesting and musically stimulating.

The R&B thing turned into psychedelia, which in Britain was very big for quite a few years from like 1966 to '71, five years. Although the British blues thing became more rock-like, like Fleetwood Mac, you would still find influences of Mose in those people. Of course, John Mayall was a big star then. Cream was sort of a combination of jazz and psychedelia, although they didn't think of themselves as being a psychedelic band. In fact, my lyrics to Cream were post-psychedelic, except for the first one when I was still taking things, but after that they dealt with sort of post-psychedelic traumas.

Something like "Politician" had the kind of cynicism of Mose, whereas something like "Dance the Night Away" and "Deserted Cities of the Heart" were not blues-based. They were going in different directions of British music, combining jazz things and whatever. The main music scene was kind of split—the psychedelic thing and the blues thing was going on at the same time. There were more musicians coming into England from America then. I know Mose played at one of those blues festivals. It was put on every year by the people who ran the Marquee. This was the National Jazz Federation and they had festivals every year. Cream played their first gig at that festival in Windsor in 1966. One was Richmond and one was in Windsor. Mose played here at one of those locations.

I didn't go to that, but the first time I saw him was at Ronnie Scott's and ever since then I've been a fan of his live thing. I once went all the way to fucking Hermosa Beach to see him at the Lighthouse. I'd had all these records of all these West

Coast people playing at the Lighthouse and I thought it was some incredibly glamorous place. It's like a filthy pub.

His influence on me has been more in recent years, I would say. There may have been some unconscious influence in the early days although I was certainly aware of what he was doing and liked it. Also, his performances I've always enjoyed. Having said that, one of the songs I wrote was for Graham Bond, which never got recorded but the words were: "You left me with the tattered fragments of the A to Z to Hell" and there was another called "Late Night Mental Tire Service." I wrote the music to those, too. When I think about them, I realize how Mose-like they are. Whether they came via other people or things I listened to, I don't know. This was in 1966 or 1967; I might have seen him by then. Later on, after I'd seen him a lot more, having been to more of his appearances in London and in America, I can see the influences. Certain things like "Middle Class White Boy" certainly had a big impact.

Once you know Mose's songs and how they're constructed, they stay with you all the time. I think everybody who's done blues, R&B, and jazz has those influences, takes those on board. Mose's work is very, very infectious and that's why people like it. Interestingly, in the days of the British R&B scene when his influence was very powerful, those guys were doing covers and went to the American blues and hip people. Mose was doubly appealing because he was hip and played jazz. The Muddy Waters thing was actually hard to do because it's so deep. O.K. Mick Jagger singing Muddy Waters doesn't really work but get somebody like Georgie Fame or Graham Bond singing those songs and they take on a different light. They make them sound convincing. Even today when I hear Cream playing "Spoonful" and then play Howlin' Wolf playing "Spoonful" I can't see the point of it. But when the blues was combined with jazz in the interesting way Mose did it, that was actually a direction people could take because it was more authentic. It wasn't just copied. Because it had such a jazz context, you could interpret. Georgie Fame did a version of "Seventh Son" in 7/4 and you could do it with those songs. You could use jazz. The classic blues performances—when you look at them now you ask, "Why the hell did all of those white people do it?" Yes, it's true they did something good for those blues guys because they made them prominent again and sold a lot of records, and used their tunes. But, when you listen to fucking Otis Rush, Howlin' Wolf, and Muddy Waters, you listen to that and you think, "How could anybody try and do that?" Whereas Mose was a contemporary songwriter, you can look at the song in a variety of ways for interpretation. The fact was that he was a real songwriter who also had roots in blues and standards which the jazzers were playing forever. Some of the things Mose plays are standards, the others are a new take on the blues. And, all of his songs are open to interpretation by others. Whereas, when you're covering Willie Dixon's "Spoonful" as done by Howlin' Wolf or "Hootchie Cootchie Man" as done by Muddy Waters, all people could do was copy and that was done badly anyway. Even the people who played it incredibly well were only scratching the surface of what was exactly there. That music came from out of very highly defined culture. And all this stuff about working-class British people relating to it; well, up to a point, yes they did. However, the main people who were successful during the blues boom were people like Paul Jones, Alexis Korner and John Mayall, who all came from incredibly privileged backgrounds and were very wealthy. Them singing Muddy Waters . . . being musicians is another matter. Anyone's entitled to do it if they've got the talent or the balls to go and do it. All of these people were copying. A lot of it has to do with this thing in Britain called "middle-class guilt." There was another guy named George Melly, another guy who came from an incredibly privileged background. He was one of the first British blues singers in the Dixieland environment. He had a very good voice and sang Bessie Smith songs. Yes, it was kind of weird, but I guess he was entitled to it. But at the same time, it wasn't very real. He had studied what he was singing about. It was like the British collecting mentality and wanting to be . . . like Tom Waits, when he sings like he's down and out, it's like shit. I know it's phony. Van Morrison singing the blues and stuff, yes, it's O.K., but I feel a lot better when he sings "Moondance." It's an original song, something he created; yes, it relates to jazz and blues a bit, but he's taken it one step further by doing something else with it. It's better.

Because Mose's work was more open to interpretation instead of just "the blues," the expression of poor black American culture, instead of being that—even if people identified with it here, being from the working class and it's authentic for them to do it and all that—actually, it sounds more convincing if people are doing more sophisticated things where you have more leeway to interpret.

Ray Charles was probably the biggest influence on the jazz people that became part of the R&B scene. Mose Allison was next. Ray Charles and Mose have a lot in common as well because they both created a body of songs which people do. The way they play, and the way that they play affecting their voices, the keyboard and voice interplay, the songs are certainly musically related. At the same time, Ray Charles was doing jazz and a couple of producers persuaded him to invent what he did because he was doing something else. And eventually, it worked.

Mose and I do have some other things in common. We actually do say no to some things and that compromise, no matter how much you suffer, is not the right thing to do. Mose is also a melancholic. And, like me, he's a gleeful cynic— listen to a song like "Ever Since the World Ended." We both can deal with a song about the end of the world, however, it's funny, because people should have known better but they didn't. It's a shame but it's also funny. That's the way that we can deal with it.

The blues, both male and female, has an element of the other gender being the enemy—my baby done gave me a dirty deal... I believe that means that my baby done gave me the clap. I think that's an Otis Rush tune. Women and men have always used the blues and related music to get back at each other. I don't think Mose's things are about the sex wars—they're more wistful than that.

Mose's image is that of someone who's been around a lot, seen it all, looks at the world with a cheerfully cynical point of view, almost like a philosopher.

You begin by becoming a composite of your influences. In a way, Mose's work is a bridge between the older blues, the straightahead blues, the deep black culture, and the next stage, which is for those musicians to begin writing original material. In other words, it was a stimulus for them to do it. And it was a bridge. There was one white face in America at that time and he was very alone. Here was somebody who was a character, he had charisma, and he wrote a body of songs, he was also blues-based and also had a base in jazz standards, which all those jazz musicians had at the time, therefore, he became a stimulus and bridge for them to do their own stuff and also for them to interpret his stuff. To me, those songs are more like standards and jazz-type material than they are the actual blues. And then again, he was a white person. Everyone loved the black blues but everyone realized they were limited in how much you could do, because you could never better that. However, it was easier to be close to Mose than to Muddy Waters. Everyone was wanting to be legendary—Graham Bond ended up sort of attaining that, as well as Alexis Korner, and Mose was also legendary because he had all those combinations of the mad artists. A body of work identifiable and interpretable.

The greatest thing about Mose is his individuality; he's an incredibly strong individual who's stayed that way.

Black Francis/Frank Black: Singer/Songwriter

I think the thing about Mose Allison is that he *does* have an impact when you hear him. It doesn't matter that I didn't grow up listening to him. Some guy a few years ago in Boston was playing Mose Allison records for me at his house. While I don't listen to a lot of jazz, I used to listen to a lot of blues. I got bored with the blues but used to listen to John Mayall and the Bluesbreakers. I went out and got a couple of Mose Allison CD compilations—like the *Best of* and one of his more recent records. I was so blown away by it. It was really interesting music. Here was this guy singing the blues who was smart, clever, and very spacey but not corny, pretentious or over-the-top. It was just the coolest of cool.

Later I had a discussion with a writer for the *L.A. Times* at a music store and we were talking about Mose Allison because I had just seen him in L.A. at a dinner club called the Vine Street Bar and Grill. He pretty much summed up Mose Allison with a single phrase. He said something like, "Yeah, Mose Allison is *right.*"

I recently got another CD and gave it to my father who's a bar owner and listens to a lot of jukeboxes all day, but he was just blown away. My father is in awe of Mose's music. He doesn't like music really—he likes Leon Redbone and George Thoroughgood and that's about it. Now he drives around in his pickup truck all day just listening to Mose Allison over and over. Same thing with my mother. My mother and stepfather went to hear him and she told Mose that I had written the song "Allison" for the Pixies.

The origin of "Allison" wasn't as dreamy as all that. I had the song and we were in the middle of recording this expensive record in Los Angeles. I hadn't written half the lyrics. There was this one little song, one of my favorite ones, a short little thing, a minute and twenty seconds, that was really fast and loud. I had the melody and a chorus that went "Allison," just because it was a girl's name, basically. I couldn't really write a girl's-name song called "Allison" because number one, I don't usually write songs like that, and another reason is that there already is a famous song called "Allison," by Elvis Costello. I kept saying I didn't want to get rid of this beautiful word Allison because I thought it was so great. Suddenly it occurred to me, why didn't I just write a song about Mose Allison? This idea appealed to me a lot because Mose had recently had a pretty strong impact on me. Also, at that time, it was my favorite one on the record. I'd never really written a song about anybody, any real person, anyway. I had a minute and twenty seconds to encapsulate what I thought Mose Allison was.

I guess I sort of think about him in sort of science-fiction terms, like he's some sort of blues hep cat traveling man going through time and space from one galaxy to the next, quietly singing the blues, which is basic people's music, very intelligently, telling it like it is. In those few seconds, I had the opportunity to write a song about the way that I felt about him and it had these science-fiction images.

Some of Mose's songs will have a sad note in them lyrically, but they always have this grin on them, sort of like, "Oh well, what are you going to do, that's the way the universe is." They come off very wise. The lyrics of my little meager song went:

From distant star
To this here bar
The me, the you
Where are we now?
Hooray, the blues
Of everyone
Allison

Keeps a smile
Around awhile.
He took no fright
And jettisoned
We'll go tonight
to hear him tell
"Oh Well"
Allison

When the planet hit the sun
I saw the face of Allison
Allison
Allison
Allison
Allison

The thing about Mose Allison: his music wasn't goofy or camp. It wasn't like some guy singing the "Monster Mash" or something. It was more "spiritual" if I can use that term. In a lot of rock over the years, sci-fi songs are sung but it comes off as camp, goofy, and sort of a joke. It wasn't a joke in Mose Allison's music. We sing science-fiction themes trying to elevate it, to also put a grin on it; it's serious but it's not serious.

During some of the songs in the Pixies' show, we project a few random slides of planets behind us. The only other image that we project is when we play "Allison," where we project an image of Mose Allison's face up on the screen. You can't really tell it's him. We took a photograph of the record covers and it looks like almost a negative of a photograph. It doesn't look silly, it looks really cool. So we have these cosmic images and then Mose Allison's face during that song.

Zoot Money: Musician

Georgie Fame introduced me to Mose Allison. Mose consolidated the idea that a white guy could actually sing in the mixture of the country-cum-blues-cum-jazz. Here in the U.K., there are segregated communities of purists in rhythm-and-blues and jazz people. Mose was the example that a white guy could actually sing in the two types of styles. Mose was "an American" influence, not just a black or white influence. His relaxed way of singing indicated a way of life for those of us who had not been to the United States. He didn't conform to the conventional music being imported at that time.

It seemed that the black blues players at that time were taking a black stance in protest over white domination, the business being pro-white. I didn't get any protest from Mose, just a lifestyle. "I Love the Life I Live" was the first song that reflected the lifestyle, and from that, I tried to glean a vibe or an approach, to ask why people lived and why compare them. Mose would sing in a relaxed style with no pretensions like the other singers. His records sold right alongside Bill Evans. Many eclectic artists existed in England, there was a whole range of music with totally different influences so that the English fan would remain true to the atmosphere and the different types of styles. England has been the country to show that it had blues to use. You wouldn't have any rock people or heavy-metal people without those musicians in England. Mose Allision was not trying to write about a black influence. His style doesn't indicate anything pseudo or phony. It was Mose Allison's delivery that interested me most. I'm more of an extrovert performer. Mose Allison had an American sound and was prone to black-influenced artists. The approach to the voice was what I was working towards in trying to sound American and Mose helped me to do that. You should sing the song phonetically whether or not you use an accent.

John Hammond: Blues Singer/Guitarist

I started my career in Los Angeles in 1962. One of my early shows was at a club called the Insomniac in Hermosa Beach. Across the street was a club called the Lighthouse, an elegant jazz room, and Mose Allison was playing there. I had heard a record called "Parchman Farm" on a jukebox in 1960 in Ohio where I went to school. There was a black ribs joint called Cobbs in Yellow Springs, Ohio where I used to go to eat and drink beer. They had a great jukebox including B.B. King, Bobby Bland and Junior Parker, and they had this one tune that was really different and cool, it was "Parchman Farm." There was a piano and there were no fleshy guitars or a big horn section or anything. The singer was real cool and it was Mose Allison.

I imagined him to be a black guy from maybe Chicago or Memphis. An old-time blues-singer guy. Was I ever surprised when I walked across the street to the Lighthouse and saw Mose Allison, a white guy, playing in this club. I was profoundly influenced, seeing somebody so into the music, and he seemed like a really cool guy. I was just starting my career and here was a guy who was getting airplay with his records and had a handle on the jazz scene, something that was way beyond my scope of ever attaining or being part of or making my mark in. Here was a guy who was doing blues, yet still into the jazz inner circle which I thought was excruciatingly hip. So, that's how impressed I was with Mose.

Mose is a great player and singer. The fact that he was white at the same time gave me some kind of an insight as to the fact that all you got to do is be it, love it and you are it. He was a reinforcement to that idea and at the same time, I just thought he was really cool. I wasn't the only one who had that impression and I know for sure that he is admired by as many black artists as white artists.

I don't think I've borrowed anything from him because I'm me, I play in my own style, but I do a few of his songs because I think they're so great. I do "Everybody's Crying Mercy," and "Ask Me Nice." I also do tunes that he didn't write that I heard him do and thought were cool. Some of the ones I first heard him do are "Seventh Son" and "Baby Please Don't Go." I've learned a lot of his songs over the years and lately made a recording of "I'm a Wildman" which I thought was his but was really written by Wildman Willis. The thing is, you're so impressed by the way somebody does something you realize that even if he didn't write the tune, in my mind, as long as I live, that's Mose Allison's tune. That's the way it is in blues, it's a traditional hand-me-down thing and nobody can really make any heavy-duty claims. Perhaps even Wildman Willis copped a lot of the words from his idol or whatever. That's the way that goes. The reality is that somebody who puts a hole in it has claim to it, in my book, anyway. I don't claim to write songs but when I do a song, it's my song.

Mose is a great piano player but to me, in my opinion, Mose's singing is the soul of him. It's his real core. That's what he sets you up for, these vocals which are so right on. His singing and his choice of material is what he sets everything up to showcase.

When I first heard him perform, his piano playing was a lot more in the groove and not as out as it is now. Not out in the sense of being weird or anything, but now he plays around with rhythms, modulations and scales. I've always enjoyed his whole persona, his whole stage thing. The fact that he'll fool around with time and feelings sort of brings you around to focus on the songs he's going to sing. I might be completely wrong and miss his whole point but to me, I think he's having fun with his life and style.

I think Mose's music has moved me so deeply that I will always be a fan of his. In terms of being a great critic, I don't hold my opinion so high as to say who's great and who isn't, but to me, Mose Allison is *great*. He's one of those players that I will always remember as long as I live. He's had a tremendous influence on me as a musician and also as a person because he's a very cool guy.

Brian Auger: Keyboard Player

I sort of came up the wrong way around in my career. I played jazz first and won jazz polls in England playing in clubs like Ronnie Scott's Club in London and the places where only jazz players were allowed.

The first time I heard Mose's music was when I was still playing jazz and would hear Georgie Fame go on. Georgie Fame was incredibly heavily influenced by Mose Allison. He sounds like Mose to me, he did all of Mose's material, and so did a lot of other people. In fact, just about every band who played in the Flamingo played at least one or two Mose Allison tunes. The ones I remember that everybody played were "Parchman Farm" and "Seventh Son," and then it ranged off into different things like "If You're Going to the City." I recorded one when I had my solo album out—"If You Live" was recorded on my first solo album in 1968.

I always thought that the rhythmic side of Mose's thing was kind of different because it wasn't really straight-out jazz with a straightahead beat. Some of it was, but a lot of it wasn't like that at all; it was a shuffling kind of swamp beat. So, I used to take that and manipulate those kinds of things and people could dance to that.

I'd say that it was more than Mose's approach that was important. The thing about Mose is this: here we are, we're English kids, right, and our dream is "America," we're musicians—it would be like going to Mecca for us if we actually ever got to America to play, and we never dreamed we ever could. It was the kind of thing we dreamed about and our idols were American musicians. Basically, everyone was influenced by American musicians, Chuck Berry and so on, and that's where we got our inspiration from. Mose's lyrics had that Southern flavor that strongly reminded us of that steamy Mississippi place or Southern America where things were settled with "Gotta go down town, gotta do what's right." We had heard black guys sing the blues. We had some understanding of that situation. Let's not say that we fully understand, because nobody in England was in their shoes. But their struggle goes on the same way as, say, Eric Burdon's, who is from Newcastle—where there are a lot of mining towns—it's a tough and grim life but people somehow overcome it and their spirit is such that they make something of it.

I come from an English working-class family and I saw my dad struggle through two wars and we were bombed out in the Second World War and I was about three years old and I remember that. While growing up there was a certain awareness of what the police mean and what it's like to be in a society where you're judged not so much by the color of your skin but by your accent. It's the same old shit. If you get into trouble and are from a working-class family, it's going to be more difficult to get out and you're going to get rousted by the authorities, probably a lot more than those who come from the right side of the tracks and have the right accent and dress the right way. And those things are the things that the people who played rock and roll in England were escaping from: the drudgery of factories and the usual nonsense that you would be put through. That was the great upsurge of creativity that started the rock-and-roll scene, and the energy that fueled it.

Sometimes in my own writing, I have used some characteristics of Mose's writing. There's a kind of laconic humor in his lyrics which I really like and that would appeal to the English sense of humor—when we understood what he was talking about! And I still love those kind of lyrics and they're to the point in a very simple way, even if he's talking about "your molecular structure." I mean, nobody could take offense at that. And another great one is "they always told me there'd be days like this." How many times did I think of that when my car had broken down on the M1 or some amp had blown up or fighting through a ridiculously horrible day, we'd get mad and sing it.

I've followed his work recently. His piano playing has changed and is much more chromatic in style. I think it's probably less accessible and I understand that. As musicians, we're all trying to move forward and the music industry is not there clapping and shouting. They're asking, "What happened to the old formulas that worked? Why aren't you doing this or that?" And we say "We have to stretch and move forward or we'll die and the music will die with it." So, I admire Mose for changing in that vein.

It's interesting that he thinks of himself as a middle-class white boy—it's the same as me. I can't say that my financial situation makes me working-class anymore, but that gives me a certain consciousness that I wouldn't want to give up for anything.

Jorma Kaukonen: Guitarist

Mose is one of those guys who has always been intellectual. I first found out about Mose in the middle to late fifties at the Showboat in Washington, D.C. Mose played a lot in D.C. at the time. I think Charlie Byrd, the jazz guitarist, may have had something to do with running that club. I haven't studiously followed his career over the last thirty years, but our paths do cross from time to time and he's still great. He's just one of those guys.

The way we do the blues is a little different. It's just a matter of personal definition. I like to blanket it all, saying it's all pretty much the same although Mose is a lot more jazzy in his approach than us, but he can certainly be funky when he wants to be. I was influenced more by Mose's early stuff. With Hot Tuna, we've covered "Parchman Farm," "Young Man Blues," "Middle Class White Boy," and songs of that ilk. I like his more lyric-oriented songs, I like what he does with lyrics.

I guess the only parallel to my work with Mose's is that

we're both middle-class white boys trying to have some fun. I think what Mose is doing is more sophisticated.

Georgie Fame: Singer/Songwriter/Keyboard Player

The first time I heard Mose was on his first record, *Back Country Suite*. I was the resident band in the Flamingo. I started there in March, 1962 for about three years. This place was frequented by a lot of black American G.I.s. Down at the Flamingo, pretty early after I started, one of these American servicemen, Carl Smith, an Air Force sergeant from Grand Rapids, Michigan—and I hope if he ever reads the book, I give him my love, because I haven't seen him since—used to stay at my place on weekends while I was working. He gave me my first Mose Allison album, *Back Country Suite*. I fell in love with what I heard. It just fitted the thing at the time. It was just what I needed to hear: the warmth of the voice, the style, the individuality. He melted my heart with the sound of his voice. I think it took me about ten years to get into the piano playing, but I love it all now.

I've written a couple of songs which have been, unintentionally but directly, inspired by Mose, just the shape, the form, and interpretation and the way they're performed. From the first five years of my playing career, he had a profound influence on my vocal sound. I had a kind of nasal sound anyway but I found myself just trying to sing like Mose for at least five years. Then I tried to shake it off as I matured. He's been one of the major influences on my vocal sound. I mean, I'm not a Mose Allison copyist anymore. I was. Hopefully, now I have my own style.

On my own album in 1963, recorded live at the Flamingo, I recorded "Parchman Farm" and also "Baby, Please Don't Go" *à la* Mose. I was influenced by his early work and I followed his career throughout. Even in 1969 or '70, I recorded "Seventh Son." I did it really differently. I did it in 7/4, which is what the time suggested and it worked. It was a good record. That was actually a hit in England in 1970.

I had all of Mose's records. I think the *Western Man* album is *the* work, the most profound work. But I think the last two records are the best. He seems to get better and better and God bless him!

Al Kooper: Keyboard Player, Producer

The first time I heard Mose Allison was in 1958, probably on the radio. New York radio didn't really play blues at all unless it was a cross-over of something that was in the top forty or something. Hearing Mose and never dreaming he was white—I probably heard "Parchman Farm" first, which was sort of a hit on those stations around that time—I really liked it. I didn't understand it at all, it was peculiar. It would come time for a solo and it was so untraditional that it was Martian—my ears couldn't take that in—of course I was only fourteen or fifteen.

Then in 1959 my parents took me and my best friend to hear some jazz. By this time, I was already making records as a rock-and-roll person in a band called the Royal Teens. We brought books with us because we thought it might be boring. What we picked out was purely a double bill—the Ray Bryant Trio and Art Blakey and his Jazz Messengers. Art Blakey at that time had Bobby Timmons on piano, Benny Golson and Lee Morgan. Needless to say, we didn't crack our books much; I was bowled over completely. Then I saw Mose in a different light entirely, and sort of understood in my own peculiar way what he was doing in the piano solos; it made more sense in that context than just in a flat-out blues context, because jazz is a wider umbrella. Mose made more sense in a jazz framework than in a blues framework, although I think he fits in both. But if he didn't play solos and just sang and played, or played traditional blues solos, he would definitely be a blues artist. Simply put, if you go to a jazz festival and hear Mose Allison, he fits right in. If you go to a blues festival and hear Mose Allison he's going to stick out because the music is more educated and brainy than just something that's from the heart.

Mose led me to the people I needed to be led to. He covered Willie Dixon and Muddy Waters—songs like "Seventh Son" and "Rolling Stone." I liked that first batch of stuff. "Eyesight to the Blind," "Parchman Farm," "I'm Not Talkin'," "Seventh Son." It was the whole package that I liked.

I didn't really hear B.B. King, Muddy Waters, Freddie King until 1965, when I joined a band. But my leanings were in this direction, so it was something that I could immediately take in, feel, understand, interpret and be a part of. One of my old partners, who is now deceased, said, "The thing about Jewish people is that they have as valid a right to be involved in the blues as black people." And I said, "Why is that?" And he said, "Black people suffer externally and Jewish people suffer internally." The blues was like a pair of pajamas to me; I could put them right on and feel really comfortable. When I was in the band and we first started, we played on the same bill with people like Muddy Waters and James Cotton, and all these people we were listening to. I was lucky enough to get piano lessons from Muddy's piano player at that time, his name was Otis Spann.

We started this resurrection of the blues in a white neighborhood. If you wanted to see people like Muddy Waters or Jimmy Reed you had to go up to Harlem. I don't know as anybody gave a shit about them in New York because they weren't covered by the media in this neck of the woods. So, all of the sudden they were playing in Village. They had never played gigs like that. We were on residency there—we were like the house band—and little by little, we built a very considerable following. We played there all the time because nobody else would have us and we weren't very good, but we played week after week. Similar things were happening all over the country. There were young people who loved the blues and were spurred on by rock and roll. Instead of being in rock bands they were forming blues bands. Mose played jazz gigs, then, but we all played Mose Allison songs: "I Love the Life I Live," "Parchman Farm."

Mose was a hero to everyone in the band and a very strong influence on sixties rock and roll. Everyone who put a band together from 1963 on that was blues-influenced at all was touched by Mose Allison, no matter what country they were in. Whether they did any of the songs or not is irrelevant. It's sort of like what Lou Reed had to say about the first Velvet Underground album—which is one of my favorite quotes—the album only sold about 40,000 copies, but everybody who bought it started a band!

Susannah McCorkle: Jazz/Cabaret Singer

I was in college at Berkeley in the late sixties, maybe 1968, when I first heard Mose. I was going out with someone who was too fast for me really—I was a freshman and at that time I still wanted to be a virgin until I got married and everything. This guy had a kind of offbeat sense of humor and I liked him, but he lived in a squalid apartment. One day he had this record on and I really liked it. It was "Seventh Son"—I was fascinated by it, not just the lyric but the sound of the singing and the piano playing. Then I didn't think any more about it for years. That was the very first time I heard Mose Allison.

Then, when I became really interested in being a singer, I was twenty-six. I started very late and was living in Paris. I went back and listened to people that I vaguely remembered the names of from the past. The main ones I listened to were Billie Holiday and Bessie Smith, and I also liked Brazilian music. But I always remembered Mose Allison and the song I remembered most that I found myself singing was the blues song "That's All Right." I really loved that song and loved it that someone who was not trying to sound black had a great, authentic blues feeling. I identify with this because people have commented to me that I also have a lot of blues feeling in my singing without trying to sound black. It's a soulfulness. There are plenty of both black and white singers whose singing sounds plastic. It's more whether a singer has music in his or her soul, whether they have pain in their soul and can communicate it through music. I always remembered this about Mose, and when I moved to London and started singing professionally on a very low scale in clubs, I wanted to do "That's All Right." The rhymes for a female-singer weren't great—it was really awkward to replace some of the words, but everybody loved it and knew that record. That was in the mid-seventies.

Mose's material, on the whole, is not very suitable for me, but at that time, I was working with a piano player who would do anything I wanted to do, which was great. Of course, he had to like it too, and he immediately did—Mose comes with such great credentials, he's always been such a great pianist. I was doing a lot of material that wasn't necessarily right for me, but we were doing a lot of Mose Allison songs. We did "Your Mind Is on Vacation," "You Can Count on Me to Do My Part," "It Didn't Turn Out That Way," and "No Special Place." I especially loved his what I think of as "evolved blues." They're songs in blues form but have a reflective, intellectual, sarcastic sense of humor that is unlike any other kind of blues. He took the blues in an entirely new direction, poetically and in terms of temperament . . . He talked about burned-out relationships and things that didn't work out on a mental basis. He wasn't just singing, "I lost my baby or my baby quit me." He was singing more about, "You did this and you did that and we can't make it because you don't understand this and I understand that and we can't communicate."

I think at first, especially in "That's All Right," I just loved the sound so much, I would slur the way he slurred. I have a light "white" voice too and a lot of feeling for the blues. In a way, I viewed myself as his female counterpart. I don't mean to compare myself with him, but in regard to my sound, the timbre and the feeling for blues and rhythm, and jazz, it came very naturally to me. It was as if he was my talented brother and I was his sister who grew up much the same way, and tuned into the same thing. And also that dark sense of humor—that's a part of me too.

I don't think I've recorded anything of his, but "Your Mind Is on Vacation" is so funny. The only time you can really do that is when people are talking. But the people who are talking aren't listening. But, it's sour and I don't like to do sour things in my performance, especially now. Now, I generally say nice things like "This room is really live, we're hearing every whisper, I wonder if you'll help us concentrate and give our best show by being a little quieter." I talk like that. I wouldn't do a put-down song like "Your Mind's on Vacation" but I love that it exists and the musicians love that song because it's so funny.

Mose is a thinking person. I really like that about him besides his great musicianship and easy, relaxed singing. The language is simple but he says a lot if you care to listen to him. In fact, one blues song I liked so much—"Nightclub"—that I wrote more choruses for it, but I never felt I could do it because that's not really the direction I've gone. It is so right on though—and I have so many things I could say about nightclubs, too. In simple language, he really captured the essence of how hard it is to play clubs and be on the road all the time.

I could have guessed that Mose would have liked Nat Cole. I liked Nat Cole best when he sang with the trio because he had that throwaway, unpretentious style then. That's what Mose has always kept. He has never become a "singing star" and the sound of his voice is so wonderful. And he's always a guy with ideas, musical and intellectual ideas, and he's always stayed that way. He has such a clear identity.

Mose's lyrics aren't really suited to women, and taking a cynical stance is not suited to me, it's not my persona on stage or off. I can be tough in the sense of a woman telling a man to shape up, a strong woman, that I can do. But not the cynical-about-life woman—because that's not how I feel and so I can't bring off a song like that very well. It's great to have models and do every kind of song when you first start out. If you're going to get anywhere as a singer and develop a clear identity, pretty soon you just know what songs are yours to sing. I felt that Mose's songs, as good as they were, were not really my songs to sing. I was singing all types of songs, when I was doing Mose's songs, Bessie Smith and some dirty blues, and those weren't my songs to sing either. Even some of the great American standards aren't my songs to sing. I still respect Mose's work very much—I just had to be more discriminating in my choice of material. That way you get a much clearer image on stage and can build an audience. In the same way, if Mose had kept doing Nat Cole songs the way Nat Cole did them, he wouldn't be Mose Allison. He took those influences and built upon them. And I think of Mose a lot when I sing, too—he has that relaxed quality in tone, good diction; Nat Cole had that and Chet Baker too. And giving something from your life. That's another thing he does. You feel he's singing about his life. He's not a guy just singing songs—there are pieces of himself in every song. All of my favorites—like Billie Holiday and Mose, he's definitely one of my favorites—have that quality of giving themselves every time they sing. They don't just give a performance, they give themselves. I try to do this, myself—you really have to know yourself pretty well to put be able to put yourself out there like that. And that's hard to do, because if people don't like your music, then, it's *you* they don't like!

I've never forgotten the way he did "Do Nothing Till You Hear From Me"—I do that song without even thinking about it, like him, without pushing, just sly and funny—the way you would talk to a person. That's another thing he does—he adds a personal quality to the song.

Another thing I like about Mose is that my favorite male singers always started as instrumentalists and then sang a little—I don't like these lugubrious, unctuous, pretty-boy singers luxuriating in the sound of their own voices. In fact, I don't like women who do that either. But, it's especially obnoxious with men—men simply can't get away with it at all. Nat Cole and Ray Charles are singers who just feel it and sing it, no phoniness. Ray Charles is probably my favorite male singer. Mose never imitated other people's sounds. A lot of people have noticed that I like a lot of male singers because they're so natural-sounding. I like a lot of the singing by instrumentalists—like Louis Armstrong, Jack Teagarden, Red Allen, Hot Lips Page, and Chet Baker. They don't have that staginess, and that sense of producing pretty notes. Instead, they're just communicating a story, a mood. My theory is that they started singing because they liked words and moods. Maybe Mose started writing to evoke some of his own moods.

Mose is unique in the world, and like all the greats, there will never be anybody at all like him. He really has his place in music, jazz and popular singing history as far as I'm concerned. I rate him very highly as a creative artist and an artist of great integrity. He found his style, his sound, and he was never diverted by popular trends. He is very respected and revered—and personally and professionally, he's been very important to me.

Ray Davies: Singer/Songwriter

I was influenced by a whole lot bunch of people—Hoagy Carmichael, for instance. I mention Hoagy Carmichael because, when I was a kid, I heard a lot of his records. In a sense, there is the same strange type of folksiness that I hear a thread of in Mose Allison's music. When I was a kid I heard "Parchman Farm." A lot of cover bands in London, like Georgie Fame, did it. I used to play the Marquee and I heard Georgie do it there. After that, I heard it on record. In fact, "Parchman Farm" was a minor hit over here.

I think appreciation of other people's work, and of music in general, is very individual and subjective. I can't give any logical reason why I should like certain types or pieces. For example, a lot of my music is influenced by stuff I heard as a child and I wasn't aware of it then. It's only coming through to me as an adult.

It wasn't until 1979 that I heard Mose Allison play live, so I have probably been exposed more to his later work. I remember flying to Atlanta to see friends, and they told me that Mose Allison was playing that night. And that name took me back. I wondered why at the time of "Parchman Farm" he never made a major breakthrough. I thought it was a great record, and I knew that he had an album or two out at that time, but I had started on my own career and had sort of stopped listening to anything.

So, as I was saying, I went down to Atlanta, walked into a club and asked the guy standing behind the bar what time Mose Allison was going on and he said, "I'm on in five minutes." I saw him standing behind the bar and thought he was the barman! He was a bit wizened then. It wasn't what I had imagined from listening to him. He didn't look like he sounded. Then he got up on stage with his trio. The musicians were much younger than him, and at first, I was kind of saddened by that, but then I realized that the bittersweetness of the situation was reflected in his music. It was a part of his music. After that, I started to familiarize myself with his work more. The next couple of times I saw him was in New York at Fat Tuesdays, then I took friends who had never heard of him to the Bottom Line in the early 1980s.

What I like about Mose Allison is that he doesn't seek star status; he keeps a low profile. I wondered why that was, and it intrigued me enough to approach him about doing a film on him. I think he is a real exponent of American music, a white American folk/blues artist, the legitimate article. I've only spoken with him briefly, but I think he is the missing link between the blues performers and his contemporaries like Elvis and Carl Perkins. They went off and played rock and roll, and it seems he stayed on his own route. This is an instinctive feeling I picked up just from listening to him play in Atlanta at that time. He appealed to my sense of humor, my sensibilities. He's a very underrated lyricist, and a very underrated pianist as well. In fact I think he's actually gotten better since I last heard him play. That was at Pizza on the Park here in London. His piano playing was definitely getting better.

I think maybe Mose Allison may not have been trendy enough for the American mainstream. He wasn't radical like Mingus, and as far as I know, he hasn't caused any great waves politically or socially. It looks to me like he's done it more to himself. He's internalized his waves. I have no idea what his personal life is like, but I got this feeling just from seeing him play and hearing his music, and I must admit, I didn't know what to expect when I met him. I was expecting a slick-looking kind of guy but he actually brought to mind my image of the biblical Moses.

In starting from zero, I've discovered there are common threads between myself and Mose Allison. I think it was a fantastic thing that happened in this country in the early sixties, when there were a lot of young people absorbing information very quickly, listening to a wide range of music and passing on ideas. I think Georgie Fame was the nearest thing we had to Mose Allison.

Until I saw him in 1979, I hadn't really had access to Mose Allison; he rarely came into my consciousness. But, after I had seen him play live I realized what a great artist he was and I wanted to go to hear him whenever I could. Not just out of professional curiosity, but for my own amusement and pleasure, which is something I can rarely do.

John Mayall: Blues Guitarist, Singer

I've always enjoyed Mose's piano playing and at that time he was one of the few jazz pianists who was calling heavily on the blues background rather than the regular jazz people who had gone before him—that sort of set him apart in my book. Everybody I know in England was raised on Mose Allison, particularly because of Georgie Fame and his band at the Flamingo. The name of Mose Allison was very strong in England in the early sixties. I got to hear *Back Country Suite* around the same time the album was released in 1957 through the shortwave broadcasts of Voice of America, which came out of D.C. These were not for airing in America but only for overseas. That was the only link we had—over the shortwave—and they were really great because as soon as the album was released and each night it was an hour of the latest music from America and our only link to what was being released.

Pete Townshend: Singer/Songwriter, Guitarist

Recently, I took my friends to listen to Mose when he was playing in England and at the end of the show they said, "Now I understand, now I understand." I asked, "You understand what?" They replied, "Now I understand why you are the way you are." Mose Allison is that much part of me.

I liked Dixieland jazz, which I used to see in rather a "Disneyland" sort of way. My father was a musician in a band, a dance band, also an English Air Force band, and they used to do a Dixieland spot which was like a gag—"Now we play this funny jazz music." Although my parents didn't sneer at blues or jazz, far from it, I never really got exposed to it at all. The Who were working then, doing clubs and pubs, and we used to play pop music like Buddy Holly, Elvis Presley, Cliff Richard, the Shadows, the Ventures, guitar music really and mainly white music. This guy, Tom Wright, befriended me in my second year of art school and started to open up this cauldron of practically all black music from his enormous record collection that he bought on the base; practically all black music, people like Ray Charles, Jimmy Smith, Snooks Eaglin—I'm naming all of those who primarily influenced me—Sonny Boy Williamson, Little Walter, Jimmy Reed, Chuck Berry, Bo Diddley, Lightnin' Hopkins and John Lee Hooker. There are a few other people, some soft blues artists that went into jazz—like the Ramsey Lewis trio and a bit of that kind of jazz. But I just got kind of lost in all this stuff and it was like a real initiation because what I really heard was new music. I mean it was really new to me. All of it.

I took the same route that I think a lot of other people of my age and my background did; I assumed that Mose Allison was black. I associated a lot of the kind of soft, cool attributes of his voice with that free-spirited but none the less subjugated black man living in the South in America, the bastion of racism where the music was obviously a signal that emancipation was going to come not just through the music but through the church, somehow, because the music was so obviously gospel-oriented and so full of spiritual vigor. A couple of years later when the album with his face on the front appeared, I think we all went crazy; I think Tom Wright did as well. This was really important for us. It was really important that blues could exist, as Miles Davis says, "on the white side." I don't know whether Miles Davis actually agreed that it can exist on the white side, but in a way, it is an interesting argument because what you have to look at is what actually happened and not what we think or feel. Miles was suffering, like a lot of black musicians, from continuing prejudice, and it breeds discomfort, anger and bitterness, and quite rightly. But that anger and bitterness was already there in the young people who lived in working-class Britain in the sixties. We associated with blues music because it sounded like our music, it sounded like our voice. It was a voice that we readily used. We didn't feel that our suffering was commensurate with the suffering of black slaves, but neither did we, in our innocence, believe that there was still such a thing as black slavery even in America. What we actually felt, what we were dealing with, like black musicians in the South, was the echoes of the indignity of man's inhumanity to man, which in the States was the enslavement of blacks. In Europe, the enslavement of the young man as cannon fodder, the enslavement and education of the young man purely to be put into the trenches and blown to bits. You have to realize that when I was fifteen years old, we were only fifteen years away from one of the most horrible wars that the world will ever see. It was fresh in everybody's mind. It was much, much, much more horrible than anything anybody has ever cared to expose or admit. The extraordinary article "The Real War" in the *Atlantic Monthly* July, 1989 describes that the news articles released in Europe and America during the war never included a photograph of a dismembered man; never, not once. Yet, the real first-hand stories from combat indicate that 50 percent of the injuries were from being hit by parts of other men's bodies. You may have seen a dismembered Asian but never a Caucasian. We felt there was kind of a conspiracy going on, that we were being educated that we were safe, that the war was over but it still felt strange.

Also, the fact was that there was still, and probably still is in England, the most extraordinarily deeply-rooted class structure, which is totally impossible to overcome. We were being told that there was this Brave New World in which our fathers and grandfathers had fought so that we could be free, and yet we knew that we weren't free. We didn't actually really have opportunities. There was nowhere for us to go. This wasn't really true for me, personally. I led a privileged life because I was the son of a musician who was earning good money and I was in that kind of classless world that musicians tend to inhabit. But the people who used to come and see the band play in the early days were young working-class kids who had just adapted the modernist lifestyle which began as a kind of jazz-based fashion ethic. I say ethic as it involved behavioral traits which were undoubtedly black-influenced through black behavior that you would see in young American blacks, say living in Paris, that kind of very dignified, well-dressed, cool, quiet kind of expensive appearance. A lot of black musicians and black concert performers went to live in Paris because they were treated with dignity there. Paris was nearby and we could see what was going on. We would go to visit their jazz clubs and hang out on the West Bank and the most beautiful girls would be with black men. So, black people became very naturally our superiors, our moral, intellectual superiors. To discover R&B, black music with a dance emphasis from that particular time as distinct from jazz actually gave us a musical root as well. I think that for me it was really important to discover that Mose was white. It was important to know that blues came from the "white side" and that there were people in the South who were white who identified with the cry of the heart and that what music is always capable of doing is dealing with much more universal emotions, the apparent hypocrisy of the white man singing the blues or whatever.

By 1962 or '63, I'd gone to the extent of distilling everything that I could learn without learning about the man, but from his music, everything I could learn about Mose Allison, into my work. I didn't go much further. I didn't go off looking for white blues performers. I didn't really have to go any further. I've always felt that Mose was a misfit in a sense in that respect. It's not just the voice, it's the person that he is. He was born in the wrong body or something.

I was very surprised when we got to the States to realize how racist the country still was. "Substitute" was the first record I wrote for the Who. In it there's a line that says, "I look all white but my dad was black, I'm just a substitute." In that I'm making a reference to the fact that I look like a white musician but my music is a black heritage. Atlantic Records, which after all had the Coasters, Ray Charles, and dozens of black artists, made me change the fucking line. They made me change it to something else and Roger had to go in and rerecord it before they could release the record. They said this was a controversial line. And that was in 1966!

We were very naïve. We didn't consciously think that we were bringing American black music back to America. In fact, this is something that has taken a long time to understand.

To structure an arch academic question you have to ask yourself what is the function of modern white music and what was the function of the original Delta blues which influenced Mose and then influenced us. If the two exist today in any form at all, do they exist in the way that the Who's music does—which I don't think is evident now in a celebratory sense—or does it have a function today. It's the idea that the form of the music follows the function. So when I go back and look at what started the blues off I'm not interested in what they're playing in clubs today. If Chicago still has a blues club it's because Chicago still likes to think of itself as the home of the blues and they serve ribs. It has nothing to do with the supply of beef or the supply of black misery. Today there should be music for people who live in cardboard boxes on the street, not just in Chicago but in every city that we played in on this tour. The other day we were coming back on the bus going back into the city after a show and passed by a bus station. I noticed that one of the people living in the cardboard boxes was carrying all of this stuff in a bag but they had a guitar and I thought, ah ha, maybe music will come out of this. That is what we're looking at. For me, the penny dropped this year in January at the Rock and Roll Hall of Fame thing that I went to where the leader of the Soul Stirrers, the band that Sam Cooke started in 1950, was there to receive an award. I'd never heard of them and this guy, Robert R.H. Harris, who is eighty-six got on the stage and said, "We waited sixty years for this recognition. It's a pity that it has to come from a predominantly white audience. Our own people have never given us any accolades. You rock-and-roll people have finally come around to recognize the importance of the Soul Stirrers and rock and roll was directly inspired by rhythm and blues and rhythm and blues was directly inspired by gospel with a swing and gospel with a swing was invented by the Soul Stirrers." He took credit for everything and everyone acknowledged it. I found out later when I talked to John Landau that the Soul Stirrers were the first band that ever took a Hammond organ into a church. You start to understand that there were seeds planted and that that was a fantastically significant moment.

I think Mose's music has adapted to the kind of audiences he's playing to, to the kind of people he's playing to, to actually take in and possibly irritate and break down preconceptions that people have to him. In the live performances that I've seen of him lately, particularly to the cafe crowds, he handles the audience in a very skillful and sophisticated way, but the most important thing is he handles them in a very honest way; he's not pretending to be what he was. He's not pretending to even come where he once came from.

There's one other interesting thing that I wanted to say to wrap up what we were talking about earlier regarding black blues music and current urban music which occurs to me now. If Charlie Parker, Miles Davis, and young hip hop and scratch musicians currently in urban black dance music are trying to use music in order to create a secret language it can never work, because music is the only thing you can't lie in. Music is the only language which tells the truth. Music is the only art form which doesn't need translation. I think this is the problem. The black heart and soul expresses itself most effectively, honestly, directly, and in the most uncluttered and simple way through music. It's, therefore, so easily exploited and I think that that's probably the tragedy. When you're as influenced as Mose has been and latterly people like the Who, the Stones, and the Beatles, and lots of others of our generation and latterly lots of other people either directly or indirectly by black music, you have to start on the premise that you're actually imitating your superiors. You have to keep telling yourself that. You actually have to read the gospel as it's laid down by the very, very bitter Miles Davis and *agree with it.* You have to agree that dance music on the "white side" is never going to have the truth or directness or the honesty of dance music from the "black side" because white people don't dance anymore. You know, they don't even really like to dance. What they actually like to do is show off, that's a bit different. You are talking about racial integrity. Sadly, it comes down to that. The African continent is an enormous continent. It's very, very pure and the racial strains are very pure, they're very ancient and genetically, if you're going to go back into it, rhythm is actually a part of the culture. Somebody said to me the other day, "Do you listen to World Music?" And I said, "What the fuck is World Music?" And they said, "You know, music from West Africa and South Africa." And I said, "Listen, that's the blues."

But to get back to Mose: I think the time that I was most influenced by him was in the early part of my songwriting career. What I think is important to remember is that in the songs that he writes himself he's an excellent poet. He shows tremendous brevity, dry wit, he doesn't use force. If you hear T.S. Eliot reading his own poetry, there's no emotion in his voice at all. That's one of the things I like about Mose. The music supplies the emotion and the voice is just a deadpan, sweet-boyish voice that just lets you hear the words. Sometimes there are terrible complaints, whining going on in the lyrics. In a sense, self-denigration, for example, "I'm a middle-class white boy." The beauty of it, at least for me, is that I learned a lot about song structure. And musically, the influences really only come up when I sit and play the keyboard. On guitar I don't get it.

The song form that Mose used, and I think continues to use, is a very straightforward and simple one, but it is capable of tremendous sophistication and I'm proud in a sense that Mose is still working with music that could be described as blues because it's about some very great deep ache—aloneness, and a sadness, and a guilt. I think the blues actually in its early form was the guilt of the impotent man, like I was talking about earlier in Soweto. You know, these are brave people but one of the things they hate is when they come to fight, they lose. This doesn't make you in any sense inferior, but if you lose too many battles you end up carrying a tremendous amount of guilt. I still hear that guilt there in Mose's music as well. That's what I identify with. There is a part of him that he can make fun of in himself. He can joke about it and he does this in the lyric. But in the music you hear this . . . you know, he's decided at some point that the recognition that he's seeking could be at any level but he knows what he's capable of handling and he's actually limited himself to what he's capable of handling. I think that's a tremendous frustration to everyone around him who realizes and recognizes in him a tremendous genius but someone who will never ever allow that genius to blossom because he hasn't the courage.

The place that he's happiest and most effective is an ultimate place. He needs a degree of intimacy to communicate. In order to sell more records, the answers are inevitable. The music does have to be reduced. The level of intimacy has to be reduced. The acuteness of the music has to be reduced. In certain ways, it would be less. It would be not as good. It would be not up to the standard that he would require. But what I meant was that within his own terms, there are people who are in contact with him who have recognized and understand him, I think, on the receiving end, who recognize him as an unbelievably important figure in music, an unbelievably vital bridge to the country blues of the late fifties in this country and an incredibly sociological bridge, an access, a right to *be* for somebody like me, for example. A right to have a voice. A right to use a white voice to sing and to share the sadness and the guilt. And hopefully, to portend some change in the future.

I think white rock kind of came along and replaced war. As I said earlier, we were trained to be cannon fodder and then told that we weren't required because all they had to do was to push a button. People wonder why young men go and fight in football stadiums in Europe, particularly in Britain which has been an incredibly brutal, violent, war-like nation for five or six hundred years or longer—thousands of years. I remember when I was a child, the whole atlas was pink; it was all British. The whole world, or at least that's the way it felt. We had a big, big empire. That's the world I grew up in and you can make a young man feel guilty if you tell him that what he's got to do to be a man is to fight to redeem his family and his country and then tell him that he's not necessary, not required, there's nothing he can do, everything he wants to do is futile, just go away, we don't need you anymore, keep out of trouble, don't speak, don't utter, don't bring me your filthy rock-and-roll music with its demons and its ghouls, and its satanic messages. In a way, it's so deeply linked to what's happening in the townships. Some people would say that this is a precious and indulgent parallel. I mean, I agree. I live in a big house. I've got two cars and a boat. I'm not pretending to live the life they do in the townships, but I identify very, very strongly, particularly with some of the kids who used to come see the Who in the early days in Shepherds Bush in the early sixties who used to look upon us as a source for music and who, therefore, happened upon Mose's music through listening to the Who and listen to it today. An Irish friend of mine, who's a postman in Cork, who went back to Ireland and he was a bus conductor for a while and now he's a postman. You know, he still earns £50 or £60 a week, lives in a very tiny house with a family, a Catholic family of five children. He's still that man. He's still living a simple life and still has no reason for being other than to deliver letters, has no great cause, yet he was one of the mods. He was one of this great army of young men that when we found R&B found music that suited our purpose, a voice that suited our frustration at the time. In a Freudian sense, it was like a great castrated generation, and the blues is the only music that was capable of providing us with a voice.

I wouldn't say that Mose was my number-one influence but if I've got five major influences he's one of them. And where he's most important is in the way he uses words and music in a tensile sense. There's some tension between the words and the music. When the Who play "Young Man Blues" it's with tremendous force and violence. That violence is not something we made up. It was there in the song. "A young man ain't nothing in the world these days" is a tremendously brutal statement. It says "I am fucking nothing . . . NOTHING IN THIS WORLD." I think that is a very studied lesson in fact distortion and presentation distortion. The fact, for example, that it makes you realize that you can take a song which is actually about "Look, when you take the cork out of the bottle and you pour the liquid on the floor it falls and then it spills." You turn that into a song and you sing it with tremendous passion. And everybody thinks "What was this about?" It was actually about what happens when you take the cork out of the bottle and spill the liquid on the floor. It works in the other direction as well. You start to realize that words in themselves actually can be used in a rhythmic sense.

I think Mose is immensely spiritual in a very Sufic sense. All of his songs are about disappearance, but not disappearance into the crowd, but disappearance in a lofty sense, disappearance with everybody else into a kind of an exodus. That is something you see in a lot of composers and musicians where you think, "Why don't they go a stage further?" I think Mose is not as aware of the spiritual messages that are carried in his work and maybe it's not something to dwell on. I recognize a longing and a yearning in it.

You have to look at him in kind of a quirky way. In India, this would be very simple and straightforward to deal with, wouldn't it? This is a greatly revered character who lives in a fucking cave and won't come out. When he does come out he comes out on his terms. He won't shake hands with anybody. He won't touch them in case he catches something. He won't work with anybody else. He won't talk to the record companies. He won't even actually look at his audience when they applaud. He stops songs in the middle just when they're starting to cook. He won't sing the songs that his audience wants him to sing. He only sings the ones that they don't want him to sing. He's a real ascetic in a sense, isn't he? Yet at the same time you can't accuse him of being a selfish man. He works hard. He continues to work. He works hard and travels and he loves music. And he's simple on the surface. It's not as though the parallels are hard to find. There's a strong spiritual parallel. If we were Indian, and we were all in Indian society, I think we'd know exactly where to put him. He would seem to be a rather yogic figure. He is one of my teachers and I am one of his disciples. The fact that I turned his teaching into good solid rocks of money is a testament to his teaching. So if you take the Eastern, mystical point of view, you get a very clear picture. The more money I make, the more successful I get at what I do, the more I can actually communicate to my audience; the more that they reward me, the more he is vicariously rewarded. To stand in a rock stadium with 85,000 people and sing "A young man ain't nothin' in the world these days" and hear 85,000 people say "Yeah," you suddenly realize that the music came from one person but is in everyone.

REFERENCES

Chapter 1: Tippo, the First Crossroad (pp. 1–19)
1. Dom Cerulli, "Mose Allison's Country Style Jazz," *Downbeat*, May 1, 1958, p. 19.
2. Paul Zollo, "Legends of Songwriting: Mose Allison, Jazz Songs in Anti-Time," *Songtalk*, Spring, 1988, p. 23.

Chapter 3: Didactics, Bartók and Curley's (pp. 35–50)
1. Robin George Collingwood, *Principles of Art* (Oxford, 1938), p. 275.
2. Ibid., p. 32.
3. Ibid., p. 81.
4. Ibid., pp. 121–2.

Chapter 4: Halcyon Days (pp. 51–67)
1. Participants at sessions at 335 East 34th Street included the following:

Trumpet
Tommy Allison
Jon Eardley
Don Elliott
Ralph Hughes
Jerry Lloyd (Hurwitz)

Trombone
Bob Bookmeyer
Clyde Cox
Willie Dennis
Jack Hitchcock
Dick Leith
Earl Swope

Saxophone
Pepper Adams
Jay Cameron
Al Cohn
Stan Getz
Bob (Bullets) Forte
Freddie Greenwell
Jimmy Giuffre
Lynn Holliday
Don Janes
Dick Meldonian
Zoot Sims
Ray Turner
Diz Utley
Phil Woods

Piano
Mose Allison
John Bunch
Bob Dorough
Bill Evans
Don Friedman
Dave Frishberg
Al Haig
Jutta Hipp
Hod O'Brien
Hall Overton
Bud Powell
Don Reitman
George Syran
Bill Triglia
George Wallington
Howard Williams
Johnny Williams

Bass
Chuck Andrus
Bill Anthony
John Beal
Sonny Dallas
Henry Grimes
Peter Ind
Buddy Jones
Taylor LaFargue
Jack Six
Ben Tucker
Wilbur Ware
Dudley Watson
Paul Worthington

Drums
Ronnie Bedford
Al Beldin
Ed Bonoff
Bill Bradley, Jr.
Sonny Carr
Ronnie Free
Frank Isola
Elvin Jones
Al Levitt
Art Mardigan
Jerry Segal
Bill Steen
Winston Welch
Mel Zelman

Chapter 5: Back Country Suite (pp. 68–82)
1. Detailed histories of the origins of the suite and Baroque instrumental music are available in Donald Jay Grout, *A History of Western Music* (New York: W.W. Norton, 1960), pp. 328–40.
2. For a discussion of Béla Bartók and the utilization of the folk idiom in art music, see ibid., pp. 664 ff.
3. David Johnson, "Mose: the Allison Viewpoint," *Zoo World*, August 1, 1974.
4. Dom Cerulli, "Mose Allison's Country Style Jazz," *Downbeat*, May 1, 1958, p. 41.
5. Richard Skelly, "Mose Allison: Forever a Free Spirit," *Goldmine*, October 5, 1990, pp. 48–52.
6. Many jazz historians point out that jazz instrumentalists emulate African-American vocal styles. This in turn means that singers who borrow elements of their own instrumental style can trace their influences indirectly from African-American vocal styles.
7. Willi Apel (ed.), *The Harvard Dictionary of Music* (Cambridge: Harvard University Press, 1972), p. 88.
8. Robert and Roberta Palmer, "Mose is Just the Same," *Penthouse*, February, 1977.
9. Ashley Conn, "Mose Allison Profile," WKCR, New York, 1985.

Chapter 6: Local Color (pp. 83–95)
1. Ira Gitler, liner notes to *Local Color*, Prestige 7121.
2. Ibid.
3. Lou Stevens, "Interview with Mose Allison," WUSB, February 2, 1977.
4. Oliver Howes, *Jazz Journal*, July, 1959, p. 1.

Chapter 7: A Prestigious Commitment (pp. 96–113)
1. Robert Franza, "Interview with Mose Allison: Jazz on the Air," WUSB, 1989.
2. Joe Goldberg, liner notes to *Ramblin' with Mose*, Prestige 7215.
3. Ibid.

4. See Willie Dixon with Don Snowden, *I Am the Blues: The Willie Dixon Story* (London: Quartet Books, 1989; New York: Da Capo, 1989). Appendix 2 lists Willie Mabon, Muddy Waters, Dion, Johnny Rivers, Nancy Wilson, Peggy Lee, Climax Blues Band, Long John Baldry, and John Mellencamp as artists who have also recorded this song.
5. Paul Zollo, "Legends of Songwriting: Mose Allison, Jazz Songs in Anti-Time," *Songtalk*, Spring, 1988, p. 23.
6. Len Lyons, liner notes to *Creek Bank*, Prestige 24002.
7. Willi Apel (ed.), *The Harvard Dictionary of Music* (Cambridge: Harvard University Press, 1972), p. 653.
8. Ibid., p. 711.
9. Ashley Conn, "Mose Allison Profile," WKCR, New York, 1985.

Chapter 8: Detribalization and Transfiguration (pp. 114-31)
1. See John B. Johnson (ed.), "White Blues Singer," *Ebony*, November, 1959, pp. 149-52.
2. Ashley Conn, "Mose Allison Profile," WKCR, New York, 1985.

Chapter 9: The Word from Mose (pp. 132-60)
1. W. Enstice and P. Rubin, *Jazz Spoken Here: Conversations with 22 Musicians* (Baton Rouge: Louisiana University Press, 1992), p. 4.
2. Les Tomkins, "Speaking My Mind: Mose Allison," *Crescendo*, March, 1966, p. 16.
3. Paul Zollo, "Legends of Songwriting: Mose Allison, Jazz Songs in Anti-Time," *Songtalk*, Spring, 1988, p. 23.
4. Ibid.
5. Peter Knobler, "Mose Allison is More Than an Influence." *Zygote*, January 8, 1991.
6. Paul Zollo, "Legends of Songwriting: Mose Allison, Jazz Songs in Anti-Time," *Songtalk*, Spring, 1988, p. 23.
7. Ibid.
8. Lou Stevens, "Interview with Mose Allison," WUSB, February 2, 1977.
9. Les Tomkins, op. cit.

Chapter 10: When You Meet Your Destiny Face to Face (pp. 161–78)
1. Kenneth Patchen, *Collected Poems of Kenneth Patchen* © 1954 by New Directions Publishing Corporation, p.437. Reprinted by permission of New Directions Publishing Corp.
2. Louis-Ferdinand Céline, *Guignol's Band* © 1954 by New Directions Publishing Corporation. Translated by Bernard Frechtman and Jack T Nile. Reprinted by permission of New Directions Publishing Corp., p. 141.
3. John Detro, "Mose Allison: Backyard Bluesman," *JazzTimes*, June, 1990, p. 9.
4. Owen Cordle, "Music Review," *Durham Herald/Sun*, April 3, 1983.

Chapter 11: Hello There, Universe (pp. 179–201)
1. Lou Stevens, "Interview with Mose Allison," WUSB, February 2, 1977.
2. Donald Truitt, "Mose Allison: Interview," *Cadence*, September 1, 1982, p. 12.

Chapter 12: Still No Top Forty Record (pp. 202–17)
1. Neil Tesser, "An Interview with Mose Allison," *Chicago Reader*, August 16, 1974.
2. W. Enstice and P. Rubin, *Jazz Spoken Here: Conversations with 22 Musicians* (Baton Rouge: Louisiana University Press, 1992), p. 11.
3. Charles Backfish and Walt Skretch, "Interview with Mose Allison," WSB, Stoneybrook New York, August 8, 1982.
4. Ibid.
5. Ibid.
6. Ibid.
7. Ibid.

Chapter 14: Towards a Piano Style (pp. 235–59)
1. Fred Bruning, "The Jazz Singer," *Newsday*, November 26, 1991, p. 44.
2. "Mose Allison," *Crescendo*, October, 1967, p. 16.

3. Ibid., p. 18.
4. Bob Ness, "Mose Allison," *Coda*, April, 1975, p. 7.
5. Kevin B. Long, "Mose Allison," *Cadence*, December, 1989, p. 5.
6. Ibid., pp. 8–9.
7. Paul Zollo, "Legends of Songwriting: Mose Allison, Jazz Songs in Anti-Time," *Songtalk*, Spring, 1988, p. 23.
8. Ibid.

Chapter 15: Mose Allison: A Source (pp. 260–7)
1. Charles Shaar Murray, "Crosstown Traffic: Jimi Hendrix and the Rock 'n' Roll Revolution", New York: St Martn's Press, 1989, p.136. London: Faber and Faber, 1989.
2. Robert Franza, "Interview with Mose Allison: Jazz on the Air," WUSB, 1991.

AD LIB
YOUNG MAN (BLUES FROM BACK COUNTRY SOITE)
F7 Bb7 C7 F
OH WELL A YOUNG MAN AIN'T NOTHIN IN THIS WORLD THESE DAYS
I SAID A YOUNG MAN AIN'T NOTHIN IN THIS WORLD THESE DAYS
IN THE OLD DAYS WHEN A YOUNG MAN WAS A STRONG MAN
ALL TH' PEOPLE STAND BACK WHEN TH' YOUNG MAN WALK BY
BUT NOW DAYS THE OLD MAN GOT ALL TH' MONEY
AND A YOUNG MAN AIN'T NOTHIN IN THIS WORLD THESE DAYS

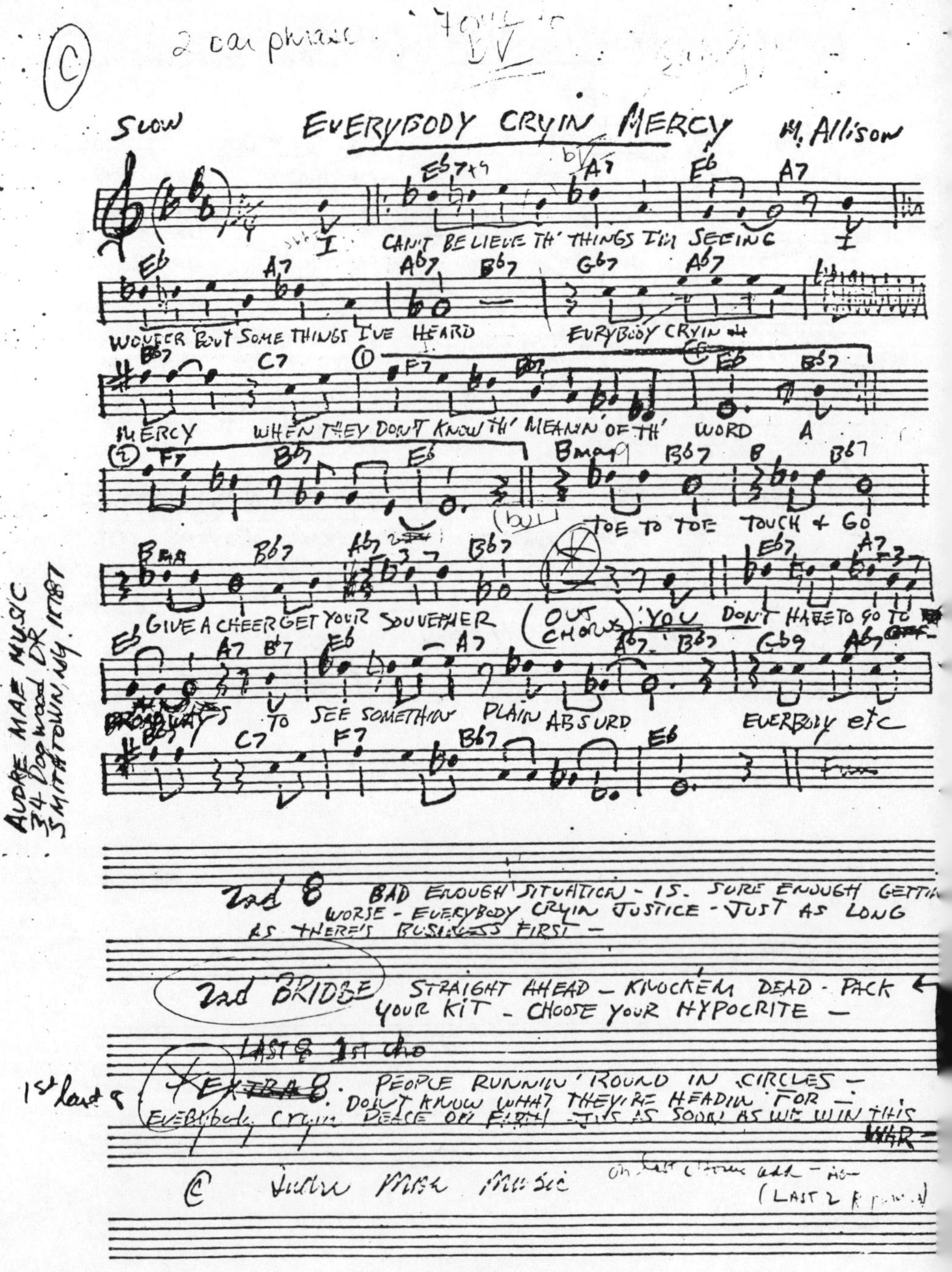

2 bar phrase
SLOW
EVERYBODY CRYIN MERCY
M. Allison
CAN'T BE LIEVE TH' THINGS I'M SEEING
WONDER 'BOUT SOME THINGS I'VE HEARD
EVRYBODY CRYIN
MERCY WHEN THEY DON'T KNOW TH' MEANIN' OF TH' WORD
TOE TO TOE TOUCH & GO
GIVE A CHEER GET YOUR SOUVENIER
OUT CHORUS
YOU DON'T HAVE TO GO TO BROADWAYS TO SEE SOMETHIN' PLAIN ABSURD
EVERBODY etc
AUDRE MAE MUSIC
34 Dogwood DR
SMITHTOWN, NY 11787
2nd 8 BAD ENOUGH SITUATION - IS. SURE ENOUGH GETTIN WORSE - EVERYBODY CRYIN JUSTICE - JUST AS LONG AS THERE'S BUSINESS FIRST -
2nd BRIDGE STRAIGHT AHEAD - KNOCK'EM DEAD - PACK YOUR KIT - CHOOSE YOUR HYPOCRITE -
LAST 8 1st cho
1st last 8
EXTRA 8. PEOPLE RUNNIN' ROUND IN CIRCLES - DON'T KNOW WHAT THEY'RE HEADIN' FOR - EVERYbody cryin PEACE ON EARTH - JUST AS SOON AS WE WIN THIS WAR -
© Audre Mae Music
(LAST 2

LET IT COME DOWN
SLOW DRAG
VOCAL LINE
TONICS
FRETTIN 'BOUT WHAT YOU'RE GOIN THRU RE GRETTIN TH'
THINGS YOU DIDN'T DO RE LYING ON COMPENSATIONS YOU'VE FOUND
GROANING BE NEATH TH' WEIGHT OF IT BE MOANING TH' FICKLE FATE OF IT COM-
PLYING JUST TO KEEP BOTH FEET ON TH' GROUND
THAT WON'T GET YOU ANY PLACE
WON'T EX CUSE YOU FROM TH' RACE WHEN YOU MEET YOUR DESTINY FACE TO FACE THERE'LL BE
NO MORE WRONG OR RIGHT AND NO MORE WISH I MIGHT AN' IF THERE'S GONNA BE
Passantino

LET IT COME DOWN (CONT)

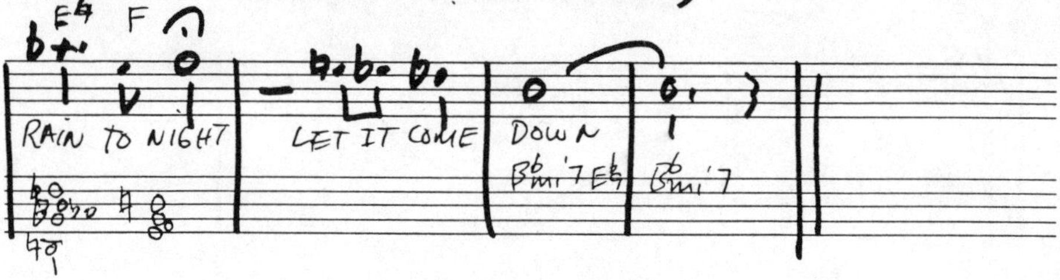
E♭ F
RAIN TO NIGHT
LET IT COME
DOWN
B♭mi7 E♭
B♭mi7

THE FOLLOWING PAGES CONSTITUTE AN EXTENSION OF THE COPYRIGHT PAGE.

Song Lyrics

All Mose Allison compositions used herein are reprinted with permission of Audre Mae Music/BMI. All rights reserved.

Chapter 1: *If You Live* (p. 1-2) © 1959, Copyright renewed, 1987 Audre Mae Music/BMI

Chapter 2: *Swingin' Machine* (p. 20-21) © 1963, Copyright renewed 1991 Audre Mae Music/BMI

Chapter 3: *Foolkiller* (p. 35-36) © 1961, Copyright renewed 1989 Audre Mae Music/BMI

Chapter 4: *City Home* (p. 51-52) © 1959, Copyright renewed 1987 Audre Mae Music/BMI
 If You're Going to the City (p.52) © 1963, Copyright renewed 1991 Audre Mae Music/BMI

Chapter 5: *Young Man Blues* (p. 68-69) © 1957, Copyright renewed 1985 Audre Mae Music/BMI

Chapter 6: *Parchman Farm* (p. 83-84) © 1959, Copyright renewed 1987 Audre Mae Music/BMI
 New Parchman (p. 87-88) © 1964, Copyright renewed 1992 Audre Mae Music/BMI

Chapter 7: *I Don't Worry a Thing* (p. 96-97) © 1961, Copyright renewed 1989 Audre Mae Music/BMI

Chapter 8: *Ask Me Nice* (p.115) © 1961, Copyright renewed 1989 Audre Mae Music/BMI

Chapter 9: *One of These Days* (p. 132-133) © 1964, Copyright renewed 1992 Audre Mae Music/BMI
 Your Mind's On Vacation (p. 144-145) © 1961, Copyright renewed 1989 Audre Mae Music/BMI
 It Didn't Turn Out That Way (p. 146) © 1962, Copyright renewed 1990 Audre Mae Music/BMI
 I'm Not Talkin' (p.148-149) © 1962, Copyright renewed 1990 Audre Mae Music/BMI
 One of These Days (p. 149) © 1964, Copyright renewed 1992 Audre Mae Music/BMI
 Days Like This (p. 151) © 1962, Copyright renewed 1990 Audre Mae Music/BMI
 Don't Forget to Smile (p. 152) © 1962, Copyright renewed 1990 Audre Mae Music/BMI
 I'm Smashed (p. 155-56) © 1966, Copyright renewed 1994 Audre Mae Music/BMI
 Tell Me Somethin' That I Don't Know (p. 156-57) © 1965, Copyright renewed 1993 Audre Mae Music/BMI
 No Trouble Livin' (p. 157-158) © 1965, Copyright renewed 1993 Audre Mae Music/BMI
 Wild Man on the Loose (p. 158-159) © 1965, Copyright renewed 1993 Audre Mae Music/BMI
 What's With You (p. 159) © 1965, Copyright renewed 1993 Audre Mae Music/BMI
 You Can Count on Me to Do My Part (p. 159) © 1965, Copyright renewed 1993 Audre Mae Music/BMI

Chapter 10: *Everybody Cryin' Mercy* (p. 162) © 1966, Copyright renewed 1994 Audre Mae Music/BMI
Your Molecular Structure (p. 169) © 1966, Copyright renewed 1994 Audre Mae Music/BMI
Look What You Made Me Do (p. 169) © 1966, Copyright renewed 1994 Audre Mae Music/BMI
If You Really Loved Me Baby (p. 170) © 1965, Copyright renewed 1993 Audre Mae Music/BMI
Feel So Good (p. 170-171) © 1965, Copyright renewed 1993 Audre Mae Music/BMI
Just Like Livin' (p. 172) © 1966, Copyright renewed 1994 Audre Mae Music/BMI
If You're Goin' to the City (p. 173) © 1963, Copyright renewed 1991 Audre Mae Music/BMI
Now You See It (p. 173) © 1966, Copyright renewed 1994 Audre Mae Music/BMI
Let It Come Down (p. 177) © 1967, Copyright renewed 1995 Audre Mae Music/BMI

Chapter 11: *Hello There Universe* (p. 178) © 1968 Audre Mae Music/BMI
Monsters of the Id (p. 182-183) © 1968 Audre Mae Music/BMI
If You Only Knew (p. 189) © 1969 Audre Mae Music/BMI
Benediction (p. 189) © 1971 Audre Mae Music/BMI
Western Man (p. 190-191) © 1970 Audre Mae Music/BMI
How Much Truth Can a Man Stand (p. 191-192) © 1969 Audre Mae Music/BMI
What Do You Do After You Ruin Your Life (p. 197) © 1974 Audre Mae Music/BMI
The Fires of Spring (p. 200-201) © 1972 Audre Mae Music/BMI
Back Down South (p. 214) © 1979 Audre Mae Music/BMI

Chapter 12: *Middle Class White Boy* (p. 202-203) © 1980 Audre Mae Music/BMI
Top 40 (big beat, rock and roll record) (p. 207) © 1974 Audre Mae Music/BMI
How Does It Feel (to Be Good Lookin') (p. 211) © 1979 Audre Mae Music/BMI
I Don't Want Much (p. 211) © 1969 Audre Mae Music/BMI
I'm Nobody Today by Rod Creagh, © 1970 Harbot Music. All rights reserved. Used by permission.
Kiddin' On the Square (p. 212) © 1977 Audre Mae Music/BMI
I'm Just a Lucky So and So (p. 212) by Duke Ellington/Mack David © 1945 by Paramount Music Corporation and PolyGram Publishing Copyright renewed 1973 and assigned to Paramount Music Corporation and PolyGram Publsihing. Used by permission.
When My Dreamboat Comes Home (p. 213) by Dave Franklin and Cliff Friend © 1936 (Renewed) Warner Bros., Inc. All Rights Reserved. Used by Permission. WARNER BROS. PUBLICATIONS U.S., INC., MIAMI, FL 33014
Back Down South (p. 214) © 1979 Audre Mae Music/BMI

Chapter 13: *Gettin' There* (p. 218) © 1984 Audre Mae Music/BMI
I Looked in the Mirror (p. 222) © 1968 Audre Mae Music/BMI
Tai Chi Life (p. 222) © 1984, Audre Mae Music/BMI
What's Your Movie (p. 223) © 1984 Audre Mae Music/BMI
Trouble In Mind (p. 224) by Richard M. Jones, © 1937 Jenkins Music. Reproduced by kind permission MCA Music Ltd and of Redwood Music Ltd., U.K. administrator.
Top Forty (big beat, rock and roll record) (p. 224) © 1974 Audre Mae Music/BMI
Ever Since the World Ended (p. 226) © 1984 Audre Mae Music/BMI
The Gettin' Paid Waltz (p. 229) © 1987 Audre Mae Music/BMI
Dr. Jekyll and Mr. Hyde (p. 230) © 1988 Audre Mae Music/BMI
You Call It Joggin' (p. 213-232) by John D. Loudermilk © Loudermilk Music/BMI. Used by Permission.
Sleepy Lagoon (p. 232) by Eric Coates/lyrics by Jack Lawrence © 1930, 1940, Copyright renewed 1958. Reproduced by permission of FirstCom Music House Chappell and MPL Communications.
Long Song (p. 232) © 1989 Audre Mae Music/BMI

Sentimental Fool (p. 233) © 1989 Audre Mae Music/BMI
Was (p. 234) © 1988 Audre Mae Music/BMI

Chapter 14: *Who's In Who's Out* (p. 235-36) © 1992 Audre Mae Music/BMI
Ever Since I Stole the Blues (p. 261) © 1989 Audre Mae Music/BMI
Allison (p. 285) by Charles Thompson Reprinted courtesy of RICE AND BEANS MUSIC.

Appendix B: Mose Allison lead sheets:
Young Man Blues © 1957, Copyright renewed 1985 Audre Mae Music/BMI
City Home © 1959, Copyright renewed 1987 Audre Mae Music/BMI
Everybody Cryin' Mercy © 1966, Copyright renewed 1994 Audre Mae Music/BMI
Let It Come Down © 1967, Copyright renewed 1995

All Music used by Permission Audre Mae Music/BMI. All Rights Reserved.

Photos:
Courtesy of Mose Allison and Ralph Hughes. Research: Amy Allison, John Allison.

Number © Art Kane. Reprinted Courtesy of the Mary Lou Williams Foundation c/o Peter O'Brien. All Rights Reserved.

THE AL COHN QUINTET FEATURING BOBBY BROOKMEYER

New York, 1956
CRL 57118

Al Cohn, tenor saxophone
Bobby Brookmeyer, valve trombone
Mose Allison, piano
Ted Kotick, bass
Nick Stabulas, drums

The Lady Is a Tramp
Good Spirits
A Blues Serenade
Lazy Man Stomp
Ill Wind
Chlo-E (Song of the Swamp)
S-H-I-N-E
Back to Back
So Far So good
Winter
I Should Care
Bunny Hunch

STAN GETZ QUARTET & SHELLY MANNE QUINTET: STAN & SHELLY LIVE IN 1956/57

Red Hill Inn, Pensauken, New Jersey
February 16, 1957
EB 407

Stan Getz, tenor saxophone
Mose Allison, piano
Frank Isola, bass
Willie "Stomp" Davis, drums

Some Blues (Bronx Blues)
Polka Dots & Moonbeams

Red Hill Inn, Pensauken, New Jersey
May 18, 1957

Theme
Jordu
Lover Man
Ain't You a Mess

THE SOFT SWING: THE STAN GETZ QUARTET

New York, July, 12, 1957
MGV-8321

Stan Getz, tenor saxophone
Mose Allison, piano
Addison Farmer, bass
Jerry Segal, drums

All the Things You Are
Pocono Mac
Down Beat
To the Ends of the Earth
Bye Bye Blues

JAZZ ALIVE! A NIGHT AT THE HALF NOTE
ZOOT SIMS, AL COHN AND PHIL WOODS

New York, February 6 and 7, 1959
United Artists
UAS5040
Produced and Directed by Jack Lewis

Al Cohn, tenor saxophone
Zoot Sims, tenor saxophone
Phil Woods, alto saxophone
Mose Allison, piano
Nabil Totah, bass
Paul Motian, drums

Lover Come Back to Me
It Had To Be You
Wee/Dot
After You've Gone

AL COHN AND ZOOT SIMS QUARTET

New York, 1960
Fred Miles FM1, Zim ZMS2002

Al Cohn, tenor saxophone
Zoot Sims, tenor saxophone
Mose Allison, piano
Bill Crow, bass
Gus Johnson, drums
Cecil "Kid Haffey" Collier, vocals

P-Town
I Like That (Cecil Collier, vocals)
Sweet Lorraine (Cecil Collier, vocals)
Autumn Leaves
The Thing
I'm Tellin' Ya
Nagasaki
Morning Fun

AL COHN AND ZOOT SIMS QUARTET: YOU 'N ME

New York, June 1 and 3, 1960
Merc MG20606, MG21030

Al Cohn, tenor saxophone, clarinet
Zoot Sims, tenor saxophone, clarinet
Mose Allison, piano
Major Holley, bass
Osie Johnson, drums

The Note (20110)
You'd Be So Nice To Come Home To (20111)
You 'N Me (20113)
On the Alamo (Cohn and Sims play clarinet) (20114)
The Opener (20115)
Angel Eyes (20116)
Awful Lonely (20117)
Love For Sale (20118)
Improvisations for Unaccompanied Saxophone (20119) (Mose Allison, Major Holley, and Osie Johnson Out)

MOSE ALLISON TRIO: BACK COUNTRY SUITE

Hackensack, New Jersey, March 7, 1957
Prest PR7091

Mose Allison, piano and vocals
Taylor LaFargue, bass
Frank Isola, drums

New Ground (1125)
Train (1126)
Warm Night (1127)
Blues*, Mose Allison, vocals (1128)
Saturday (1129)
Scamper (1130)
January (1131)
Promised Land (1132)
Spring Song (1131)
Highway 49 (1134)
I Thought About You (1135)
In Salah (1136)
You Won't Let Me Go (1137)
One Room Country Shack, Mose Allison, vocals (1138)
Blueberry Hill (1139)

* Recorded as "Young Man" on Prestige 7279 and Stateside SL10106

MOSE ALLISON TRIO: LOCAL COLOR

Hackensack, New Jersey, November 8, 1957
Prestige PR7121

Mose Allison, trumpet, piano and vocals
Addison Farmer, bass
Nick Stabulas, drums

Town (1382)
Mojo Woman (1383)
Crepuscular Air (1384)
Carnival (1385)
I'll Never Be Free (1386)
Don't Say Goodbye (1387)
Ain't You A Mess (1388)
Trouble in Mind, Mose Allison, (trumpet) (1389)
Lost Mind, Mose Allison, vocals (1390)
Parchman Farm, Mose Allison, vocals (1391)

MOSE ALLISON: YOUNG MAN MOSE

Hackensack, New Jersey, January 24, 1958
Prestige PR 7137

Mose Allison, piano, trumpet and vocals
Addison Farmer, bass
Nick Stabulas, drums

Somebody Else Is Taking My Place (1439)
Bye Bye Blues (1440)
How Long Has This Been Going On (1441)

Don't Get Around Much Anymore (vocal) (1442)
I Hadn't Anyone Till You (vocal) (1443)
My Kinda Love (1444)
Sleepy Time Gal (1445)
I Told Ya I Love Ya, Now Get Out (1446)
Baby, Let Me Hold Your Hand (vocal) (1447)
Stroll (trumpet) (1448)

MOSE ALLISON: RAMBLIN' WITH MOSE

Hackensack, New Jersey, April 18, 1958
Prestige PR 7215

Mose Allison, piano and vocals
Addison Farmer, bass
Ronnie Free, drums

Saritha (1499)
Stranger (1500)
Ingenue (1501)
You Belong To Me (1502)
Old Man John (1503)
Ramble (1504)
The Minstrels (1505)
I Got A Right To Cry (vocal) (1506)
Ol'Devil Moon (1507)
Kissin' Bug (1508)

MOSE ALLISON: CREEK BANK

Hackensack, New Jersey, September 15, 1958
Prestige PR 7152

Mose Allison, piano and vocals
Addison Farmer, bass
Ronnie Free, drums

Creek Bank (1555)
Moon and Cypress (1556)
Mule (1557)
Dinner On The Ground (1558)
Prelude To A Kiss (1559)
If I Didn't Care (1560)
Cabin In The Sky (1561)
If You Live (vocal) (1562)
Seventh Son (vocal) (1563)
Yardbird Suite (1564)

MOSE ALLISON: AUTUMN SONG

Hackensack, New Jersey, February 13, 1959
Prestige PR 7189

Mose Allison, piano and vocals
Addison Farmer, bass
Ronnie Free, drums

Spires (1714)
Promenade (1715)

It's Crazy (1716)
The Devil In The Cane Field (1717)
Autumn Song (1718)
Strange (1719)
That's All Right (vocal) (1720)
Do Nothin' Till You Hear From Me (vocals) (1721)
Eyesight To The Blind (vocal) (1722)
Groovin' High (1723)

MOSE ALLISON: TRANSFIGURATION OF HIRAM BROWN

New York, December 21, 1959*
Columbia CL 1444   CL 8280

Mose Allison, piano and vocals
Addison Farmer, bass
Jerry Segal, drums

How Little We Know (CO64532)
Baby, Please Don't Go (CO64533)
Hiram Brown Suite (CO64534)
Barefoot Dirt Road
City Home
Cuttin' Out
Gotham Day
Gotham Night
Echo
The River
Finale
Make Yourself Comfortable (CO64535)

New York, December 23, 1959
Columbia CL1444

'Deed I Do (CO64539)

New York, January 11, 1960
Columbia CL1444

Love For Sale (CO64540)

* Bruyninckx listing differs from Electra/Asylum Records Discography which lists a May 9, 1960 recording date and CS 8260

I LOVE THE LIFE I LIVE: THE VOICE AND PIANO OF THE MOSE ALLISON TRIO

New York, June 28, 1960–September 9, 1960
BA 17031 Columbia RM 52318

Mose Allison, piano and vocals
Addison Farmer, bass
Jerry Segal, drums

Night Ride
Fool's Paradise
You Turned the Tables on Me
Mad With You
Path

Henry Grimes, bass
Paul Motion, drums

I Love the Life I Live
Hittin' On One
News
You're A Sweetheart

Bill Crow, bass
Gus Johnson, drums

Isobel
Can't We Be Friends
I Ain't Got Nobody

MOSE ALLISON: TAKES TO THE HILLS

New York, June 16 and June 23, 1961
Epic LA 16031

Mose Allison, piano and vocals
Aaron Bell, bass
Osie Johnson, drums

V-8 Ford Blues
Please Don't Talk About Me When I'm Gone
Hey Good Lookin'
Back On the Corner
Life is Suicide
Ask Me Nice

New York, December 9, 1959

Addison Farmer, bass
Jerry Segal, drums

Baby, Please Don't Go

New York, January 11, 1960

'Deed I Do

New York, June 28–September 9, 1960

Mad With You

New York, June 28–September 9, 1960

Henry Grimes, bass
Paul Motion, drums

I Love the Life I Live
You're a Sweetheart

New York, June 28–September, 1960

Bill Crow, bass
Gus Johnson, drums

I Ain't Got Nobody

MOSE ALLISON: I DON'T WORRY ABOUT A THING

New York, March 15, 1962
Atlantic Atl LP1389

Mose Allison, piano and vocals
Addison Farmer, bass
Osie Johnson, drums

I Don't Worry About A Thing (vocal) (6031)
Stand by (6033)
Idyll (6034)
Your Mind Is On Vacation (vocal) (6035)
Meet Me At No Special Place (vocal) (6036)
Let Me See (vocal) (6038)
Everything I Have Is Yours (vocal) (6039)
The Well (6040)
It Didn't Turn Out That Way (vocal) (6041)
The Song Is Ended (vocal) (6042)

MOSE ALLISON: SWINGIN' MACHINE

New York, November 8, 1963
Atlantic Atl LP1398

Mose Allison, piano and vocals
Addison Farmer, bass
Frankie Dunlap, drums
Jimmy Knepper, trombone
Jimmy Reider, tenor saxophone

Do It (6577)
Promenade (6578)
If You're Goin' To The City (vocal) (6579)
I Ain't Got Nothing But The Blues (vocal) (6580)

New York, November 9, 1963

Saritha (6581)
Swingin' Machine (vocal) (6582)
Stop This World (vocal) (6583)
So Rare (6584)

MOSE ALLISON SINGS

Compilation, August, 1963
Prestige PR 7279

Mose Allison, piano and vocals
Addison Farmer, bass
Ronnie Free, drums
NIck Stabulas (*), drums

The Seventh Son
Eyesight to the Blind
Do Nothin' Till You Hear From Me
Lost Mind*
I Got a Right to Cry
Baby Let Me Hold Your Hand*
Parchman Farm*

If You Live
Don't Get Around Much Anymore*
One Room Country Shack (Taylor LaFargue, bass; Frank Isola, drums)
I Hadn't Anyone Till I Had You*
A Young Man (Taylor LaFargue, bass; Frank Isola, drums)
That's All Right

MOSE ALLISON: THE WORD FROM MOSE

New York, March 10, 1964
Atlantic Atl LP1424

Mose Allison, piano and voclas
Ben Tucker, bass
Ron Lundberg, drums

Don't Forget to Smile (7667)
I'm Not Talking (7668)
Days Like This (7669)
Wild Man (7670)
One Of These Days (7671)
New Parchman (7672)

New York, March 12, 1964

Your Red Wagon (7680)
Foolkiller (7681)
Rollin' Stone (7682)
Lost Mind (7682)
Look Here (7684)

MOSE ALLISON: MOSE ALLISON ALIVE!

"Lighthouse Club," Hermosa Beach, California
October 22 to 31, 1965
Atlantic Atl 587007

Mose Allison, piano and vocals
Stan Gilbert, bass
Mel Lee, drums

Love For Sale (9561)
Seventh Son (vocal) (9562)
Since I Feel For You (vocal) (9563)
The Chaser (9566)
Smashed (vocal) (9567)
Fool's Paradise (vocal) (9569)
Parchman Farm (vocal) (9574)
I Love The Life I Live (vocal) (9577)
Tell Me Somethin' (vocal) (9578)
That's Alright (vocal) (9580)
Baby Please Don't Go (vocal) (9582)

Reissued, 1985
Edsel Records, ED 153

MOSE ALLISON: WILD MAN ON THE LOOSE

New York, January 26, 1965
Atlantic Atl 587031

Mose Allison, piano and vocals
Earl May, bass
Paul Motian, drums

Never More (vocal) (8528)
What's With You (vocal) (8529)
Wild Man On The Loose (vocal) (8530)
No Trouble Livin' (vocal) (8531)
You Can Count On Me To Do My Part (vocal) (8532)

New York, January 28, 1965

That's The Stuff You Gotta Watch (vocal) (8538)
Power House (8540)
War House (8541)
Night Watch (8542)

DOWN HOME PIANO

Reissue, August, 1965
Prestige PR 7423

Mose Allison, piano
Addison Farmer, bass
Nick Stabulas, drums
Ronnie Free, Drums*

Dinner on the Ground
Crepuscular Air
Mule*
Creek Bank*
Town
Devil in the Cane Field
The Minstrels*
Moon in Cyress*
Carnival
Mojo Woman

MOSE ALLISON PLAYS FOR LOVERS

Reissue, 1966
Prestige PR 7446

Mose Allison, piano and vocals
Addison Farmer, bass
Taylor La Fargue, bass
Ronnie Free, drums
Nick Stabulas, drums
Frank Isola, drums

It's Crazy
You Belong to Me
I Told Ya I Loved Ya, Now Get Out
Hoe Long Has This Been Going On
Somebody Else Is Taking My Place

My Kinda Love
I Thought About You
Kissin' Bug
Strange
If I Didn't Care

MOSE ALLISON SINGS AND PLAYS THE V-8 FORD BLUES

Reissue, Columbia BA 17031, CL 8280, Epic BN 26183 16031
January, 1966
Epic LN 24183

Mose Allison, piano and vocals
Addison Farmer, bass
Jerry Segal, drums
Henry Grimes, bass
Paul Motion, drums
Aaron Bell, bass
Osie Johnson, drums

V-8 Ford Blues
Please Don't Talk About Me When I'm Gone
Baby, Please Don't Go
Hey, Good Lookin'
I Love the Life I Live
I Ain't Got Nobody
Back On the Corner
Life Is Suicide
'Deed I Do
Ask Me Nice
You're a Sweetheart
Mad With You

MOSE ALLISON: I'VE BEEN DOIN' SOME THINKIN'

New York, July 9, 1968
Atlantic Atl SD1511

Mose Allison, piano and vocals
Red Mitchell, bass
Bill Goodwin, drums

Jus' Like Livin' (vocal) (14828)
City Home (vocal) (14829)
If You're Goin' To The City (vocal) (14830)
Everybody Cryin' Mercy (vocal) (14831)
Look What You Made Me Do (vocal) (14832)
Feel So Good (vocal) (14833)

New York, July 10, 1968

Let It Come Down (vocal) (14834)
If You Really Loved Me (vocal) (14835)
Now You See It (vocal) (14836)
You Are My Sunshine (vocal) (14837)
Your Molecular Structure (vocal) (14838)

New York, July 12, 1968

Back On The Corner (vocal) (14879)

MOSE GOES: MOSE ALLISON

Reissue of CS 8280 *Transfiguration of Hiram Brown*
Columbia Jazz Odyssey 32-160294, October, 1968

Mose Allison, piano and vocals
Addison Farmer, bass
Jerry Segal, drums

Transfiguration of Hiram Brown Suite:
Barefoot Dirt Road
City Home
Cuttin' Out
Gotham Day
Gotham Night
Echo
The River
Finale
How Little We Know
Baby, Please Don't Go
Make Yourself Comfortable
'Deed I Do
Love For Sale

MOSE ALLISON: ALLISON MOSE

Reissue
Prestige PR24002

Mose Allison, piano and vocals
Taylor LaFargue, bass
Addison Farmer, bass
Frank Isola, drums
Nick Stabulas, drums

Back Country Suite
New Ground
Train
Warm Night
Blue Blues
Saturday
Scamper
January
Promised Land
Spring Song
Highway 49
Blueberry Hill
You Won't Let Me Go
I Thought About You
One Room Country Shack
In Shalah
Parchman Farm
Carnival
Crepuscular Air
Mojo Woman
Town
Trouble In Mind
Lost Mind

I'll Never Be Free
Don't Ever Say Goodbye
Ain't You A Mess

MOSE ALLISON: HELLO THERE, UNIVERSE

New York, 1969
Atlantic Atl SD1550

Mose Allison, piano and vocals
John Williams, bass
Joe Cocuzzo, drums
Jimmy Nottingham, Richard Williams, trumpet
Jerome Richardson, alto saxophone, flute
Joe Farrell, tenor saxophone
Pepper Adams, baritone saxophone
Bob Cranshaw, guitar

Somebody Gotta Move (vocal) (17963)

Joe Henderson (tenor sax) replaces Joe Farrell
Bob Cranshaw, bass replaces John Williams

Monsters Of The Id (vocal) (17916)
I'm Smashed (vocal) (17915)

Joe Farrell, tenor sax replaces Joe Henderson
Seldon Powell, baritone saxophone 1
Pepper Adams, baritone saxophone 2
John Williams, bass replaces Bob Cranshaw

Wild Man On The Loose (vocal) (Seldon Powell, baritone saxophone) (17917)
Hymn to Everything (Pepper Adams, baritone saxophone) (17962)
Hello There, Universe (vocal) (18426)
Blues In The Night (vocal) (18426)
No Exit (18480)
I Don't Want Much (18481)

MOSE ALLISON: THE BEST OF MOSE ALLISON

Atlantic Atl SD1542

Your Mind Is On Vaction (from *I Don't Worry About a Thing*)
Swingin' Machine (from *Swingin' Machine*)
Stop This World (from *Swingin' Machine*)
Seventh Son (from *Mose Alive!*)
New Parchman (from *The Word From Mose*)
Rollin' Stone (from *The Word From Mose*)
I'm The Wild Man (from *The Word From Mose*)
If You're Goin' To The City (from *Swingin' Machine*)
I Don't Worry About A Thing (from *I Don't Worry About A Thing*)
Your Molecular Structure (from *I've Been Doin' Some Thinkin'*)
Everybody Cryin' Mercy (from *I've Been Doin' Some Thinkin'*)
I Love The Life I Live (from *Mose Alive!*)

MOSE ALLISON: WESTERN MAN

New York, February 2, 1971
Atlantic Atl SD1584

Mose Allison, piano, electric piano and vocals
Chuck Rainey, electric bass
Billy Cobham, drum

Ask Me Nice (vocal) (21125)
Tell Me Something (vocal) (21126)

New York, February 3, 1971

How Much Truth (vocal) (21128)
If You Only Knew (vocal) (21129)

New York, February 11, 1971

Benediction (21303)
Night Club (vocal) (21304)

New York, March 3, 1971

Mountain (21355)
Western Man (vocal) (21356)

New York, March 4, 1971

Meadows (21357)
If You Got The Money (vocal) (21358)
Do Nothin' Till You Hear From Me (vocal) (21359)

MOSE ALLISON RETROSPECTIVE

Reissue, April, 1971, *Transfiguration of Hiram Brown, I Love the Life I Live and Takes To the Hills*
Columbia C 30564

I Love the Life I Live
Fool's Paradise
You're a Sweetheart
I Ain't Got Nobody
Baby, Please Don't Go
'Deed I Do
Back On the Corner
Love For Sale
Can't We Be Friends
V-8 Ford Blues
Please Don't Talk About Me When I'm Gone

MOSE ALLISON: MOSE IN YOUR EAR

Live "In Your Ear," Palo Alto, California, 1972
Atlantic Atl SD1627

Mose Allison, piano and vocals
Clyde Flowers, bass
Eddie Charlton, drums

Look What You Made Me Do
Fool's Paradise
I Don't Worry About a Thing

Powerhouse
Hey, Good Lookin'
I Ain't Got Nothin' But The Blues
You Can Count On Me To Do My Part
You Are My Sunshine
Don't Forget To Smile
The Seventh Son

MOSE ALLISON-SEVENTH SON

Reissue of *Mose Allison Sings*
Prestige PRT-10052
Distributed by Fantasy Records, Berkley, Calif

The Seventh Son
Eyesight to the Blind
Do Nothin' 'Till You Hear From Me
Lost Mind
I Got a Right to Cry
Baby Let Me Hold Your Hand
Parchman Farm
If You Live
Don't Get Around Much Anymore
One Room Country Shack
I Hadn't Anyone Till I Had You
A Young Man
That's All Right

MOSE ALLISON: CREEK BANK

Reissue, 1975 of *Young Man Mose* P 7137 and *Creek Bank* P 7152 P 24055

Somebody Else Is Taking My Place
Don't Get Around Much Any More
Bye Bye Blues
How Long Has This Been Going On
I Told Ya I Loved Ya, Now Get Out
Baby Let Me Hold Your Hand
Stroll
I Hadn't Anyone Till You
My Kind of Love
Sleepy Time Gal
The Seventh Son
If I Didn't Care
Cabin In the Sky
If You Live
Yardbird Suite
Creek Bank
Moon and Cypress
Mule
Dinner on the Ground
Prelude to a Kiss

MOSE ALLISON: YOUR MIND IS ON VACATION

New York, April 5, 7, 8, 9, 1976
Atlantic SD1691

Mose Allison, piano and vocals
Jack Hannah, bass
Jerry Granelli, drums
Al Porcino, trumpet (1)
David Sanborn, alto saxophone (1)
Joe Farrell, tenor saxophone (1)
Al Cohn, tenor saxophone (2)

No Catalogue Numbers listed for songs

Your Mind Is On Vacation (1)
One Of These Days (1)
Fires of Spring (1)
If You Only Knew (1)
Your Molecular Structure (1)
Foolin' Myself (2)
I Can't See For Lookin' (2)
No Matter
I Feel So Good
What Do You Do After You Ruin Your Life
Swingin' Machine
Perfect Moment

MOSE ALLISON: MIDDLE CLASS WHITE BOY

Los Angeles, February 2 and 3, 1982
Electra/Asylum E1-60125

Mose Allison, piano, Yamaha electronic piano
Putter Smith, bass
John Dentz, drums
Joe Farrell, tenor saxophone, flute
Phil Upchurch, guitar
Ron Powell, conga drums, percussion

How Does It Feel? (To Be Good Looking)
Rollin' Stone
I Don't Want Much
Middle Class White Boy
When My Dreamboat Comes Home
I'm Nobody Today
I'm Just A Lucky So-And-So
Back Down South
The Tennessee Waltz
Hello There, Universe
Kiddin' On The Square

MOSE ALLISON: LESSONS IN LIVING

Montreux, Switzerland, July 21, 1982
Electra/Asylum 60237

Mose Allison, piano
Jack Bruce, bass

Billy Cobham, drums
Lou Donaldson, alto saxophone
Eric Gale, guitar

Lost Mind
Wild Man On The Loose
Your Mind Is On Vacation
You Are My Sunshine
Seventh Son
Everybody Cryin' Mercy
Middle Class White Boy
I Don't Worry About A Thing
Night Club

MOSE ALLISON: EVER SINCE THE WORLD ENDED

New York
May 11 and 12, 1987
May 21 and June 2, 1987
Capitol/Blue Note B4J 48015

Mose Allison, piano and vocals
Dennis Irwin, bass
Tom Whaley, drums
Bob Malach, alto and tenor saxophone (1)
Arthur Blythe, alto saxophone (2)
Bennie Wallace, tenor saxophone (3)
Kenny Burrell, guitar (4)
Ever Since The World Ended (1, alto) (2, solo) (3)
Top Forty (4)
Puttin' Up With Me
Josephine (1, tenor)
I Looked In The Mirror (4)
Gettin' There (1, tenor) (2)
Tai Chi Life (1, alto) (3)
What's Your Movie (4)
Trouble In Mind (1, alto) (3)
I'm Alive

MOSE ALLISON: THE BEST OF MOSE ALLISON

Reissue, 1988
Atlantic Jazz
1542-2
Reissue of earlier "Best of" with
Eight added bonus tracks:

It Didn't Turn Out That Way (from *I Don't Worry About A Thing*)
I Ain't Got Nothin' But the Blues (from *Swingin' Machine*)
Don't Forget to Smile (from *The Word From Mose*)
What's With You (from *Wild Man on the Loose*)
That's The Stuff You Gotta Watch (from *Wild Man on the Loose*)
Jus' Like Livin' (from *I've Been Doin' Some Thinkin'*)
Nightclub (from *Western Man*)
One Of These Days (1) (from *Your Mind is on Vacation*)

MOSE ALLISON: GREATEST HITS, THE PRESTIGE COLLECTION

Reissue, 1988
Original Jazz Classics 6004
Originally Prestige PR 7279 *Mose Allison Sings*

MOSE ALLISON: MY BACKYARD

New Orleans, December 5, 6 and 7, 1989
Capitol/ Blue Note B1 93840, B4-93840, CDP 7 93840

Mose Allison, piano and vocals
Tony Dagradi, tenor saxophone
Steve Masakowski, guitar
Bill Huntington, bass
John Vidacovich, drums

Ever Since I Stole the Blues
You Call It Joggin'
Big Brother
Sentimental Fool
Stranger in My Own Hometown
Was
The Gettin' Paid Waltz
Dr. Jekyll & Mr. Hyde
That's Your Red Wagon
Long Song
Sleepy Lagoon
My Backyard

GIANTS OF JAZZ: MOSE ALLISON AT HIS BEST

Reissue, 1990
Warner Special Products
OPCD-1596
JCD-3651
Your Mind Is On Vacation
I Don't Worry About a Thing
Your Molecular Structure
Everybody Cryin' Mercy
Feel So Good
I'm Not Talkin'
What Do You Do After You Ruin Your Life
Perfect Moment
Hello There Universe
Do Nothing Till You Hear From Me

MOSE ALLISON SINGS AND PLAYS

Reissue, 1991: *Mose Allison Sings plus ten extra tracks*
Prestige CDJZD 007

The Seventh Son
Eyesight to the Blind
How Long Has This Been Going On
Do Nothing Till You Hear From Me
My Kind of Love

Lost Mind
Moon and Cypress
I Got a Right to Cry
Creek Bank
Baby Let Me Hold Your Hand
Stranger In Paradise
Parchman Farm
If You Live
Somebody Else Is Taking My Place
Don't Get Around Much Anymore
Bye Bye Blues
One Room Country Shack (A Thousand Miles From Nowhere)
I Told Ya I Loved Ya, Now Get Out
I Hadn't Anyone Till You
A Young Man
You Belong To Me
That's All Right
Yardbird Suite

MOSE ALLISON: I DON'T WORRY ABOUT A THING

Reissue, 1991
Rhino R271417
Originally Atl LP1389

I Don't Worry About A Thing (vocal) (6031)
Stand by (6033)
Idyll (6034)
Your Mind Is On Vacation (vocal) (6035)
Meet Me At No Special Place (vocal) (6036)
Let Me See (vocal) (6038)
Everything I Have Is Yours (vocal) (6039)
The Well (6040)
It Didn't Turn Out That Way (vocal) (6041)
The Song Is Ended (vocal) (6042)

MOSE ALLISON TRIO: BACK COUNTRY SUITE

Reissue, 1991
Original Jazz Classics 075
Originally Prest PR7091

New Ground (1125)
Train (1126)
Warm Night (1127)
Blues*, Mose Allison, vocals (1128)
Saturday (1129)
Scamper (1130)
January (1131)
Promised Land (1132)
Spring Song (1131)
Highway 49 (1134)
I Thought About You (1135)
In Salah (1136)
You Won't Let Me Go (1137)
One Room Country Shack, Mose Allison, vocals (1138)
Blueberry Hill (1139)

* Recorded as "Young Man" on Prestige 7279 and Stateside SL10106

MOSE ALLISON TRIO: LOCAL COLOR

Reissue, 1991
Original Jazz Classic 457
Originall Prestige PR7121

Town (1382)
Mojo Woman (1383)
Crepuscular Air (1384)
Carnival (1385)
I'll Never Be Free (1386)
Don't Say Goodbye (1387)
Ain't You A Mess (1388)
Trouble In Mind, Mose Allison, (trumpet) (1389)
Lost Mind, Mose Allison, vocals (1390)
Parchman Farm, Mose Allison, vocals (1391)

THE EARTH WANTS YOU: MOSE ALLISON

New York, September 8, 9, 10, 1993
Capitol/Blue Note CDP 724382764021

Mose Allison, piano and vocals
Paul Motian, drums
Ratzo B. Harris, bass
John Scofield, guitar
Joe Lovan, alto saxophone
Bob Malach, tenor saxophone
Randy Brecker, trumpet
Ray Mantilla, conga
Hugh McCracken, harmonica

Certified Senior Citizen
This Ain't Me
You Can't Push People Around
My Ideal
The Earth Wants You
Cabaret Card
Red Wagon
Children of the Future
I Don't Love You
Who's In, Who's Out
Natural Born Malcontent
What a Shame
Variation On Dixie

MOSE ALLISON: PURE MOSE

Recorded Live at Keystone Korner, San Francisco, CA
date unknown, approximately the late seventies
Ram Records, 1994
R–81001

Mose Allison, piano and vocals
Tom Rutley, bass
Jery Granelli, drums

Lost Mind
Wildman on the Loose

Your Molecular Structure
It Feels So Good
Swingin' Machine
You Can Count on Me to Do My Part
I Love the Life I Live
If You're Goin' to the City
I Ain't Got Nothin' But the Blues
Hey Good Lookin'
Meet Me At No Special Place
Seventh Son
Wildman
Show Closer
Bonus track: Your Mind Is On Vacation

THE MOSE ALLISON TRILOGY: HIGH JINKS!

Reissue, 1994
Columbia/Epic/Legacy
MOSE ALLISON: TRANSFIGURATION OF HIRAM BROWN
Columbia Legacy, CK57879
Originally Columbia CL 1444

How Little We Know (CO64532)
Baby, Please Don't Go (CO64533)
Hiram Brown Suite (CO64534)
  Barefoot Dirt Road
  City Home
  Cuttin' Out
  Gotham Day
  Gotham Night
  Echo
  The River
  Finale
Make Yourself Comfortable (CO64535)
Love For Sale (CO64540)B
Barefoot-Dirt Road* previously unissued, alternate version

I LOVE THE LIFE I LIVE: THE VOICE AND PIANO OF THE MOSE ALLISON TRIO
CK57880
Columbia Legacy, 1994
Originally Columbia RM 52318

Night Ride
Fool's Paradise
You Turned the Tables on Me
Mad With You
Path
I Love the Life I Live
Hittin' On One
News
You're a Sweetheart
Isobel
Can't We Be Friends
I Ain't Got Nobody
Am I Blue* previously unissued
The Pretty Girl Is Like a Melody* previously unissued

MOSE ALLISON: TAKES TO THE HILLS
Epic/Legacy
EK57878, 1994
Originally Epic LA 16031

V-8 Ford Blues
Please Don't Talk About Me When I'm Gone
Hey Good Looking'
Back On the Corner
Life Is Suicide
Ask Me Nice
Baby, Please Don't Go
Mad With You
I Love the Life I Live
You're a Sweetheart
I Ain't Got Nobody
High Jinks* previously unissued
So Rare* previously unissued
The Hills* previously unissued

ALLISON WONDERLAND: THE MOSE ALLISON ANTHOLOGY

Reissue, 1994
Rhino/Atlantic Jazz Gallery R2 71689

Back Country Suite: Blues (Young Man Blues)
Parchman Farm
If You Live
Seventh Son
Eyesight to the Blind
Baby, Please Don't Go
Fool's Paradise
V-8 Ford Blues
Ask Me Nice
Hey, Good Lookin'
Back On the Corner
Your Mind Is On Vacation
Meet Me at No Special Place
I Don't Worry About a Thing
I Ain't Got Nothing But the Blues
Swingin' Machine
Stop This World
I'm Not Talkin'
I'm the Wild Man
Your Red Wagon
Foolkiller
Wild Man on the Loose
You Can Count on Me to Do My Part
Smashed
That's Alright
If You're Goin' to the City
Everybody Cryin' Mercy
Feel So Good
Your Molecular Structure
Monsters of the Id
Hello There, Universe
I Don't Want Much

How Much Truth
Western Man
I'm Just a Lucky So and So
The Tennesse Waltz
Ever Since the World Ended
Top Forty
Josephine
Gettin' There
Ever Since I Stole the Blues
You Call It Joggin'
Big Brother
The Gettin' Paid Waltz

MOSE ALLISON: MIDDLE CLASS WHITE BOY

Reissue, 1994
Discovery Records 71011
Originally Elecktra/Asylum E1-60125

How Does It Feel? (To Be Good Looking)
Rollin' Stone
I Don't Want Much
Middle Class White Boy
When My Dreamboat Comes Home
I'm Nobody Today
I'm Just a Lucky So-And-So
Back Down South
The Tennessee Waltz
Hello There, Universe
Kiddin' On The Square

MOSE ALLISON: LESSONS IN LIVING

Reissue, 1994
Discovery Records 71014
Originally Elektra/Asylum 60237

Lost Mind
Wild Man On The Loose
Your Mind Is On Vacation
You Are My Sunshine
Seventh Son
Everybody Cryin' Mercy
Middle Class White Boy
I Don't Worry About A Thing
Night Club

INDEX

Abramson, Herb, 134
Adams, Pepper, 182, 186
Adolphos Hotel, 46
Aeroplane, 224, 272
Ain't Misbehaving (revue), 172
"Ain't She Sweet", 123
Al and Zoot, 56
Al Cohn Quintet, 56
Alcott family, 241
Allen, Red, 298
"Allison", 284-6, 285
Allison, Alissa (MA's daughter), 44-5, 50, 66
Allison, Amy (MA's daughter), 66
Allison, Audre (née Schwartz, MA's wife): children, 44-5, 66; first meets MA, 29; marriage, 29, 32-3; Miami trip, 47-8; New York, 41, 55, 66-7; Orlando gig memories, 49-50; work, 46, 49-50, 66
Allison, Farris (MA's aunt), 4

Allison, Frances, *see* Butts
Allison, Janine (MA's daughter), 66
Allison, John (MA's son), 66
Allison, John Robert "Papa" (MA's grandfather), 3-7, 9
Allison, Johnnie (MA's aunt), 4
Allison, Joy (MA's sister), 10
Allison, Lacey (MA's uncle), 3
Allison, Maxine (née Collins, MA's mother), 4-9, 11-13, 17, 86-7
Allison, Minnie (née Holland, MA's grandfather's first wife), 3
Allison, Mose John (MA's father), 4-8, 10-12
Allison, Ollie "Mom" (née Cox, MA's grandfather's third wife), 4-6, 12
Allison, Sammie (MA's aunt), 4

Allison, Texana (née Paul, MA's grandmother), 3, 6
Allison, Tony (MA's brother), 10
American Armed Forces Radio, 81
Ammons, Albert, 13
Anderson, Cat, 273
Armstrong, Louis: comparison with MA, 248; 276; influence on MA, 18, 22, 43, 98, 237; singing style, 298; Southern style phrasing, 80
Art Blakey and his Jazz Messengers, 293
"Ask Me Nice", 115, 129, 190, 288
Atlantic Monthly, 303
Atlantic Records, 64, 116, 119, 128, 130, 131, 133-7, 140, 143, 146, 147, 154, 157, 158, 163, 167, 172, 180-1, 187, 192, 193, 194, 203-8, 212, 213, 219, 224, 238, 244, 263, 268, 304

Atomic Mr Basie, The, 89
Auerbach, Art, 183
Auger, Brian, 88, 90, 267, 289–91
Autry, Gene, 101
"Autumn Song", 107, 108
Autumn Song, 106–9, 112, 147

"Baby, Let Me Hold Your Hand", 98
"Baby Please Don't Go", 124, 125, 127, 129, 130, 147, 154, 288, 292
Bach, J.S., 130, 176, 239–40
Back Country Suite, 39, 60, 68, 69–82, 84, 88, 97, 106, 111, 120, 143, 137, 236, 238, 239, 273, 292, 301
"Back Down South", 213–14
"Back on the Corner", 129
Baez, Joan, 268
Baker, Chet, 57, 238, 298
Baker, Ginger, 273–4, 278
Baker's Lounge, 57
Baldry, Long John, 90
"Ballad of Bonnie and Clyde, The", 90
Barber, Chris, 278
Barber, Samuel, 240
"Barefoot-Dirt Road", 121, 123
Bartók, Béla, 39, 71–2, 239–40
Basie, Count: Buck Clayton's performances, 17; influence at Ole Miss, 22; influence on MA, 13, 18, 43; "Let Me See", 146; playing in London, 273; popularity, 266; style, 108
Bass, Lester, 28
Bauzá, Mario, 54
BBC, 135, 266
Beale Street Auditorium, 27
Beatles, the, 268, 276, 306
Beck, Jeff, 148–9
"Bemsha Swing", 150
"Benediction", 189
Bennett, Bill, 32, 43–4, 46–8, 58
Berry, Chuck, 209, 268, 289, 302
"Big Brother", 230
Big Maceo, 14
Billboard, 134
Birdland, 53, 57–8, 246
Bivens, Birk, 223
Black, Brown and Beige, 71
Black, Frank, *see* Black Francis
Black Francis, 283–6
Blakey, Art, 293
Bland, Bobby "Blue", 42, 287
Blood, Sweat and Tears, 92, 187
Bloomfield, Mike, 93, 266
Blue Cheer, 94
Blue Moon, the, 40
Blue Note Records, 95, 123, 125, 189, 207, 209, 219, 220, 228, 270

"Blueberry Hill", 81
"Blues", 75, 76–7, 80
"Blues in the Night", 182
Blues Project, the, 92, 266
Bluesbreakers, John Mayall and the, 88, 90–1, 283
Blythe, Arthur, 220, 221, 225
"Body and Soul", 31
Bogart, Humphrey, 196
Bond, Graham, 273, 274, 278, 280, 283
Bottom Line, the, 300
Boudreaux, Buddy, 40
Bowles, Paul, 81
"Bringing in the Sheaves", 242
Britishers, the, 88
Britten, Benjamin, 276
Brookmeyer, Bobby, 55
Brooks, Don, 27, 47
Broonzy, Big Bill, 2, 14, 82, 262
Brown, Charles, 43, 78, 269
Brown, Clifford, 98–9
Brown, Les, 22
Brown, Pete, 277–83
Brown, Rick, 90
Browne, Jackson, 269
Brubeck, Dave, 50, 118
Bruce, Jack, 80–1, 91, 214–15, 273–7, 278
Bullet Records, 28
Burdon, Eric, 290
Burrell, Kenny, 220, 223

347

Butts, Frances (née Allison, MA's aunt), 4, 6, 7, 17
"Bye Bye Blues", 98
Byrd, Charlie, 291

"Cabin in the Sky", 105
Cafe Bohemia, 53, 64
"Call the Po-lice", 45
Calloway, Dick, 22
"Can't We Be Friends", 126, 128
Capitol/EMI, 219
Carlo Listi's Bar, 31
Carmichael, Dr., 36
Carmichael, Hoagy, 78, 124, 299
"Carnival", 84–5
Caseres, Rick, 49
Castle to Castle, 164
CBS, 118, 125
Cecil, Tommy, 257
Céline, Louis-Ferdinand, 164–5, 184
Cerulli, Dom, 71
Charles, Ray: Atlantic Records, 304; "Baby, Let Me Hold Your Hand", 98; comparison with MA, 282; influence, 74, 268, 282, 302; MA's interest in, 65; singing, 298; status, 74, 270, 273; Townshend on, 92; work with Walter Miller, 40
Charleston High School, 15–17
Chase, 187
"Chaser, The", 154
Chatham, Sarah, 26
Chicago, 187

Chicago Reader, The, 205–6
"City Home", 51–2, 121–2, 123, 125, 141, 173
Clapton, Eric, 91, 148
Clark, Sonny, 123
Clash, The, 149–50, 267
Clayton, Buck, 17, 22, 98
Clyde's, 61
Coasters, the, 304
Cobham, Billy, 187–8, 214–15
Cohn, Al: MA's work with, 55–7, 60, 64, 74, 116, 126, 195–6, 238, 277; "Saritha", 112; 34th Street loft, 61; work with Brew Moore, 40
Cole, Nat: influence on MA, 18, 22, 31, 45–6, 78, 79–80, 94, 98, 108, 237, 297–8; "Meet Me at No Particular Place", 146; popularity, 266, 272
Coleman, Ornette, 81, 134, 274
Collingwood, R.G., 37–8
Collins, Cliff (MA's grandfather), 5
Collins, Maurine (MA's aunt), 5
Coltrane, John, 58, 70, 134, 136, 246–7
Columbia Records, 91, 118–20, 124–5, 126, 128–31, 133–4, 136, 154, 205, 208, 212, 219, 238, 263
Columby, Harry, 150

Concerto for Orchestra, 72, 240
Concord Sonata, 241
Connick, Harry, 272
Cooke, Sam, 305
Cooper, Hog, 186
Copland, Aaron, 71
Corber, Gene, 49
Corea, Chick, 187
Cork and Bib, the, 57
Costello, Elvis, 154, 173, 284
Cotton Country Suite, see *Back Country Suite*
Cotton, James, 294
Cowan, Joel, 44
Cox, Clyde: career, 53–4; memories of MA, 53–4, 65–6, 67; 34th Street loft, 53, 59–60, 62, 69
Creagh, Ron, 211
Cream, 80, 91, 214, 265, 279, 280
"Creek Bank", 105
Creek Bank, 101–2, 104–5, 107, 112, 124, 193, 212
"Crepuscular Air", 84
Crescendo, 237–8, 242–3
Crosby, Stills and Nash, 134
Crow, Bill, 126
CTI Records, 187
Curly's, 47
"Cuttin' Out", 121, 122

Dagradi, Tony, 228, 230, 233
Daltrey, Roger, 76, 304
Dameron, Tadd, 28
"Dance the Night Away", 279
Dane, Barbara, 117

348

Davies, Ray, 299–301
Davis, Jimmie, 171
Davis, Miles: black music, 302, 306; Columbia Records, 118; influence, 98; Prestige Records, 70; style, 66, 274; work with Gerry Mulligan, 117
Day, Doris, 268
"Days Like This", 150, 151, 182
Death on the Installment Plan, 164
Decca Records, 90
"Deed I Do", 124, 129
Demon Records, 154
Dempsey, Maudie, 47
Dentz, John, 209
Desert Island Discs, 232
"Deserted Cities of the Heart", 279
"Devil in the Cane Field", 107, 108
DiAgostino, JoJo, 49
Diddley, Bo, 302
"Dinner on the Ground", 105
Discovery Records, 158
Dixon, Willie: friendship with MA, 102; "I Loveced the Life I Live", 91, 126–7, 211; "Seventh Son", 3, 92, 94, 102–4, 112, 184, 193, 252, 293; "Spoonful", 281; work, 88, 102, 274; work with Barbara Dane, 117
"Do Nothing Till You Hear From Me", 109–10, 188, 271, 298
"Dr. Jekyll and Mr. Hyde:", 230–1
Dolphy, Eric, 274
Domino, Fats, 81
Donaldson, Lou, 215, 216
"Don't Forget to Smile", 152, 159
"Don't Get Around Much Anymore", 98
Dorn, Joel, 180–1, 186–7
Dorsey, Tommy, 22
Dowd, Tom, 134, 135–6, 146, 207
Downbeat, 71, 74–5
Dreja, Chris, 148
Driscoll, Julie, 90
Duke, Vernon, 105
Dylan, Bob, 174, 260

Eaglin, Snooks, 302
"Early Autumn", 57
"Echo", 123
Eckstine, Billy, 29
Edwards, Esmond, 209
Either Way, 56, 126
Electric Hot Tuna, 93
Elektra/Musician, 158, 184, 187, 208–9, 214, 219, 245
Eliot, T.S., 307
Ellington, Duke: "Do Nothing Till You Hear From Me", 109–10, 188; "Don't Get Around Much Anymore", 98; "I Ain't Got Nothin' But the Blues", 146, 193; "I'm Just a Lucky So and So", 212; influence on MA, 18, 71, 136; playing in London, 273; popularity, 266; "Prelude to a Kiss", 105
Elwood, Phillip, 253
Emerson, Ralph Waldo, 241
EMI, 89, 123, 219, 224, 270
Entwistle, John, 76
Epic Records, 93, 119, 130, 190, 193
Ertegun, Ahmet, 134–5, 180
Ertegun, Neshui, 134–5, 146, 180, 181, 204, 207
Esquire, 88
Evans, Bill, 286
"Ever Since I Stole the Blues", 229, 261, 272
"Ever Since the World Ended", 225–7, 226, 228, 282
Ever Since the World Ended, 95, 207, 220, 223, 227–8, 270
"Everybody Cryin' Mercy", 162, 168, 171, 173–4, 180, 182, 190, 212, 216, 225, 288
"Everything I Have Is Yours", 146
"Eyesight to the Blind", 108–9, 166, 294

Falkenhagen, Sparky, 45, 46–7
Fame, Georgie: career, 89–90; MA's influence, 77, 89,

264, 289, 292; on MA, 292–3; performs MA's songs, 88, 89, 190, 267, 292, 299; spreads MA's reputation, 264, 289, 301
Fantasy Records, 113
Farmer, Addison, work with MA, 64, 98, 99, 102, 107, 120, 126, 146
Farmer, Art, 64, 117
Farrell, Joe, 182, 186, 195, 209, 211, 213
Fat Tuesdays, 300
Faulkner, William, 61, 163–4, 204, 260
Fedric, Dudley, 23
"Feel So Good", 168, 170–1, 184, 196
Feet Warmers, The, 17–18
Ferguson, V.P., 164
"Finale", 123
"Fires of Spring, The", 195, 198–201, 200–1
Flack Roberta, 180
Flamingo Club, the, 89, 90, 264, 273–4, 278, 289, 292, 301
Fleetwood Mac, 91, 279
Fontana, Carl, 40
"Foolkiller", 35–6, 68, 147, 167, 182
"Fool's Paradise", 126–7, 149, 193, 211
"Fools Rush In", 29
Forbidden Planet, The, 184
Fortier, Lee, 40

Four Satans and an Angel, 31
"Fourteen Day Palmolive Plan, The", 11–12
Francis, Connie, 268
Franklin, Aretha, 134, 269
Franks, Michael, 77
Free, Ronnie, 59, 60, 61, 99, 102, 107
Friedman, Don, 61
Frishberg, Dave, 60–1, 62
Frizzell, Lefty, 188
Fuller, Johnny, 126, 193, 211

Gaillard, Slim, 277
Gale, Eric, 215
Garaldi, Vince, 183
Garner, Erroll, 31, 45, 108, 130, 237
Garrison, Jimmy, 247
Gaye, Marvin, 272
Gentry, Bobby, 3
George, Don, 146
Georgie Fame and the Blue Flames: Rhythm and Blues at "The Flamingo", 89
Georgie's, 274
Gershwin, George, 98
"Gettin' Paid Waltz, The", 229
"Gettin' There", 218–19, 220–1, 228
Getz, Stan: influence, 277; MA's work with, 57, 58, 63, 64, 74, 116, 125, 126, 238, 277; 34th Street loft, 61
Gilbert, Don, 29
Gillespie, Dizzy, 20, 43, 98, 107

Gitler, Ira, 84–5
Goldberg, Barry, 93
Goldberg, Joe, 101
Golden Slipper, the, 40
Golson, Benny, 293
Goodman, Benny, 118
Gordon, Max, 101
"Gotham Day", 122
"Gotham Night", 123
Gould, Glenn, 130
Granelli, Jerry, 183, 195, 196, 198, 202, 249–50
Greenwell, Freddie, 57, 61
Grey, Bob, 44
Grimes, Henry, 61, 126
"Groovin' High", 107
Guignol's Band, 164–5
Guthrie, Woody, 82
Guy, Buddy, 275

Haig, Al, 61, 106, 108, 122, 237
"Half Neslon", 28
Half Note Cafe, 56
Hammerstein, Oscar, 233
Hammond, John, 88, 93, 118, 287–9
Hampton, Dale, 29, 30–1
Hampton, Lionel, 28
Hancock, Herbie, 187
Hannah, Jack, 195, 196, 198
Harris, Robert R.H., 305
Harris, Wynonie, 277
Harrison, Benjamin, 23
Harvey, Bill, 42–3, 44
Hawes, Hampton, 65

Hawkins, Screaming Jay, 277
Hawthorne, Nathaniel, 241
Haymes, Dick, 63–4
Haymes, Margaret, 63
"Hello There, Universe", 107, 179–80, 181, 182, 183, 185, 190, 197, 200, 213, 225
Hello There, Universe, 154–5, 158, 163, 180–1, 184, 186, 195
Henderson, Joe, 182, 186
Hendrix, Jimi, 94, 266
Herman, Woody, 31, 56, 57
Hextall-Smith, Dick, 274, 278
"Hey Good Lookin'", 129, 193
High Jinx, 130
"Highway 49", 75
"Hills, The", 129
Hindemith, Paul, 13, 104, 107, 176, 240, 243–4
Hines, Earl "Fatha", 13, 18
"Hittin' on One", 126, 128
"Hold Tight", 16
Holiday, Billie, 94, 272, 295, 298
Holly, Buddy, 302
"Honeysuckle Rose", 41
Hooker, John Lee, 2, 43, 269, 302
Hopkins, Anthony, 277
Horwitz, Murray, 172
Hot Tuna, 88, 93, 291

House, Son, 2
Houston, Joe, 40
"How Does It Feel to be Good Lookin'", 210–11, 214, 220
"How Little We Know", 124
"How Long Has This Been Going On", 98
"How Much Truth Can a Man Stand", 107, 181, 184, 191–2
Howes, Oliver, 88–9
Howlin' Wolf, 42, 262, 274, 280–1
Hubbard, Freddie, 187
Hughes, Ralph, 46–9, 59, 60
Hughes, Susan (née Staton), 46
"Hungarian Sketches", 39, 72, 239
Huntington, Bill, 228
Hurwitz, Jerome, *see* Jerry Lloyd
"Hymn to Everything", 185

"I Ain't Got Nobody", 126–7, 129
"I Ain't Got Nothin' But the Blues", 146, 193
"I Can't Get Started", 31
"I Can't See For Lookin'", 196
"I Don't Want Much", 184, 211
"I Don't Worry 'bout a Thing", 96–7, 143–4, 146, 184, 193, 215–16

I Don't Worry 'bout a Thing, 119, 143, 167
"I Got a Right to Cry", 100
"I Got Fish for Supper", 45
"I Hadn't Anyone Till You", 98, 100
"I Just Want To Make Love to You", 102
"I Looked in the Mirror", 220, 222
"I Love the Life I Live", 91, 126–7, 129. 154, 211, 286, 294
I Love the Life I Live, 119, 128, 129, 279
"If I Didn't Care", 105
"If You Got the Money", 188
"If You Live", 1–2, 104–5, 112, 137, 166, 289
"If You Only Knew:, 189, 196, 271
"If You Really Loved Me Baby", 169, 170
"If You're Goin' to the City", 52, 146, 167, 171, 172–3, 252, 289
"I'm Alive", 189, 220, 221–2, 227
"I'm Just a Lucky So and So", 212
"I'm Just a Wild Man", 151, 158, 288
"I'm Just Foolin' Myself", 195
"I'm Nobody Today", 211–12
"I'm not Talkin'", 148, 149, 167, 190, 294
"I'm Smashed", 154–6, 168, 182

"I'm Your Hootchie
  Coochie Man", 102,
  281
Imperial Records, 94
"In-a-Gadda-Da-
  Vida", 94
"In Salah", 81
In Your Ear, 192–3
Insomniac, the, 287
Iron Butterfly, 94
Irwin, Dennis, 220
"Isobel", 126, 128
Isola, Frank, 61, 70
"It Didn't Turn Out
  That Way", 145–6,
  296
"It's Crazy", 107
I've Been Doin' Some
  Thinkin', 163, 166,
  168, 171, 172, 176,
  209, 239
Ives, Charles, 13, 104,
  122, 240–4

J. Geils Band, 92
Jackson, Chubby, 31
Jagger, Mick, 260,
  278, 280
Jamerson, James, 275
Janes, Don, 61
"January", 75
Jarrett, Keith, 209
Jazz Journal, 88–9
Jefferson Airplane,
  88, 93
Jet, 117
John Mayall and the
  Bluesbreakers Featuring
  Eric Clapton, 90
Johnny Birch Band,
  the, 274
Johnny Garner Trio,
  45, 49, 50
Johnson, Gus, 126
Johnson, Harry, 47
Johnson, Osie, 146

Johnson, Pete, 13
Johnson, Robert, 2, 88
Jones, Buddy, 61
Jones, Elvin, 246–7
Jones, Paul, 281
Jones, Richard M.,
  16, 95, 151, 223–4,
  231
Jones, Ronnie, 273
Joplin, Janis, 266
Jordan, Louis, 11, 13,
  14, 31
"Josephine", 220, 223,
  228
Journal of Albion
  Moonlight, The, 165
Journey to the End of
  Night, 164
"Jus' Like Livin'",
  171–3, 172

Kahn, Gus, 223
Kaukonen, Jorma, 93,
  291–2
Kelly, Wynton, 65
"Kiddin' on the
  Square", 211, 212,
  229
King, B.B., 27, 28, 42,
  44, 287, 294
King, Freddie, 294
King, Wayne, 223
Kirk, Roland, 186
Knepper, Jimmy, 146
Kooper, Al, 92, 130–1,
  266, 293–5
Korner, Alexis, 273,
  278–9, 281, 283
Kotick, Teddy, 55

L.A. Times, 284
LaFargue, Taylor: Back
  Country Suite, 70–1;
  in Baton Rouge, 40;
  influence on MA,
  45; memories of

work with MA, 30–
  2, 45–6, 49, 50, 70–
  1; 34th Street loft,
  59; work with Getz;
  63; work with MA,
  29, 30–2, 44–7, 70–1
Landau, John, 306
Lane, Bunky, 47
"Late Night Mental
  Tire Service", 280
Lawrence, Jack, 105
Leadbelly, 82
Led Zeppelin, 265
Lennon, John, 276
Lessons in Living, 152,
  158, 210, 214–15,
  245
Lester, Ketty, 272
"Let It Come Down",
  107, 176–8, 177–8,
  180
"Let Me See", 146
Lewis, John, 106, 108
Lewis, Meade "Lux",
  13
"Life Is Suicide", 129
Liggins, Joe, 100
Lighthouse, the, 239,
  279–80, 287
Lightin' Hopkins, 43,
  73, 126–7, 199, 302
"Little Red Rooster",
  102
Little Richard, 268
Little Walter, 302
Live at Leeds, 76
Live at The Beacon
  Theatre, 190
Live at the Whiskey A Go
  Go, 94
Lloyd, Jerry, 61
Local Color, 16, 83–5,
  88, 92, 94, 95, 97,
  111
Lockwood, Robert Jr.,
  109

Logos, Paul, 46-7
"Long Song", 232
"Look Here", 149-50, 167
"Look What You Made Me Do", 169, 193
"Lost Mind", 94, 151-2, 216, 271
Loudermilk, John D., 231
Louis Armstrong plays W.C. Handy, 89
Louisiana State University (LSU), 33, 36-7, 39, 41-3, 71, 72, 117, 238, 239
Love, Willie, 129
"Love for Sale", 125, 126, 154
"Love Letters", 272
Lundvall, Bruce: Blue Note, 209, 219, 270; Columbia Records, 125; Elektra/Musician, 187, 208, 214; memories of MA, 125, 260; Robert Palmer meeting, 270

Mabon, Willie, 78, 103
Macbeth, 176
McCarty, Jim, 148-9
McCorkle, Susannah, 77, 295-9
McDade, John Earle, 28
McDowell, Mississippi Fred, 269
Macero, Teo, 119, 120, 124, 272
McFerrin, Bobby, 228
Machito, 40, 54

McLaughlin, John, 187
McVie, John, 91
"Mad with You", 126-7, 129, 130
Mahivishnu Orchestra, the, 187
"Make Yourself Comfortable", 124-5
Malach, Bob, 220, 224
Mann, Herbie, 64, 134
Marius the Epicurean, 36
Marquee, the, 278, 279, 299
Marsh, George, 208, 247-9, 256-7
Masakowski, Steve, 228-9, 231
Massengale, Burt, 32
Mayall, John: background, 281; influence, 279, 281, 283; MA's influence, 80, 91; on MA, 301; performs MA's songs, 88, 90-1, 267; work with jazz musicians, 278
Mayfield, Percy: comparison with MA, 204; influence on MA, 78; "Lost Mind", 94, 151, 216; playing in Jackson, 44; "Life Is Suicide", 129; "Stranger in My Own Hometown", 231
"Meadows", 188
"Meet Me at No Particular Place", 146, 296
"Melancholy Baby", 238
Melly, George, 281

Memphis Minnie, 14
Memphis Recording Service, 42
Memphis Slim, 14, 117
Mercer, Johnny, 124
Mercury Records, 92, 126
Merrill, Bob, 124
Meters, the, 171
"Middle Class White Boy", 202-3, 214, 216, 220, 229, 280, 291
Middle Class White Boy, 152, 184, 209, 210, 212-13, 219, 220, 228
Midler, Bette, 180
Miller, Walter, 40
Mingus, Charles, 70, 134, 300
"Minstrels, The", 100
Minton's, 135
Mississippi State Penitentiary, 85
Mississippi State University for Women, 4
Mississippians the, 18, 22, 53
Mitchell, Charles, 171
Mitchell Hotel, the, 28
"Mojo Woman", 84
Money, Zoot, 286-7
Monk, Thelonious: "Bemsha Swing", 150; Columbia Records, 118; influence, 242; influence on MA, 106, 108, 122, 123; Prestige Records, 70
Monroe, Vaughn, 232

"Monster Mash", 285
"Monsters of the Id", 182–3
Montreux Jazz Festival, 214–17, 245, 275
Moon, Keith, 76
"Moon and Cypress", 105
"Moondance", 282
Moore, Brew, 40
Moore, Marilyn, 55
Morgan, Lee, 187, 293
Morganfield, McKinley, *see* Muddy Waters
Morrison, Van, 189–90, 267, 281–2
Morrow, Buddy, 63
Mose Allison Alive!, 135, 153–4, 188, 239
Mose Allison Plays for Lovers, 113
Mose Allison Sings and Plays V–8 Ford Blues, 119, 130
Mose Allison Takes to the Hills, 128–9, 130, 190, 193
Mose Allison Trio, the, 63–4, 66, 70, 115–16
Mose Goes, 130
Mose in Your Ear, 152, 192, 195
Motian Paul, 56, 64, 126, 246–7
Motorhead, 272
Motown, 268, 275
"Mountains", 188
"Move", 65–6
Mozart, W.A., 241
Muddy Waters: background, 2; influence, 43, 73, 229, 260, 262, 269, 280–1, 283; MA's encounters with, 73, 86; "Rollin' Stone", 92, 151, 210, 211, 221, 293–4; songs, 88, 92; UK impact, 73, 262, 274, 278, 280–1
"Mule", 105
Mulligan, Gerry, 57, 117
Murray, Charles Shaar, 260
Musicians' Union, 54–5, 277
Musselwhite, Charlie, 93
"My Backyard", 233
My Backyard, 152, 228, 231–2
"My Kind of Love", 98

Nat Garner Trio, the, 31, 45
National Public Radio, 123–4
National Records, 134
Navarro, Fats, 99
"Never More", 160
"New Ground", 75
"New Parchman", 87–8, 152, 154
New York Times, 43
New York University, 41
Newborn, Phineas, 27
Newman, Randy, 174, 260, 271
"News", 126, 128
Night at the Half Note, A, 56
"Night Ride", 126, 128
"Night Watch", 160
"Nightclub", 190, 215–16, 229, 297
Nighthawks, the, 93
"No Exit", 184–5
"No Matter", 196
"No Trouble Livin'", 157–8, 167
Noble, Ray, 98
Nolan, Bob, 223
Nonesuch/Folkways, 199
Norris, Walter, 31–2
North, 164
Norwood, Cookie, 41
"Now You See It", 171, 173

"Ode to Billy Joe", 3
Odetta, 268
Ol' Devil Mose, 113
"Ole Devil Moon", 100, 113
Oliver, "Miss Jimmy", 9–10
"On the Run", 184
"One of These Days", 132–3, 140, 149, 152, 168, 196
"One Room Country Shack", 79, 80, 166

Page, Hot Lips, 298
Page, Jimmy, 148
Palmer, Robert, 207, 224, 267, 270–3
Papa, Tony, 28
"Parchman Farm", 83–4, 83–95, 103, 136–7, 152, 154, 166, 181, 200, 214, 274, 279, 287, 289, 291, 292, 293, 294, 299
Parker, Charlie: bebop, 43; black music, 306;

comparison with MA, 248; style, 59, 251-2, 254; work with Jerry Lloyd, 61; "Yardbird Suite", 105
Parker, Horatio, 241
Parker, Junior, 287
"Parker's Mood", 252
Patchen, Kenneth, 161-2, 165
Pater, Walter, 36, 37
Patey, Bill, 31, 40
"Path", 126, 128
Paul Butterfield Blues Band, the, 266
"Perfect Moment", 197-8, 200, 233
Perkins, Carl, 300
Pete Baggett's 49 Club, 46
Pete Townshend's Deep End Live!, 109
Phillips, Sam, 42, 266
Piano Bar, 135
Picasso, Pablo, 186
Pidgeon, Walter, 184
Pine Hill Club, 48
Pixies, the, 284, 286
Pizza on the Park, 300
Plantation Club, 27
"Please Don't Talk About Me When I'm Gone", 129
"Politician", 279
Polygram, 189
Porcino, Al, 195
Porter, Cole, 125
Powell, Bud, 62, 106-7, 108, 123, 237-8
Powell, Ron, 209
Powell, Seldon, 182
"Power House", 160, 193, 250
"Prelude to a Kiss", 105

Presley, Elvis, 42-3, 300, 302
Prestige Records, 16, 63, 69-71, 84, 94, 96-9, 101-3, 106-7, 110-13, 116, 118-20, 131, 133, 135, 136, 147, 166, 187, 193, 209, 212, 219, 227, 238, 262
"Pride", 271
Principles of Art, 37
Prokofiev, Sergei, 240
"Promenade", 107, 147
"Promised Land", 75
"Puttin' up with Me", 220, 221, 229
Pyle, Harry, 146

Raitt, Bonnie, 173-4, 266, 268-70
"Ramble", 100
Ramblin' with Mose, 99-102, 112, 147
Ramsey Lewis trio, the, 302
Rault, Philippe, 214
Ray Bryant Trio, the, 293
Reagan, Ronald, 211
Red Hill Inn, 57
Redbone, Leon, 186, 284
Redding, Otis, 134, 272
Reed, Jimmy, 260, 294, 302
Reed, Lou, 295
Reider, Jimmy, 146
Relf, Keith, 148
Retrospective: The Best of Mose Allison, 130, 283
Reynolds, R.J., 49
Richard, Cliff, 302

Richardson, Jerome, 186
Rigandon, 164
Rising Sun, the, 17
"River", 123
Rivers, Johnny, 88, 94
Roach, Max, 237
Robinson, J. Russell, 146
Rock and Roll Hall of Fame, 305
"Rock Around the Clock", 28
Rodgers, Jimmie, 109
Rodgers, Richard, 233
Rogers, Roy, 223
Rogers, Will, 236
"Rollin' Stone", 92, 151-2, 210, 211, 221, 294
Rolling Stones, the, 265, 268, 306
Rollins, Sonny, 61
Ronnie Scott's, 273, 279, 289
"Rosetta", 41
"Route 66", 45
Royal Teens, the, 293
Ruggles, Carl, 240
Rush, Otis, 281, 282
Russell, Leon, 155
Rym, Shelly, 44

Sam and Dave, 134
Sammy's Restaurant and Bar, 31
Samwell-Smith, Paul, 148
Sanborn, David, 195, 196
"Saritha", 100, 107, 112, 147, 250
"Saturday", 75
"Scamper", 75
Schmidt's piano exercises, 243

355

Schoenberg, Arnold, 176, 239
Scriabin, Alexander, 104, 107, 122, 240, 242
Seamen, Phil, 274
Second Piano Concerto, 72
Seeger, Pete, 82, 268
Segal, Jerry, 120, 126
Sense of Wonder, A, 189
"Sentimental Fool", 233
"Seventh Son", 3, 92, 94, 102–4, 112, 124, 147, 154, 181, 184, 193, 215–16, 252, 279, 280, 288, 289, 292, 293–4, 295
Shadows, the, 302
Shakespeare, William, 176
Shapiro, Nat, 120
Showboat Lounge, the, 144, 291
Sidran, Ben, 38, 77, 123, 228
Silver, Horace, 64, 65, 123
Simpson, Sonny, 54
Sims, Zoot: MA's work with, 55–7, 60, 64, 74, 116, 125, 126, 238, 277; "Saritha", 112; 34th Street loft, 61, 62; UK tour, 277; work with Brew Moore, 40
Sinatra, Frank, 219
"Sleepy Lagoon", 232
"Sleepy Time Gal", 98
Smith, Bessie, 118, 281, 295, 297
Smith, Carl, 292
Smith, Jimmy, 92, 302

Smith, Putter, 209
Soft Swing, The, 126
"Somebody Gotta Move", 184
Sonny and Cher, 136
Sons of the Pioneers, 223
Soul Stirrers, the, 305–6
Spann, Otis, 294
"Spoonful", 102, 280–1
"Spring Song", 65, 75
Springfield, Buffalo, 134
Stabulas Nick, 55, 98
Staples Singers, the, 270
"Stardust", 31, 41
Staton, Elizabeth, 18–19
Staton, Marianna, 41
Staton, Ruth, 6, 41
Stax Records, 268
Steampacket, 90
Stevenson, Robert Louis, 230
Stewart, Rod, 90
"Stop This World", 146, 168
"Strange", 107
"Stranger in My Own Hometown", 231
"Stranger in Paradise", 100
Stravinsky, Igor, 71, 276
"Stroll", 16, 97, 98
"Substitute", 304
"Summertime Blues", 94
Sun Records, 42, 266
"Sweet Sue", 7
"Swingin' Machine", 20–1, 146, 167, 196

Swingin' Machine, 146, 147, 172, 193
Swinging Guys and Dolls, 119
Sykes, Roosevelt, 14
Symphony Sid, 92

"Tai Chi Life", 222
Takes to the Hills, 119
Tampa Red, 14
Tatum, Art, 108, 248
Taylor, James, 269
Taylor, Mick, 261
Taylor, Puddin, 86–7
Teagarden, Jack, 298
Tehnet, Toby, 47
"Tell Me Something I Don't Know", 154, 156–7, 167, 188
"Tenderly", 17
"Tennesse Waltz", 214
Terker, Arthur, 146
"Thank God for Self Love", 189
"That's All Right", 109, 295, 296
"That's Your Red Wagon", 231
"This Masquerade", 155
Thoreau, Henry, 241
Thornton, Theo, 7
Thoroughgood, George, 284
"Tight Rope", 155
Till, Emmett, 3
Time, 50, 150
Timmons, Bobby, 293
"Top Forty", 207, 220, 224–5, 267, 270
Topham, Tony "Top", 148
Totah, Nabil "Knobby", 56
"Town", 84–5

Townshend, Pete:
"Eyesight to the
Blind", 109; on *Back
Country Suite*, 68, 81–
2; on MA, 301–11;
on MA's influence,
91–2, 307, 309;
"Young Man
Blues", 76
Tracy, Spencer, 230
"Train", 75
*Transfiguration of Hiram
Brown, The*, 119–25,
127–30, 154, 173,
238
Trinity, the, 90
Tristano, Lennie, 106,
108, 237–8
"Trouble in Mind",
16, 84, 95, 220,
223–4
Tuff Green and His
Rocketeers, 27–8
"Tumblin'
Tumbleweed", 223
Turk, Tommy, 25
Twain, Mark, 163
"Twelfth Street Rag,
The", 7
Tyner, McCoy, 247

UCLA, 135
"Unanswered
Question, The",
191
University of
Mississippi (Ole
Miss), 1, 18, 20–6,
29–31, 36, 41, 42,
46, 53, 163
Upchurch, Phil, 209,
211
Utley, Dizzy, 62

"V-8 Ford Blues", 129
Van Gelden, Rudy, 70

Velvet Underground,
295
Ventures, the, 302
Vernon, Mike, 91
Verve Records, 126
Vidacovich, John,
228–30, 232
Village Vanguard,
the, 53, 101, 144,
294
Vonnegut Kurt, 150,
164, 165

Waits, Tom, 281
Walker, Percy, 7
Walker, Shenny, 27,
42
Walker, T-Bone,
78
Wallace, Bennie, 220,
222, 224, 225
Waller, Fats, 16, 18,
172
Waller, Mickey, 90
Wallington, George,
61, 69–70
Walton, Cedar, 44
Walton, Mercy Dee,
79
"War Horse", 160
Ward, Peter, 91
"Warm Night", 75
Warner Brothers
Entertainment, 194,
204, 208
"Was", 233, 234
"Washington and Lee
Swing", 16
WEA Records, 187
Weinstock, Bob, 69–
70, 119
Welty, Eudora, 5
"We're Gonna Rock
This House
Tonight", 28
West, Bill, 47

"Western Man", 181,
190, 191
Western Man, 163, 184,
187–8, 292
Wexler, Jerry, 134,
135, 204, 205, 207
Whaley, Tom, 220
"What Do You Do
After You've
Ruined Your Life",
196, 197
"What's with You",
159
"What's Your Movie",
222–3, 228, 230,
232
"When My
Dreamboat Comes
Home", 212–13, 232
White, Bukka, 83
Who, the, 76, 94, 265,
267, 304–6, 309
"Who's In Who's
Out", 235–6
"Wild Man on the
Loose", 158, 167,
182, 193, 216, 239,
252
Wild Man on the Loose,
157–9
Williams, Hank, 129,
193
Williams, J., 124
Williams, Johnny, 61
Williams, Richard, 186
Williamson, Sonny
Boy (John Lee
Williamson), 2
Williamson, Sonny
Boy (Rice Miller),
27, 108–9, 148, 260,
302
Willie Dixon Dream
Band, The, 102
Willis, Wild Man, 151,
158, 288

357

Wilson, John S., 43
Wolf, Peter, 92
Wolfe, Thomas, 231
Wolftrap, 269
Woods, Bill, 18, 26
Woods, Phil, 56
Word from Mose, The, 87, 140, 147, 149, 151, 152–3
Worthington, Paul, 54
Wright, Tom, 82, 302

Yancey, Mama, 117
"Yardbird Suite", 105
Yardbirds, the, 148, 265, 267
"Yeah, Yeah", 90
Yerbie, Mr., 17
Yiengst, Bill, 41
"You Are My Sunshine", 168, 171, 193, 216
"You Belong to Me", 100
"You Call It Joggin'", 231–2, 272
"You Can Count on Me to Do My Part", 159, 296
"You Can't Go Home Again", 231
You 'N Me, 56, 126
"You Turned the Tables on Me", 126, 128
Young, Lester: dance solo, 249; influence, 22, 43, 59, 75, 96, 98, 237; military service, 23; sound effects, 254
"Young Man Blues", 68–9, 76, 112, 140, 143, 176, 208, 291, 309
Young Man Mose, 16, 97–9, 100, 111, 209
"Your Mind's on Vacation", 95, 103, 143–5, 144–5, 146, 167, 168, 181, 196, 205, 214, 215, 296–7
Your Mind's on Vacation, 194–5, 196, 205, 210, 244
"Your Molecular Structure", 140, 168, 169, 193, 196
"Your Red Wagon", 151–2
"You're a Sweetheart", 126–7, 129

Zen and the Art of Motorcycle Maintenance, 259